Mind over Media
Creative Thinking Skills
for Electronic Media

Mark von Wodtke

McGraw-Hill, Inc.

New York
St. Louis
San Francisco
Auckland
Bogotá
Caracas
Lisbon
London
Madrid
Mexico
Milan
Montreal
New Delhi
Paris
San Juan
Singapore
Sydney
Tokyo
Toronto

**Mind over Media:
Creative Thinking Skills
for Electronic Media**

Acknowledgements appear on pages D-1–D-3 and on this page by reference.

1 2 3 4 5 6 7 8 9 0 DOC DOC 9 0 9 8 7 6 5 4 3

ISBN 0-0-067633-X

The cover was designed by Joan Greenfield.

The book design and layout was by Joe Molloy, Mondo Typo, Inc.

Graphic production was by Long Ha.

The editors were B. J. Clark, John Morris, David Damstra, and Judy Duguid; the production supervisor was Janelle S. Travers.

R. R. Donnelley & Sons Company was printer and binder.

Library of Congress Cataloging-in-Publication Data

von Wodtke, Mark.
Mind over media: creative thinking skills for electronic media/ Mark von Wodtke.
  p. cm.
Includes index.
ISBN 0-07-067633-X
1. Multimedia systems 2. Thought and thinking I. Title.
QA76.575.V66 1993
006.6'01'9—dc20
92-27328

Trademarks
Amiga is a registered trademark of Commodore Business Machines, Inc.
ARCH INFO is a registered trademark of ESRI.
ARCH VIEW is a registered trademark of ESRI.
AutoCAD is a registered trademark of Autodesk, Inc.
Hypercard is a registered trademark of Apple Computer, Inc.
LANDCADD is a registered trademark of LANDCADD International.
Macintosh is a registered trademark of Apple Computer, Inc.
MS-DOS and MS-Windows are registered trademarks of Microsoft Corporation.
NeXt is a registered trademark of NeXt Computer Corporation.
PS/2 is a registered trademark of IBM Computer Corporation.
Unix is a registered trademark of A. T. & T.
VMX is a registered trademark of Digital Equipment Corporation.

I dedicate this book to my students —
past, present, and future.

Past students have helped me learn
about teaching creative thinking skills.

Present students provide a proving
ground for developing approaches for
using electronic media creatively.

And, I hope, future students — and
others — will find these approaches
useful when working with the new
media and tools which are emerging.

Contents

Chapter 3: Perceiving, Thinking, and Acting

Chapter 10: User Interfaces   250

Chapter 11: Mixing Media   272

Chapter 12: Change   296

Appendixes   323

Preface

The goal of this book is to help you discover more creative ways to use electronic media. This book should enable you to develop beyond conventional cognitive computing and learn creative thinking skills for multimedia computing. Using conventional computing, you typically work with rational modes of thought which emphasize logic. You use a narrow range of media generally involving only data, text, or numbers. Computers are mainly tools, typically with keyboards as the primary user interface. Using more creative approaches to multimedia computing, you can draw upon your whole brain. These approaches work with a broader bandwidth of media involving graphics, images, spatial models, animation, and even video and sound — as well as data, text, and numbers. Electronic media enable you to use computers as a vehicle for accessing shared media space involving a variety of user interfaces. You work with more of your mental capacity when using these approaches.

This goal is rather ambitious. Yet there have been many people who have helped me pursue it, and I greatly appreciate their help. This book really represents a collaborative effort in which I (as the author) have given focus to ideas from many different sources while adding my own insights. I have also found it very helpful to interact with people who have served as sounding boards for presenting these ideas. This book is therefore a product of many people's efforts, and I wish to share the credit. Responsibility for any shortcomings, however, rests with me — the author.

Not much could be written about electronic media were it not for a burgeoning computer industry. This industry is providing a plethora of computer-aided design, multimedia, and virtual reality tools. I am hoping this book will, inturn, help stimulate user demand for the new media and tools which are emerging. As an educator, I find an interesting challenge is helping people learn to use these tools creatively and effectively.

Many people have influenced this work. I only have space to acknowledge a few: The people who have helped me in developing different sections of the book include Russ Pielstick, Rick Moore, and Doreen Nelson. The people I have worked with in developing the case studies are Jules Bister, Dale Lang, Tony Palmisano, Mark Sorensen, and Clark Briggs. In addition, authors such as Betty Edwards, John Lyle, Robert McKim, Robert Johnson, and Ken Wilber have written works that I have drawn heavily upon. Throughout the book, I have made every effort to reference the work of others.

I am deeply indebted to a team of technical reviewers who have provided comments on the manuscript at different stages of its development. These include Steve Harrison, researcher, Xerox Park; William Larson, professor emeritus of behavior science, Cal Poly, Pomona; Paul MacCready, inventor and engineer; Robert McKim, writer, educator and engineer; Joel Orr, writer, computer consultant, and Autodesk fellow; and Michael Schrage, writer and MIT Media Lab fellow. The review team also includes Christopher Rennie, chair of engineering graphics and design, Pennsylvania Institute of Technology; Kim Manner, lecturer in mechanical engineering, University of Wisconsin – Madison; James Mallory and Anthony Spieker, professors, Rochester Institute of Technology; Sandra Helsel, editor of *Virtual Reality Report, Multimedia Review,* and consultant; as well as Nohl Lyons, graduate student, University of Arizona.

My colleagues at Cal Poly, Pomona, have helped me with this project in different ways. Some have read parts of the manuscript; others have provided a stimulus in team-teaching situations. At the university level I wish to thank Dr. Weller, our former vice president, who granted me a leave in 1983 which started me on this journey. I also wish to thank Carol Holder, director of faculty development, for her encouragement and exceptional workshop, "Writing across the Disciplines." In our College of Environmental Design, I thank Marvin Malecha FAIA, our dean, for continued support which has included a sabbatical leave in 1990 to work on this manuscript. I also want to thank many colleagues in our College of Environmental Design. Sylvia White guided me in developing the proposal for this book. Branko Kolarevic, Jeff Olson, John Lyle, Felix Barreto, Hersh Farbarow, and Robert Perry gave me helpful comments on the manuscript.

My architectural and landscape architectural firm — CEDG, Inc. (the Claremont Environmental Design Group) — has provided a tremendous amount of support for this project. It has also been a proving ground for many of the ideas. My partner Brooks Cavin has engaged in discussions on many facets of the book and continually brought new material to my attention. Mary Reeves has been an able assistant preparing the manuscript and getting the necessary permissions. Long Ha has handled the graphic production effectively and with flair. Others including Curtiss Johnson, Diann Durant, Ignacio Sardines, Woody Smeck, and Steve Pomerenke have offered helpful comments on the manuscript.

My father and my brother Henry as well as my sister-in-law Janet von Wodtke have provided important moral support for this project. And finally I wish to thank my own family for patience and understanding while I have been physically at home but mentally in media space when working on this book. My children, Kirsten, Erik, and William have taught me a great deal about learning and growing. And last, but not least, special thanks goes to my wife, Carla. Not only has she endured living with this book; she has helped in many ways.

Mark von Wodtke

About Using This Book

You probably already have some favorite ways to explore ideas, but you may not be using your full potential. This book will help you discover ways you can use electronic media more creatively. A key to exploring ideas is to learn creative thinking skills. They are rather abstract notions which I find easier to diagram than to just write about. Consequently, I am presenting these thinking skills to you by integrating graphics with the text in this book. The diagrams will help you quickly catch on to approaches for using electronic media creatively.

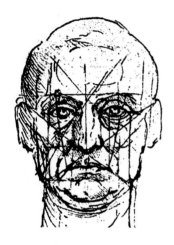

Sketch
by Leonardo da Vinci

There are long traditions of exploring ideas through sketching and writing. Leonardo da Vinci's sketchbooks are classic examples. The layout of this book, *Mind over Media*, involves two channels — visual and verbal. The visual channel appears on the left side of the page and contains images, diagrams, or sometimes illustrative quotes and definitions. The verbal channel, or text, appears on the right side of the page. Graphics or text may take the whole page where appropriate. Some of you may relate more to the text and others more to the graphics. Absorb the text and graphics together. The images help visualization and recall. The text provides elaboration needed for fuller understanding.

Preview each chapter by browsing the graphics and skimming the text. Previewing provides a sense of the contents and organization. Where you find the material new, draw upon both channels to gain an understanding of the chapter. This may be particularly helpful if you are reading English as a second language. Readers familiar with many of the concepts can use the visual channel to get an overview and quickly find areas of interest. This will also help you continue to use this book as a guide after you have read it.

Appendix A contains a chart that provides an overview of the approach this book presents for learning creative thinking skills for electronic media. The goals are ambitious; however, ambitious goals can help you reach your full potential. The chart summarizes principles related to the goals. There are also strategies for using the principles. This chart also lists the activities provided at the end of each chapter. The activities provide challenging ways of experiencing the thinking skills. They help you relate these goals, principles, and strategies to your own discipline and computer environment.

Activities to Experience

Use this book on universal thinking skills with other books which provide the knowledge base needed for your discipline. *Mind over Media,* used together with current software and hardware application guides, can help you learn to work with electronic media more creatively.

Each chapter of this book begins with a brief overview. Headings provide a sense of the objectives and organization. Diagrams illustrate important ideas and procedures. Examples demonstrate thinking skills presented in this book. Italics identify terms with definitions that appear in the left column. The definitions appear again in Appendix B, which is a glossary at the end of the book. Here you can look the terms up alphabetically.

The body of this book presents creative thinking skills that relate to many disciplines. Chapter 7 presents four case studies. The first examines how an award-winning animator uses these approaches. The second describes how architects, landscape architects, and engineers can work together using electronic media. The third discusses how planners use electronic media to plan new communities in Japan. The final study shows how scientists and engineers create models of space vehicles to design and test hardware for outer space exploration. Cross-fertilization of thinking is beneficial. You will discover useful approaches can grow from disciplines other than your own. Ideas come from your mind; computer applications are simply tools to explore ideas using electronic media. Many disciplines involve similar creative thinking skills. Although disciplines deal with different knowledge bases, the computer applications we use are often the same. We can share this common ground in *Mind over Media*.

There are three parts to this book. The first part focuses on the mind by discussing creative thinking skills and how you can use them. The second part of the book focuses on the interaction between your mind and electronic media by presenting approaches that will help you use computers creatively. The third part of the book helps you use your mind to master using electronic media by teaching you how to draw from deeper levels of consciousness, approach user interfaces, and mix the media you are using. This last part of the book also helps you address changes involved in using electronic media to a greater extent.

Each chapter of this book ends with activities. They have no finite solutions, but are intended to get you thinking. You can do some of the exercises in your head. Others you can do with pencil on paper. Still others involve various computer applications. All involve creativity. Try the activities; they provide a crucial step in making these approaches your own. These mental exercises can massage your mind. They provide a focus for each chapter of this book. Through the activities you can transfer the goals, principles, and strategies, described in each chapter, into experiences. Those experiences help you apply creative thinking skills to your discipline and computer environment. The activities are challenging in order to help you develop your mental capacity. They will help you learn thinking skills necessary for multimedia computing.

Each activity contains a brief demonstration and explanation of the thinking skills involved. Then it suggests an exercise you could do to experience these ideas. In addition, the exercise proposes approaches you could use to apply these thinking skills to case studies of your own.

Part I: Thinking

Part II: Interacting

Part III: Mastering

ABSTRACT

goals

principals

strategies · — · experiences

activities

CONCRETE

Relating Goals to Experiences

Also included are suggestions on how you might evaluate your experiences.

Appendix C contains a bibliography listing references alphabetically. There is also an index at the end of the book.

You can obtain the *Instructor's Guide* from the publisher when you adopt this book for your class or workgroup. This guide contains masters for transparencies of key diagrams from each chapter for use in lectures and workgroup discussions. These diagrams are also available in color slides. You can purchase the set of 114 high-resolution, color, 35-mm slides of the diagrams in the *Instructor's Guide* by ordering it through your McGraw-Hill representative or the McGraw-Hill Electronic Bookstore on CompuServe. I can also make the graphic files available to you should you wish to incorporate them into supplementary material. These digital graphics should work with computer programs that can display Encapsulated Postscript files.

Mind over Media (and the *Instructor's Guide*) will be available through Primis — McGraw-Hill's electronic publishing system. They can print and deliver any portion of this material you order specifically for your course or workshop. Contact your McGraw-Hill representative for details.

You understand your own disciplines and changing computer environments better than I do. Tell me about the discoveries you make when doing the activities in the book. Please share supplementary material you develop for your own disciplines and favorite computer environments. Maybe you also have ideas for other activities that help you learn creative thinking skills. You can share supplementary material and activities with colleagues online.

Reach me via Internet at MJVONWODTKE@CSUPOMONA.EDU. It is my hope that this book can continue to evolve, responding to the needs and interests of you — the user — as well as to the developments in the computer industry.

Part I

Thinking

**Part I
Thinking** provides a foundation in visual thinking and creative thought processes. This is especially helpful in **design methods courses.**

**Part II
Interacting** provides approaches for involving electronic media more creatively. This is especially helpful in **case study courses.**

**Part III
Mastering** provides a direction for getting the most out of your mind when using electronic media. This will help you **address change.**

1

Exploring Images in Your Mind

Who can use computers creatively? Many people can — in disciplines ranging from art and design, to architecture and engineering, planning and business, and even medicine and science. Students, professionals, educators, executives, clerical workers, and technicians all have the potential to visualize and explore ideas using computers. Keys to being able to do this are thinking skills you can learn. This chapter introduces those thinking skills. Typically, when working with conventional computing, you use primarily left-brain or deductive modes of thought. When working with multimedia computing you need to learn to use right-brain or inductive modes of thought that are more visual and intuitive. This chapter will make you aware of how you can increase your productivity and enhance your creative capabilities using computers.

Mental Images

Imagine being able to record your dreams. Imagine having the ability to walk through, or even fly through, your mental images, reviewing and refining alternatives as you go. Imagine being able to share your visions with others in multimedia, not just using computer text, but also using graphics, video, and sound. New media for creativity are emerging. You can learn to access these media using computers.

Computing originally meant counting and dealt only with numbers and data. You may associate computing with punch cards, keyboards, and near-sighted people wearing horn-rimmed glasses. Today computers transcend that original meaning. The image of computing is changing significantly. In addition to numbers and data, computers now also deal with text, graphics, three-dimensional models, video images, and even sound. You really have new media for expression. Data processing machines have become word processing machines. Graphic workstations have become visualizing machines. You can explore your mental images by using computers, or perhaps put more accurately, by using electronic media.

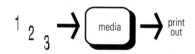

Conventional Computing

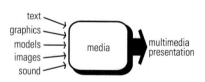

Multimedia "Computing"

Creative Thinking Skills

mind That which thinks, perceives, feels, or wills; combining both the conscious and unconscious together as the psyche. The source of thought processes that facilitate the use of computers for artistic expression, design, planning, management, or other problem-solving and issue-resolving applications.

medium, pl **media** The intermediate material for expression. Using computers people work with ideas and information expressed in electronic media.

The purpose of this book is to help you learn to use computers more productively and creatively. In essence it is a manual for learning to use the operating system of your *mind*. Most books on computers start by telling you about thinking skills. It relates these thinking skills to electronic *media*. The mind is extremely complex and still contains many mysteries. Consequently, this book is not a definitive work on this topic. This book will instead provide you with useful approaches for using your mind more effectively.

To realize what thinking skills can do, consider how much more quickly you can do something a second time. Or consider how much easier it is to do something once you know an approach. This may be as simple as finding someone's home. Once you know where it is, you can go right to it. Or it may be more involved such as the type of thinking you do when using computers. For example, possibly you have already experienced losing a computer file that took you some time to create. After your initial frustration and anger, you decide to redo your work. In less time than it took you before, you find that not only have you been able to redo the work, but you have probably been able to refine it. What accounts for the increase in speed? The *hardware* you used was no faster, and the *software* you used was probably the same. The difference was most likely your method. Not only did you know what you wanted to do, but you knew how to do it.

hardware The computer and its peripherals such as the central processing unit and monitor; includes input devices such as the keyboard and mouse and output devices such as a printer.

software Computer code that transfers instructions. The program that enables the computer to carry out commands.

Knowing how to approach a task enables you to do it much more quickly and easily. You can visualize new and better ways to work and discover short cuts that may make it quicker and easier. Being able to do this is the key to undertaking creative endeavors. This is what *Mind over Media: Creative Thinking Skills for Electronic Media* is all about.

Goals, Principles, Strategies, and Activities

Buckminster Fuller used to tell a story about a magic log. He would relate how a primitive tribe found a log that appeared to have magical powers. In the forest this log was positioned over a rock in a way that enabled a person to lift a huge load by leverage. The natives dragged this log back to their camp and worshipped it not knowing how to use it. What they did not understand was the fulcrum principle behind the log's magic. Sometimes it seems that people treat computers like magic logs. They drag them into a work environment without understanding key *principles* behind using them effectively. Or they may use computers only in one particular way and don't realize their greater potential.

principle A fundamental truth upon which others are based.

This book addresses approaches for using computers effectively and creatively. Each chapter identifies goals related to creative thinking skills for electronic media. Next, the chapter distills principles that will help

abstract

goals

principles

strategies

activities

concrete

Relating Goals to Activities

you address these goals. Each chapter also discusses strategies that will help you when working with a variety of computer applications. At the end of each chapter are activities that will challenge you to apply these approaches to projects you are doing in your own discipline and computer environment. The activities will help you translate the ideas presented in this book into experiences you can learn from.

Who Can Use Computers Creatively?

A shift in who uses computers is occurring. Until recently, specialized technicians and typists were the computer operators. Today, professionals, executives, teachers, and students of all kinds have access to computers. Each can learn to make more creative use of computer applications.

A New Breed of Computer Users

Gene Bylinsky, writer
Fortune Magazine

Gene Bylinsky found a new breed of computer users which he wrote about in *Fortune* magazine, ("Saving Time with New Technology," *Fortune,* December 30 1991). These computer users include top managers and professionals—all using computer work environments. In his article, Bylinsky described the following users of this new technology:

Philippe Kahn
Combines work & play.

Of course, one would expect Philippe Kahn, the CEO of Borland International, to work with computers. He runs this multimillion dollar software company using telecommunications from wherever he happens to be. The French-born entrepreneur also uses telecommunications for play. With a lap-top computer, ship-to-shore phone, and FAX on board his 70-foot sloop, he was able to find time to sail in the biennial Pacific Cup race from San Francisco to Oahu. Using his computer-communication setup, he avoided a delaying weather system and calculated a course that enabled him to win the race in record time.

James E. Clark
"Anytime, anywhere, computing"

James E. Clark, a vice president for AT&T's new NCR subsidiary, practices what he calls "anytime, anywhere, computing" using "a post office in the sky." Armed with AT&T's Safari notebook computer, he can bounce messages off a SkyTel satellite as he travels around the world. In this way, he is able to stay in touch through media space.

W. Thomas Stephens
Navigates with his own notebook computer.

W. Thomas Stephens, the CEO of Manville Corporation, uses a chauffeur and a limo to get him through city traffic. He uses a pilot for the company jet, which takes him around the country. But when it comes to navigating in his information environment, he operates his own notebook computer and FAX modem to help stay in touch with the large company he is managing. Many other executives are also using electronic media to help them manage their companies, although they may have computer and communication operators that function as chauffeurs as they navigate their information environment.

Patricia Seybold
Electronic Newsletter

Patricia Seybold is a management consultant and computer newsletter publisher. She travels around the country working in media space with her equally nomadic staff. They publish their information electronically, enabling customers to access it online. She would like to use a pen computer to incorporate graphics into her reports so she could portray the work flow of the companies for whom she consults — many of them Fortune 500 corporations: "You could project the image on an overhead screen so that a group could see it and work together to make that particular process more efficient."

John M. Lavine, the director of the Newspaper Management Center at Northwestern University, creatively uses his portable computer and printer — even right in meetings. When interviewed by Bylinsky, he said, " . . . under pressure, I can compose and edit a proposal or a presentation on a computer. When I'm done, I push a button and the proposal comes out right in a newspaper or a consulting company's office." He has a word of caution on using computers: "The goal is to have electronics serve me, not for me to become a captive of it. Executives should guard against doing on computers what their assistants can do for them, such as some of the more menial computer work. Ask yourself, 'What's the best use of my time?'" Lavine concludes: "Computers and telecommunications have made possible much higher quality work."

Bernard Krisher is an American journalist-entrepreneur. He carries a palm-top computer and cellular phone with him, and runs his enterprises from New York, Tokyo, or his vacation home near Japan's Mount Fuji. He uses communication services such as MCI to keep in touch with clients and friends no matter where he is. "An on-line life has freed me from the straitjacket of being confined to any given place," says Krisher. "I've become totally self-reliant so that I can easily mix business and pleasure. I'm able to receive and send messages and manuscripts to and from practically anywhere. And no one even needs to know where I am."

Regis and Dianne McKenna live very full lives together in Sunnyvale, California. Their home is linked to their work environments via modem. Regis communicates with five regional offices of his marketing consulting and public relations firm as well as with the venture capital firm of which he is a partner. He works with people in his offices as well as outside consultants, such as a free-lance editor, using his media space work environment. His wife, Dianne, is the chairperson for the Santa Clara County board of supervisors. She often writes letters on her computer at home and sends them electronically to her eight-person staff in San Jose where they print the letters out and mail them. In addition, she uses her computer at home to do the family banking. The McKennas can even select music on their CD player with the click of a mouse.

This Book Is for You

This book is dedicated to those of you who want to learn to use electronic media to assimilate information and explore and express ideas. This especially includes:

Students in fields using visual thinking and graphic communications such as art, design, architecture, landscape architecture, planning, and a range of engineering disciplines, as well as medicine, science, and mathematics. Working with electronic media is also important to students in business and education. All these students can learn to model information electronically and develop multimedia presentations.

Professionals in a variety of disciplines who want to expand their creative capabilities and collaborate using computers. These professionals can learn to use electronic media to communicate more easily.

Educators who want to learn more about creative thinking. Computers can help prepare and present educational materials, but more importantly, thinking skills will help prepare the next generation to use computers creatively. These educators can use electronic media to open new channels for working with students and engaging their creativity.

Executives — managers and decision makers — who need quick access to information and work collaboratively when planning. They may not use computers themselves but may prefer to be chauffeured by a computer operator when on their mental journeys. Electronic media provide these executives access to information anywhere, anytime. These executives can learn to benefit from new freedom in dealing with space and time.

Clerical workers and technicians (many of the present computer operators) who already know how to push the buttons, but who want a better understanding of what else they can do with these tools. These workers can learn to use electronic media to tap their creative energy.

And, finally, **hardware and software developers**, who need clear strategies for relating their tools to creative users' minds. These toolmakers can help people to more easily use their mental capacity.

tool An object that helps the user to work. This may be a traditional tool — such as a pencil — or a computer tool — such as hardware and software for word processing, computer-aided design, animation and many other applications. Used to optimize efficiency where cost-effective.

This book is for all of you — the creative computer users of tomorrow. It will enable each of you to work with these *tools* and use electronic media more effectively when pursuing your creative endeavors.

Creative Endeavors Involving Electronic Media

cognitive Knowing; recognizing what you perceive. Cognitive computer applications use primarily deductive modes of thought.

Even the typical *cognitive computer applications* have the potential to let you express your creativity. For example, you could write on almost any computer by using word processing programs that combine tools for outlining, editing, and formatting text. You could also create spreadsheet models and databases and work with them interactively.

With computer graphics you could work with images using paint programs or drawing programs as well as drafting programs. You could integrate geographical information with maps using geographic information systems (GIS). Similarly, you could integrate attributes with drawings using computer-aided drafting and design (CADD). You could also build three-dimensional models using CADD programs. For example, these may be wire-frame, shaded, or even solid models. Then you could enhance these models (and other graphic images that you produce) using rendering programs.

Conventional Computing -
emphasize logical modes of thought

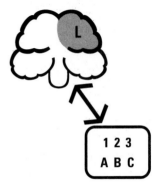

Cognitive Approaches to Conventional Computing -
transfers primarily numbers and text

multimedia Integrating more than one medium. Computer systems can enable the integration of electronic media combining text, graphics, animation, spatial modeling, imaging, video, and sound.

Multimedia computing helps you to undertake an even greater variety of creative endeavors, enabling you draw upon more areas of your mind. There is continuous debate over the definition of *multimedia*. Marketing people keep looking for the "killer application" that will be all encompassing. Instead, multimedia encompass many applications. It is best to define multimedia simply as integrating more than one medium. Multimedia are pervasive. You have already been using multimedia for a long time. Electronic media are opening new and exciting possibilities. For example, you could explore movement and change using animation programs, in effect, giving your graphic images life through movement. You could transform images in imaginative ways. You could present "walk-throughs" or "fly-throughs" of environments you are exploring or shaping. You could work with scanned images of photos or capture images from video. Multimedia computing helps you to manipulate and enhance images in very realistic ways, enabling you to explore and to express new ideas. You can work with audio as well as video. For example, you could compose music by working with a musical keyboard attached to a computer. Not only could you play your own notes, but also you could record and even integrate synthesized sounds generated by a computer. Using computers, you could even create a *virtual reality* that you could experience with stereo goggles and glovelike pointing devices. This enables you to, in effect, enter and navigate within an information environment.

Creative Approaches to Mutimedia Computing -
draw upon the whole brain

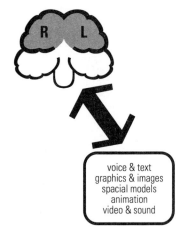

Multimedia computing -
transfers a wide range of information

Media integration could occur in a variety of ways, relating multimedia computing to telecommunications, publishing, video, and TV, as well as manufacturing and construction.

For example, electronic mail and telecommunications are rapidly evolving from being media for transferring simple text messages and binary files. Telecommunications can now integrate phone and FAX messages as well as graphic images. Interactive video is also emerging, enabling more people to do video conferencing. It is likely cellular phone technology will provide more computer users with even greater mobility.

Desktop publishing programs enable you to integrate text and graphics, and produce documents by either laser printers or high-quality printing presses. Hypermedia databases provide many possibilities to combine text, graphics, video, and audio on laser disks through which people could interactively navigate at their own pace. Multimedia is making it possible to integrate text, graphics, imaging, three-dimensional models, animation, video, and even sound to produce video programs. Desktop video is beginning to make it possible to do many things that were

Palmtop Computer

Pen Computer

Notebook Computer

Desktop Computer

Tower Computer

formerly only done in a TV production studio. Of course, you may still work with studios to produce broadcast-quality videos. However, as high-definition television (HDTV) emerges, remarkable changes will enable you to work with digital television images using multimedia computers. This presents exciting possibilities for the entertainment industry, the arts, and the design disciplines. It also has potential for medical imaging and scientific visualization as well.

Using computers, you can plot or print graphic images on paper; you can also generate slides and project video images for viewing by large groups. In addition, it is possible to work three-dimensionally inputting forms using sonic digitizers. And it is possible to output three-dimensional models using stereolithography, as well as holography. CADD programs can now be linked directly to machine tools using numerical controls, making it possible to manufacture prototypes or custom components more easily. You will also probably see multimedia computing become more integrated with the construction process, making it possible to lay out construction sites and do grading directly from three-dimensional computer models. Construction documents may even incorporate instructional videos showing how to assemble key components.

Consumer electronic devices such as telephones, televisions, and electronic toys are gaining computer capabilities. Computers are also now available in a range of sizes. Small, hand-held, *palm-sized computers* are becoming personal assistants enabling you to do more than keep a daybook and diary. *Pen computers,* the size of a pad of paper, let you take notes, sketch, and enter data using quick gestures of a penlike device right on the computer screen. Portable *notebook computers* the size of a three-ring binder can have a full-sized keyboard and pointing device such as a mouse or roller ball, as well as a FAX/modem, giving you access to all the functionality of a personal computer. *Desktop computers* can have larger screens than portable computers. They may also be tied to peripherals such as digitizing tablets, musical instrument digital interface (MIDI) keyboards, networks, modems, video disks, printers, plotters, and sound systems. These computers may have central processing units that either sit on a desk or can be placed on the floor like small towers under a desk, leaving more workspace for the user. *Microcomputers* have evolved into powerful workstations that can function either on a stand-alone basis or as a part of a network linked to minicomputers and mainframe computers. These large systems no longer need entire rooms with specially controlled environments, but can be placed in small cabinets. The power of computers continues to increase and migrate toward smaller, more affordable devices. They are also becoming easier to use. This has tremendous potential for empowering you — the creative individual.

Obviously, what you do with computers will be influenced by the discipline you are studying (or your profession) and the computer environment you have access to. What you do will also be filtered by your

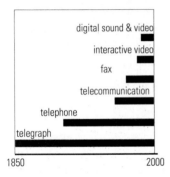

digital sound & video

interactive video

fax

telecommunication

telephone

telegraph

1850 — 2000

Evolution of Electronic Media

interests. If you have access to the right equipment, and the interest, you can learn to do many of these things. You may also elect to work with computer operators using high-end equipment. So long as you know where you want to go, you can develop thinking skills to get there. You will also come to realize that not everything you can imagine is possible using the computer systems available today. Who knows what tomorrow will bring?

Key Principles

Here are a few key principles for using computers productively and creatively.

Viewing vs. Interacting

Viewing - simply watching without responding

interact To view and do what you visualize.

Viewing involves simply watching without responding — the way most people watch TV. Western society has become a viewing society — influenced first by photography in the last century, then by moving pictures in the 1920s and 1930s. The popularization of TV in the 1950s brought televised images into almost everyone's living room. People gather more and more of their impressions and information from pictures, whether they are photographs, movies, or televised images. Today, most children voluntarily spend hundreds of hours sitting in front of the television, before becoming an adult in this viewing society. Most of that time is spent passively viewing images on a screen.

Marshall McLuhan heralded the impact of media on society in his book *The Medium Is the Massage*. Yet a significant shift is occurring. Whereas the medium used to be the massage, we can now massage the medium.

text

graphic

models

sound

images

Interacting - alternately viewing doing what you visualize

Interacting involves viewing and doing what you visualize — the way people use computers. This is changing how society relates to electronic media. As people enter the next century, they are also entering a new information age which will be highly visual. For example, children no longer just passively view TV; for better or worse, they become interactively involved in video games. With amazing speed, they intuitively visualize their moves and strategies. Adults, too, no longer need to take a passive role, simply viewing electronic media. Using multimedia computing, they can manipulate electronic media right on their desktop. They can also access digital information more interactively.

The ability to visualize is intimately linked with creative capacity. *Mind over Media* presents the principles behind visualization and creativity so you can use these capabilities to work interactively with electronic media. It will help you link you mental energy with electronic media.

Mind over Media

To work effectively with any tool requires more than simply having the tool. You must have the skill or technique to use the tool. You also need strategies or methods for working with it. In addition, you need a goal or objective that provides a positive mental attitude to open your mind to the possibilities the tool affords. Lacking any of these limits the benefit of the tool. As a result, the tool can even be a source of frustration.

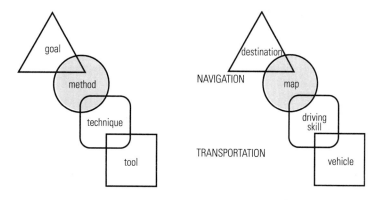

Generic Levels   **Vehicular Transportation**

Transportation involves using tools to move people and goods. For example, you are familiar with how to use an automobile for transportation. To get anywhere, you need a good vehicle, but you also need to be able to drive (or have a driver). In addition, you need a mental image or map of where you are going. And, of course, you need a destination and the ability to navigate. Although you usually don't consciously think about it, you need to address all of these levels to be able to use an automobile effectively.

Communication involves moving ideas and information. Consider how you can relate your mind to media when using computers for communication. To be able to access electronic media, you need a good computer, but you also need to be able to use it (or have a computer operator). In addition, you need a mental model of where you are going. And, of course, you need an objective and the ability to find your way in what you are doing. As you can see, this involves both mind and media. You need to know more than how to just access the media—as you would just turning on a television. To work interactively with media using computers, you need to develop your mind, learning thinking skills that will help you navigate.

Different media are more effective in certain circumstances. Just as it is important to have access to multimodal transportation systems, it is also important to have access to multimedia communication systems. In some situations it makes sense to talk on the phone, or to write a handwritten note, or to make sketches you can FAX. Using telecommuni-

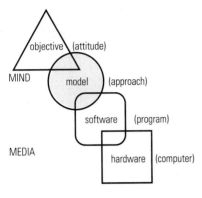

Mind over Media

bandwidth A range. Typically refers to the transmission of a signal, but may also refer to the richness of a message. Multimedia encompass a wide bandwidth.

cations, you can access databases, move documents, or even interact with video. Both transportation and communication can give you a sense of freedom. With transportation you have the potential to go places and move goods. With communication you have the chance to explore ideas and transfer information.

Linking Your Mind to Multimedia

Multimedia is changing the way people think when using computers. Conventional computing dealt primarily with numbers and text. Today, you access electronic media through different devices such as telephones and FAX machines, computers and graphic workstations, as well as interactive video devices. In effect, you can draw from a broad *bandwidth* of information. You can engage many of your senses electronically — almost as if you were working with reality. Multimedia computing enables you to express ideas using many modes — in effect, offering more channels of communication. In this way multimedia can help you draw upon more of your mental capacity when you learn, create, and communicate.

By using multimedia computing to link your mind with electronic media, you can work more interactively with ideas and information. Imagine having a model of what you are designing right in front of you. Imagine being able to manipulate it using your computer. This has tremendous potential for creative thinking because it enables you to refine and test ideas before you carry them out. Since the model may be a mock-up of what you are producing, it also enables you to develop production procedures concurrently as you develop the design. You can also recycle creative energy and information.

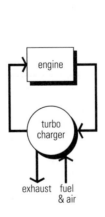

Turbocharger

Coupling MInd & Media

Linking your mind to media in this interactive manner is much like turbocharging an internal combustion engine. Turbocharged engines use energy from the exhaust to pump more fuel and air into the combustion chambers. Using a computer interactively, you can direct a flow of information to your mind which can spark new ideas. If you use computers linked by networks, others can also work interactively with the models you are working on setting up opportunities for creative collaboration. In effect, you have a creative engine with more than one cylinder. These models also enable you to communicate using electronic media. Not only can you transfer digital information directly to our models, but you can also transfer information from your models to others. This could be in the form of presentations or could even embody information needed to build the models. This is done, for example, with electronic publishing and with computer-aided design and computer-aided manufacturing (CAD CAM).

This interaction represents a significant shift in the way people think and use information. At one time, education stressed memorizing information. Today, the emphasis of education is on learning thinking skills to access and use information effectively. While people need a certain knowledge base to be informed and operate in most disciplines, there is too much information to learn. Also, since disciplines are constantly evolving, information can become obsolete rather quickly.

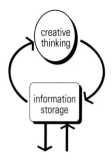

Computer

There is another significant shift in the way people work with information. Multimedia computers enable you to relate directly with visual images and sound without having to translate into words. Printed medium has emphasized text. Electronic media are largely visual and audible. Using multimedia therefore draws upon more of your mental faculties when you learn and create. It also offers more channels for communication. Typically, education has favored verbal thinkers; however, multimedia can make learning easier for those more visually inclined. While it is important to continue to develop verbal literacy, it is important to develop visual literacy as well. Graphics, video, and other modes of multimedia have great potential for conveying information and giving expression to ideas.

Enhancing Enjoyment

Initially, you may find that using computers is not particularly enjoyable. You may use them primarily because you have to and not because you like to. Yet using computers can become intrinsically rewarding. I have seen students go through changes in attitude where they find that working with electronic media can become satisfying in itself. To me, the excitement that they generate makes teaching pleasurable. It helps both students and teachers endure the difficulties that they may encounter achieving these truly rewarding experiences.

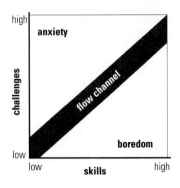

The Flow Channel
adapted from *Flow: The Psychology of Optimal Experience* by Csikszentmihalyi

In his book *Flow: The Psychology of Optimal Experience,* Mihaly Csikszentmihalyi indentifies the elements that make experiences enjoyable. These include:

A challenge requiring skills

A chance of completion

The opportunity to concentrate, merging action and awareness

Clear goals

Immediate feedback

Deep involvement transcending distractions and the awareness of time

A sense of control over actions

Absorption of self

Expansion of self through experience

Multimedia computing potentially has all these elements.

Imagine a model of a landscape appearing on your computer screen. Assume you can easily move around this terrain model. As you look in different directions, the other views of this landform unfold. You begin to feel almost as if you are walking on this landscape. Suddenly, you discover a magnificent panorama. You begin to play with this site, adding features you have in mind. Then you move to where you would enter the site and see what your design would look like from there. You lay out an access road, checking soils, drainage, and other important considerations as you proceed. Soon you capture a series of views so you can show to others what they would experience moving down this access road. You realize it would have taken you several days of difficult hiking to explore these possibilities in reality. You look forward to going to the site again to see how these ideas would work. Then you could return to your computer model and begin to refine your design.

You only need to relate to your own optimal experiences using computers to realize you can achieve flow and find genuine enjoyment. Have you ever lost track of time when you have played a computer game or used a graphics program? You probably have. You also realize that if a computer application is too challenging, it can cause anxiety. If it is too simplistic, it can lead to boredom. Knowing your flow channel will help you find a path between anxiety and boredom as you work with electronic media.

Increasing Productivity and Capability

You can increase productivity for some tasks by using computers — mostly through automation of routines. For example, if you had to replicate the same form — say, a graphic symbol — you can do this more quickly using a computer.

Computers also enable you to increase your capabilities — by enhancing your perception and by augmenting your abilities to create and give expression to ideas. For example, if you had to develop variations on a form — say, new ways of looking at and expressing a graphic symbol — you could explore possibilities more quickly using a computer.

There are different ways to increase productivity and capabilities. Typically people focus on hardware and software. (This is what they read about in advertisements.) But you can probably achieve greater gains in productivity and capabilities by learning good techniques and methods for using those tools. Obviously, you need good hardware and software as well as good techniques and methods to be able to achieve your goals.

Increases in the speed of computers are measured in split seconds. Computer chips are classified by the number of bits of information they process simultaneously. (Most computers today use 16-, 32-, or 64-bit chips.) The more bits, the faster the machine. Computer chips also have clock speeds measured in megahertz. Parallel processing machines are emerging which use several computer chips to process even more information simultaneosly, making them faster yet. Aside from the speed of the central processing unit, which is measured in nanoseconds, accessing information on disks takes only milliseconds. These split seconds are important to the feel of the machine. Faster machines are more responsive, inviting interaction. Fast computers can relate better to the pace of your flow of thoughts, especially when processing graphics. In this way you don't lose the pattern or rhythm of your thinking. You can stay focused and avoid distractions. Of course, these split seconds saved also add up, making it possible to carry out complicated tasks more easily.

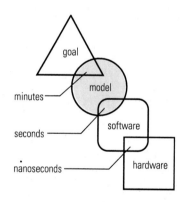

Speed Enhancement

Increased productivity of software, however, is measured in seconds. Throughput measurements, taken from benchmark tests, indicate how quickly various programs perform tasks such as opening files, accessing information, or saving files. Faster software permits more tasks to be automated. Good software can also provide more possibilities for the users to involve their mental capabilities.

Increases in productivity due to user training are measured in minutes or even hours. A baseline is 1:1 productivity — that is, being as productive with a computer as you are manually. Productivity enhancements, using computers, can achieve rather high ratios when automating repetitive tasks such as replicating data. You can also learn techniques for doing standard procedures such as manipulating data.

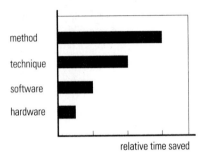

relative time saved

Potential for Productivity Increases

In addition, you can learn new approaches or methods that enable you to use electronic media more effectively. The enhancements in productivity and capabilities you can achieve through effective use of media may be dramatic. Used intelligently, computers can enhance productivity by enabling you to work with information more interactively and transfer it more easily. For example, you can learn to build models (a spreadsheet or a three-dimensional spatial model) which provide a focus for your workgroup's collaboration. However, using computers with the wrong mind-set, you can actually waste time and effort even though you have access to good hardware and software and know techniques for using the computer.

Electronic media can help creative people visualize more than they readily can in other ways. Computers can also help people overcome perceptual or even physical handicaps. After all, aren't we all handicapped when it comes to peering into outer space, comprehending large patterns on earth, or investigating microscopic realms? Using computers, you could compile information, clarify concepts, and bring more precision to developing ideas. Models you generate electronically are easier to evaluate and change than prototypes or drawings on paper. This reduces the risk and the time necessary to bring ideas to fruition. Finally, once you develop and evaluate ideas, you can present them more easily with electronic media. These media can be linked directly to your audience, or to manufacturing, or even to construction.

Insights, from which ideas are born, originate in your mind as you interact with the world around you. However, you need media to express them. The next chapter will help you explore electronic media further. Electronic media may enable you to express ideas in ways that were not possible before. Learning more about thinking and expressing mental images electronically may change the way you think. This could improve your capabilities to act upon ideas you generate. You may need to expand your mind-set to assimilate new tools successfully. However, recognize that the computer age is here. Electronic media could be another outlet for expressing your creative genius.

Summary

In summary, you can see there are many ways to relate your mental energy to electronic media. A key principle is learning to work interactively. You can go beyond passive viewing—what you typically do when watching TV. You can find ways to interact, alternatively viewing and doing what you visualize—by using computers.

When learning to use computers, or any tool for that matter, you need to learn techniques and methods that relate to your goals. When using computers, this means not only learning to work with the hardware and software; it means learning how to develop useful methods and models, as well as clearly identifying your objectives. This process involves media—the files you access through your computer and program. It also involves your mind—the thinking skills you use and the attitudes with which you use them. Develop goals that will enable you to enhance your creativity. Seek to improve your productivity by adopting new approaches and attitudes when working with electronic media. Conventional computing emphasizes logical modes of thought. Multimedia computing draws upon the whole brain. You can learn to couple your mind with the new media that are emerging.

The following activities will help you begin to explore these approaches. Get in the habit of keeping a journal, and do these activities in it. This will help you see how your thinking develops and how your mind-set (your attitude) evolves. You can keep your journal in a notebook or sketchbook. You can also keep your journal in a digital file using computer software that enables you to both write and draw if you have access to your own computer. Don Schoen's reflective design practices can help you if you need some guidance on keeping a journal. (See the bibliography in Appendix C for this and other supplementary reading.)

Be sure to do the activities. They will cause you to think about how you can use computers more creatively.

Activities

1. Get the Picture

You probably read newspapers and magazines that publishers produce electronically. When you turn on a television, you frequently see flying logos and weather maps composed of digital images. When you go to the movies, you may see special effects that are clearly computer-generated. At times, you may not even be aware that the images on the screen are sometimes electronically enhanced. Early films such as *Star Wars, Tron,* and *Star Trek II* featured special effects generated by computers. *The Abyss* and *Terminator 2* set new standards for realism of computer-generated imagery in the entertainment industry. Many of the multimedia computing techniques that produce dazzling special effects potentially have much broader application. You are a passive viewer when you simply read a magazine, watch TV, or view a movie. But when you use the telephone, send a message over a FAX machine, or play video games, you are more actively involved. You enter the realm of electronic media when you use a computer for telecommunications or interact with video images on laser disks.

You are an active viewer when you work with multimedia computing—selecting what you want to see and playing or working with it using a computer.

Begin simply with passive viewing. Consider this book, which was produced electronically. The writing was done using computers, as were most of the drawings. Some images (for example, those drawn by Leonardo da Vinci) were obviously hand-drawn but were scanned by an optical scanner so they could be electronically integrated for printing. What other examples of electronic publishing can you find?

In addition, visit the fantasy worlds of entertainment to find examples of multimedia computing. You will see computer-generated images on televi-

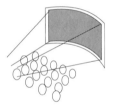

sion and in major movie theaters. You will also find animation film festivals that feature short works frequently done with computers. How could you relate the results you see to what you want to do with electronic media?

Look for opportunities to work with interactive video. You can find interactive video in arcades, at art and science exhibits, in some schools, and even in stores. Multimedia computers enable you to work interactively with electronic images and even sound. Surprisingly sophisticated technology is migrating to consumer electronic devices and more affordable computers. Research centers, schools, professional offices, and service bureaus are also emerging which can provide access to more expensive equipment and to personnel who have the expertise to use it. Consider how active viewing could relate to your endeavors.

2. Play Games

Watch children play computer or video games. Notice how they can become absorbed in a game. Remember your own experiences playing games. Remember how you could flow with the pace of the game when the controls became an extension of your being. As your skills developed, you looked for new challenges. If the game became boring, you dropped it. If it was too difficult, you quit.

Select a computer or video game and practice the controls, starting at very basic levels. Find a quiet place where your activity does not disturb others. (A classroom or office may not be the ideal place for this activity.) Play the game until you are comfortable with the controls and are able to move into more challenging levels. Notice how initially the controls may seem strange

and clumsy; eventually they become part of you. You can internalize the goal of the game and learn to react almost automatically. Are you able to achieve a flow experience as you interact with what you see and hear? Notice how absorbing flow experiences can be. Try word games, graphic games, and number games. Try simulations and video games. Make your own games using graphic or music programs if you can. See if you can achieve flow using different channels of perception and expression. Be careful—these experiences can become addictive.

3. Identify Creative Endeavors

Many people pursue creative endeavors in which they express their own ideas and feelings or solve problems as part of individual or collaborative efforts. They express their creative energy by writing, drawing, composing images and music, or making models and objects that can become a virtual reality. Most people find creative endeavors very satisfying. These endeavors are important expressions of a culture and are often essential for economic survival.

Write down creative endeavors that you do in your work, studies, and avocations. Identify the tools and media you are now using. Are you already using computers as a vehicle for your creativity? For what other creative endeavors might you use electronic media?

4. Develop Goals

Everyone has goals. That is probably why you are reading this book. Your immediate objectives may have to do with getting through a course. Or you may wish to learn to use some application software to develop marketable skills. You may also want to improve your productivity, enhancing your professional capabilities. What about even more fundamental goals? Can computers help you access and learn to work with the knowledge base of your discipline? Can computers contribute to basic drives such as creative freedom and happiness? Can they stimulate your self development and enable you to achieve basic goals in life?

Ask yourself: "What are my basic goals?" "What creative freedoms am I looking for?" "What type of experiences make me happy?" Contemplate and list some basic goals that relate to your vocation and avocations. You will need to sort them out if you can, so that you can relate your goals to what electronic media have to offer. This process may involve some fundamental shifts in your modes of thought as well as some changes in the way you use computers, telecommunications, and television. Being convinced of your goals will help you commit to these changes.

Write your goals down in a journal. This will cause you to take some time to contemplate these questions. Also add your thoughts about your creative endeavors. As noted before, keep your journal in a notebook you carry with you or in a digital file if you have regular access to a personal computer someplace where you can quietly reflect. Add to this journal as you read the book and do the activities. Keeping a journal will give you a chance to think more about your basic goals and approaches to media. Your goals will probably evolve as you go on through the book and do the activities. You may find it interesting to record where this book and related experiences are leading you.

2

Exploring Electronic Media

This chapter will help you use computers to set up a work environment in media space. It will show you how to map your media space and develop a sense of place so you can navigate electronically. It will help you learn to transfer information and ideas to media space as directly as possible so you can work interactively using computers. This chapter identifies syndromes that can block the transfer of ideas to electronic media. Addressing these common problems can help you overcome them. It also shows you how to diagram information and data flow. Visualizing how to move information helps you go beyond using computers as single-purpose tools. By learning to use a media space environment you can gain more freedom over where and when you work. Understanding media space can enable you to work collaboratively and access shared information when using computers. After you have read the chapter, do the activities—on your own or with your class or workgroup. The activities will help you relate these possibilities to your discipline and computer environment.

A New Renaissance

renaissance Rebirth; revival. The revival of art, literature, and learning in Europe during the fourteenth, fifteenth, and sixteenth centuries, marking the transition from the medieval to the modern world. The term can also refer to a revival of creativity and understanding stimulated by multimedia computing, empowering individuals to make a transition into a new information age.

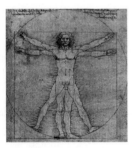

Over the centuries, civilization has developed media for human expression. In the fourteenth, fifteenth, and sixteenth centuries, the *Renaissance* demonstrated the impact of traditional media. For example, Florence became the focus for writing, painting, and fine sculpture as well as architecture, engineering, and scientific investigation. These traditional arts and sciences are still here today. Beginning in the fifteenth century the printing press made the written word more available to the public. Publishing revolutionized the way information was transferred. Some refer to this mode of expression as "the press." In this century, society has experienced the impact of radio and TV which has again brought many changes. Some refer to these forms of communication as "the media." Now society is moving into an information age where computers enable people to work interactively with multimedia. This may stimulate a new Renaissance if people can learn to use these tools creatively.

The challenge is to mesh your mind with these new media. How do you transfer your mental images into a digital format? Or, conversely, how do you relate to what you see on a computer screen? How can you work with anything as abstract as electronic media and be able to find your way?

Media Space

media space The information environment connecting real and imaginary places, objects, and the people within them. The context in which people can use representations to work with artificial reality.

Media space is an important notion that enables you to develop a sense of place when working with electronic media. Researchers in the System Concepts Laboratory at Xerox PARC coined the term *media space* in about 1985. Two of the researchers, Bob Stults and Steve Harrison, began to work in media space, using video as a design medium. They were looking for ways to extend physical space electronically. Their primary concern was the way in which the environment of electronic media interacts with the environment of physical space. They used video as an extension of their work setting for design and other collaborative endeavors. Their media space dealt with "the connection of real and imaginary places and the people and objects within them." They conducted several design projects using media space in this way.

By accessing electronic media using video and computers you can, in effect, experience and create information environments. *Artificial reality*, a term coined by Myron Krueger in 1974, refers to "graphic worlds that people can enter from different places to interface with each other and graphic creatures." *Virtual reality*, a term coined by Jaron Lanier, refers to environments you can enter and experience using hardware and software which provides a sense of immersion, navigation, and interaction. William Gibson, a science fiction writer, calls information environments *Cyberspace*. Michael Sorkin points out that through TV and other media we experience the *Electronic City*.

artificial reality Models or graphic representations people can access from different places to interact with objects and with each other. People can develop these representations using information in media space.

virtual reality Simulations using information to provide multisensory experiences. People can create these simulations by using computer-generated images in media space.

cyberspace Media space connected to the human brain, enabling people to experience this information environment interactively.

mindscape The inner world of your own mind, involving both conscious and subconscious levels.

Media space really has several frontiers. As you substitute information for matter, you can begin to experience artificial environments constructed electronically. These can be models or representations of reality. You can also suspend the rules of reality to create new constructs. Media space is the context in which all this occurs. This outer world can grow more vivid as the bandwith of communications expands. You can also shape media space using your own experiences and imagination — in that way exploring your *mindscape* — the inner world of your own mind. (Chapter 9, "The "Zen" of Regeneration," will help you explore your inner world.)

Peter Drucker, a renowned writer on business management, talks about moving ideas instead of people. There are many implications. Organizations can move ideas faster than they can move people. People can access information whenever necessary from wherever they are. People who can work together effectively in media space gain the freedom to be where they want to be. If they can maintain contact using electronic media, they can also gain more freedom over when they work.

Cities are being choked by moving people to work every day on a regular schedule. Most cities no longer have space for more highways and parking, if they are to be humane places to live. Growing businesses and schools often lack physical facilities. Furthermore, the world's resources

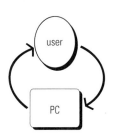

Personal Media Space

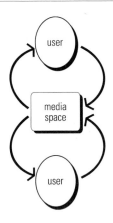

Shared Media Space

cannot sustain these patterns of commmuting. The environmental impacts are too significant. The quality of life is in jeopardy because of the way people use transportation and physical space.

Communication and media space could be used to improve the quality of life. Telephone and cable communication networks could effectively tie homes, communities, universities, businesses, and public services to media space. The global village that is beginning to emerge in media space could offer more opportunities for interaction than broadcast networks and telephone now provide.

As already mentioned, some computer operators could function like chauffeurs operating the communication vehicles in this global village. They could help people access media space. Some established executives who use the telephone extensively may wish to have a media chauffeur and not bother with learning to operate and maintain computers and video equipment. However, they still need to know how to navigate in media space if they want to access information. They also need to know how to transfer ideas if they want to work with others in media space. But can you afford a media chauffeur all the time, and what would that do to your creative freedom?

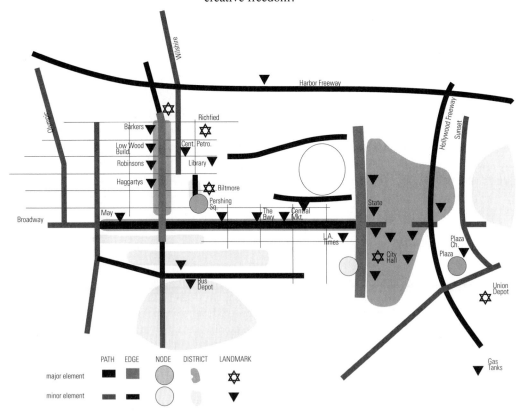

Image of Downtown Los Angeles
adapted from *Image of the City* by Kevin Lynch

Mapping Media Space

directory A guide. The directory of a computer disk will provide a guide to its contents.

subdirectory A folder contained within a directory. A computer disk can be divided into many subdirectories.

cognitive map A visual representation of your perception. A cognitive map can show spatial or conceptual relationships.

In his book *Image of the City*, Kevin Lynch observed that people develop a mental image of a city. They identify nodes, paths, edges, and focal points to develop a sense of place so they can navigate. Cities with identifiable images are more accessible. The maps people draw of their image of a city depend upon what they understand and have access to. Children might know just the area around where they live. A taxi driver knows the districts of a city and the routes to get there. You use these images to develop a sense of place, not only in cities, but also work environments such as offices and schools. You have a mental image of where you put things in your file cabinet, desk, briefcase, and notebook.

Similarly, when working with electronic media, you need to develop a sense of place. You can do this by creating a clear image of the media space you work with. For example, you can make a branching diagram showing *directories* (folders) and *subdirectories* where you place files. Or you can diagram nodes you have access to and identify the paths you use to get there. These *cognitive maps* will help you develop a mental picture of where you are, what you can access, and how you can get there. This helps you remember where you put computer files; it also helps others

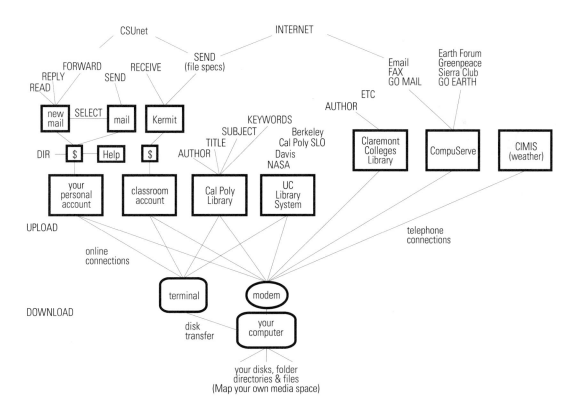

Map of Media Space - Cal Poly, Pomona

find them. You can even diagram the frames of references you use in different application programs. This helps you access information when working in those programs. Identify what focal points (such as menus, icons, or markers) help you navigate. By working with familiar metaphors such as desktops, mailboxes, and classrooms you can quickly begin to develop a sense of place in the media space you use. Your media space will expand as you learn to use new applications and reach other computer environments through telecommunications. If you can clearly map your media space, then you can work more successfully with computers. With that comes a sense of confidence. Your whole attitude toward using electronic media can change.

map of media space A visual representation of your information environment. Shows how to connect with and navigate in media space. Can include what is accessible on disk, as well as what is accessible through networks and via telecommunications.

You can sketch your *maps of media space* using a pencil and paper. You may also develop them using a graphic program on a computer. This way you can change your diagram as your perception of your media space expands. You can also share your map of media space with others in your workgroup so they know how to find information you share. Learn to diagram the media space environments you have access to using different devices.

Information Environments

voice mail Verbal messages transmitted to a computer account, usually from a telephone. These messages can be picked up anytime, from anywhere, using a telephone.

E-mail (Electronic mail) Messages transmitted to an account, usually from a computer that is online. These messages can be picked up anytime, from anywhere, using a computer that can access the account.

telecommunications Electronic transfers of information. Can take the form of FAX, E-mail, or especially binary transfers of digital files such as programs, formatted documents, or drawings.

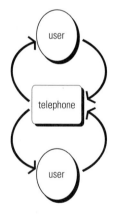

Telephone System

The telephone is probably the most pervasive electronic media device you use interactively. Through the telephone, your voice can travel around the world. You can figure out how to connect by just noting a few numbers — the access line or credit card number you are using, the country code, the area code, and of course the phone number. This media space is immediate and intimate — people like these qualities, although they can be intimidating. Pauses provide the cues to hand off the verbal exchange. You glean a great deal from not only what is said but how it is said. The manner of speech, as well as the tone of voice, is very revealing. Telephone answering machines that record messages are in widespread use. They enable you to leave messages for people when they are not there, giving you and them some control over time and space. The answering machine, of course, records voice messages in the sequence they occur. *Voice mail*, now becoming an integral part of some computer *E-mail* systems which are emerging, can permit you to reorganize messages and work with them more interactively. Using *telecommunications* you can transfer formatted text and graphic files.

mosaic A series of images. Used to preview a collection of digital graphic files so a user can select an image to call up on a computer.

hypertext A collection of keywords linked to information. Used to present associated information so a user can quickly access what he or she is interested in, using a computer.

hypermedia A collection of keywords, graphics, images, video, and sound linked by associations. Used to present digital information in ways a user can explore interactively.

operating system The programmed interface between computer hardware and application software. It permits the software to function on the computer and enables the user to perform simple functions such as searching for, copying, or deleting files.

user shell A computer program that provides a user interface making an operating system easier to use. Most user shells incorporate metaphors such as a desktop or windows to help users relate to the interface more intuitively.

file management utilities Computer programs that help users navigate around their information environment. Permit pruning of the branching structure of file directories and easily move branches and files.

Audio and video recordings are linear. They follow a time sequence. To navigate in this media space you need to remember the sequence of events. To do this, you can use a counter as a reference, but more likely you will use certain sounds or scenes to judge where you are on the tape. To find something, you fast forward or reverse through the tape. Obviously, this medium is well suited for listening to music or viewing movies — sequences you want to experience from beginning to end. Video editing machines enable you to change that sequence.

Compact discs enable you to access large amounts of information non-linearly. For example, you can randomly select from *mosaics* of images. Or you can use links to navigate in non-linear ways through *hypertext* or *hypermedia*. In this way you can explore information more interactively. Hyperlinks are built upon associations which should reflect your thinking patterns.

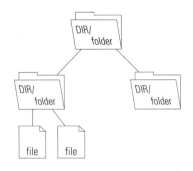

Operating System

Computer operating systems enable you to access files on disks. You can picture directories of computer files as tree diagrams, showing subdirectories as branches or roots. You can access files randomly by using the commands of an operating system. Graphic user interfaces with pull-down menus have made it easier to use these commands. The user can select them by pointing and clicking with a mouse or other pointing device. The Macintosh System uses a desktop metaphor, drawing upon intuition derived from the familiar desktop setting. *User shells* such as Windows for the MS-DOS environment and X-Windows for the Unix environment use window metaphors, enabling users to peer into several different places simul-taneously. The PenPoint system uses a notebook metaphor to access files and programs together. The Amiga also has a graphic user interface. Older operating systems such as MS-DOS and VMX require the user to remember commands and type them in. This can be a fast and effective way of operating a computer, if you know the commands and have good keyboard skills.

File management utility programs can also help you navigate around your disk. They enable you to prune this branching structure and move the branches easily. By developing a consistent file-naming system, you can select and sort files more easily using operating system commands. For example, MS-DOS and the VMX operating systems have "wildcards" such as * and ? which can substitute for characters in a file name when searching for or selecting files. *Menus* are like signs on pathways, helping you find your way. *Icons* are like landmarks, helping you recognize where you have been, where you are, and where you are going in media space.

menu A list of choices. Provides pathways and commands to help computer users find their way and function in their information environment.

icon A graphic representation. Used in graphic-user-interfaces to represent files, disks, or objects which the computer user can pick.

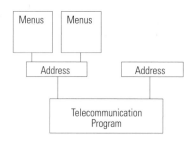

Telecommunications

Telecommunications enable you to extend your media space around the world. You can explore beyond what you access on the disks at your desktop computer. Using a network you can reach servers that share programs and files. With a modem you can access computer accounts, bulletin boards, and information services as well as other computers and even FAX machines. A lightweight portable notebook computer with a FAX/modem can connect to almost any telephone. This empowers you to reach your media space from almost any place, any time.

upload To transfer digital information from a local computer to a remote server (often a mainframe computer).

download To transfer digital information from a server (or mainframe computer) to a local computer.

Of course you need phone numbers, account numbers, and passwords to work with telecommunications. But you also need to develop clear cognitive maps of the servers, networks, and hubs you can reach. Your map can take many forms. Usually it is easiest to diagram paths starting from your workstation. Communication software refers to *uploading* and *downloading* — as well as send and receive commands. Consequently, you need to develop a sense of place — to know what is up. You can organize your diagram to show uploading of files in an upward direction and show downloading of files to your computer disks in a downward direction. You also need to know where you send and where you receive.

Diagramming Workspace in Application Programs

You can also develop cognitive maps or diagrams of the workspace you use in application programs. This enables you to keep track of where you put information. It helps you navigate within your application files. Have you ever been lost in your own word processing documents? You can also get lost in a drawing or three-dimensional model. The following paragraphs briefly suggest how to map the media space of a variety of application programs. You may not be working with all of them, but understanding how to organize information in these applications will help you eventually learn to use them more easily. Quite possibly you will find some of these applications are presently not useful to you in your discipline, or you may not have access to them in your computer environment. But that may change. If you know how to use these applications, you will realize how important these simple cognitive maps are for finding where you are, where you put information (or where someone else put something), and how you can access other information so you can work with it creatively.

word processing A computer application that enables users to compose statements by writing and editing digital files.

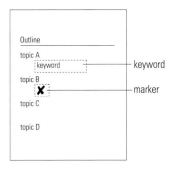

Word Processing

You navigate in *word processing programs* using outlines. You may also keep the outline in your head or print it out. Some programs have outlining commands that permit you to expand or collapse areas of the document, offering both detail and an overview. An outline in one part of a screen and the document in another can help you work with both the overview and details interactively. By using search routines, you can quickly find keywords that are like focal points. Some programs enable you to set markers. Headings and markers function like landmarks in a document. Diagrams can show relationships between keywords and ideas. Although you can generate these diagrams quickly on paper, some word processing programs now enable you to incorporate simple diagrams into your word processing media space.

spreadsheet program A computer application that enables users to organize information in rows and columns and do calculations.

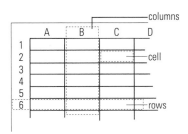

Spreadsheet

Spreadsheet programs organize information in rows and columns. This arrangement enables you to find cells of information very easily. You can embed formulas into this format to carry out calculations. A two-dimensional matrix provides a very handy frame of reference. It can handle information ranging from simple charts to complex ledgers or financial models. Some spreadsheet programs provide three-dimensional frames of reference. Others permit you to link information from a cell in one spreadsheet to a cell in another spreadsheet. These become more difficult to visualize; however, you can picture linking layers of spreadsheets together. Diagramming is helpful for using multi-dimensioned spreadsheet

database program A computer application that enables users to sift information by selecting attributes.

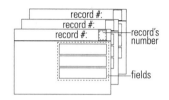

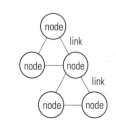

Database

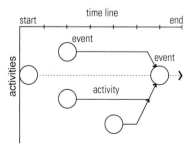

Hyper Media

capabilities effectively. Graphic programs, integrated with spreadsheets, enable you to generate line graphs, bar charts, and pie charts. This capability lets you visually express the quantitative information you are working with in your spreadsheet model.

Some *database programs* can display information on a spreadsheet. You can also picture databases as a stack of filecards. Each file contains records and fields. You can generate lists by sifting and sorting these records and fields of information. Hypermedia now enable you to nest information more freely and even integrate graphics and video images. You can map hypermedia stacks as a network of choices. Each choice has information nested at different levels within a hierarchy.

project management program A computer application that enables users to keep track of resources, activities, and time for doing projects.

Project Management

Some applications, like *project management software*, integrate several different frames of reference. Project management involves dealing with a time line. You can graphically relate activities and events to a time line using a Gannt chart or work flow diagram. You can assign activities and generate lists indicating start and end dates.

You can relate all this to a calendar. Most project management programs also enable you to track resources using databases or spreadsheets.

drawing and painting programs
Computer applications that enable users to draw and paint digitally.

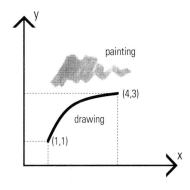

Drawing / Painting

Drawing and painting programs enable you to work graphically in media space using two dimensions — x and y coordinates. It is helpful to use a "ruler" or grid as a frame of reference. The compositions you develop may also offer spatial cues that help you organize your graphic information. Most programs let you navigate by zooming in and out and panning around your drawing area. People typically draw full scale. It is important to set your drawing limits and scale so you can print drawings out on a piece of paper or integrate them into other documents.

desktop publishing program
A computer application that enables users to lay out and integrate text with graphics.

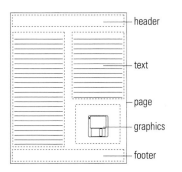

Desktop Publishing

Desktop publishing software enables you to lay out and integrate text with graphics. The page formats and numbers become the spatial reference with which you work. In effect, you are creating an electronic mock-up or prototype of what you are producing. What you see should relate very closely to what you get when you print.

computer-aided design and drafting program (CADD) A computer application that enables users to model and develop drawings of designs.

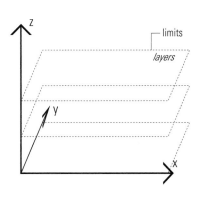

CADD / Modeling

Computer-aided design and drafting programs enable you to draft two-dimensionally on many different layers. You can turn these layers on and off to composite your graphic information in different ways. It is important to develop a clear layering system to keep track of which layer you put information on. Architects, for example, will sometimes use layering systems that relate to the construction specifications they generate. That way they can relate the organization of their drawing files to their written specifications. You can also set up certain base layers over which you draw unique information. That way you can generate several drawings from the same graphic file sharing base information.

When drafting in two dimensions, it is also important to set drawing limits. This prevents you from getting lost in media space. If you set your limits incorrectly, your drawing may become only a small dot on your screen. On the other hand, the benefit of drafting electronically is that you never run out of drawing space. You only have to redefine your limits. (You may run out of disk space, however.) Of course, you may need to recompose or rescale your drawing when you print it out.

Many CADD programs also enable you to build three-dimensional models electronically. So you need to develop a three-dimensional frame of reference involving x, y, and z coordinates. You need to define drawing limits three-dimensionally. When drawing in three dimensions, you also need to set up user coordinates because you are typically drawing using a two-dimensional digitizing tablet and looking at your model on a two-dimensioned screen. Three-dimensional digitizers and viewing devices are emerging which can make three-dimensional modeling easier to work with. In effect, by working this way, you are beginning to create a virtual reality of what you are working with. When moving around this space, you need cues like the ones you normally experience in reality so you can orient yourself and navigate. Otherwise you can get lost in a three-dimensional model. You also need to learn how to distinguish between model space and paper space. Model space is the spatial construct you are working with. Paper space is how you compose a printout on paper. For example, a single three-dimensional model could generate many different views you could print out in paper space. You can also export models or views of objects into *rendering programs* that enable you to add colors and textures. Some artists are now painting in three dimensions.

rendering program A computer application that enables users to add colors and textures to graphic images.

CADD also enables you to use parametrics to generate spatial models. For example, you can draw a staircase by simply entering the rise and run of each tread into a program that has an algorithm to generate stairs. This provides another way of drawing, and of exploring forms. CADD also enables you to attach attributes to objects. For example, you can add specifications — such as a manufacturer's model number — to objects in a drawing. In this way you can combine databases with your spatial models.

geographic information system (GIS) A computer application that enables users to develop spatial models with layers of information linked to databases of attributes.

Geographic information systems (GIS) enable you to develop spatial models with layers of information. You can composite this information to generate suitability models. GIS links databases to these spatial models and updates them as the spatial models change. It is very important to relate the spatial models to the earth's coordinates. That way the user can relate the information in media space accurately to the reality on the ground. Many of the spatial characteristics found in GIS systems are similar to those found in CADD systems. The way you orient in these media space work environments is also very similar.

imaging program A computer application that enables users to work with and enhance digital images.

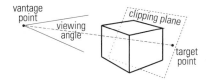

Imaging

You can now capture graphic images electronically by using either a scanner or a video capture board. These images provide their own frames of reference which you need to interpret so you can work with them. Images involve perspective and scale references as well as resolution, color, and contrast. *Imaging* is now becoming integrated into many other applications such as desktop publishing, CADD, and GIS.

animation program A computer application that enables users to portray movement.

Animation

Animation provides movement by manipulating space in time. Most animation programs are two-dimensional, although some involve three-dimensional spatial models. To work with animation requires visualizing movement. You can do this by planning positions and picturing the extremes. This enables you to develop the in-betweens (sometimes called "tweening") with key gestures and movements. You can compose this movement into flicks, sequences, and scenes related to a time frame. You can also plan how to transform an object from one morphology to another (sometimes called "morphing"). This lets you change objects over time. In this way our media space takes on the dynamic qualities of movement and change.

music program A computer application that enables users to compose and mix sounds digitally.

Music

Music programs involve yet another type of media space — the acoustical environment. You modulate sound in tempo and pitch to generate rhythms and themes. You can recognize patterns of sound using modes of thought related to your auditory senses. Yes, what is really being discussed here is music — an acoustical environment you experience in emotionally stirring ways. Using a

desktop video program A computer application that enables users to create multimedia productions involving text, graphics, images, video, and sound.

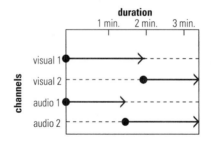

Multimedia

computer you can both synthesize and compose sound into musical arrangements.

People typically watch multimedia — video and TV. To author multimedia productions, however, may involve a studio. *Desktop video* enables you to create multimedia productions using computers. Using the multimedia software that is emerging you can integrate images and sound. You can combine many different channels including text, graphics, video, and sound. Multimedia workspace involves a score that enables you to relate different channels of media to a time frame. In this way you can develop a storyboard and integrate media over time. You can have some things play concurrently, others in sequence.

simulation A computer hardware and software setup that represents real environments. Enables users to work with computers to rehearse what it would be like to do something, like fly an airplane, in reality.

Simulations are another way of working with multimedia. In effect, you can use a media space that simulates a real environment. You can use controls to interact with this artificial reality. For example, flight simulators enable you to look out the window of a simulated airplane and view the horizon as well as the instruments. Expensive simulators include actual controls with tactile feedback. Personal computer versions use the keyboard, or various pointing devices, to simulate the controls.

As you can see, there is a wide range of applications for electronic media. Visualizing how to organize media space is an important first step to work with it. Of course, you need the right software and hardware and must learn how to use them. You also need to develop the skills and be able to apply them to your discipline.

Transferring Information to Media Space

Now that you have a sense of media space, you need to learn how to transfer information into it. Only then will it become real and useful to you.

Everyone is familiar with personal interaction. If you are engaged in a conversation, you are alternately listening and talking. The conversation is paced by what you can comprehend and express. You also usually find out immediately if the person you are talking to does not understand what you are saying. You also can indicate when you don't understand. You can even can guide the conversation to things you find more interesting. You do this in face-to-face conversations. You can also do this using a telephone or interactive video. While there are certain advantages to real-time interaction, unless you can remember what is said, take notes, or record the interaction, you don't have the information to work with later.

Using electronic media, you can record and work with information interactively in media space. This gives you certain freedoms over time and space. You don't have to respond right away. You can also distribute information to people in other places. For example, working with a computer, you can compose a message. When your message contains what you want to say, you can send it by E-mail or other forms of telecommunications — distributing it rather easily that way. Other people can read your message and respond at their own pace. It is also possible for them to forward your message (and their comments) to others. In this way more people have this information to work with interactively.

Beyond just working with messages, you can build models representing objects your discipline may be working with. For example, planners and businesses often work with spreadsheet models for budgeting purposes. Architects and engineers typically work with drawings; they can also work with three-dimensional spatial models to create new designs. These models become an artificial reality that a project team can work on together in shared media space.

The trick to being able to use electronic media interactively is learning how to effectively transfer ideas and information into media space. You need to learn to quickly capture ideas and information and avoid getting stuck or wasting time when moving them. You can also learn to use *templates* which have *generic information*. For example this could be as simple as a *form* or *clip art* which you can add information to or modify for your purpose. Templates can also be much more elaborate such as those uses in spreadsheet models, or in standard drawing layers. Realize that generic information is just a starting point. You really need to adapt it to your own purposes, by adapting information and adding your own ideas. A common pitfall is using the wrong tools. Beyond that, you need to develop good approaches for using the tools you have access to.

template A standardized format that presents generic information. For example, this could be as simple as a form or clip art that computer users can add information to and modify for their own purposes.

You transfer information and ideas to media at different rates. The rate

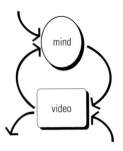

Video - real time sound and images

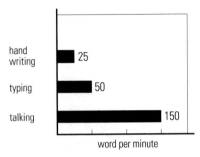

hand writing 25

typing 50

talking 150

word per minute

Comparative Transfer Rates

often depends upon the tools you use. For example, you can capture images in real time on video actually faster than your mind can assimilate them. No doubt you have had the experience of seeing an instant replay. This helps you discover much more of what happened than you were aware of when you saw the image the first time. You can also translate your mental images to drawings that express your thinking. Translating images into words is a comparatively slow process since you think visually at an equivalent of thousands of words per minute.

A difficulty you may have expressing your creative thinking is to keep pace with your mind. For this reason, you should do initial transfers in the form of quick notes or idea sketches that enable you to record your thoughts as they are occurring. The next quickest mode of expressing words is through talking. Most people can easily speak at between 90 and 180 words per minute — typically, 150 words per minute. While shorthand can almost keep up with verbal expression, typing is the next fastest mode for expressing words. People generally type between 30 and 90 words per minute — typically, about 50 words per minute (or about a third of the rate at which people talk). Handwriting is a slower mode for expressing words. People can typically handwrite between 15 and 30 words per minute — on the average, 25 words per minute (about one-half the rate at which people type or about one-sixth the rate at which people talk). Develop transfer modes that are quick and effective for you. Relate these to the computer environment you have access to.

Unless your initial transfers are quick, you risk not getting your ideas down. So you need ways to compress information — using keywords and outlines or idea sketches and diagrams. When working verbally, you can capture keywords. You can make outlines on a notepad using a pencil or, in electronic media, using a word processor. Or working from notes, you can dictate on tape and then transcribe the tape using a word processor. Or you can work from an outline and expand your outline using a word processor. Similarly, working graphically, you can make idea sketches on paper and then scan them into a digital format. Or you can develop your

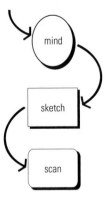

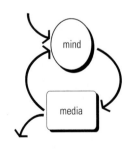

Indirect Transfer

Direct Transfer to Electronic Media

idea sketches using a graphics or CADD program. Once you have a composition and some symbols in the computer, you can manipulate them electronically. Drafting by hand, like writing by hand, is slow compared with the other methods you have available. Handwriting and sketching are very effective means for mental note taking, but you can go beyond these basic tools. Keyboard skills enable you to express written compositions digitally. A mouse or stylus enables you to express your mental images graphically in electronic media.

The more easily you can transfer your thinking into a digital form, the more readily you can use computers to develop your thoughts creatively. Many forms of electronic media are extremely fluid. You can add information and make changes rather easily. As more people begin to work electronically, it will also be easier to share information. You can also communicate over long distances in less time.

Transfer Syndromes

Productivity studies of white-collar workers have generally shown a disappointing improvement in productivity due to computerization. This causes me to wonder why.

The students and professionals who I find make the greatest strides using computers creatively and productively are those who most directly transfer their thoughts to electronic media. There they can work more interactively. Those who have problems with this often suffer from some of the following *syndromes*. Yet these syndromes can be overcome. Identifying problems can often help you turn them into opportunities for personal improvement and growth.

syndrome (from Greek, *syn*, together, and *dromos*, running) Conditions running together. A number of symptoms which together characterize a problem.

The "I Can't Create on a Computer" Syndrome

Some people find it difficult to sit down in front of a computer and access media space. Or they may stare at a blank screen and not have a mental picture of what to express even if they know how to use a computer application. Computers sometimes intimidate people, making it difficult for them to transfer ideas to electronic media. (People can also have difficulties concentrating on what is on paper. Or they may stare at a blank piece of paper with a pen in hand unable to make a mark.) They may not yet be comfortable using these tools, or they may fear making mistakes.

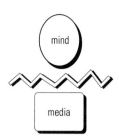

I Can't Create on a Computer

Fortunately, when working with a computer, you can quickly access information. Once you are familiar with the user interface and application commands, it is also not that difficult to express ideas even in multimedia. You can change your mind or correct mistakes without any tell-tale erasures. Although computer user interfaces may seem difficult to learn, they are easy if compared with learning to play a violin, a flute, a trombone, or a pipe organ. Certainly these instruments enable people to play beautiful music. Obviously, well-designed interfaces are needed so users can easily engage the new instruments that are emerging.

You may feel using computers is difficult compared with using familiar tools such as pencils or pens. But did you ever consider how long it took you to learn to print letters, or write in script, or draw with a pen? If you have no hand-drafting or computer-drafting skills, you can learn to use both of these tools at about the same rate. It takes a while to master ink drafting. Similarly, it takes a while to master electronic drafting.

Many creative thinking skills relate to both paper and electronic media; however, your approach to each should differ because what you can do with paper and with electronic media is not the same. You need to find hardware and software with which you are comfortable and productive. Give yourself time to develop familiarity with applications so you can work with them creatively.

The "Paperless Office" Syndrome

The aim of some people is to do away with paper — to try to do everything with a computer; but frequently this is impractical. That is because your better ideas often strike you when you are not sitting in front of a computer. Don't be embarrassed to jot down notes when ideas occur using any tools and media that you have available. Sometimes you can make mental notes and then sit down at a computer and proceed. Usually, however, it helps to have a few notes or scribbles on paper. There is a crucial point, however, at which you can do your scribbling and note taking more productively using a computer. The key is knowing when to shift vehicles while transferring ideas.

You should use the transfers that make the most sense based on your capabilities, the tools you have available, and the tasks at hand. You should seek the quickest and easiest way to transfer ideas into electronic media if you want to use computers creatively.

Small hand-held computers could be especially useful in situations where you generate ideas and information, making it easier to do this transfer directly with electronic media.

The "Product" Syndrome

Some people feel they have to have a tangible product. In a traditional office, this is usually a piece of paper that is an artifact of their efforts. Previous education or work experience may have conditioned them to have a paper to put in their notebook or file. They may also be driven by a need to show a product to a computer-illiterate instructor or employer. But instead of printing out paper, it is better to enable others to access a digital file. Then they can work with it electronically and make revisions more directly. (You can also secure files you don't want changed.) A printout requires extra steps not only for printing, but also for transferring the revisions back to a digital document, although this does give the

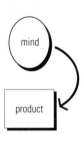

Paperless Office

Product

author of the document a way to consider changes proposed by others. Sometimes it is productive to print out drafts or plot check sets especially when dealing with large documents that require an overview. Then checking can also be done without tying up a computer. Using printouts in these situations does provide definite benefits. However, too many printouts can undermine productivity and profits when using electronic media. It can be more productive to get each member of a workgroup to relate to objects in a computer. This digital product can become the object focusing a team's activity, enabling each of the group members to work with it directly and interactively.

The "Typist" Syndrome

Some people use a word processor only as a typewriter. First they may gather their notes in traditional ways. Then they may write a complete draft by hand, using the computer only for typing a final copy.

Working this way they convince themselves there is no real advantage to using computers. In their case this is true because they lose the benefits of electronic media. The transfer of their ideas takes too many steps and involves processes that are comparatively slow and less interactive. They ignore the opportunities to use the evaluative tools a computer provides — spell checkers, grammar checkers, etc. They ignore opportunities to use more attractive fonts and formats.

However, typing papers from handwritten drafts is a way to develop the skills necessary to become comfortable with a computer keyboard. Only after you have typing skills can you compose with a keyboard. Also, many people seek a quiet place to do their creative work. They may not have a computer to use where they can work creatively. In noisy computer labs, all they can do is type. Under those circumstances it may be easier to work from a handwritten draft.

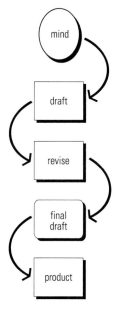

Typist

The "Draftsman" Syndrome

Similarly, some people may sketch on tissue and then develop their designs by hand on paper. If they use the computer only for drafting the final presentation, they lose the real benefit of electronic media. Their transfer of ideas takes too many steps and is comparatively slow.

Using computers only as a drafting machine misses opportunities computer-aided design provides. The drafting syndrome, like the typing syndrome, is a legacy of transfer processes learned when using paper. The process of drafting and then redrafting is tedious and time-consuming. With electronic media you can transfer information from one draft to the next. Computers enable you to refine documents more interactively.

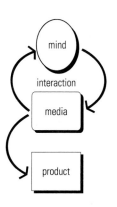

Draftsman

Most of my students don't have access to CADD stations where they can work on their project whenever they would like. Consequently, they often work on paper and then transfer their ideas to electronic media when they can use a CADD station. I try to get them to quickly sketch their ideas by hand and then use the computer to develop more precise drawings. I also suggest they get an inexpensive drafting program that can run on their own personal computer if they have one. Then they can do simple portions of drawings and transfer their files to integrate them into larger drawings they assemble on a CADD station. Many basic drafting programs are compatible with more advanced CADD and graphic programs. This gives students more convenient access to electronic media and a way of uploading their files so they can work with advanced features, such as three-dimensional modeling and shading, when workstations are available

The "Single Application" Syndrome

Many people use only one computer application. For example, they may do only word processing or work only with numbers using a spreadsheet. Or they may work only with CADD.

You can explore different applications that give you more ways of transferring information and ideas to electronic media. You can learn to work not only with text, but also with graphics, imaging, three-dimensional models, video, and sound. Ideally, you could learn to relate all your channels of perception and expression to electronic media. This opens more avenues for communication and creative thinking.

The "Clip Art and Cliché" Syndrome

Clip art provides images people can re-use, much like they use verbal clichés (stock phrases). Some people use clip art in very superficial ways — as decoration, not communication. Similarly, they use written clichés in almost the same way — as words without meaning, noise.

Developing a capacity for critical thinking enables you to recognize the trite and meaningless. People need to go beyond this to use computers creatively. However, templates can often be useful as a starting point or guide. And clip art and stock phrases can sometimes stimulate more creative thinking.

The "Computer Programming" Syndrome

In the past, computer literacy usually meant knowing how to write programs. At one time you had to develop your own programs to use a computer. Today, this is no longer true. Yet there is confusion between toolmaking and tool using.

Programming is for toolmaking. Although it is a useful and creative endeavor, you don't need to know how to write computer programs to use them. Similarly, you don't have to know how to forge a hammer to drive a nail.

To work with computers creatively, however, you do need to know how to work interactively with electronic media. You especially need to know

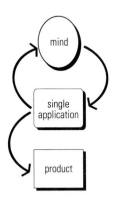

Single Application

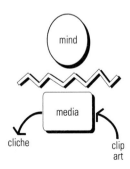

Clip Art & Cliche

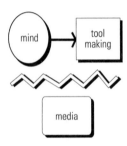

Computer Programming

how to transfer your own ideas into the media. Learning creative thinking skills, learning to use software applications, and becoming familiar with the hardware should be the basic focus for computer literacy.

The "Computer Phobia or Anxiety" Syndrome

Computer Phobia or Anxiety

Some people's aversion to computers may come from computer literacy courses that offer an overdose of programming or applied user training. Many people may relate better to learning to use computers in regular courses and real-life situations where the applications are clearly helpful to them.

Some peoples' anxieties have more to do with the place than the machine. Computer labs in many universities and offices can be hostile environments. They may produce anxieties related to noise, glare, and crowding. There are often too many people and too few machines. Experienced users can get impatient with neophytes who need time to explore and learn. Sometimes, people derive phobias from crashes —losing a file or bumping the hard disk they did not back up. People have difficulty relating to computers when they can't picture the media space they are working in. If they have no sense of place, they can't navigate. Then they lose confidence in being able to find files they leave in a computer.

Good facilities and appropriate instruction can help overcome phobias and anxieties. Developing a passion for electronic media helps you engage yourself creatively. If you can work intimately, you will find fertile media for growing ideas.

The "Computer Frustration" Syndrome

Computer Frustration

Frustration often results when people expect so much but have so little. This formula for frustration seems almost unavoidable for students who become aware of the computer's possibilities, but who have to rely on their own computer resources. How wonderful it would be if schools could provide students access to good computers. (Unfortunately, often what schools typically can afford compounds students' and educators' frustrations.) High expectations are actually healthy. You do need to temper them, though, with the reality of the situation with which you are working.

Fortunately, students move on to offices. Usually, in this environment there are economic incentives for using good tools. Then, some of this frustration will subside.

Configuring computer systems can also be very frustrating. You can usually survive the configuration blues and forget all your troubles when you get the system working right. It is hoped that you can find the technical support you need to help you through these frustrations. Given the complexity of the hardware and software, it is amazing that people can make computers work at all.

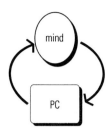

Personal Computer

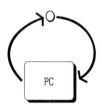

User Training

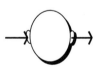

Why Bother

Wait for It to Get Better

The "Personal Computer" Syndrome

Using personal computers as stand-alone workstations can isolate people. What good is an idea if you can't share it? Linking computers by using networks and telecommunications promotes communication. You can work with others using electronic media.

The real potential for electronic media is what it can do for workgroup productivity, not just individual productivity. Workgroups need to share common media, models, and methods. Then people can interact more creatively and productively. Chapter 6 provides approaches for helping you and your workgroup learn to do this using computers.

The "User Training" Syndrome

Many people and schools focus on user training, stressing hardware and software application skills. This kind of training can perpetuate the myth that people just need to push the right buttons and, "the computer will do it all." Training alone may produce computer operators who quickly become obsolete. While there is a need for good user training, people have to go beyond training and also learn creative thinking skills related to electronic media. Computer applications can be interjected into the many disciplines where people can use them creatively. Also people must get the knowledge base necessary to pursue their disciplines.

Computers are only a means, not an end in themselves, unless you build hardware and software. They are a tool, just as a calculator is. Rarely do you find a calculator course. Instead, you use calculators in any course where they are helpful. In the same way, disciplines need to integrate computer applications into their coursework.

The "Why Bother" Syndrome

"Why bother to use computers?" is a question established professionals sometimes ask. They have invested a great deal in learning their current skills. Naturally, they may feel threatened by new tools and techniques.

Some older professionals may have a hard time justifying the investment. Others see the use of computers as a challenge and enjoy the learning experience and the capabilities they can develop. Young students, who are just learning a discipline, are usually eager to learn computer applications.

The "Wait for It to Get Better" Syndrome

Hardware and software are constantly getting better. Methods embodying thinking skills also continue to evolve. For example, the multimedia wave is cresting and merging with HDTV, bringing many changes to the way people use computers. You can easily talk yourself out of investing in new tools and wait for them to get better. They may even get less expensive. However, software and hardware are already good enough to benefit many disciplines if you know how to use them well. You can transfer what you learn about thinking skills to new computer systems. Much of what you learn about using software continues to be useful through upgrades. Even the hardware you purchase initially can continue to be useful, although it may not continue to be the state-of-the-art.

In these syndromes I have compiled observations from teaching and working with computer applications. Sometimes people learn most from mistakes; however this book presents approaches that can help you avoid these syndromes. This will help you to learn more quickly and with less misguided effort.

Information Flow

Information flow changes as tools and the work environment change. When I started teaching more than twenty years ago, we worked in a traditional tool-based environment to produce course materials and correspondence. We would write by hand, type, edit, retype, copy, and

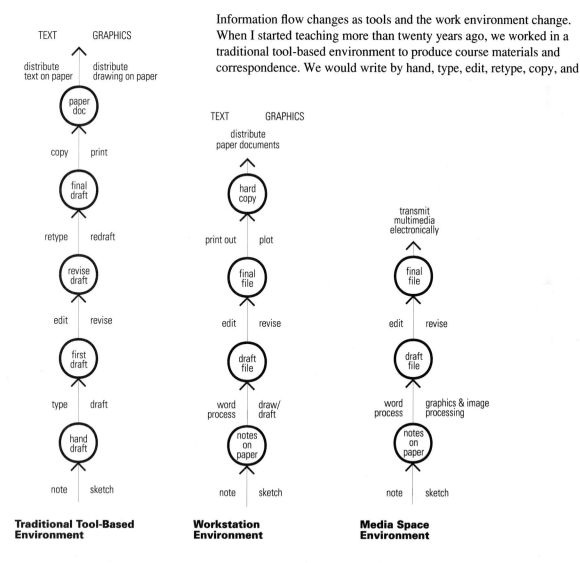

Traditional Tool-Based Environment

Workstation Environment

Media Space Environment

distribute paper documents. During the 1980s many of us changed to a workstation environment using personal computers. Then we could word-process, edit, print out, and distribute course materials and correspondence on paper. Word processing made written documents easier to produce. Today, I try to work mostly in a media space environment. I word-process, edit, and transmit course materials and correspondence electronically. I also work on other types of digital files such as drawings and models, which I can transfer electronically.

A change is occurring in communication costs as computers and telecommunications become more available. Until now, memos, mail, and meetings have been the least expensive modes for communication and interaction. However, telecommunications are starting to become less expensive than those modes. With the right equipment, it is easier, quicker, and less expensive to use E-mail than to mail a paper memo or letter. For example, because we have E-mail at my university, it is less expensive for my department if I work in media space and distribute course materials online than have them typed out in the department office, reproduced, and distributed on paper. E-mail enables me to get written information to my students more quickly and update it more frequently.

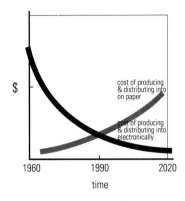

Information Distribution Cost

As telecommunications evolve to include interactive video, this mode of communication can even replace some meetings. It can cost less to move information than to move people. It is also becoming less expensive to arrange and distribute electrons through media space than to arrange and distribute graphite on paper, or dyes on film. It is even becoming less expensive to store information digitally than to store it using traditional media. (And you may have a better chance of finding information electronically than finding it in a paper file.) Maybe the most compelling benefit is providing people more freedom over where and when they work.

As a result of these changes in communication costs and benefits, disciplines are undergoing changes in the way people work with and move information. Managing information flow is becoming more complex, particularly as people use different media. Consequently, it has become important to learn to visualize the transfer of information involved in a project.

Information Flow Diagramming

information flow diagram A graphic representation to visualize how to transfer information from one object to another. Especially helpful when integrating information from many different sources and using computer document-oriented interfaces to transform it into a range of products.

Think of information as being embodied in objects you work with. Each file, document, model, or graphic representation contains information. You can show how you transfer information from one object to another, or how you transform objects from one stage of a project to another. Graphically diagram your objects as boxes. Then link those boxes with lines showing the pathways through which you are transferring information. These diagrams help you develop strategies for transferring information more effectively. *Information flow diagrams* are helpful when

	source info	final product
text		
graphics		
images		
video		
sound		

info types

Format for Information Flow Diagram

working with traditional media such as paper or film. The thinking skills involved are especially important when working with electronic media.

You can develop information flow diagrams for projects you are working on. Simple information flow diagrams drawn with pencil on paper are fine. You can also draw them using almost any computer graphic program. In these diagrams, show how you will proceed from your source information to a final product. Examine the type of information you are working with — be it text, graphics, images, even video or sound. Establish a frame of reference to help you diagram information flow. For example, I usually have my students set up a chart showing the source information in columns on the left and final products in columns on the right. This chart can also show different channels of information in rows. You will find this will help you examine how to transfer and coordinate text, graphics, etc. You can see how you are moving information back and forth between different channels which often involve different work environments. Another approach is to keep information related to different topics in separate rows. For example, when working with a landscape you might keep site information in one row, user information in another. Then you can see how you will merge this information to develop a design that addresses both site and user needs.

Two approaches can help you develop information flow diagrams. One approach is to start with the information you have and diagram strategies for what you can do with it (relative to the problem you are addressing). The second approach is to envision what the final product will be and work backward (deriving what information will be necessary to design and develop your project). You can use both of these approaches together to develop a more complete picture.

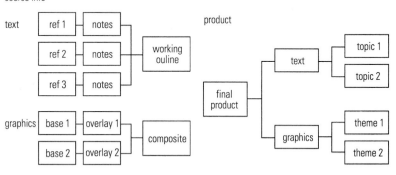

Start with Source Information and Visualize Forward

Start with Final Product and Visualize Backward

Visualizing strategies for transferring information can help you in many ways. You can avoid gathering information you don't need before you invest a lot of time and effort. You can also discover where there are dead ends or missing pieces of information. By diagramming information flow, you can examine transfers at each stage of the project and determine the most effective way to integrate the information into your final product.

As you gather information, you get a better idea of how to work with it in the media space you are using. Often, information you thought you could acquire isn't available. Having a clear picture of information flow enables you to work with surrogate information or proceed with assumptions you can verify later. Sometimes you will discover new information that is useful to your project. Or you may also change or refine your project goals as you proceed. Obviously your information flow diagram evolves as you find out more about your project. Your information flow diagram may also evolve as you learn more about the media you are using. For that reason it can be helpful to draw the diagram electronically in order to modify or update it more easily. Flow diagramming programs are even available in some software packages.

There are different attitudes for using maps of media space and information flow diagrams. You can develop clear strategies for attaining a predetermined goal — using your diagrams as you would use a map of a transit system and an itinerary. Or you can simply establish a general direction and see what you discover as you work — using your diagrams as you might use a road map when you are exploring. Then your diagrams will help you to reassess where you are and where you are going.

Try not to replicate traditional approaches when using new tools. For example, a map developed for traveling in a horse-drawn buggy would be different from a map developed for driving in a car. A map for flying would be different yet. Make sure that your information flow diagram fits the tools you are using. For example, a flow diagram developed for transferring information using traditional handwriting and drafting techniques is different from the diagram you would develop for working with electronic media. Electronic media offer new possibilities. In fact, using traditional procedures can make new tools ineffective. For example, constantly transferring between electronic media and paper printouts is like taking an airplane down a horse and buggy trail. By developing effective thinking skills, you can transcend traditional approaches and find new routes for working with information applying the new tools that are emerging.

Data Flow Diagramming

data flow diagram A graphic representation to visualize how to transfer digital files. Especially helpful when working with different file formats where it is necessary to figure out the best way to move files from one program or computer platform to another.

Data flow diagramming helps you visualize how to transfer digital files. This is useful when you work with different file formats. Diagramming key steps can help you figure out the best ways to move files from one program or computer platform to another. Otherwise you risk not being able to make the transfer and may have to start over, digitizing information again. Boxes can represent the files in different formats. Arrows can represent the transfers involved. The framework you work with can relate to your media space. For example, you can visually show how to upload and download files to a mainframe computer. Once you develop a strategy by using your diagram, it is important to test it with sample files.

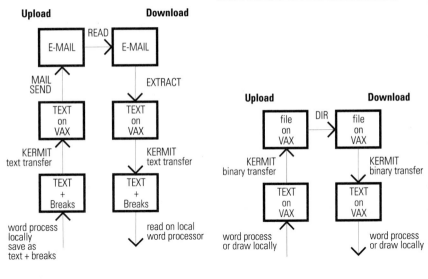

Upload   **Download**

READ

E-MAIL → E-MAIL

MAIL SEND   EXTRACT

TEXT on VAX   TEXT on VAX

KERMIT text transfer   KERMIT text transfer

TEXT + Breaks   TEXT + Breaks

word process locally save as text + breaks   read on local word processor

**E-Mail Transfers
(Working Locally)**

Upload   **Download**

DIR

file on VAX → file on VAX

KERMIT binary transfer   KERMIT binary transfer

TEXT on VAX   TEXT on VAX

word process or draw locally   word process or draw locally

Binary File Transfers

For example, transfer sample text and graphic files to your desktop publishing program. Then transfer a pilot of your composited file to whatever device you are going to print it on. This will let you know if your data transfers work before you commit a lot of effort.

Some applications now provide for *dynamic data exchanges*. For example, changing information in one file, such as a spreadsheet, will change information in another file, such as a word processing document. GIS and some CADD programs also dynamically link objects (such as polygons) with attributes. Changing the object updates the attributes. *Document-oriented interfaces* are emerging which will provide more powerful and intuitive ways to work with "living files."

dynamic data exchange The automatic transfer of information from one application to another as you work in any of the applications linked by the exchange.

document-oriented interface The DOI focuses on documents rather than on applications. Object-oriented applications, as well as attributes, are imbedded in documents which users can work on using a variety of computers.

As already shown, a map of your media space is much like a map of a transportation system. Your data flow diagrams involve the same thinking you go through when figuring out what your schedule is, where to transfer, and what tickets you need. You go through that mental exercise when taking a journey (although you may internalize the thought process). Similarly, you need to go through that thought process when transferring computer files. Sometimes you may find yourself stumped like the old New Englander, who, when asked directions, simply said, "Don't reckon you can get the'ah from he'ah." If you take the time to picture how to get there, you usually can do it. Maps of media space and data flow diagrams can help you find your way — especially when you venture into areas and applications you haven't used before. Even when working with familiar applications, these visualization techniques can help you find shortcuts.

Simple cognitive maps and data flow diagrams can also help others in your workgroup understand how to organize your shared media space work environment. Each person in a workgroup should know how to navigate, where to put files, and how to transfer them efficiently. Transfers can involve handoffs from a person, or group, working in one computer environment to another person, or group, working in another computer environment. Good communication can help solve problems you may encounter.

Collaboration

collaboration The act of working together. Electronic media offer new opportunities for workgroup collaboration.

Most creative endeavors today involve teamwork. Consequently, you need to be concerned about effective *collaboration*. Some people look at media (and the tools related to media) as a way of getting their own ideas out — a dialogue with themselves. Others look at media (and related tools) as a vehicle for collaboration — a dialogue with others. The emphasis depends upon the nature of the creative work they do. You can focus inwardly in reflection; you can focus outwardly in collaboration. Endeavor to do both. You can learn to carry on these dialogues using the new tools and media that are emerging.

When working creatively in a group, find ways to get everyone's ideas down. Work together to organize the ideas. Then evaluate them and generate shared products that reflect your group's thinking. This provides an effective record for collaboration. It works especially well if you have a shared object that you can relate to in media space. For example, you could work with a draft or mock-up of the actual document you are producing together. You could also work together on a financial model or a three-dimensional spatial model of whatever you are producing. Object-oriented meetings enable a workgroup to build something together in media space. Such meetings can be much more productive than ones where people just get together to talk and then have their discussion

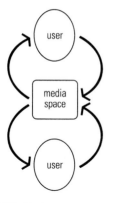

Shared Media Space

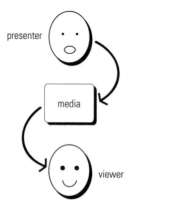

Presentation

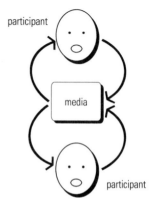

Collaboration

recorded in minutes. You can even assemble teams of consultants and work in shared media space without being in the same place or working at the same time.

Working in media space also provides opportunities for audience or client participation. People typically think of making presentations to their audiences or clients. When people present information, they need their audience's reaction. By working in electronic media space, it is possible to invite participation. For example, people can work interactively with client groups, making them part of the collaboration. Doing this can reduce the need for making elaborate single-direction (from consultant/ performer to audience) presentations. It sets up opportunities for more effective multidirection (from consultant to client to consultant, etc.) multimedia interactions.

Michael Schrage's book *Shared Minds: The New Technologies of Collaboration* discusses opportunities for working together using computers. He points out how this can enhance group interaction, particularly in large organizations. However, this is also very important to small independent consultants — especially if they wish to locate in remote areas. Aside from using the telephone, consultants can send ideas and information back and forth on disk. They can correspond via FAX or transmit information electronically via modem. Using networks, they can interact with the same database shared by others.

Groupware is emerging, designed to give network users better access to shared information. This is beginning to affect the basic structure of the workplace. It is especially helpful to large organizations that have offices in different regions. It can improve coordination and group input in making decisions. It also has potential to shorten product development cycles and delivery time.

Computers and electronic media space can enhance group meetings in much the same way traditional tools such as pencil and paper, or chalk and a blackboard, have. However, you will not run out of space as easily. You can also print out the document you work on together at the end of the meeting, or you can store it for future efforts. I have seen discussions revolve around a computer workstation where the participants spontaneously take turns adding ideas and information to the file. A few people can also pass a notebook computer around a coffee table. These computer-augmented discussions are particularly effective when people sit down together to get their first ideas out before they work individually on their assignments. These discussions also work well when editing a working document or manipulating an existing drawing or model. Of course, it helps if the participants are all computer-literate when carrying on this type of interaction. But this is not essential if someone is willing to record for the group.

Bernard DeKoven's booklet, *Connected Executives*, describes some helpful procedures for larger group sessions. A key to running this type

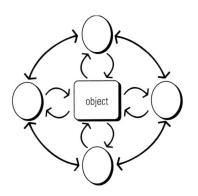

Computer-Augmented Workgroup

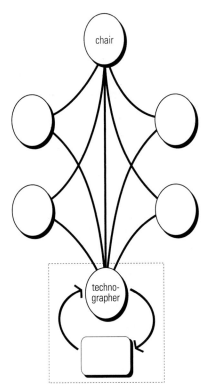

Computer-Enhanced Meeting

technographer A technical recorder for computer conferencing. This person uses electronic media to record a group's thinking, so the group can work interactively to collaboratively.

of meeting is to have a *technographer* who develops the collaborative document to which all can contribute interactively. DeKoven suggests meeting in a room set up with a computer and video projector. This helps keep people focused and enables the technographer to work with the ideas and information coming from the group in ways that wouldn't be possible using chalk or a marker. The participants need not use the computer themselves. He points out that the group leader should also not try to function as the technographer. The computer needs to be neutrally controlled in the background to reflect the group discussion.

You can also work with a much broader range of information using video. I sometimes videotape presentations my students make so they can see their presentations as others do. The tape shows them things that are very difficult to comment on constructively. Using this feedback positively can help them improve. Video can also reveal a great deal about the dynamics of discussion groups. It can actually be very instructive to have participants review tapes, provided they are aware they are going to be taped and are comfortable with the medium. Video also provides a record you can share with others. It is nice for a student who missed a presentation to be able to see it at another time.

interactive video Video that is both sent and received. Enables users to interact in real time involving both audio and video transmitted electronically.

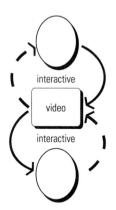

Interactive Video

Interactive video provides even more possibilities. The participants need both viewing and transmitting video setups, enabling them to communicate in much the same way they use a telephone, although with a dramatically broader bandwidth of information. There are now commercial video conference centers that enable you to confer with people at centers in another city. Some school systems are starting to use interactive video for education. This enables specialized instruction to reach a much bigger audience, especially in remote areas, giving that audience a chance to participate in interesting ways.

Electronic media typically elicit a whole range of reactions. Many people's preconception is that working in media space must be very impersonal. Actually, I find this is not true. You know how personal using a telephone can be. Interactive video could be even more engaging. Using E-mail or telecommunications, you can pick up messages and send them when you want to, thereby giving your responses more thought. Meetings in media space are less limited by time because people don't have to sit there waiting for the response. They can do other things and then, whenever they have the time, tune in to get the latest messages or files. Having a modem can permit you to respond from a quiet, comfortable place where you can concentrate. When working in media space, anyone with computer literacy has the chance to respond. People also have a chance to edit their responses before they send them. In some ways, this process can draw more out of people. Also, each person can see when he or she is off the topic. Some people can dominate verbal discussions, but media space provides an opportunity for everyone to participate. A good workgroup can productively focus its interaction in media space.

multidisciplinary Involving more than one discipline. Enabling disciplines to work together.

multidirectional Involving more than one direction. Enabling computer users to both receive and send digital information.

Computers provide a vehicle for multimedia, *multidisciplinary*, and *multidirectional* collaboration. As the bandwidth of electronic media widens, people can use more of their perception, and hence more of their mental capacity. Disciplines can collaborate in this shared media space. At one level people can easily learn to navigate in media space — much like a tourist — simply viewing what is there. With more effort people can learn to work creatively in media space — more like an artist — studying and interacting with what is there.

Multimedia computing is becoming a vehicle for learning the knowledge base in many disciplines. Developing the thinking skills needed to interact and work together using electronic media should also become a common concern for education. Learning to interact effectively in media space could open new opportunities for creative collaboration. What people do could reach a wide variety of audiences using electronic media. Possibly a new Renaissance could emerge.

Summary

Now you realize that you can picture media space. You can learn to navigate in it. Key principles involve establishing both personal and shared media space using a range of computer applications you have access to. Developing maps of media space helps you remember where you put information and how you can access it. The following activities will help you develop a mental picture of your media space.

You can also learn to transfer information to your media space effectively. Understanding syndromes can help you overcome problems related to transferring information and working with electronic media. Information flow diagrams help you visualize these transfers. The activities that follow engage you in establishing ways to diagram information flow so you find more direct transfers to electronic media. This will help you receive and present information when working with electronic media. Using a matrix as a frame of reference helps you diagram information flow — forward from your information sources or backward from your final product.

Data flow diagrams help you sort out transfers of files from one digital format to another. The last activity in this chapter involves using data flow diagrams to figure out transfers between formats you use in your computer environment. This can also help you access media space using FAX, a computer with modem, or even video. Working through these activities enables you and your workgroup to be more productive and creative when using electronic media.

Activities

1. Map Media Space

Everyone creates cognitive maps. Think of your mental image of your community or home. You also have a mental map of your office or studio, your desk or file drawer, your briefcase or notebook. You use this to help organize and navigate in each of these places. Life might be simpler if you didn't try to keep track of so much, but then you would also be limiting what you have access to. Typically, the more access you have, the more freedom you enjoy. Of course, you need to know how to use this freedom, and there should not be too much burden maintaining it. You experience anxiety when you lose track of something — especially when you need it. For example, remember how you felt when you have said, "Where are my keys?" Similarly, you need to keep track of commands to access different areas of your media space. You have also asked; "Where did I put that book?" In media space you need to remember where you put your files.

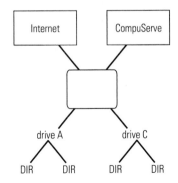

If you develop a clear picture of the electronic media space you put computer files in, you can gain confidence in electronic media and find information more easily. This will also help you develop a sense of place so you can learn to navigate electronically and work interactively using computers. Develop clear cognitive maps you can share with others. That way each of you can find places where you put information when you work together in shared media space. It is now possible even to develop virtual realities using electronic media that enable you to transcend time and space. To do this you need to learn how to navigate and use computer systems that are a vehicle for accessing this environment. Use metaphors that can help you navigate. For example, a desktop metaphor can help you find familiar tools in your work environment. A cockpit metaphor can make a simulator more realistic. Ask yourself, "From where can I access this media space? Can I reach it from my classroom or work environment? Can I reach it from my home? Can I access my media space when I am traveling and call it up any time of the day? Can I extend my media space to include information services or colleagues I may wish to communicate with around the world?"

Develop a map of the media space you can access interactively. Sketch a diagram of it on paper. This may be simply your collection of floppy disks or perhaps partitions and directories on a hard disk. It may involve several different computers you have access to. You can expand your media space by using networks and telecommunications. To use media space effectively, not only do you need to know where to go, but also you need to know the commands necessary to get there. You also need mental maps to navigate within applications. For example, you need to orient yourself to navigate within a word processing or spreadsheet file to know where you are within a document. Similarly, you need to be able to orient within a CADD drawing or three-dimensional model, as well as within a database or hypercard stack. Get in the habit of drafting outlines or sketching diagrams of your media space. This will help you develop the mental picture you need in order to navigate and work with electronic media more effectively. Initially, your maps may be very crude and your media space limited. Save your first diagrams. Do them in your journal or fold them up and tuck them into this page of the book so you can look at them later. Eventually, as you continue on in this book, you will learn more about visualization. This will help you develop clearer mental pictures of your media space. You will also find that your media space will be expanding. After you read this book, you might find it fun to come back to this early map of your media space and redo this exercise. You will probably find it amazing how clearly you can visualize this abstract realm and how extensive your media space environment can become.

2. Diagram Information Flow

Each discipline deals with a flow of information. Most professions have established patterns for processing information. For example, artists observe and derive inspiration from settings, develop interpretations using whatever media they are working with, and produce art objects or performances. Architects and engineers derive design criteria (taking into consideration client requests, user needs, and environmental conditions), develop designs, produce implementation documents, and monitor the construction process. Medical professionals examine patients, administer tests, interpret results, make diagnoses, and prescribe appropriate treatment. Scientists develop hypotheses, conduct experiments, interpret results, derive conclusions, and publish findings.

You can visualize each type of project as a flow of information. Your discipline has sources for information. They establish ways to perceive the information and work with it. There are also ways to transfer information to produce results. What is significant here is that these procedures are changing as better tools become available, enabling you to use more electronic media. This two-part exercise will cause you to consider changes in information flow related to your discipline.

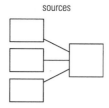

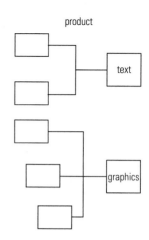

a. Impressions

Consider how you gather information for your creative endeavors. Use any project you are now doing as a case study. Diagram the flow of information from your data sources to your applications. What tools and media are you presently using as the vehicles for transferring your information? How are you currently using computers and electronic media?

After you carefully consider what you are now doing, evaluate it. What hardware and software do you presently have access to or could you possibly acquire? Could you use these tools to gather and transfer information more effectively? Are there ways you can transfer information more directly into electronic media? For example, can you gather information (or take notes) directly using a computer? Are there information services you could use to access existing information already in digital formats? Can you transfer information into formats that you can work with more easily? Can you use telecommunications to reduce the time and effort involved in transferring information? Draw simple data flow diagrams to develop strategies for how you might gather and transfer information more efficiently.

b. Expressions

Consider how you now do your creative work. Use the same project again as a case study. How do you develop your ideas? What tools and media are you using to give expression to your thoughts? How do you interact with the information you are working with? How do you share information when you collaborate with others? What objects or computer models embody the information with which you are working? Trace where that information goes. Consider how you are transferring it.

Again, evaluate what you are now doing. Can you recognize any of the transfer syndromes that may inhibit the way you work with information? Consider how you could use electronic media to develop ideas more interactively. Consider how you could collaborate more effectively if you could share files with other people on your project team. How could you transfer ideas and information more directly to your presentations and final products? Diagram strategies for how you might express and develop ideas using electronic media.

Relate the information flow diagrams you sketched for part *a* to those you just sketched in this part. This should provide you with a picture of how you are presently transferring information in your case study. Consider the strategies you began to identify in your evaluations. This exercise can help you begin to visualize how you might make better use of computers and electronic media.

3. Diagram Data Flow

You can diagram data flow showing how you transfer digital files from one file format to another. The example on this page is a data flow diagram done by students in one of my landscape design courses. Focus your data flow diagram on key transfers you need to work out. Determine the appropriate level of detail for diagramming each project you deal with. If you haven't done a particular type of project before, a more detailed data flow diagram can help you think through how you are going to convert formats. Diagramming familiar projects will enable you to recognize the patterns involved. Sometimes it is beneficial to reexamine the data flow to discover better ways of moving your files. Data flow diagrams are also very helpful in collaborative efforts. They enable each member of the workgroup or project team to better understand how they can get or handoff digital files.

Data flow diagrams are especially helpful when sorting out how you can transfer files from different devices. For example, you can move information from FAX to computer in an ASCII (American Standard Code for Information Interchange) format, or from computer to FAX without printing it out. Using a modem, you can transfer files between many application programs and hardware platforms provided you have the proper conversion programs or filters. You can also scan images from photos or convert them from video and work with them in a computer. You can also convert vector drawing files into raster images. Or raster graphic files into vector drawings. (You will learn more about transformations in Chapter 11, "Mixing Media.")

Select a case study project and develop a data flow diagram. Pick a team project if you can. That way you can work with the diagram collaboratively. Develop your diagram by identifying data sources on one side of a chart and linking them to your presentation or products on the other side of your chart. What is the format of your data sources? How are you transferring files? What files are you integrating into the final product? Are there ways to transfer files more efficiently? Are there possibilities for dynamic data exchanges? Can you transfer data more directly to your final product? Data flow diagramming provides a procedure for learning to work with digital files more effectively when using multimedia. As you do this exercise, you might also begin to ask yourself, "What channels of perception am I using? What modes of thought am I involving?"

Example of Student Work
by Tony Exter, Scott Shrader, and Greg Unti from the Department of Landscape Architecture, Cal Poly Pomona

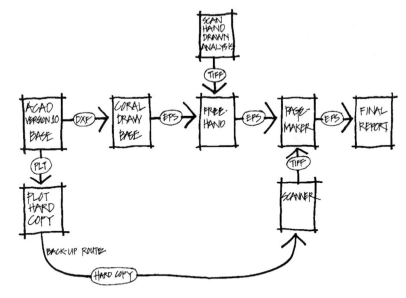

3

Perceiving, Thinking, and Acting

In this chapter you will learn strategies for handling transfers of information and ideas through different channels of perception. You will learn which modes of thought are important to creativity and how you can act upon your creative impulses. This chapter looks further into media space by discussing artificial reality and presentation reality — different realities you will find yourself involved with when using electronic media. You will learn to mock up multimedia models so you can begin to work with these objects more interactively.

You will also learn approaches to generating multimedia presentations using computers. Again, the activities at the end of the chapter should help you apply these approaches to your discipline and computer environment.

Consider How You Presently Perceive, Think, and Act

Each of us comes from different disciplines that influence the way we look at the world, the way we think about it, as well as the way we act upon what we think. Take a moment to ponder how the discipline you are pursuing is influencing your perceptions, thoughts, and actions. You should be comfortable with that mind-set, but you probably also realize there are other ways to relate to the world. Multimedia computing provides possibilities to draw upon more of your perceptions, to use different modes of thought, and to express ideas and information in much richer ways. You can expand your mind-set to develop these capabilities.

Channels of Perception

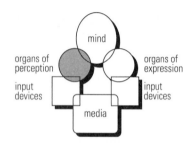

Mind-Media Perception

You experience the world through your organs of perception: your eyes, your ears (which help you perceive not only sound, but balance and motion), your skin, tongue, and nose. They offer different channels for relating to real-life experiences. You use many of these channels of perception when interfacing with computers. For example, you can see high-contrast color images on monitors. With animation you can follow movement. Certain devices — such as stereo goggles — enable you to view computer images in three dimensions. Digital video enables you to explore realistic images. Computers are also now capable of emitting more than simple beeps and buzzes. When integrated with stereophonic sound systems, they enable you to work with rich digital sound patterns—mixing recordings with synthesized music and voices. You also relate to the feel of a keyboard, the feel of a mouse, or to the response of a program. "Look, sound, and feel" are very important attributes of computer and audio/video programs.

Researchers are finding that experiencing virtual reality by using stereo goggles also provides visual cues related to the perception of movement and balance. In addition, simulators can provide tactile feedback. For example, a computer-aided flight simulator can cause the cockpit to move in response to a pilot's actions, providing a more realistic simulation of flying an airplane. Electronic media stimulate a wide range of perceptions.

Impressions: Receiving Information

Impressions

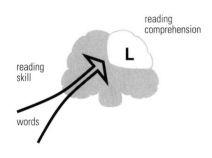

Reading

Look at the place you are in. Take a moment to observe what you see, hear, feel, and smell. You draw your most vivid impressions from life's experiences. Reality stimulates many channels of sensations and relates to the full capacity of your mind. Life's experiences are rich with information. By focusing you can make conscious observations. Most impressions simply seep into the subconscious levels of your mind.

Now consider how you experience representations. You can explore what you can't perceive directly. For example, electron microscopes, remote sensing equipment in satellites, and other devices help transcend human physical limitations. Infrared, x-rays, ultrasound, and magnetic resonant images enable you to experience what you could not normally see with your naked eye. With the emergence of multimedia computing, it is also becoming possible to create models in virtual reality you can experience interactively. Virtual reality presents opportunities for exploring what doesn't exist. For example, you could explore models of new landscapes or buildings if you can access these artificial realities. These realistic experiences enable you to draw extensively upon your mental capacity when working with computers. Just as you can learn to make perceptive observations when dealing with reality, you can also learn to work perceptively with representations or models of reality.

Much of your education focuses on printed material found in books. Yet you are gathering more and more information from other media as well—particularly electronic media (television and video). You can develop your abilities to glean information effectively from these media as well as from books.

Some training focuses on single channels of perception such as reading. For example, reading dynamics exercises develop visual reading skills. They teach people to avoid verbalization, or translating words into sounds. They train people to read with larger fixations (seeing more words at a time). They even teach learning to read vertically (fixating on

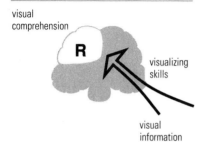

visual
comprehension

R

visualizing
skills

visual
information

Seeing

visual thinking skills Approaches that help you comprehend what you perceive, and help you give expression to patterns. Visual thinking skills enable people to work with representations — drawings, diagrams, models, animation, video, and sound — so they can use multimedia.

electric circuitry -
an extension of the central nervous system
adapted from *The Medium is the Massage*
by McLuhan

whole lines at a time). This leads to increased reading speed. Speed reading, coupled with previewing, reviewing, and visualization techniques, leads to increased comprehension. These approaches also can carry over to develop better listening and note-taking skills.

Training for reading provides an example of the type of training, or skills, which can develop other perceptual channels. You can learn to become more visually literate by practicing similar approaches. The activities in this book will give you some guidance in doing that. You can learn to see more perceptively and express yourself graphically. *Visual thinking skills* can help develop more awareness and comprehension of what you perceive. This will enable you to work with representations — drawings, diagrams, models, animation, and videos — so you can express yourself better using multimedia.

You can also immerse yourself in electronic media as you did in the activities at the end of the first chapter. An activity at the end of this chapter encourages you to play with hardware and software, stimulating different channels of perception. Doing this activity will help you learn to work with more channels. (Chapter 8, "Applications — Tools and Toys," has activities that will help you explore, practice, and plan how you can use new media that are emerging.)

Your education should be helping you learn to use more channels of perception and expression. Go beyond reading, writing, and numerical skills. You will find that drawing, painting, modeling, or sculpture courses as well as animation, video, or music courses can help you develop other channels. You can transfer much of what you learn about perception and expression to electronic media even though you may learn it using traditional media. For example, I have found that students who can draw well on paper are usually also successful visualizing ideas using electronic media. Try to work with a range of electronic media. As you can see, learning to work creatively involves more than learning software commands and routine computer applications. You can develop thinking skills and a passion for a medium which compels you to explore its potential (as well as your own).

For democratic societies to work, people must be able to effectively gather information from a broad range of media. Media sometimes influence public opinion by the way information is selected and presented. However, if people are perceptive, they can also become better informed using media they have access to today. The Media Lab at MIT is researching imaging technologies, relating them to the human cognitive system. Their research examines information flow in different ways:

For example, when reading a typical newspaper, you can browse information selecting what interests you. Editors act as a filter in selecting the news they consider fit to print. You read stories written by reporters, who are either relating their experience or using information from AP, UPI, Reuters, or other sources. Newspapers and magazines are dominant

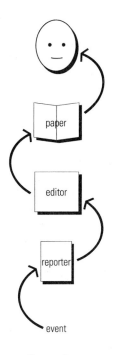

Newspaper Reporting

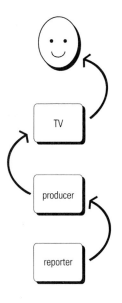

TV Reporting

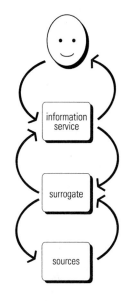

Information Services

modes of transferring information on current events, although television network news has a tremendous impact. CNN now presents "history as it happens."

Viewing TV provides little opportunity to browse information. You either watch the whole program or tune out when the presentation doesn't interest you. Network producers select information to present. News stories are aired in sound bites, usually with live action from the scene. Time constraints often make the content superficial. The programming is designed for everyone to watch passively together. Some browsing capability is emerging today that gives viewers the choice to select from multiple TV channels using split-screen viewing capabilities.

You usually need to browse individually, however, so you can control your own interaction. My oldest son, Erik, flicks through TV channels in a way that can drive me crazy. He has an inquisitive mind and naturally likes to take control of the TV. The crux of the problem is our interests are not always the same. I, too, like to control what I am watching. When he was a child, we could read books together. Of course, as a parent, I selected books of interest to him. As adults, we prefer to read and browse written material on our own. Obviously, the same is true when watching TV.

Computer services, such as CompuServe, can act as your surrogate, compiling information. You can identify topics you are interested in and then view what the news service compiles for you. It is also possible to access databases, encyclopedias, weather information, etc. For example, using a computer with a modem, you can call up WeatherBrief and view weather maps. Many libraries also have computerized card catalogs you can access using a modem. I put course material online for my students at the university where I teach. For example, my students can access the course outline, and problem statements, as well as our schedule of discussions, meetings, and reviews which I update each week. They can access these materials either using computer terminals on campus or using a computer with a modem from somewhere else. We use primarily text files; however, we can transmit formatted documents and graphics as binary files. For example, sometimes I will put a basemap online for students to use.

Beyond selecting and receiving information, telecommunications enable you to act upon information. For example, information services enable you to communicate through bulletin boards, electronic mail, and FAX. You can download computer programs and files so you can work with them. You can shop and conduct financial transactions electronically. You can plan trips by booking accommodations and making airline reservations. I have my students submit some of their assignments electronically. I can review them, add comments, and send them back, accessing our computer system either from my office at school or from my study at home.

Computers have the potential for providing a much broader range of stimulus when they include video. Fiber optics and other improvements in telecommunications, along with data compression, are making it possible to transmit digital video images. Personal computers and TV are just now being integrated in ways that will empower individuals to browse electronic media more effectively. For example, consumer products are emerging which enable users to select video coverage of current events, or even communicate with other people using interactive video.

Levels of Perception

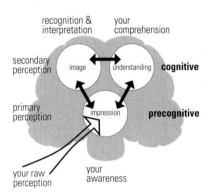

Perceptual Process

You have several levels of perception. Consider how you perceive an interesting painting. What you see provides an initial impression that you may not be totally conscious of. From this impression you derive an image that becomes the basis for your awareness of that painting. Ideally, you can derive understanding from the image you develop. Understanding can also come from other sources (what you are told or what you read). For example, if you don't recognize the artist of a painting, you might find out who painted it — in what period, the techniques used, etc. — by reading the label or catalog. An interplay occurs in your mind, enabling you to transform your image of the painting into understanding through recognition and interpretation. You can also transform your understanding of the painting into an image that can help you develop greater awareness involving your whole being.

In general, this is how you perceive paintings, people, and most anything on which you focus your attention. You are using this approach right now to develop your awareness and understanding of your mind and media. You are viewing diagrams on one side of this page and reading this verbal description on the other.

Science and engineering disciplines stress understanding as a basis for comprehension. The arts and design disciplines emphasize imaging as a basis for awareness. An engineer and an architect can look at the same thing but perceive it quite differently. This is the source of many communication problems (but it is also the basis for effective collaboration). These different points of view are even the basis for different learning styles. Some people seek awareness; they derive images that provide them with a sense of what they experience. Others seek comprehension — deriving understanding from what they see, hear, or read. Ideally, you can develop both your awareness and comprehension.

Primary perceptions (impressions) sometimes register only in your subconscious. *Secondary perceptions* (images and understandings) relate more to cognitive modes of thought. Each channel of perception has primary and secondary levels as shown on the chart listing channels of perception.

Channel	Primary Perception	Second Perception	Comprehension
SEEING	contrast, color	patterns, objects, characters, numbers	recognition, words, meanings
	distance	space	place, orientation
	motion	sequence	path or procedure
HEARING	loudness, pitch reception	character, phonetics rhythm, tunes	calls, words music
SENSING	temperature pressure texture	hot/cold sharp/dull, heavy/light rough/smoothe hard/soft	comfort pain
SMELLING	aroma	putrid/fragrant	associations
TASTING	taste	sour/sweet/bitter	pallatability
MOVING	balance movement	up/down moving/still	direction progression

Channels of Perception

Multimedia computer applications integrate a range of these channels. Originally, computers were used primarily to improve understanding — to do calculations or manipulate data. Today, multimedia computers are also used to increase awareness — by enhancing and manipulating images. For example, using a computer program such as CHAOS: The Software, you can generate fractal images that appear like crystals. (This software, available from Autodesk, is based on James Gleick's book *Chaos: Making a New Science*.) Changing the variables in the algorithms that generate these images helps you understand how they are generated. Viewing the colorful images the program generates helps you develop greater awareness of this intricate order.

Classic ways in which you refine awareness and enhance comprehension include discussion, writing, drawing, modeling, and composing. Computers enable you to work with very flexible media to develop your dialogues, writings, drawings, models, and compositions, thereby enabling you to enhance your perception. Using computers, you can refine observations interactively, share them, and transfer them to other applications. For example, you can take notes on what you observe. Then, using a word processor, you can write about it. And, of course, you can integrate what you write into a letter or a report. You could follow similar approaches using a computer graphics program. You could also compose using a music program.

Modes of Thought

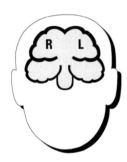

L-mode -- deductive thought processes based on logic

R-mode -- inductive thought processes based on intuition

Right & Left Brain

"R" Mode (Right Brain)	"L" Mode (Left Brain)
impression	understandings
wholistic	segmental
inductive	deductive
"in" words	**"de" words**
induce	deduce
innovate	derive
invent	develope
inspire	describe
intuit	define
primary creativity	**secondary creativity**

Modes of Thought

Your mind has many facets. It has been found that the right side of the brain relates more to visual and inductive thinking skills. The left side of the brain relates more to verbal and deductive thinking skills. Researchers sometimes attack theories about *right-brain* and *left-brain* thinking as being too simplistic. It is difficult to generalize about something as complex as thinking, especially when there is still much to discover. However, this simple dichotomy can help characterize fundamentally different modes of thought so you can learn to work with them more effectively. People often refer to what they feel in their heart as opposed to what they understand in their head. Right-brain thinking tends to involve the whole body, which people associate with the heart. Left-brain thinking tends to be more cerebral — related to the head.

In her book *Drawing on the Right Side of the Brain*, Betty Edwards distinguishes between right-brain and left-brain activities. In her second book, *Drawing on the Artist Within*, Edwards refers to these two types of activities as a dichotomy between the *R-mode*, which deals with visual thinking, and the *L-mode*, which deals with verbal thinking. The R-mode is more holistic; the L-mode more segmental. In R-mode you use inductive thinking to deal with perception and comprehension of relationships. In L-mode you use deductive thinking to deal analytically with sequences and details. Inductive thinking tends to be intuitive; deductive thinking is more logical. R-mode relates to what you perceive; L-mode relates to what you conceive. You can shift between right-brain and left-brain modes of thought — between what you see and what you (verbally) think.

The same dichotomy exists between modes of thought characterized by *in* words and *de* words. The *in* words are *induce*, *innovate*, and *invent*. The *de* words are *deduce*, *derive*, and *develop*. The *in* words characterize primary creativity; the *de* words characterize secondary creativity. Both modes of creativity are important. Primary creativity is more characteristic of the arts. Secondary creativity is more characteristic of the sciences. However, art and science both involve invention and development. Often, intuitive leaps can provide new breakthroughs for understanding. New levels of understanding, in turn, provide platforms from which you can take further intuitive leaps. The interactive nature of electronic media lends itself to shifting between inductive and deductive thinking, though initially computers were considered highly deductive tools.

Internal Transfers

Often, people have the tendency to favor one mode of thought over another. This may be like the tendency to favor one hand over another. We all know "right-handers" and "left-handers." Similarly, we can also identify "right-brainers" and "left-brainers." Most people seem to be right-handed but left-brained.

Certainly, you can learn to use both hands and your whole brain. Just as each hand can perform important functions when you do physical tasks, each mode of thought is crucial to creative thinking. You need to learn how to make internal transfers from your R-mode to your L-mode. For example, get in the habit of drawing or diagramming a whole image of what you are dealing with, while you also examine the parts. Robert McKim, in his book *Experiences in Visual Thinking*, calls using both modes of thought *ambidextrous thinking*.

Creative thinking involves alternating between right-brain and left-brain modes of thought. When you alternate between modes, you also shift between internalized thinking — reflection — and externalized thinking — expression — when proposing and disposing of ideas. My colleague John Lyle, in his book *Design for Human Ecosystems*, calls this the alternating current of the creative process. You shift between these modes of thought naturally — almost like breathing in and breathing out. Sometimes, however, you may get stuck in one mode or another. Then you need to return energy to this alternating current. You need to breathe life into your creative approach.

Alternating Current of Design
adapted from *Design for Human Ecosystems*
by Lyle

Different modes of thought also relate to different modes of learning. R-mode learning is more experiential and is characterized by a statement such as "I have a feeling for that" or "Let me get into that." Your learning experience is more holistic as you derive impressions related to this mode of thinking. L-mode learning is more rational and is typified in a statement such as "I understand that part" or "Let me read about it." Your learning experience for L-mode thinking is more segmental, like putting together pieces of a puzzle.

Alternating Approaches to Learning

Imaging

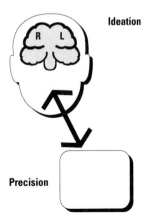

Ideation

Precision

Mind and Media

Understanding imaging languages can help you to comprehend what you perceive as well as express what you visualize. As already discussed, perception involves a variety of your senses. Since ideas originate in many parts of your brain you can learn to comprehend and express images using a wide range of media. Multimedia provide a means for doing this. Each channel has a different lexicon with basic units for comprehending and expressing ideas. You can learn the syntax for understanding and making statements using each channel. For example, you learn to do this to listen and speak, or read and write. You can also learn to understand and express yourself graphically or in music. Each channel has different formats for packaging meaning into an organized work that others can relate to.

In general, there is a consistency in the way people construct imaging languages. The *chart of imaging languages* summarizes the syntax used by different channels.

Channel	Lexicon		Basic Unit	Idea	Statement	Grammar	Meaning	Work
SYMBOL								
written	dictionary		letter	written word	sentence	paragraph	chapter	book/essay
	data		cell	field	file	record	sort	database
			digit	number	equation	therom	proof	treatise
AUDIO								
verbal	phonetics		diphthong	spoken word	phrase/ sound bite	line/statement	story/lecture	epic/course
musical	sounds		note	chord	stanza	theme	composition	album/concert
VISUAL								
graphic	symbols library		point	line	texture/color	pattern/image	composition	drawing/ painting
3-D model	primatives		facet	elements	form	object/space	construct	model
4-D animation	frame/cell		flic	scene	movement	strip	sequence	feature/film
performance	repertoire		gesture	expression	mood	scene	act	play
CULINARY								
	menu		ingredient	taste	serving	course	meal	cuisine

Imaging Languages

Traditionally, in school, you learn to use symbols, be they written words or numbers. With words, the basic units are letters and syllables, which make up written words. Statements are in the form of sentences, which build paragraphs. Paragraphs build chapters, which compose an article, essay, or book. With numerical symbols, the basic units are digits, which make up numbers. Statements are in the form of equations, which build theorems. Proofs test theorems. Similarly, you can develop imaging languages for constructing databases. Basic units of data are in cells, which make up fields. Statements are in the form of records, which build data files. You can derive meanings through various strategies for sorting or navigating to query the data. The complete work is a database or a stack—such as a hypercard stack.

Probably the most familiar channel is audio, which you learn to use even before you go to school. Almost from birth you learn to make sounds from which you construct spoken words. Soon you learn to comprehend sound bites and express phrases. Beyond that, your mind can create verbal statements that you can express with great fluency.

The audio channel also relates to appreciation and expression of music. Even babies enjoy music. Although most people can express musical ideas, this isn't developed unless a person becomes involved with music informally or pursues musical instruction. With music the basic units are notes, which make up chords. Musical statements are in the form of stanzas, which build themes. Themes build musical compositions, which make a concert or an album.

While most people gather information visually, fewer people can express themselves graphically. This could change, however, given the visual nature of electronic media and the tools computers provide. The construct of visual imaging languages is relatively simple. You need to learn a visual vocabulary (or develop your own) and a sense of composition. For two-dimensional graphics, the basic units are points, which make up lines. Lines, texture, and color, which build patterns and images, express visual statements. Compositions comprise a drawing or a painting.

Another visual channel is three-dimensional visualization. Here the basic units are facets, which make up elements. Forms become three-dimensional statements. Forms create objects and space, which construct the spatial model. You can now build three-dimensional models electronically using a fast desktop computer with the right software. Different disciplines develop their own vocabulary of forms.

Beyond three dimensions, there is a fourth dimension—time. Working with space and time, you can create animation. With animation the basic units are frames or cells drawn in sequences to create flicks. Flicks express movement. Movements create the strips, which compose the scenes of the film or feature. Similarly, in the performing arts, the primary units for acting are gestures, which make up expressions. The expressions, in turn, set the mood. The mood creates the scenes, which make up the acts. The scenes and acts make up the play.

Even taste—the culinary arts—has an imaging language. The basic units are the ingredients, which, when artfully combined, create delightful flavors. The culinary statement is the serving. Servings create the courses, which make up the meals, which are satisfying. Computers will probably never be able to simulate a delicious meal. However, you can create images in your mind which can make your mouth water.

Movement—kinesthetics—also has an imaging language. There are basic positions, movements, and rhythms for dancing as well as for sports. Visualizing rhythm helps you work with computers (as discussed in the next chapter and explored further in Chapter 9). Using a computer-aided simulator, you can experience flying an airplane. Using the right computer setup, you can even move in virtual realities.

Organs of Expression

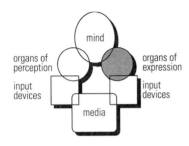

Mind-Media Expression

Your eyes, voice, and body are all organs of expression. People "look you in the eye" to get a sense of how you feel, what you are thinking, and where you are going to move. Your body movements give expression to your feelings and thoughts. Some of your movements are primary — natural gestures involving impulses. These are spontaneous. Others are secondary — controlled gestures involving more conscious direction. You can condition your movements to use tools and toys. Think of how you use a pencil or a ball. This involved training.

When you work with computers, you can use many of your organs of expression. You probably are familiar with a keyboard, mouse, or pen (digitizing stylus). Other types of interfaces are emerging. For example, voice commands offer tremendous potential for working with computers. In addition, the Media Lab at MIT has been experimenting for some time with pointing devices that can follow your eye movements. By bouncing light off your cornea, a computer can detect where you are looking and move a cursor so you don't have to point. All these developments can help able-bodied, as well as disabled, people interface with computers. It is conceivable that the types of interfaces envisioned in science fiction such as *Star Trek* will eventually become a reality.

You can use multimedia computing to enhance your expression. You can change the scale of an environment in media space expanding your reach or increasing the speed by which you can move from one place to another. You can increase your strength and capabilities by connecting your actions to robotics or computer-aided manufacturing. For example, even a physically impaired person could create a three-dimensional digital model that a computer could use to construct a massive steel component. You can also increase the amplitude of sound or the intensity of color. You can reach distant audiences electronically via telecommunications, desktop publishing, or desktop video. Electronic media can enable you to work with a wider range of expression. To give expression to your creativity using electronic media, you need to learn to effectively transfer your mental impulses to electronic media. There you can learn to work interactively to refine and share your ideas.

Channels for Expression

Your imagination is linked to all your senses. You derive images and ideas from many areas of your brain. To find ways to transfer these images, you need media that relate to many channels of expression.

Each channel — such as writing, composing music, or drawing and painting — has art forms with long traditions. People specialize — as writers, poets, composers, painters, sculptors, designers, architects, or engineers — to master the knowledge required of a discipline and the complexity of the traditional media they use. However, some — like Leonardo and Michelangelo, regarded as Renaissance men — worked in multiple media centuries ago.

The tools available today are making it easier to work in multimedia, providing people with the potential for fuller expression. It is because of that I believe a new Renaissance may be emerging. More people may be able to express their creative thinking using multimedia. From this, new art forms and products can emerge. Multimedia can make learning more stimulating. As already discussed, computers also enable people to use electronic media for collaboration. Creative workgroups can coordinate their expression into collective compositions involving many modes of expression. Multimedia workgroups may involve the collaboration of individuals each working with different modes, however each contributing to a coordinated effort.

The following chart lists channels of expression and identifies related basic functions and primary and secondary forms of expression. Basic functions are involuntary. Primary forms of expression are rather intuitive; secondary forms of expression involve more training.

Channel	Basic Function	Primary Expression	Secondary Expression
visual	eye movement	glance gaze	fixation
audio	utterances	modulation	speak sing
kinesthetic	heartbeat breathe touch	anxiety/relaxation natural ryhthm feel/ press	anger/composure controlled breathing write sketch draft type point/click digitize steer
			keyboard foot pedal finger valve
	move	balance/ rhythm	swim walk run bike ski skate throw swing
olfactoral	perspire salivate	excrete swallow	cool eat

Channels of Expression

Computer user interfaces are considered more intuitive if they draw upon primary expression. For example, it is easier to gesture than to type. Consequently, pointing and clicking with a mouse are more primary and therefore easier to learn. As a result, the mouse has become a popular user interface.

Pen-based computers, which respond to gestures and can recognize handwriting, have promise for making the power of computers even more accessible. More people know how to use pens than keyboards. Pen computing is also an easy-to-use interface for very small personal computers. However, when writing alphabet-based western languages, many people can type faster and with less effort than they can letter by hand. The pen interface may open new possibilities for people using character-based languages such as Japanese and Chinese. Similarly, pens hold promise for visual note taking — sketching — using electronic media.

Verbal expressions are even more natural than writing. Primary audible expressions are simple utterances that babies make. A one-year-old learns to modulate sounds and speak. A two-year-old can learn to sing. A three-year-old can talk on the telephone. Computers now provide voice mail and can even recognize and synthesize words. Vocalizing is a primary gesture that most people are relatively comfortable with once they get over the inhibitions of talking to a machine. Computers, using this type of interface, could also transfer what you say into digital formats you could work with interactively.

You can learn to interact effectively with computers through conditioned actions. For example, you can learn typing. Once mastered, typing becomes automatic and you no longer have to think consciously about it. Learning to master user interfaces for different channels of expression will permit your interactions with the computer to become more automatic. You can then focus on transferring your ideas using different modes.

Most people can learn to use many different devices to interface with a computer, especially if these devices relate to primary gestures. Hardware developers should provide simple-to-learn user interfaces which, when mastered, can increase the speed of interaction between the user and the computer. Standardized formats for interfaces help you move between hardware platforms and software applications. However, standards should be based on good interface design that responds to all channels of expression. An intuitive user interface frees up cognition for creative thinking and problem solving. This is particularly important when using computer applications creatively. More basic actions generally provide more successful interfaces.

Creative thinking also involves moving between the conscious and subconscious levels of your mind. Chapter 9, "The "Zen" of Regeneration," will help you learn to do that. Right now, just recognize the need to

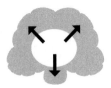

Internalization

internalize much of what you do when working with computers. Learn to work with your hardware and software so you become less conscious of using them. The more you can do subconsciously, the more you can focus your conscious efforts on your creative endeavors and the problems at hand.

Expressions: Sending Ideas and Information

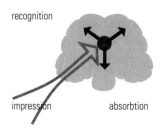

recognition

impression   absorbtion

Absorbing

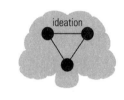

ideation

Contemplating

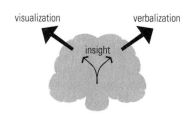

visualization   verbalization

insight

Expressing

The mind provides the ideas — the inspirations, brainstorms, hunches, feelings, and connections or associations. Computers provide a vehicle for using electronic media to develop ideas and give expression to them. Think about how this happens and you will realize there is a progression you go through in transferring ideas from your mind to any medium. This progression usually starts internally with some sort of insight or muse.

Initially, you may not even express your ideas. You may simply reflect on them internally. Given the opportunity, you can express your muse with simple gestures — making verbal statements, writing down keywords, or sketching visual notes. You may even whistle or hum a tune you have in your head. Beyond these primary expressions, your draft statements are more elaborate, often involving writing, drawing, modeling, composing, or other creative modes of thought. You can create drafts in a variety of media including paper, film, or, as will be explored here, electronic media.

A trick to using your creativity is to learn to get ideas into a medium that you can work with. Previously, this trick involved mostly learning to get ideas down on paper. To use computers creatively, the trick involves learning to transfer your ideas to electronic media. A key goal is to help you learn to make primary statements of ideas using electronic media. Mastering any medium permits ideas to flow more freely.

For example, take a thought and express it as a gesture — or maybe as a diagram or a few keywords. Then make a statement that you can work with interactively. You may tape-record your statement so you can listen to it and transcribe it to a digital file. Or you may develop a digital file directly with a word processor. Once the draft statement is in a digital form, you can edit and refine your ideas more easily. You can package your ideas for communication using a variety of computer applications.

Creative thinking involves working with whole impressions. You can use visual images, symbols, feelings, and sounds, as well as verbal statements. Usually, your insights or hunches are an integration of all your mental faculties. Your first expression of an idea is often just a change in heart rate, or perhaps a smile (or a frown). Ideas flash through your mind at a tremendous rate. The easiest transfers from your mind relate to quick abstract notes. If you can produce primary expressions quickly, there is less chance of losing ideas. Make quick diagrams or idea sketches, or note keywords — providing hooks for remembering your insights.

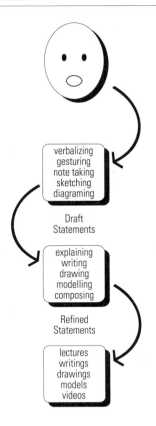

verbalizing
gesturing
note taking
sketching
diagraming

Draft
Statements

explaining
writing
drawing
modelling
composing

Refined
Statements

lectures
writings
drawings
models
videos

Expressing Ideas

Once you get these primary expressions down, you can transfer them into a more complete statement. The draft may be a verbal discourse or a written statement — prose or poetry. Drafts can also involve a wide variety of drawings or diagrams. You can even develop multidimensional models — using three dimensions in space or more abstract variables such as coordinates on a graph. Your statements may be musical expressions — sequences of sound in time. Your expression may also involve planning processes or operations — a sequence of events on a time line. The expression may even involve multimedia sequences for doing animation, choreographing dances, scripting plays. Or it may involve scripts or storyboards for movies or video. Following those basic approaches, you can link your mind with media.

Each of us has different ways of expressing ideas. We become comfortable with certain transfers and media. Yet you can learn more ways of transferring your insights. With practice, you can become comfortable with using a wider range of media creatively.

Assimilating Information

Assimilating information is like digesting food. Sometimes you can suffer from overeating. Similarly, you can suffer from information overload. On the other hand, you can become hungry. In the same way you can develop an appetite for good information. You need an appropriate information flow. Multisensory stimuli provide a balanced diet; they nourish the whole mind. You can browse information, finding what interests you in the same way you can sample foods. You consume kernels of information (often in sound bites or in visual fragments) like you consume bites of food. Pursuing trivia is much like nibbling. Studying should be like eating a well-balanced meal. Absorbing information nurtures your psyche as digesting food nurtures your body.

Richard Saul Wurman's book, *Information Anxiety*, describes a malady of the information age. Wurman identifies symptoms of information anxiety, describes this illness, and offers cures. Most of the approaches to dealing with information anxiety that Wurman offers have to do with attitudinal changes. For example, accept what you don't know as a learning opportunity. Recognize that you can't deal with all the informa-

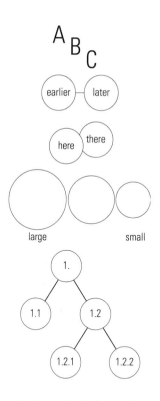

Ways to Organize Information

tion that is available. Select what interests you. Find ways to connect ideas using various "hat racks" for storing information. Think about opposites.

Wurman identifies five generic ways to organize information:

1. The alphabet

2. Time

3. Location

4. Continuum or magnitude

5. Categories

These approaches to organizing information are both verbal and visual. Alphabetical lists are primarily verbal although you can often visualize what is at the top and the bottom of the list. You record and calculate time numerically, but a watch face, or a time line, enables you to picture it. You can describe locations verbally; however, diagrams or maps provide a clearer picture of locations. You can work with a continuum and magnitudes numerically, although graphs and charts provide ways to visualize these relationships quickly. You can describe categories verbally — as lists or outlines. Branching structures provide ways to diagram categories.

Edward Tufte's book, *Envisioning Information,* provides examples for displaying complex information visually to increase comprehension. These examples include many well-designed maps, charts, and scientific visualizations, as well as diagrams, statistical graphs, and tables. Tufte also shows stereophotographs, guidebooks, timetables, and computer screens.

Hypermedia

Hypertext and hypermedia provide ways of organizing information by association — which can relate to the way your memory works. Using these types of programs, you store information in stacks. Hypermedia offer associations or links for the reader to explore. You can do this by selecting subtopics and probing them further. For example, your hypermedia stack may deal with plant materials. You could select plants which grow in a particular climate zone, and then find those with blue flowers. Hypermedia could also offer you pictures of what the plants you are interested in look like. In his book *Hypertext and Hypermedia*, Jakob Nielsen provides many approaches to using hypermedia. He helps you learn to navigate through this media space so you know where you are. This also helps you find your way back to where you were, and ascertain if you found all the available information you are seeking.

Hypermedia make it possible to package information in ways that users can explore interactively. These approaches have tremendous potential

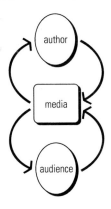

Hypermedia

for education since they provide great flexibility to reach users with different interests and capabilities. For example, you can access reference information, like encyclopedias on CD-ROM disks, using hypermedia interactively. People typically browse reference material. Hypermedia enables you to do that using not only text and graphics, but audio and video as well. Hypermedia also have potential for packaging implementation documents. For example, some of my graduate students explored using hypermedia to package landscape construction documents so plan checkers, bidders, and contractors could work with the information more interactively. (In their project, David Briley, Anthony Diaz, and Gary Tom even envisioned ways of controlling grading equipment using information from computer-generated three-dimensional landform models.) Hypermedia also have potential for presenting training programs. For example, mechanics could click on part of a diagram showing an automobile. If they wished, they could see a video of how to service that part, or they could quickly just get a listing of part numbers. They could select the parts they needed. Companies could update this electronic training program/service manual as new models of the product evolved.

Computer Modeling

To work creatively using computers, you need to go beyond just assimilating and storing information. You need to be able to use information interactively to generate new ideas, develop them, and give them expression. You can do this by building computer models to represent objects you are working with. Real objects are multisensory. Computer models can be multimedia. You can base these models on the *intrinsic order* of the realities you are working with. For example, if you are working with an area of land, you can develop a digital map that represents that area. You could even develop a three-dimensional terrain model using a computer.

intrinsic order The natural or inherent order. Recognizing the intrinsic order of what you are working with enables you to model or represent it using a computer.

Mapping and *modeling* help sort out observations of phenomena that have a spatial or functional order. Using computers to work interactively with this information helps you explore the intrinsic order of what you are observing. You can recognize textures, patterns, objects, space, orientation, sequences, and rhythms. This has interesting implications for the arts, which involve visual images, spatial forms, or movement. It is particularly useful for scientific inquiry and medical imaging. It also applies to interpreting geographic information. Maps and models relate to environmental design and planning disciplines such as urban and regional planning, landscape architecture, and architecture. Models of objects and movement are especially important to a wide variety of engineering disciplines. For example, engineers work with microscopic maps — such as circuit diagrams — as well as dynamic models — such as space platforms.

map To represent spatial order.

model To represent functional order.

Database models enable you to search information that may not be locationally or functionally related. You can find patterns that are intrinsic to attributes you select. For example, you may search a demographic database to find the distribution of people in different age groups. Spreadsheets enable you to explore relationships between numbers. You can manipulate quantitative data and even chart them electronically. This provides graphic representations of relationships and patterns that enhance awareness of these quantitative observations. For example, you can plot costs and revenues and see where the break-even point is. Spreadsheet models may help you derive insights that can lead to new possibilities.

artificial intelligence The ability to carry out programmed responses. Computers can carry out programmed responses.

Using *artificial intelligence,* you can set up computer models to check selected information and automatically carry out programmed responses. For example, with programmed trading, computers evaluate stock market trends and then carry out transactions to buy or sell stock. Another example of a programmed model is a quality control system that can measure attributes of parts and compare them to predetermined parameters. The computer can then quickly accept or reject these parts. In these models the programmer does the real thinking by predetermining what the responses should be.

Computers can enhance your primary perception (your recognition) and aid your secondary perception (your interpretation). However, you do your cognitive and connative thinking in your mind. Your mind recognizes images, written words, symbols, and patterns, attaching meanings to them. You develop a sense of orientation that helps you discover and express new possibilities. You determine what information means to you and what you are going to do about it. Judgments, involving qualitative considerations, are the domain of your mind.

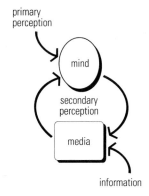

Primary & Secondary Perception

Your mind does free associations more easily than computers can. Despite extensive research in artificial intelligence, computers cannot yet really learn without being programmed. A lot of effort is going into developing neural networks. People are still discovering the extent to which computers can recognize, interpret, and comprehend information.

Working with your mind using multimedia models provides a means for drawing upon the abilities of your whole brain. To do this well requires developing your perception and thinking skills. Using computer models can enhance your recognition, your interpretation, and your comprehension involving different channels. Using multimedia can help you sharpen what you perceive through each of your channels of perception. Multimedia computer models can help you recognize and interpret key information and give expression to your ideas using different channels.

Learn to use media that are fertile for growing the ideas you develop. This, of course, will relate to your discipline and to the computer environment you have access to. Electronic media offer a special richness because of their wide range. They relate to most of your channels of perception — what you see, what you hear, as well as your sense of touch and movement. Electronic media also provide many channels for expression — talking, writing, drawing, modeling, etc. You can learn to build multimedia computer models. You can, in effect, learn to create virtual reality.

Realities

"Imagination is more important than knowledge."
— Albert Einstein

An interesting interplay of realities exists when working with electronic media. Growing up, you learn to work with the dichotomy between the real world you perceive and your mental construct of the world you can imagine. Your mind can usually distinguish between what is real and what is imaginary. With computers the distinction between viewing reality and viewing artificial realities is becoming more subtle. Reality can relate to virtual reality. Physical space can relate to media space. Virtual reality and media space can also become their own domains.

reality relates to virtual reality

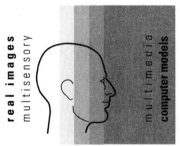

physical space relates to media space

Realities

model space The information environment where you work on your models.

presentation reality The information environment others will perceive. This may involve the layout of pages or drawings you produce on paper, or it might be the sequence of a video production.

paper space A representation showing what you will see when you print a document on paper.

video space A representation showing what you will see when you integrate media to produce a video.

The realities you work with using electronic media can take many forms. Artificial realities may be abstract models diagramming or calculating relationships. You might even use programming to develop these models. Virtual realities may include many qualities of the real world. For example, these representations may be three-dimensional models incorporating realistic images. In fact, you can even give these information environments unreal qualities if you wish. Why not change colors, forget about gravity, change scale or almost anything else? *Model space* is a way of referring to the information environment where you work on your models.

Another reality you have to learn to deal with is *presentation reality* — what others will perceive. This may involve the pages or drawings you produce on paper (*paper space*) or animated images and sound you

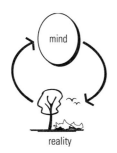

Recognizing Reality

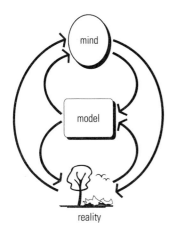

Representing Reality

produce on video (*video space*). Artificial reality and presentation reality may be one and the same if your audience can experience and directly interact with what you are working on. More typically, you transfer information from your model to some presentation format. This format may involve layouts on paper, slides on film, or video sequences on magnetic tape or laser disk. You can select views of the artificial reality you are working with and package them for an audience.

There is a lot to learn about making good observations from either reality or representations. You learn to involve all your senses in observing reality. You can also learn to make more holistic observations from representations that involve multimedia. Different disciplines refine different types of observations. A physician, for example, observes key symptoms in a patient. A landscape architect sees key characteristics of the land. However, multimedia can make representations almost as rich as, or in some instances even richer than, reality. Representations may contain information you cannot readily perceive directly from reality. For example, physicians can learn from an x-ray or CAT scan things they may not find out just by looking at the patient. Landscape architects can discover overall patterns of the land from an air photo, or a digital terrain model, that may be difficult to perceive when walking a site.

You still need to distinguish between reality and the artificial reality that can be created in media space. You derive source data directly from reality. You derive interpreted data from some representation of reality. There is a saying about "garbage in, garbage out" related to conventional computing. That saying remains true with multimedia computing as well. Maintaining close contact with reality where possible enables you to ground truth or verify the models you are working with in media space.

The Impact of Media on Current Events

The media can impact current events. As a graduate student at Berkeley in the 1960s, I remember experiencing the events related to the People's Park that were occurring on campus. Some of these events were given national media coverage in the press and on TV. I found it interesting to compare my impressions of what was going on with perceptions derived from the news media. I could begin to see the events of that time feed on media coverage. This also provided me with some healthy insights into the distinctions between these realities.

Electronic media are having a greater impact on people's lives every day. People gather more and more of their impressions from representations. Television and telephone communications are linking people to a global village, or what Michael Sorkin calls the electronic city. Consider the information that television brings into your home every day. Consider also the contact you have with others simply by using the telephone. These media extend your consciousness and your contact. For example, the video coverage of the 1989 San Francisco earthquake focused on "live action" such as the fires in the Marina District or the rescue efforts where the Nimitz Freeway collapsed. This gave the viewer the impression of total disaster. Television coverage of the Iraqi War also developed an immediacy. CNN reported events as they happened. This coverage was distributed worldwide. Although most people were far away from these events, they developed some perception of these grim realities.

In 1992, many people watched in dismay as riots broke out on a sad Wednesday evening in Los Angeles, seemingly fed by video coverage from helicopters. This event was triggered by the verdict in the Rodney King beating. We are now in an age where the public is privy to information that enables it to make its own judgments, and most people, who had seen the video of this beating, could not understand how the jury was able to acquit the policemen involved. Media coverage of events as they occur also provides powerful feedback that influences events. This can have detrimental results, as it seemed on that Wednesday night in Los Angeles. By Friday night the public got to see Rodney King on television — not as an icon, but as a person — pleading, "Can we all get along?" By Saturday, television seemed to provide positive feedback as the Los Angeles riot turned into a rally for peace. The television showed thousands of people marching with banners, brooms, and shovels. Because of that, many more people turned out to join the peaceful event they saw unfolding on television. The real healing, of course, will take much longer, but electronic media will continue to be a part of that process.

Just as you need to make accurate observations from reality, you also need to make good observations from artificial realities emerging in the media. The daily barrage of images from TV make it vital for people to learn to interpret and to derive meaning from those images so they use information effectively. There are new opportunities to involve electronic media in positive democratic action.

The Impact of Media on Design Endeavors

The evolution of media is also changing the way in which people pursue design endeavors. It enables them to do more with models or representations of reality. This presents both problems and opportunities. For example, centuries ago landscape architects, such as Capability Brown, would work directly with the land. Only two realities existed. These were the actual reality (consisting of the landscape and social context with which the landscape architects worked) and the vision (or mental image they used to develop their design). It was difficult to communicate the vision without implementing the design. Implementation of the actual landscape took considerable effort and resources. So landscape architects most often worked for rich patrons who had the resources to construct these visions. There was little review of the design before they carried it out. The landscape architects often worked the design out on the site.

As drafting and delineation evolved, designers worked more plans out on paper. Paper space became a design and presentation medium for communicating with clients, users, review bodies, and construction workers. However, this is changing. Using computers, landscape architects can in effect create artificial realities in electronic media space. The actual site can be photographed from an airplane or satellite. From this, a digital survey can provide a three-dimensional model of the landform. The planning and design team can work with this model in a computer. They can add information showing invisible attributes such as geology, buried utilities, and zoning. The planning and design team can do site analysis and interpretations using this information. The landscape architect can use this information to model the site development and design. Others — such as architects and engineers — can use the models as a focus for collaboration. Even the users of the environment can get involved.

Environmental design professionals can take selected views of a computer model and integrate them with video images taken of a site. This presents a realistic picture, or walk-through, of the proposed project. The client, user groups, and local jurisdictions can view this presentation. Design professionals can develop the design in an artificial reality (or model space) and work on drawings electronically. They can plot these models and drawings on paper for review and for use as implementation documents. Of course, the design professionals need to experience the real site as well. That helps them relate to the models they can develop using multimedia.

Media space enables people to create a new reality. As engineering, architectural, and landscape architectural practices continue to evolve, it is likely that more implementation will be done directly from the models of the artificial reality. Engineers, for example, can link the manufacturing of products directly to models created with computers, without doing traditional presentation and construction drawings. They can develop implementation procedures for manufacturing, or building, concurrently as they develop the design. This can result in better coordination and quicker implementation. There are similar opportunities in many other disciplines where it becomes possible to model objects in media space and transfer them electronically for implementation. For example, you could even mock up the layout of a report electronically while still working on the manuscript and graphics. That way you could get a sense of what the final product would look like and also be able to make sure your files will transfer for printing.

Object Orientation

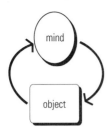

Object Orientation

object-orientation A focus on products, documents, or data to be processed. People can work with representations of objects in media space using in computers.

process-orientation A focus more on procedures or actions to be performed. People can program procedures using computers.

object-oriented programming An approach to computer programming that enables people to build from modules that have attributes that transfer from one program to another.

soft prototypes Three-dimensional models built in media space using computer software.

actual prototypes Three-dimensional physical models.

Your thinking can emphasize either objects (nouns) or actions (verbs). However, both nouns and verbs are necessary to construct sentences. Emphasizing objects or procedures can result in different paradigms for programming and using computers. *Object-orientation* involves focusing more on documents or data to be processed. This is characteristic of object-oriented programs which are emerging. For example, when you bring up a document using Penpoint, it already has the applications related to it. A traditional *process-orientation* involves focusing more on procedures or actions to be performed. This is characteristic of many specialized computer applications. To use these applications you typically load the program and then open your data file.

Object-oriented programming has certain advantages over traditional computer programming. Objects can contain many attributes. Objects can inherit some attributes from other objects. This permits building computer programs in modules by transferring attributes. This has promise for making programs more stable as well as making it easier to implement changes.

Object or document-oriented interfaces can provide computer users with advantages. Documents can become a natural vehicle for interaction between users and computers. They can provide a focus for tasks. Document-oriented interfaces also have the potential for making transfers of information more seamless. Ultimately, they could make the integration of applications easier.

You can learn to work with objects as well as procedures. Engineers use mathematical models, three-dimensional models (*soft prototypes*), and physical constructions (*actual prototypes*). Architects and landscape architects can now also develop drawings and three-dimensional models using electronic media. Artists instinctively focus on objects such as paintings or sculpture they are creating. These objects could even become constructs of information in media space which can have special meaning and represent a new genre of expression. Just as you can learn to write papers, do drawings, and build scale models using traditional media, you can learn to write, draw, and model using electronic media. Working with objects enable you to work with assemblies or constructs of information. These may be components of a program, a format for writing, a symbols library for graphics, or primitive forms for three-dimensional models. For example, maybe you have already built spreadsheet models using templates with formulas enabling you to do certain types of calculations. Maybe you are already working with computer-aided design programs which include symbols libraries and overlays. Data flow diagrams help you visualize ways of transferring information that objects or products contain. Work flow diagrams can help you visualize activities that make up procedures. A successful project involves managing both products and procedures.

You may be familiar with a game called Dungeons and Dragons. This game is an exercise in mapping and creating objects with attributes. A dungeon master creates a map or game for characters to play. The players invent their own characters and assign attributes to them according to the guides and rule books that are available. These attributes include strength, intelligence, wisdom, dexterity, constitution, charisma, hit points, armor class, and experience points. My youngest son, William, and his friends have spent hours playing this game. On the surface it seems frivolous. Some parents may even be disturbed by how obsessed children become. I see the game, however, as an exercise in creative thinking. The players develop mental maps and learn to orient in their imagination. They attach attributes to objects which have real meaning to them. Games like this can help develop thinking skills that can transfer to learning to navigate in media space. The exercise of attaching attributes to objects is helpful in learning to organize information. The concept is similar to object-oriented programming. Young children (and even adults) like to play these games. They are a fascinating means of learning thinking skills useful in electronic media space without even needing to access a computer. (However, there are also computerized versions of this game.)

There are also distinct advantages to object orientation in workgroups. One advantage is motivation. Swedish automobile manufacturers find their workers will produce better — achieving higher quality with greater satisfaction — if they are part of a small team building whole cars than if they are part of a large production line simply turning a bolt. Another advantage is orientation. Objects can help people find their way, especially in an information environment. Workgroups, which can clearly relate to objects, have a focus that enables team members to recognize their contribution as part of the whole. People can very quickly see what part is done and what part needs work. A third advantage (already mentioned) is transportability. Often, objects built for one model can be transferred to another. This enables the transfer of whole assemblies of information, reducing the time and effort involved. Note that people using telecommunications can access the objects they are working on from many different locations. In effect, that is what you are doing when you reach your bank account using your ATM card.

We are all familiar with the typical committee meeting. The agenda usually begins with a review of the minutes of the last meeting, followed by announcements, old business, and new business. While recording meeting minutes in chronological order provides a useful record, these procedure-oriented meetings are not very conducive to creative work. It is sometimes difficult to keep the group discussion focused and build upon the ideas that are generated. To make a committee meeting productive you need to transfer their discussion into producing some object or action.

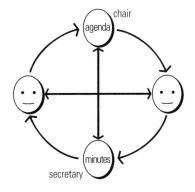

Record-Oriented Meeting

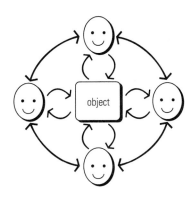

Procedure-Oriented Meeting

You have probably also experienced work sessions where a workgroup focuses on some object, model, or document. Object-oriented meetings enable participants to relate directly to what the group is developing together. This may be a physical object in the field or a scale model; it can also be a paper document at a conference table. Today, with electronic media, these objects and the group's interaction can take new forms. For example, now objects can involve text and graphic documents or databases online, spreadsheet models, three-dimensional computer models, or even video images with sound. People can access these objects from different places and at different times and still be part of an interactive, object-oriented work session. This sets up new opportunities for workgroups to work together creatively. When a workgroup does meet they can use electronic media to enhance their meeting by focusing the group on what they are producing and recording their ideas in that context. Using media space can even help overcome problems finding a common time and place to meet. Using telecommunications, you can have meetings in media space where the individuals of a workgroup can interact from wherever they are, and whenever they have time. Object-oriented meetings can make it easier to transfer the decisions made by the workgroup into products, such as reports or implementation documents, that can initiate actions.

Mock-ups

The last chapter introduced media space. As you learn to map your media space, you will discover different domains. Your media space includes workspace — your desktop or windowing environment, which enables you to access your programs and files. Your media space also includes model space — which may involve many types of representations of reality that you and others can work with interactively. And, finally, your media space includes presentations — which may involve paper space or even video space you use to package information for others. As you have probably already found out, mapping media space can help you and others in your workgroup navigate in these different domains. You will also discover that mocking up your models and presentations can help you and others relate to them more readily as objects.

mock-up A representation. People use mock-ups to show how the pieces of an object or the parts of a presentation come together.

Mock-ups can take many forms. They show conceptually how the pieces of a model or presentation come together. Mock-ups can use the frames of reference already described in Chapter 2 for diagramming workspace in application programs. For example, you can mock up a written document with a simple outline. You can mock up a drawing by outlining the major graphic components. You can mock up pages or layout sheets of drawings with thumbnail sketches. You can mock up a three-dimensional model with a quick wire frame diagram. You can mock up animation or video presentations with a script or storyboard. You can mock up each object you work with in media space. Doing mock-ups helps you and your workgroup visualize what you are working on together. This can also help you work concurrently on design and production. It improves coordination and can reduce the time involved in going from the inception of an idea to a finished product.

Multimedia

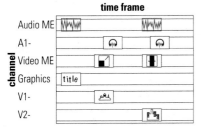

Multimedia Storyboard

Multimedia programs enable you to rearrange video sequences and develop presentations to fit a time frame. You can also integrate different channels — such as text, graphics, video, and sound — into multimedia presentations. Just as you can integrate text and graphics on a page using desktop publishing software, you can now also integrate animation, video, and sound on a tape or laser disk using multimedia software. To do this effectively you need to learn to develop storyboards or mock-ups of these presentations as well as learn to use the application software and related hardware. Chapter 11, "Mixing Media," will give you some approaches to doing this.

Debate rages over the definition of multimedia. Some groups refer to multimedia as media integration. The roots of the word multimedia obviously suggest that information is transferred through more than one medium at a time. More fundamentally, the concept of multimedia not only involves more than one of your senses of perception, it also involves more than one mode of thought. In addition, it can involve more than one means of expression. There is a tendency to focus multimedia rather narrowly on the new technology that is emerging. Through extensive promotion, impressive new hardware and software packages make claims to being "the multimedia platform." But there is no single multimedia platform. People can work with multimedia in many different ways, integrating not only typical text and graphic computer applications, but also telecommunications and video. As faster multimedia computer platforms evolve, media integration will become easier and more seamless. The creative thinking skills that are developed to use multimedia computing will also continue to evolve, opening new possibilities for human interaction.

Most multimedia packages focus on presentations. The audience may view a multimedia presentation passively, as people do watching videos and films. Or the audience may explore multimedia presentations interactively using laser disks controlled by computers. For example, people could select and play segments of full-motion video related to topics of interest to them. Yet there is a difference between being a viewer and a presenter, just as there is a difference between being a reader and an author. Multimedia software must also be geared to authors — people who can generate ideas and creatively assemble multimedia information. Ideally, multimedia computer literacy could evolve to mean learning to perceive, develop, and express ideas and information using more than one medium at a time. If that level of literacy could be established, then it would be easier to establish media space work environments where people view, interact with, and express ideas and information using multimedia computing. Workgroups could achieve new levels of collaboration. The type of close personal interaction people experience working with physical objects in reality could also become possible when working with imaginary objects in virtual reality.

Tom Yager, a technical editor for *BYTE Magazine*, who oversees *BYTE*'s Multimedia Lab, aptly summarized the hope of multimedia in an article entitled "Information's Human Dimension" (*BYTE Magazine*, December 1991, Vol. 16, No. 13, pp. 153–160). He stated:

> . . . *better* [presentation] means a shorter path from a concept in one person's mind to comprehension of that concept in another person's mind. The further hope is that if people can understand new concepts more quickly and thoroughly, their performance in intellectual tasks will improve. For anyone, better comprehension holds the promise of a richer fund of ideas and information. It is this fund that provides the raw materials on which the human mind—with its unique talents for associative reasoning, pattern discrimination, and intuition—performs its magic.

Summary

You can employ a range of electronic media. Multimedia stimulate channels of perception and expression which relate to each of your senses. Use multimedia to draw upon a wider range of perception and expression. The first activity that follows encourages you to explore different media.

You can use different modes of thought when working with multimedia computing. Multimedia enable you to work creatively with both your understandings and feelings, drawing upon both your deductive and inductive modes of thought. The second activity will help you learn to use different modes of thought.

You can also develop models to represent reality. These objects can be computer files such as documents or graphics, as well as spatial or quantitative models. These representations can help your mind absorb, contemplate, and express ideas.

Media enable you to work with ideas and refine them interactively. Models can represent objects you are working with. Reality can relate to virtual reality. Physical space can relate to media space. Real objects are multisensory. Computer models can be multimedia. You can develop models of objects to represent the realities you are working with. The third activity will help you learn to use models of objects as a focus for creative thinking and collaboration. The fourth activity will help you learn to mock up multimedia, enabling you to begin to visualize how you can integrate your presentations.

Activities

1. Explore Different Media

You can, using a pencil, give expression to your observations. You have probably already been exposed to many fine writing and drawing exercises that help you learn to express yourself on paper. Similarly, you can learn to express yourself using a computer and a variety of electronic media. Multimedia computing enables you to integrate different channels of perception. However, you need to learn to work with the channels you find interesting and useful.

Play with hardware and software that enable you to use different channels of perception. For example, try drawing with a simple graphics program. Or build a basic three-dimensional model using a computer-aided design program. You might play with programs that enable you to manipulate images either scanned from photos or captured from video. Or try an animation program to create a moving object. Even play with programs that can record sounds and compose music. Also try programs that can integrate text and graphics, video and sound. Explore how you could use different channels of perception for your projects. This will help you discover programs you will want to learn to use for your creative endeavors. You will need to invest some time learning to use the hardware and software you select. The more complete the program, the longer the learning curve will be, but as your skills develop, so will the challenges you can meet.

	time line		
Audio ME	ᴡᴡᴡ		ᴡᴡᴡ
A1-		🎧	🎧
Video ME		▮	▮
Graphics	title		
V1-		ᴀᴫᴫ	
V2-			ᴦ⁴ᴪ

2. Use Different Modes of Thought

You are capable of using different modes of thought—*L-modes* and *R-modes*—what you understand and what you feel. For example, when you think about a person, your impression involves both your "head" and your "heart." You may get the impression that a person is not credible if your understandings and feelings don't match. Writing emphasizes what you understand. Viewing emphasizes what you perceive. Television is a powerful medium for political debate because it enables the audience to get a more complete impression of the candidates. Working with a more complete impression is also important to creative thinking. Creating an impression is important to the arts as well as to many other endeavors.

Give expression to your different modes of thought so you can experience the internal transfers your mind makes. Pick something you know very well. Choose, for example, your shoe, or perhaps a familiar object in your room. First picture it in your mind and draw what you know about it. Then look at the object as if you had never seen it before and draw it from your observations. The results should show expressions of different modes of thinking. Compare the results. Practice shifting between what you understand and what you experience—between R-modes and L-modes of thought. This exercise can help you learn to use your understanding and sensitivity together.

3. Develop Models to Represent Reality

There are long traditions for creating models to represent reality. These objects may be icons. They can also be scale models such as those used in architecture since medieval times. Making maps is also an ancient tradition. Many types of drawings are, in a sense, a model of reality. Representations can also be quantitative models. People now make very elaborate quantitative models in computers by programming algorithms or using spreadsheets. They can work interactively with these models to explore *if-then* relationships. People are now beginning to be able to create spatial models in computers which represent virtual realities they can enter and experience in different ways.

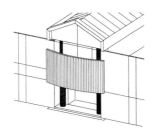

Develop a multimedia model, or object, you can work with interactively and collaboratively. This may simply be the page layout for a presentation of text and graphics. It could be a spreadsheet model that you can represent both numerically and graphically. It could be a wire-frame model of an object you are designing. It could be the topography of a landform or the images of a site you are working with.

It could even be an animation flick or a musical segment. You can also work with object-oriented programs that have transferable attributes. Use your model to compile base information. Use it to generate alternative ideas and save different versions. Work with your ideas interactively. Share the object with others on your project team and work collaboratively. Make sure each team member can access and navigate in the media space where you keep the model so you can work collaboratively.

4. Mock up Multimedia Presentations

Mock-ups enable you to visualize what you are producing. They may consist of verbal descriptions (or treatments), thumbnail sketches, storyboards, scripts, branching diagrams, musical scores, and flowcharts. All these examples provide ways for visualizing how to integrate different channels of perception. Thumbnail sketches help organize text and graphics spatially on a page or drawing. Treatments, scripts, and storyboards describe video or animation. Branching diagrams show hierarchical levels of organization of database files or hypermedia stacks. Flowcharts relate procedures to a time frame. Musical scores relate sounds to stanzas. These are all ways to preview what you are going to produce so you can create cohesive products or conduct well-coordinated performances. Multimedia may simply involve the integration of text and graphics or video and sound. But there is even greater potential. New object-oriented programs employ techniques that permit you to arrange icons in

flowcharts for planning multimedia presentations. They enable you to integrate text, numbers, graphics, and imaging, as well as animation, audio, and video, into electronic productions. There are also programs that enable you to author and navigate in hypermedia which you can map hierarchically using branching diagrams. In addition, it is becoming possible to create multimedia environments in virtual reality which you can mock up with three-dimensional wire frame models.

Mock up a presentation you are working on. Consider what channels you are working with and develop appropriate ways of visualizing how you use them. You may initially want to sketch concepts with a pencil on paper. Once you have a direction you are happy with, you can develop a format for picturing your product more easily using computer graphics, particularly where you reuse a basic format that you can replicate quickly. Multimedia programs enable you to integrate text, graphics, images, and sound by working with simple icons. You may use these programs for planning your production, but give some careful thought to how you use them.

4

Visualization — A Key to Creativity

This chapter will teach you visual approaches for working with computers. Through visualization you can comprehend your perceptions, clarify your thoughts, and coordinate your actions. Visualization helps you transfer information and ideas to electronic media effectively, so you can work interactively. It helps you to work with models you can create in artificial reality. Using computers in this way, you can enhance your perception, develop your thoughts, and amplify your actions. The exercises at the end of the chapter will help you apply approaches to visualization when working with your discipline and computer environment.

Consider How You Visualize

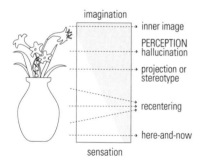

Perceptual Filter
adapted from *Experiences in Visual Thinking*
by McKim

What comes to your mind when you dream or imagine things? I typically see images — forms and colors. I can feel movement and rhythms. My wife, Carla, relates to conversations she may have in any of the languages she knows. When she is in Holland (her native country), she dreams in Dutch. In California she usually dreams in English. If she is in France, after a short time, she will dream in French. (That is when she feels she has really arrived.) Other people may imagine sounds — even music. We have all had tunes stuck in our heads. The point is, each of us has ways of visualizing.

What comes to your mind when you experience things? Your perception is filtered by many factors, as illustrated in the diagram to the left. What you perceive is a blending of sensation and imagination. Your mind-set is very important to your perception. The visualization techniques that follow will help you develop your perception and transfer your thoughts to electronic media.

Gestalt

gestalt, pl gestalten (German) The recognition of integrated patterns that make up an experience. The overall style or personality that one senses. This whole is more than a sum of the parts.

You have an innate capacity to comprehend a painting, or music — really anything — in ways that transcend physical reality. Overriding feelings characterize your impressions. This overall style or personality that you sense is sometimes called *gestalt*. Gestalt manifests itself in many ways. For example, a good painting is more than just pigment on canvas; music is more than just a sum of the notes; a personality is more than just a set of traits. Christian von Ehrenfels discussed this notion in the essay "Über

Gestaltqualitäten," which he wrote in the latter part of the nineteenth century. The term *gestalt* is used in many languages because there is often no equivalent. This notion has had a significant impact on psychology and art. Gestalt psychology has provided a way of appreciating and nurturing the more intuitive aspects of perception. It also applies to how you perceive the artificial reality you can access using electronic media.

You can derive gestalten from multimedia computing and video. For example, a video that combines rich visual images and music can be very stimulating. Just think of some of the music videos you may have seen on MTV or in music stores. There can be a synergy in what you perceive in electronic media which is greater than the sum of the parts. However, there is more to comprehension than gestalt. As Robert McKim points out in *Experiences in Visual Thinking*, "Seeing only the gestalten of visual imagery, without also seeing the diverse detail embedded in these larger patterns, is much like gulping down food, without savoring it." Certainly, you can sense the whole, but you can also learn how to visualize the detail.

Pattern Seeking

Patterns
adapted from *Experiences in Visual Thinking* by McKim

visualization technique Ways to perceive and comprehend based largely on pattern seeking and pattern recognition.

Look at the diagram to the left. You will find your mind automatically seeking patterns. Can you see the circles? Can you see patterns repeat? Can you recognize other patterns in this composition of little squares?

The capacity to recognize patterns helps you comprehend what you perceive. You can derive patterns symbolically from words you read, graphically from what you see, and audibly from what you hear. You can also derive patterns tactilely from what you touch. Think of all the patterns you relate to. You use patterns to recognize objects and understand speech. This is how you find meaning. Patterns also help you orient. Patterns of movement enable you to perform. Visualizing patterns can also help you use multimedia computing. There are techniques for doing this.

Visualization techniques are based largely on pattern seeking. For example, Dr. Russell Stauffer has developed *speed learning* techniques to help improve reading comprehension. Speed learning takes you beyond speed reading by addressing thought processing involving visualization. Stauffer's speed learning techniques include:

1. Surveying: By surveying you develop an overview of the material you are reading so you don't get lost in the details. Surveying also helps you manage your reading time.

2. Focusing on questions: Questions guide your attention, causing you to pique your interest when you read.

3. Pacing: Pacing helps you read with the flow of your thoughts.

4. Speculating: Speculating enables you to remember what you read by visualizing connections to your past knowledge and experience.

5. Instantly accessing information: If you understand how information is organized, you can locate key items. This technique helps you review and remember more and use information more effectively.

6. Sharpening your analysis: This last technique addresses analytical thinking and decision-making skills. If you have a clear conceptual framework, you can analyze information more effectively. You can also use it to make decisions more easily. For example, you can decide where you need more information.

You can relate these techniques to different channels of multimedia. For example, when viewing a graphic image or three-dimensional model in a computer you can:

1. *Survey* the whole image or model to gain an overview.

2. *Focus on questions* to pique your interest.

3. *Pace yourself*, letting your attention follow the flow of your thoughts.

4. *Speculate*, visualizing connections to your knowledge and experience.

5. *Instantly access information* by visualizing the composition of the image or the organization of the model. (This will help you navigate when you pan and zoom.)

6. *Sharpen your analysis* by visualizing the conceptual framework. (This will enable you to organize information you have and fit in new information you are adding.)

You can apply these techniques to using hypermedia and interactive video as well.

1. surveying
2. focusing
3. pacing
4. speculating
5. accessing
6. analysing

Speed Learning
adapted from Stauffer

Levels of Detail

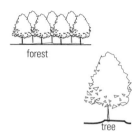

forest

tree

leaf

The Forest and the Trees

You naturally consider different levels of detail. You can look at the whole or examine parts. Comprehending the whole gives you an overview and a sense of the context. Examining detail lets you understand the parts. You recognize some things by their outline or overall form; some things you recognize from details. For example, how many trees can you recognize by just seeing their form from a distance? How many can you recognize by just seeing a leaf, the bark, or a section of wood? There is a saying that a person "can't see the forest for the trees," which means that a person can get stuck on different levels of detail.

Everyone is capable of dealing with an overview and also giving attention to detail. Some people naturally seek an overview. Others go for details. People's personalities reflect these two styles. So does the work of artists. Sometimes the overview is most important; sometimes the

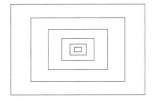

Boxes Within Boxes

outline

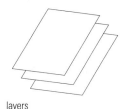

layers

parts

Levels of Detail

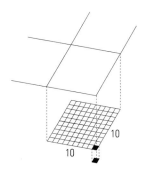

Hierarchy of Scale

detail is crucial. As you will see from the approaches described below, you can work with both styles using electronic media.

Computers can help you work with different levels of detail rather easily. For example, using a word processor with an outlining program, you can expand or collapse an outline, selecting the level at which you want to work. You can have an outline in one window of your computer screen and detailed information in another. Or you can expand only the portion of the outline you are working on. Similarly, working with a graphics or CADD program, you can have a base layer for your drawing and layer more detailed information on top of that. CADD programs enable you to select the layers you work on and display. You can zoom in or zoom out, depending upon how closely you want to examine the drawing. You can also have a key drawing in one window of your computer screen, while working on details of the drawing in another. This provides you with an overview while you focus on a portion of the drawing. Working electronically, you can even add layers to sound tracks. Each layer adds accompaniment to the score much like a traditional orchestra adding sections of instruments. The old Beatles' albums, such as *Sgt. Pepper's Lonely Hearts Club Band*, provide wonderful examples of electronic mixing.

Like changing levels of detail, you can also change scale. The Charles and Ray Eames film *Powers of Ten* graphically shows this by simulating what you would see if you were in a rocket lifting off the ground. Usually detail and scale are intertwined — the larger the scale, the greater the detail. Yet there is a scale continuum from microscopic to macroscopic realms. No matter what you are looking at, the continuum of scale extends beyond comprehension — at both the small and large end of the spectrum. You can add or subtract detail at any scale. So you need to select a focus that is at the right level of scale, detail, and speed (when viewing animated objects). Computers enable you to work with everything from microscopic detail to the vastness of outer space. They also enable you to slow down or speed up movement. Computer companies compete to provide higher-resolution photo-realistic images, as well as real-time movement.

When working with information, you need to determine what is the appropriate level of detail needed for a given task. Often "less is more." Architects strive to apply this Bauhaus principle, which is also evident in

art. A simple statement or soliloquy can have more meaning than an elaborate dissertation. A simple line drawing can convey more meaning than a fully rendered image. A solo can sometimes be more powerful than a symphony. When using electronic media, you need to select the appropriate density of information to work with, even though you may have the information or technical capability to add more. You should get beyond just processing information. Strive to visualize and communicate meaning.

Simple Line Drawing

Vertical and Lateral Thinking

dichotomy A division into two parts. A set of two (usually opposites).

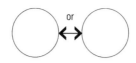

Dichotomy

Typically, you work most comfortably with *dichotomies*—sets of two (usually opposites)—or *trilogies*—sets of three. With practice you probably can work (in your mind) with about nine patterns at a time before you get confused. (Try visualizing three sets of three.) Using computers, you can store more patterns and recall them more easily than you could using only your mind. This enables you to work with more possibilities. Computers provide the means to manipulate patterns as well. You can add or update information, restructuring it to gain greater insight and visualize new possibilities.

trilogy A discourse consisting of three parts. A set of three.

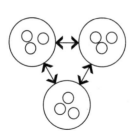

Trilogy

po A positive maybe.

In Edward de Bono's book, *Lateral Thinking: Creativity Step by Step*, he uses the word *po* (a positive maybe) as a way of identifying possibilities. De Bono says, "Po is an insight tool. Po is the laxative of language. It acts to relax the rigidity of the tight patterns so easily formed by [the] mind and to provoke new patterns." With vertical thinking you usually deal with *yes* or *no*. With lateral thinking you need to add the word *po* to keep possibilities alive.

vertical thinking An approach to creative thinking typically involving a linear, logical progression of steps.

lateral thinking An approach to creative thinking typically involving consideration of alternatives.

You can shift between vertical thinking and lateral thinking. *Vertical thinking* typically involves a linear, logical progression of steps. *Lateral thinking* typically involves consideration of alternatives. Vertical thinking requires that you make immediate judgments. Lateral thinking permits you to delay judgments so you can interact with information and generate new ideas. Vertical thinking is convergent, selective, focused on details. Lateral thinking is divergent, generative, opening new possibilities.

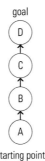

goal

D

C

B

A

starting point

Vertical Thinking

vertical

alternatives

Vertical Thinking
adapted from *Lateral Thinking* by de Bono

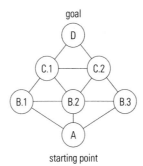

goal

D

C.1   C.2

B.1   B.2   B.3

A

starting point

Lateral Thinking
adapted from *Lateral Thinking* by de Bono

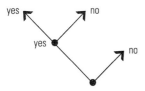

Defined Logic

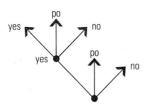

Fuzzy Logic

Obviously, both modes of thought are useful. Use vertical thinking to solve problems logically and work out details. Use lateral thinking to restructure patterns you perceive and to develop insights.

Of course computers are marvelous machines for vertical thinking. They process data using programs based on logical modes of thought: *on-off, yes-no, if-then.* But you can now use lateral thinking more effectively by working with interactive multimedia computing. The artificial reality you can create with computers helps you visualize new possibilities — artificial reality is the *land of po.* Some of the most exciting possibilities for using computers creatively have to do with applying lateral thinking. You can work interactively to restructure patterns, recognize new possibilities, and quickly manipulate them. In this way, computers can enhance both vertical and lateral thinking.

Thinking Analogies

You can see similarities. You often develop your comprehension of similarities in the form of analogies. Here is how you can use this capacity to explore relationships — to make connections.

symbolic analogy A similarity or likeness that involves abstract qualities that you can relate from one situation to another.

In the book *Synectics: The Development of Creative Capacity,* William J. J. Gordon identifies four types of analogies that you can use for creative thinking. These are symbolic analogies, direct analogies, personal analogies, and fantasy analogies.

Symbolic analogies involve abstract qualities that you can relate from one situation to another. These may be abstractions of form. For example, the form of the Sydney Opera House, in Sydney, Australia designed by Jorn Utson, abstractly appears like sails in the Sydney Harbor. Architects often use symbolic analogies to help generate forms for buildings.

Sydney Opera House   **Statue of Liberty**

Symbolic analogies can also involve abstract concepts. The Statue of Liberty, which France gave to America, commemorates the freedoms embodied by both the French and the American Revolutions. Chinese students replicated this symbol in Tiananmen Square and used it as a rallying point for their uprising. Symbols are very powerful analogies. People use them as a focus for social and political action as well as for form making. Artists use symbols creatively — in literature, painting, sculpture, and music. You can now create and communicate symbols, icons, and logos electronically.

direct analogy A similarity or likeness that involves similar physical characteristics or processes that relate to different contexts.

Direct analogies involve similar physical characteristics or processes that relate to different contexts. You can use direct analogies to transfer concepts from one situation to another. For example, communication and free speech are keys to democracy. These concepts helped propel the American Revolution. Printing presses provided a medium for communication at that time. There is a direct analogy between the role of the printing press in the American Revolution and that of electronic communication in the recent uprising in China. At Tiananmen Square, TV coverage and FAX machines spread communication around the world. However, the government in China gained control of the communication media there and suppressed the uprising.

printing press

FAX machine

Communication Devises

Direct analogies apply to many situations. Nature often provides a source of inspiration and understanding. For example, a bird's wing provides a direct analogy to an airplane wing. Birds in flight inspired Leonardo da

Bird in Flight
adapted from Leonardo da Vinci

personal analogy A similarity or likeness that involves your identification with elements of a problem.

anthropomorphic Related to human-like forms or attributes.

fantasy analogy A similarity or likeness that relates to an ideal.

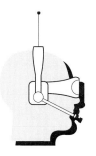

Fantasy Headset

Vinci to examine fluid dynamics. Using direct analogies, he developed concepts for human flight centuries ago. Leonardo wrote, "To give the true science of the motion of birds in the air it is necessary first to give the science of the winds, which will be confirmed by means of the motion of water in itself, and by means of this visible science [i.e., currents in water] you will arrive at understanding" (Paris MS. E, f. 54r). Leonardo da Vinci filled sketchbooks with observations of nature. He explored natural phenomena and derived direct analogies that provided the basis for many of his inventions. You too can derive and manipulate direct analogies. Now you can do this using electronic media.

Personal analogies relate to your identification with elements of a problem. For example, personal analogies are useful in dealing with interpersonal relations. They enable you to project yourself into another person's point of view and develop empathy for that person's situation. You could also use personal analogies to give computers personality traits or artificial intelligence. This can sometimes help you to relate to these machines and to envision attributes they might acquire. However, there are certain limitations and delusions to an *anthropomorphic* point of view that you should be careful of. Not everybody, or everything, thinks the way you do.

Rain Drops

Personal analogies also enable you to use all your senses when exploring phenomena in nature. For example, imagine if you were a raindrop. What would you experience? This can lead you to interesting discoveries and inventions. Computers set up opportunities to explore personal analogies electronically using multimedia. For example, you can mentally project yourself into the models you are working with.

Finally, Gordon identifies the *fantasy analogy*, which describes an ideal. Although this analogy is detached from reality, it can provide a source of ideas that can help you visualize real possibilities. For example, start with the outrageous fantasy of implanting a computer chip in your brain to enhance your mental capabilities. Using today's technology, this fantasy might be developed into a headset — something like a jogger's radio or a helmet. In addition to having radio and TV, this headset could also include a miniature computer as well as a portable telephone. If this computer were capable of voice recognition (translating spoken words into digital formats), you could interact with it using voice commands — spoken words. Maybe you could use your eyes and tongue as pointing devices. This computer might even detect your temperature and galvanic skin response through the headband or helmet. Then it would know how you are doing and might help induce a good frame of mind. The computer might provide you with audio feedback through stereo earphones and with a video display on your eyeglasses.

Thus, through fantasy you can transcend the boundaries of reality. In effect, then, the only boundaries become the limits of what you can imagine.

Bird in Flight

Wing Structure

Flying Machine

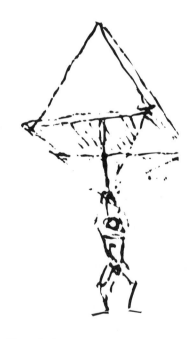

Parachute
all sketches adapted from Leonardo da Vinci

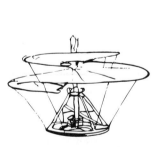

Helicopter

Transformations

transformation A change, or visualization of change.

Transformations help you visualize change. You can explore and express transformations by visualizing the integration of objects or parts of models that you are working with. You can also visualize the disintegration of objects you know and understand. Visualizing transformations enables you to put things together, take them apart, and put them together again. Transformations can also help you explore new possibilities.

Consider disintegration and integration at many different levels. You can physically take objects apart and put them together. You can also abstractly take concepts apart and put them together, exploring ideas and symbols.

Electronic media provide a marvelous vehicle for making transformations. Once you have objects in a computer, you can put them together or take them apart rather easily. These objects may be documents, procedures (like programs), drawings, images, three-dimensional spatial models or even audio and video. For example, you can build three-dimensional models in a computer, using primitives such as blocks or modular components. You can also take constructs (whole objects) apart in a deconstructive manner.

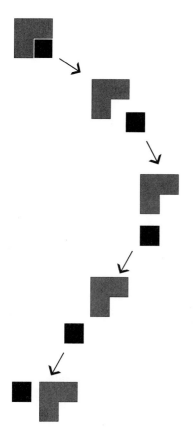

Transformations

Animation artists work with transformations in fascinating ways. They can change the morphology (or form) of an object, showing all the different shapes in between. This is *polymorphic tweening*. Animation studios have many techniques for doing these transformations. For example, Pacific Data Images used bend and stretch, or a "squish box," in the award-winning computer animation *Locomotion*. Many of these techniques are finding their way into commercially available animation programs that run on desktop computers. This development enables you to explore and express animated transformations using a personal computer.

polymorphic tweening A change in morphology (or form) of an object, showing all the different shapes in between.

In some ways, the urge to explore transformations makes working with virtual reality even more intriguing. It may also be why children find viewing the imaginary world of cartoons and video games so compelling. However, care must be taken not to confuse artificial reality with the real world. The constraints you work with in artificial reality are obviously different from those you work with in reality.

Levels of Abstraction

abstraction An operation of the mind involving the act of separating parts or properties of complex objects. Enables you to simplify information and clarify relationships you perceive.

By developing *abstractions*, you can simplify information and clarify relationships you perceive. For example, take something you can see right now and visualize it as a simple geometric form. Abstractions also help you develop concepts that you can express. For example, imagine simple geometries such as circles and parabolas, and then (in your mind) develop them into a more intricate object like a bright yellow sunflower.

Abstractions let you understand larger patterns. Using abstractions, you can work with relationships that you cannot readily comprehend at concrete levels. Insights derived at abstract levels are open to more applications. Abstractions can also relate to many channels of perception and expression. You can work with abstractions using any media. For example, you can abstract not only what you see, but also what you hear or write, by using electronic media. You can do this with graphic programs, music programs, and of course word processors. These media open new possibilities for using abstractions. Some approaches for developing the thinking skills needed to work with abstractions using electronic media are outlined below.

Developing Thinking Skills

S. I. Hayakawa derived an illustration of the "abstraction ladder" for verbal and written language. He used a cow for this illustration. In reality, you can see and smell a cow. You can call her *Bessie*. The word *cow* abstracts general characteristics commonly related to *Bessie*. You can also refer to cows as *livestock* — further abstracting their characteristics. *Livestock* relates to *farm assets*, which in a more abstract sense are just *assets*. At an even more abstract level, you can use the term *wealth*. You can abstractly relate this term to *Bessie*. Each level of abstraction leaves out certain information. But it enables you to consider further understandings.

In his book *Experiences in Visual Thinking*, Robert McKim presents a "graphic abstraction ladder." He shows how to use graphic languages both concretely and abstractly for visual thinking and graphic expression. He identifies concrete graphic languages as involving working models, three-dimensional mock-ups, perspective projections, isometric and oblique projections, and orthographic projections. Abstract graphic languages include schematic diagrams, graphs, and charts. McKim's book presents many fine examples of graphics used at different levels of abstraction. Computer graphics can now be used to express this visual language.

Multimedia computing can relate to different levels of abstraction. For example, working with virtual reality can involve rather concrete experiences. Working with computer programs can involve rather abstract relationships. A multimedia abstraction ladder can be developed to move ideas from reality to abstraction (or from abstraction to reality). Most computer users relate more to reality than to abstractions. Computer programmers, on the other hand, relate to abstractions and consider machine languages at the level that makes things work. You can learn how to move up and down an abstraction ladder. Simulators with visual, audio, tactile, and kinesthetic feedback provide realism. At the next level there are interactive video and audio and then animation with sound. Three-dimensional models are a bit more abstract; they range from rendered solid models to wire frame models. Beyond that there are two-

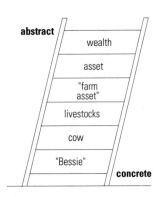

Abstraction Ladder
adapted from *Experiences in Visual Thinking* by McKim

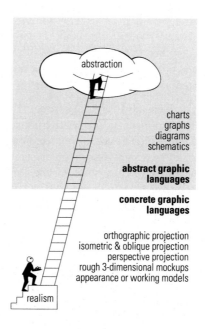

Graphic Abstraction Ladder
adapted from *Experiences in Visual Thinking*
by McKim

dimensional orthographic drawings such as the plans and sections typical of most architectural and engineering construction documents. At more abstract levels are graphic layers or sound track channels. Still more abstract are attribute databases. Beyond that are programs with algorithms. Probably the most abstract level of electronic media comprises the machine languages that computers use. Programmers usually have compilers to attain that level of abstraction. Few people can program in machine language.

Initially, those who worked with computers had to use abstract machine languages such. Later, programming languages such as C and Basic permitted programming to use a less abstract syntax. Now the push is toward object-oriented languages that enable programmers to work more visually.

The computer industry is also striving to provide photo-realistic images. Adding detail requires storing and processing more information, resulting in a need for computers with more memory and speed. Higher resolution usually requires larger and more expensive monitors. Even with these new systems, however, you still need to find effective ways to develop abstractions so you can comprehend what you are dealing with. Abstractions also provide quick ways of expressing insights to use as a starting point

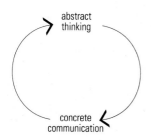

Alternating Between Abstract and Concrete

when developing ideas. Photo-realism may not really help you do this.

When mastering computers, you want to be able to use them in both abstract and concrete ways. This helps you interpret and express your thoughts. Many designers and writers find themselves most comfortable sketching and writing notes on paper and, initially, not composing at the computer. While this is fine in many situations where ideas are flowing and no computer is at hand, you can learn how to reflect and compose at a computer. Using different levels of abstraction can help you do this.

There are advantages to abstract thinking. It helps you simplify information and focus on key relationships to quickly explore solutions. There are also advantages to concrete thinking. Concrete thinking helps you examine details and communicate what solutions will be like. The real benefit of realism is not in generating ideas, although it could certainly help you develop thoughts more concretely. The real benefit is in communicating. A realistic presentation can provide enough detail for other people to abstract their own understandings and responses. Multimedia also help present abstract ideas. Audiences can get lost in abstract presentations unless they are familiar with the topic. Presenting abstract ideas with multimedia, using different channels, can help comprehension.

Visualization Techniques Related to Perception and Thinking

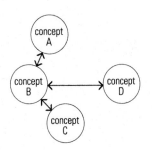

Concept Map

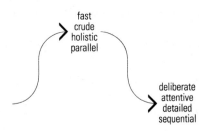

Cognition

Cognitive Mapping

By developing cognitive maps you can clarify and express concepts and interrelationships. This helps you sort out what you understand. It also helps you identify and clarify what you don't understand. Putting your understanding into a visual form helps you work with it more readily then if you were just working symbolically using words or numbers. Visualization helps you see connections. Cognitive maps can make it easier to relate information. Concept diagrams help you express new insights. You can also communicate your understanding and insights to others using concept diagrams.

There are many approaches to doing cognitive maps and concept diagrams. Ulric Neisser points out in his book, *Cognitive Psychology,* that two stages are related to cognition. "The first is fast, crude, holistic, and parallel." The second is "deliberate, attentive, detailed, and sequential." Neisser observes that cognition involves both abstract and concrete observations. Think of how you visualize ideas and you will realize you often go from forming abstractions to working out details. You may see evidence of this process in a sequence of idea sketches you produce. Develop the capacity to move back and forth between abstract and concrete levels of thinking. Also try developing cognitive maps for different channels of perception.

bubble diagram A graphic representation that shows the relationships between functional areas. Can describe patterns evident in a map or a plan.

flow diagram A graphic representation that shows the sequence of a process. Can describe movement of material or energy in natural processes.

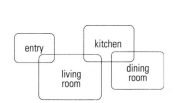

Bubble Diagram

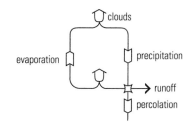

Flow Diagram

The visual track of this book includes cognitive maps and concept diagrams. For example, cognitive maps may simply show relationships between different concepts. *Bubble diagrams* can show the relationships between functional areas such as in a building. *Flow diagrams* can show movements of energy or material such as water in natural processes. Simple concentric arrangements can show the organization of elements in many objects such as an atom. Axial arrangements can show the anatomy of an organism. The possibilities are really endless. You can develop cognitive maps and concept diagrams that reflect the intrinsic order of what you are working on. Initially your diagrams may be fast and crude. As you develop your concepts, these models become more deliberate and detailed.

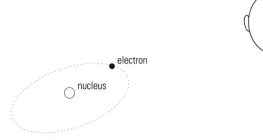

Concentric Arrangement

Axial Arrangement

icon An image or representation. Used to express ideas graphically.

Pattern
adapted from *Pattern Language* by Alexander, Ishikawa, and Silverstein

Graphic languages have evolved *icons* to express ideas. Icons are used in many different ways. For example, the icons on international signs communicate across cultures. They provide an international language. Good examples are the clever icons developed for each venue of the Olympics. Computer user interfaces often use icons as well. These symbols relate to commands or files that the user can activate by clicking on the icon. For example, the keys on the computerized cash registers in some fast-food establishments have icons representing the menu. People can simply ring up orders by pressing the icons. The computer will total the sale and record the transaction. Users can develop quick and clear recognition of icons.

A pattern language was developed for use in architecture by Christopher Alexander, Sara Ishikawa, and Murray Silverstein in their book *Pattern*

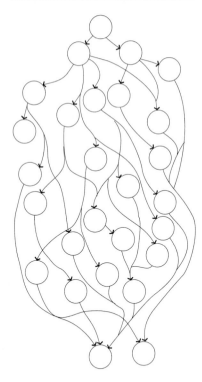

Pattern Language Cascade
adapted from *Pattern Language*
by Alexander, Ishikawa, and Silverstein

Language. Their patterns, shown as concept diagrams, usually have a behavioral basis and relate to how people use living space. In addition, their pattern language describes each concept and documents related research. In this way, pattern language can distill information related to many useful concepts. It is a way of recording observations and insights and appling them to design.

Patterns are integrated using a "language cascade." In this form of concept mapping, patterns that influence other patterns appear higher on the page. Patterns of equal significance appear at the same level horizontally. Arrows connect patterns that have important relationships. This approach can help a designer synthesize concepts for complex problems. One technique for creating a cascade is simply to record patterns on file cards. (Draw the pattern on one side and the description and documentation on the other side of the card.) You can then arrange the cards in cascades and in other conceptual frameworks that help you sort out and integrate important concepts. Another technique is to sketch key patterns on tracing paper and draw the interrelationships in cascade diagrams or other concept maps. Obviously, there is tremendous potential for working with patterns in electronic media attaching attributes to them. Computer-aided design programs are emerging that essentially develop pattern languages for conceptual design.

In his book *Environment, Power, and Society*, Howard T. Odum presents a language for diagramming material and energy flows. Systems ecologists and landscape architects use this diagrammatic language to describe ecosystems. Electrical engineers use similar diagrammatic languages for electrical circuits. In Odum's diagrammatic language, key transformations, such as photosynthesis, are given symbols. These symbols can then show the transformations that occur in material and energy flows. For example, they can show how solar energy moves through an ecosystem.

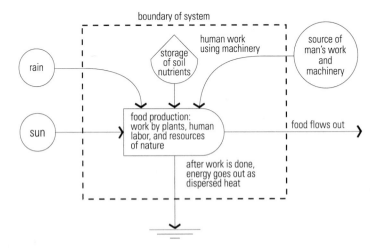

Model of Ecosystem
adapted from *Energy Basis for Man and Nature* by Howard T. and Elizabeth Odum

They can also track the flow of a key nutrient, such as nitrogen. For clarity, these diagrams often show just one flow at a time. For example, typically water flow is shown separately from nutrient flows although they are interrelated. This diagrammatic language provides a way for visualizing natural processes which helps people develop an understanding of how ecosystems function. Working with students and colleagues in the Department of Landscape Architecture at Cal Poly, Pomona, I have adapted this diagrammatic language and worked with it in environmental planning and design. We use this diagrammatic language as an analytical tool. We also use it for synthesis when developing ways to restore or carefully modify natural processes. We can also use it as a tool for assessing environmental impacts. John Lyle has documented this approach in his book *Design for Human Ecosystems*. He provides many fine examples of how to use maps and conceptual diagrams — including material and energy flow diagrams — to better understand and design the environment.

Today, techniques are emerging which enable you to use graphic languages to manipulate many patterns and processes. You can build cognitive maps of what you are doing right in the computer application. For example, multimedia programs enable you to move icons on a storyboard to integrate different channels into your presentation.

Hierarchical Orders

hierarchy The governing or intrinsic order. Can be categorical as well as spatial and temporal.

Examining *hierarchies* can help you understand the intrinsic order of what you are working with. There are categorical as well as spatial and temporal hierarchies. Most hierarchies exist in a continuum without boundaries. That is, there are entities within entities, within entities . . . . You readily relate to only a small band of this continuum. Each discipline has a different focus on it. Science helps expand comprehension of this continuum.

You can work with hierarchies by establishing frames of reference for building your models. You can use a topical frame of reference — such as a branching diagram of a directory. You can choose a spatial frame of reference — two or three dimensions in space (using *x*, *y*, and *z* axes). You can also establish a time frame — such as a time line.

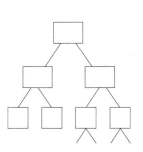

Hierarchy

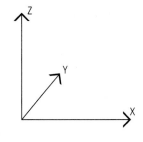

Spacial Frame

Time Frame

Topical models have hierarchical structures. There are topics within topics within topics. For example, you can arrange topics in outlines. Your outline should contain both overview and detail for the topic you are focusing on. You can also create hypermedia stacks that have a hierarchical order. This gives your hypermedia stacks clear paths for accessing more specific information.

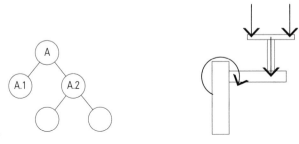

Topical Hierarchy   **Structural Hierarchy**

Spatial models also have hierarchies. There are places within places within places. When using spatial models, you need to recognize the scale of concern that you are dealing with. Then consider at least one scale above and one scale below your level of concern. For example, you can model a structural hierarchy. Recognize the main structure as well as the supporting structure for anything you are dealing with.

Temporal models have hierarchical time frames. There are moments within moments. Again, you should recognize the time frame you are working with. For example, you can model a system's hierarchy by diagramming flows through black boxes. Systems have processes within processes, each with its own inputs and outputs. Here again, recognize the level of understanding that is useful for your purposes. Also, look at the next higher level of function. And where necessary, look at lower levels to understand how the parts work. You could also develop temporal models for audio and video presentations. You can do this by developing scripts and storyboards.

Hierarchical orders are built into many computer applications. By recognizing them you will be able to work with these applications more easily and more creatively.

Parameters

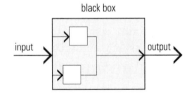

System Hierarchy

Parameters are key variables that govern the shape or performance of models. Engineers and planners often work with quantitative models to explore parameters.

parameter A key variable that governs the shape or performance of a model.

Aside from working with parameters in mathematical models, you can use parameters in CADD programs to generate forms. For example, using LANDCADD, landscape architects can simulate plant growth. They simply select the growth rate of a plant (fast, medium, or slow) and give

first year

fifth year

Growth Simulation
adapted from LANDCADD Program
by Greg Jamieson

the plantan initial and an ultimate size. Then the program can simulate the growth for one, two, or however many years landscape architects wish to specify. This helps both the landscape architects and their client understand how a planting plan will evolve. Integrated spreadsheet and business graphics programs also enable you to transfer quantitative information into graphic expression. For example, you can express the quantitative relationships on spreadsheet models as bar or line graphs or as pie charts. Visualization can help you understand these quantitative relationships better. These quantities can relate to parameters you can manipulate.

Smart Drawings

Computers enable you to link objects and *attributes*. In effect, you can create smart drawings by attaching database information to them. You can do this using computer-aided design systems. For example, you may have a drawing of a room layout which shows the furniture. You could include information about the furniture (manufacturer, model, cost, etc.) in the drawing and be able to extract and work with it in a database. You can do this even more extensively using geographic information systems. For example, many communities are compiling geographic data on their land resources and utility infrastructure. These data can include both locational information for mapping and database attributes for tracking key information. Linking maps and attributes enables computer users to keep track of resources in ways that were not possible when using only hand-drawn maps.

attribute A property, quality, or characteristic that describes an object.

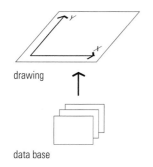

drawing

data base

Linking Drawings and Attributes

Summarizing the Techniques

Visualization techniques such as cognitive mapping are a vehicle for clarifying your thinking. They are the essential vehicle for transferring insights and understandings into a visual form that you can begin to work with. Hierarchies enable you to recognize the intrinsic order of what you are working with. Working with parameters enables you to explore options even faster and to develop designs according to set criteria. Smart drawings enable you to integrate nonvisual information. Now that you have explored visualization techniques related to perception and thinking, it's time to turn your attention to visualizing techniques for carrying out coordinated actions.

Visualization Techniques Related to Coordination

Aikido

visualization The formation of a mental image that can help you coordinate your mental and physical activities.

Visualization

aikido (Japanese) A martial art that focuses on three elements: **Ai** refers to harmony or coordination; **ki**, spirit or inner energy; and **do**, the method or the way.

hara (Japanese) A reference to a person's center. Your center of gravity, as well as your focus of concentration, and even your spiritual center.

Visualization can also help you coordinate your actions. You already do this when playing a game, participating in a sport, or even driving a car. Visualizing your actions enables you to perform well. Using multimedia computers often involves rather complex actions. There are ancient approaches to visualizing actions which you can apply when using computers.

The Japanese word *aikido* contains three elements: *Ai* refers to harmony or coordination; *ki*, spirit or energy; and *do*, the method or the way. *Aikido* is a benevolent and sophisticated form of martial arts focusing on self-defense. It provides the mental approach and moves for self-defense. *Aikido* teaches how to integrate the powers of mind and body. This discipline also integrates philosophical ideals and ethical motives. Some of the principles and techniques used in *aikido* have been practiced for more than 700 years. Today, people all over the world practice *aikido*. They do this not only as a form of self-defense, but especially as a way to integrate their mind and body, exercising this harmony. *Aikido* teaches coordination. The Japanese also approach calligraphy and traditional drawing in much the same way, integrating mental activity with coordinated body moves.

In their book *Aikido and the Dynamic Sphere*, Westbrook and Ratti show how to work with the *hara* — a person's center. You can consider this your center of gravity, as well as your focus of concentration, and even your spiritual center. They also teach how to draw on the *ki* — your inner energy. This relates to your physical strength, as well as what you can

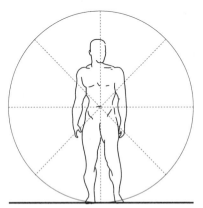

Centering
adapted from *Aikido and Dynamic Sphere*
by Westbrook and Ratti

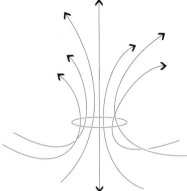

Extension
adapted from *Aikido and the Dynamic Sphere*
by Westbrook and Ratti

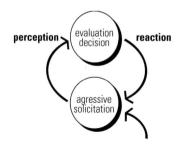

Defense

visualize mentally, and even your inner drives. This fusion of mind and body provides techniques that enable you to deflect an aggressor's attack by moving dynamically in a sphere. If you can do aikido, your actions can control by leading or redirecting the aggressor's energy rather than using any great force of your own.

Westbrook and Ratti describe the process involved. It starts with an *aggressive solicitation* (a threat). It then leads to *perception* (sensing the threat). The next step is an *evaluation decision* (instantaneously deciding how to respond). This results in a *reaction* (decisively applying the technique and movement). With practice this response becomes a conditioned reflex artfully combining the *hara* and *ki*. Important aikido principles are "The mind leads the body" and "Spirit rules matter."

Western sports such as skiing, tennis, and golf—if approached as an integration of mental and physical activity—can achieve much the same harmony of body, mind, and spirit. Skiers learn basic turns. Eventually, good skiers have rich repertoires of moves they can use for any terrain. Sometimes they will visualize a line down a particularly challenging slope. They respond to natural conditions—gravity, bumps, and snow conditions—as they jubilantly glide over the terrain. Similarly, tennis players also develop a repertoire of moves. They learn strokes and how to use them in different situations. They can visualize strategies using strokes that will be particularly effective against certain opponents. Tennis players need to respond instantaneously to each shot their opponent returns. Golfers also learn swings and visualize shots that help coordinate their approach to a hole.

There is a distinct difference in performance between an athlete who can combine body, mind, and spirit and one who just goes through the motions. You probably can relate to your own experiences verifying this. Some of the gold medal success of athletes relates to mind/body training techniques developed in Eastern European countries. In those countries considerable research and training have helped athletes reach peak performance. Some of the techniques used by athletes, such as "visual motor behavior rehearsal," involve approaches to using mental imagery. These techniques can carry over into other endeavors such as playing video games and using computers.

Visualization can help you coordinate your mental and physical activities when working with computers. It can help you focus on and visualize what you are working with. Visualization can also help you draw upon your creative energy and direct it toward addressing the problems at hand. You can combine a western understanding of creativity and visualization techniques with Far East traditions in coordinating mind and movement. You can also draw upon the type of mental imaging techniques used successfully by athletes from Eastern Europe.

Metaphors

metaphor Transferring to one situation, the sense of another. For example, transferring to a computer application, the organization of a desktop. Helps you relate to previous experience upon which you can build familiarity.

Metaphors help you relate to previous experience which you can build upon. For example, you can use a desktop metaphor—using what you know about organizing a desktop—to help you relate to your media workspace. You can use a soft prototype—or a model of the object you are creating—to help you relate to the artificial realities you are working with in shared media space. You can use metaphors to orient yourself in electronic media space. This helps you visualize how you organize electronic media. Metaphors enable you to use your intuition, drawing upon experiences with actual objects and applying knowledge you have internalized. In this way, metaphors help you coordinate actions when working in artificial reality.

Metaphors are useful only if you have experience with the reality of the metaphor. The desktop is a popular metaphor because most people can relate it to their own experiences. This metaphor enables people to draw intuitively upon what they already know about organizing a desktop workspace. If a person hasn't worked at a desk, however, this metaphor would have limited value. Many other workspace metaphors can be useful. For example, some painting and drawing programs use a drawing table as a metaphor. Appropriately enough, they have icons to represent the tools that are available. Consequently, anyone who has experience with a real drawing table and related tools can easily learn software using this metaphor.

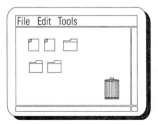

Desktop Metaphor

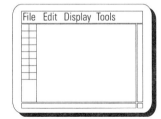

Paint Program

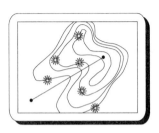

Mountain Model

Metaphors can even represent large environments, by using models or simulations. For example, at some ski areas, artificial snowmaking is controlled electronically using a model of the mountain. Instead of having to send a crew out in the cold night to turn on and adjust snow-making machines, an operator can sit in a command post and touch the snow-making guns in a model on the computer screen. The operator can turn on the individual guns and adjust them relative to the temperature, humidity, and wind being sensed at each location on the mountain. Similarly, factory processes can be controlled from a computer screen showing their layout in the factory.

Simulators provide metaphors for training. The objective is not so much to transfer experience from reality to the metaphor; rather it is to learn by

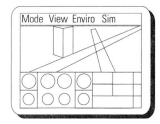

Flight Simulator

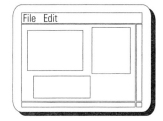

Windows

using a simulator and then transferring that experience to coordinate actions in reality. There are simulators for learning to pilot airplanes, ships, and other vehicles. These simulators can help people learn to coordinate their actions in artificial reality before venturing into the real world with an expensive vehicle. They are also fun to use. Training programs usually work back and forth between the real controls and the simulator, enabling people to visualize what they are learning.

Metaphors can go beyond being physical representations. They can be symbolic. Graphic user interfaces, such as Windows, use a windowing concept to provide ways of accessing both workspace and artificial reality using multimedia. Standardizing these interfaces helps the user shift from one program to another (also from one medium to another).

Using metaphors, people can carry habits into a new medium. This can be both good and bad. Metaphors may help people work more comfortably in media space; however, some of the habits they transfer may not be helpful or productive. For example, someone who habitually stacks his or her desk in reality, and never throws anything out, will probably use the desktop metaphor in media space the same way. (I know that from personal experience.)

Another difficulty with using metaphors is that the capabilities people have in artificial reality can transcend the capabilities people have in reality. Consequently, workspace metaphors are limiting, unless program-mers cleverly extend them to cover new capabilities. People with real experience are sometimes dissatisfied with the look and feel of the new electronic workspace and tools. Metaphors that are too literal can elicit these reactions by trying to be something they aren't. Also, as noted before, people may have no experience using the traditional tools and workspace upon which the metaphor is based. This metaphor does them little good when learning to use electronic tools and workspace. It may even complicate the learning process. In the long term, it may make more sense to learn to use new metaphors specifically designed for electronic media.

You can learn to develop your own metaphors in media space picturing the reality you are working with. Doing this can enhance your perception, clarify your thinking, and help coordinate your actions. You can use most of the visualization techniques presented in this chapter to develop metaphors. Your metaphors can relate to your work environment (where you keep your tools and information) or to the objects that you are working on — such as a product or building. They can also relate to the context you are working in — such as a landscape.

To work effectively in media space you need to link your experiences in reality with your experiences in artificial reality as much as possible. Metaphors can help you do that. For example, a road map means a lot more to you if you have been to the places shown on the map. When working with an abstract model, you have to develop a real sense for the frames of reference for a sense of which direction is up or down; which direction is hotter or colder, louder or quieter, faster or slower, earlier or later. Metaphors enable you to draw deeply upon your senses and intuition when working with computer models.

Manipulating Images

While the images you express can become a source for generating new images, you can also interact with existing images and manipulate them in many ways using computers. It is likely that more digital information will become available online. You can also scan images from drawings or photographs or capture images from video. You can also record samplings of sounds. This provides a new starting point that you can work with creatively. No longer are you staring at a blank screen or sitting with a silent computer.

There are many techniques for working creatively with existing digital information. These techniques depend upon what computer environment you are using and whether you are working with text, graphics, digital images, or sound. The basic approach for interacting with existing images, however, is like aikido or the sports described previously. You see how each situation presents itself and then derive your perceptions. This provides a basis for your decision so you can respond. Your response brings about a new situation to which you can respond again.

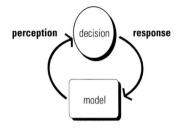

Interaction

This interaction can absorb your whole being. It can happen again and again with each new situation that presents itself on your screen. Through this interaction, you can attain a harmony of body, mind, and spirit. You can relate reality to artificial reality. To coordinate your efforts you need to visualize what you are going to do. You also need to internalize how you are going to do it. Then you direct your energies toward what you are visualizing. You can learn a repertoire of techniques or moves much like in aikido, skiing, tennis, or golf. Each type of software embodies these techniques. Learn what these techniques do and practice to make them part of your repertoire. Only then will you be able to use them interactively.

Experiencing Virtual Reality

The notion of exploring new realities is an ancient one. We all do this in our fantasies. A story, a picture, music, even a map, stimulates images in the perceiver's mind. You experience this through your imagination. Many people enjoy fantasy to escape reality. This is what much of popular entertainment is all about. Disney's Fantasy Land is an ever-popular place. However, it is sometimes disturbing if your mental images doesn't coincide with reality — for example, if a description or map doesn't match the setting. Sometimes artificial realities themselves don't coincide, for example, when the images you generate reading a book don't match the images you see in a movie.

There are different approaches to fantasizing. You can visualize fantasies in your head by dreaming, or through meditation. You can fantasize by responding to external stimuli, such as a sunset, or a movie, or a musical performance. Now, using multimedia, you can actively explore new realities. You can look through the window — your computer monitor — and visualize ways to work with the artificial realities you see there.

User interfaces that are emerging can make this experience a virtual reality. In effect, you can step through the window and enter a new reality, experiencing it interactively. One way to do this is to use a simulator that has realistic controls. The monitor showing the electronic image becomes part of the reality like the windshield of an airplane. Another approach is to use a *mandala* to interact with a video setting you walk into and interact with. You (and others) can see where you are on a TV screen in front of you. For example, TV production uses this technique to show the weather forecaster pointing to images of the earth taken from satellites. Another approach is to enter a virtual reality, sometimes called cyberspace, by looking through stereo goggles and controlling your movement through a power glove or a suit that senses your movement. Using these devices, you can enter virtual reality alone or even interact there with other people, creating a shared experience.

mandala A video setting you walk into and interact with.

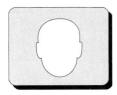

Cyberspace

Stereo Goggles and Data Glove

Let me share with you a brief adventure I had in virtual reality. While at the first meeting of the North American AutoCAD User Group (NAAUG) in California, I had the opportunity to experience cyberspace (which Autodesk is researching). The monitor was a stereo viewing device — much like a set of goggles. The pointing device was a data glove that fit on my hand. These peripherals were attached to a desktop computer with two graphics boards (one for each eye) to provide binocular vision. I could direct my movement in space by using the data glove. Pointing my finger enabled me to move in the direction I pointed. Closing my fist would stop me in space. Moving my head enabled me to look to either side, as well as up and down.

I visualized a vivid experience in this virtual reality, although the spaces and the objects were simple shaded models. The major sensation for me was a sense of floating in space, much like swimming in a pool. It took me a short time to learn to direct my movement with my finger without crashing through a wall. When I crashed, however, I simply went right through the wall and found myself outside the space I was in before. Orientation was easy; however, at times I did develop the sensation of being lost in space. But I could reorient myself by finding objects I recognized. And I could pick up and move objects such as a chair and a book. By going though a door in this model I could reach other settings.

A peculiar sensation occurred when I came out of cyberspace. Taking the stereo goggles and data glove off, I found myself suddenly back in a bustling convention center. While in cyberspace I had become oblivious to the real context that I was in. I then realized that in cyberspace I had a sensation of being almost weightless. It felt peculiar to start walking again in reality. I had the desire to point my finger and go, but I felt the pull of gravity and quickly realized I had to walk. Compared to the freedom of movement I had experienced in cyberspace, I felt very earthbound returning to reality.

Back to Reality

Often the real trick is getting what you are working on in artificial reality back to reality. Traditionally, artists work directly with a medium to create a new reality such as a sculpture or a painting. Working with electronic media, the artist often transfers to another reality. The final product may be a printout, a slide, or a video. On the other hand, with some computer art as well as with simulators, electronic media may contain the final object. Here, the perceiver may enter the artificial reality and bring back experience. As artists, architects, engineers, and scientists work more with artificial reality, they may find it more practical to package information electronically and have the audience experience it directly in media space rather than transferring it to paper or film.

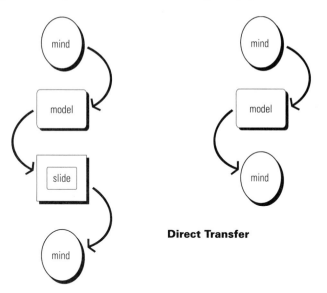

Direct Transfer

Indirect Transfer

When you work directly by hand using traditional drawing formats on paper, the size of the drawing is determined by how small you can draw legibly, unless you enlarge or reduce your drawing photographically or with a copy machine. Therefore, hand-drawn sheets are usually rather large. However, working electronically you can zoom in and draw at any size you wish. Consequently, you can produce drawings that are much smaller than you could by hand because the limit is no longer how small you can work. The limit is how small the print and detail can be in the

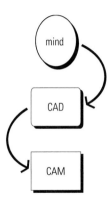

CAD / CAM

final document and still be legible. You can also work directly with models of objects you are producing. You can electronically transfer information from model to model which others can experience online using computers. You can transfer some models developed in artificial reality to reality without having to produce intermediate construction documents. For example, computer-aided design can link with computer-aided manufacturing software to run tools using numeric controls.

You need to keep your mind centered by moving back and forth between reality and artificial reality. Make sure you distinguish between these realities as you move back and forth. There is a risk of becoming lost in artificial reality. For example, a statistician may become deluded by a mathematical model if the sampling doesn't relate to reality. An architect may become enamored by a three-dimensional model that doesn't suit the actual site or situation. A landscape architect may begin to find more meaning in a map of the site than in the site itself. By moving back and forth between artificial reality and reality, you can verify the information you are working with. You can also test the ideas you are generating. Moving back and forth is also necessary to give more meaning to what you visualize in artificial reality.

Bear in mind that artificial reality is still abstract. You need to relate it to all of your senses. Experiencing the actual reality of a situation enables you to attach these experiences to your model. Then you can go into artificial reality, related to that situation, and imagine a richer experience. This richness is important to creativity and communication. Virtual reality is not entirely in a computer. You visualize it in your imagination.

Use visualization to integrate your body, mind, and spirit. Learn to do this not only in reality; also learn to do it in artificial reality. In reality, you use visualization to relate to your surroundings, consider possibilities, and coordinate actions. You visualize how to work with tools as well as play with toys or sporting equipment. In artificial reality, you can use visualization to relate to media space. This can involve your workspace, such as a metaphorical desktop. It can also involve what you can see in media space through windows. You can even extend your creative energy to interactions with objects in brave new worlds you can model. Visualization will help you to work creatively in electronic media space.

Summary

This chapter presents many visualization techniques. It takes a lifetime to master these approaches. You have already begun; and now you understand better what these techniques and approaches are and how you can apply them when using electronic media.

Visualization helps you learn to work with patterns. You can recognize patterns that relate to all your senses. Patterns relate to the intrinsic order of what you are working with. Picturing patterns helps you to comprehend what you perceive. Modeling patterns helps you to visualize and develop concepts you conceive. Develop models that relate to the intrinsic orders you work with. Use computers to build the models you can work with. The first activity helps you to develop this visual perception.

Visualize abstractly and concretely using cognitive models. Alternate between abstract and concrete models. Initial cognitive models are fast, crude, and holistic. Later cognitive models become more deliberate, attentive, and detailed. The second activity that follows helps you clarify thinking through visualization.

Coordinate actions by visualizing. You can transform models to create new entities. Use computers to transform models. Save different versions of models as you proceed. Use models to focus your perception, compile information and ideas, and coordinate your actions. Work with models interactively involving your body, mind, and spirit. Use models as a focus for collaboration. Involve your audience in experiencing your models. Transfer your models to reality as directly as possible. The third activity will help you coordinate actions using visualization techniques.

Activities

1. Develop Visual Comprehension

a. Abstracting Images

You can learn to work with very complex objects and situations by abstracting key information. For example, when reading, you can focus on keywords or outline the statement to comprehend it more clearly. When viewing, you can abstract the basic composition of a pattern, You can also diagram the structural system of a building, or you can map the attributes — such as roadways, topography, and vegetation patterns — of a landscape. You can even enhance images of tissue — and muscles and bones — of an organism. Electronic media enable you to abstract and enhance images to improve your visual comprehension. You can separate this information graphically on layers or save it with different versions of a file.

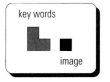

Abstract a written statement you find worth examining. Pull out keywords and organize them into an outline. Do this using a word processing program you are comfortable with. Next, take a visual image and abstract it. Diagram, map, or enhance some key visual attributes of something you find interesting. The image you work from can be a detailed drawing, a scanned photo, or a captured video image. Use any paint, drawing, or drafting program you are comfortable with. This will help you discover how you can begin to manipulate images electronically. If you do not have access to a computer, you can practice these exercises with pencil on paper. Take notes using a pencil to outline the key ideas of a written statement. Put a layer of tracing paper over an image and abstract it drawing with a pencil. Practicing with pencil and paper will help you visualize how you can do these things using computers and electronic media. Although initially you may find pencil and paper more comfortable and accessible, you can discover the tremendous potential computers offer for visualizing abstractions by learning to use a range of computer applications. There are many things you can do electronically you can't do with pencil and paper. For example, using a music program, you can even abstract the theme of a song if you wished to play with it electronically.

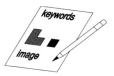

b. Developing Images

You can also learn to develop very complex ideas and objects from simple concepts. For example, speakers use notecards or teleprompters with keywords they can elaborate upon. Writers often find it easier to organize their thoughts and write from an outline. Artists may first block out images and then add detail. Designers typically use concept diagrams to work up schematic designs that they can then develop adding more precision and refinement. Composers usually begin with some musical theme that they then develop. Think about your own creative endeavors and you will realize that you begin with some abstract vision or concept and then proceed to develop it into a reality.

Take a keyword that excites you and speak about it into a tape recorder. Or write about it using a word processor. Express your thoughts as quickly as you can without worrying about diction, spelling, or editing. You can also organize keywords into an outline, develop the outline using a word processor, and then use the outline to write a draft. Save your work at each step — save your outline as a file, save your expanded outline as a new file, and save your first draft as yet another file. Compare each file and you can see how you developed your ideas. It is often helpful to have these different versions in case you want to go back and change the direction you are taking.

You can also do this exercise visually. Draw a simple diagram expressing an abstract image or concept you have in your mind. Make a new layer or file and, using a drawing or CADD program, develop that diagram into a more realistic image. Does your developed design relate to your original concept? How did it evolve? What alternative images can you generate using that concept diagram? Draw some alternatives. This exercise will help you discover how to use electronic media to develop ideas visually.

You can even do the same thing with sound if you like. Play a simple theme on an electronic keyboard connected to a computer. Add background using a music program with a synthesizer. Try out different effects. Electronic media not only let you work with voice messages; they can help you integrate sounds and even compose music.

Note: Again, you can do some of these exercises without a computer. You can write on lined paper. You can graphically abstract and express images using a pencil and tracing paper. You can even manipulate (copy, rotate, enlarge, or reduce) paper images using scissors, tape, and a copy machine. If you do these exercises with paper, however, pretend you are doing them with a computer. Visualizing can help you learn to work creatively with any medium. The thinking skills you learn will carry over to the time when you have access to good computers and are more comfortable using them.

2. Clarify Thinking through Visualization

The well-known work of Leonardo da Vinci demonstrates how he clarified his thinking by sketching and diagramming what he observed in nature. He developed design ideas using this approach as well as built models of some of his "machines." In a few instances he actually had prototypes built for testing. For example, a prototype of his flying machine was launched from a hill in Fiesole, Italy. Unfortunately, the athlete powering this machine was killed.

Designers often develop models to help visualize what they are working with. Models can take many forms. Traditionally, designers have worked with full-size prototypes, as well as scale models, in addition to drawings and diagrammatic representations. Quantitative models have become helpful in a wide variety of disciplines. Computers now also enable the creation of three-dimensional solid models with considerable detail. They can even make three-dimensional wireframe models to dynamically show deflections. Diagrammatic models can show key relationships of many situations. Computer spreadsheet models and algorithms can represent qualitative relationships. The advantage of models is they can be easier to interact with and change than reality itself. Models are artificial realities that abstract selected considerations so people can work with them more clearly. They are extremely useful for communicating — helping others visualize design ideas. They also provide lower-risk ways of testing ideas. Computer models do not injure people or damage the environment.

Take a project and develop models to help you visualize what you are working with. Recognize the intrinsic order of your subject. Develop topical, spatial, temporal, or quantitative models to clarify your understanding. For example, you may be working with a landscape. Develop a three-dimensional model or work with images of the landscape so you can view it from important vantage points. Map locational attributes showing soil, slope, and vegetative patterns. Consider how seasons and succession change these patterns over time. What is the structure of key elements such as the drainage pattern? Diagram the flows of material and energy to examine how the ecosystem functions. What are the opportunities and constraints? You can use this approach to visualize anything you are working with. You can even use visualization techniques to model abstract things — such as the organization of a database. Use your models to identify what you know and what you don't know about your subject. Recognize hierarchies. Determine your level of concern, but also consider the next higher and lower levels. For example, when considering a landscape, focus on your site, but also consider the surroundings as well as the subtleties of detailed concerns such as the soils. Relate the artificial reality you are modeling to the actual reality of the situation you are working with. When working with a computer model of a landscape, keep on visiting your site so you continue to experience it in reality. Can you relate your model and reality, enabling you to draw upon more channels of perception and expression? Models will help you assimilate new information and work with it creatively.

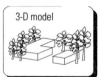

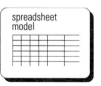

3. Coordinate Actions Using Visualization Techniques

The first chapters of this book explored techniques for visualizing how you can use media space, transfer information, and mock up presentations. This chapter explored how you can model the realities you are working with. All these techniques can help you visualize how to use multimedia computing creatively. Similarly, before a competition, good athletes visualize their event to achieve peak performance. From your own experience, you know that if you can visualize an action — a dance step, a tennis stroke — you can more easily go through the appropriate motion and rhythm. If you can't visualize it, your actions become hopelessly uncoordinated. Visualization techniques can also help you coordinate your actions when using computers creatively, particularly as you move beyond routine procedures and try new things. You can also develop rich metaphors that help you visualize new actions by relating them to more familiar experiences.

Consider the same project you are working with in the last exercise and use some of the approaches you have learned in the first chapters of this book. This will help you better visualize how you can do your project using electronic media.

Visualize Media Space

source info   final info

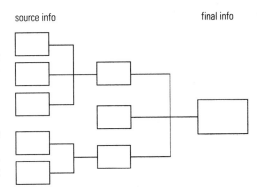

Visualize Information Flow

Visualize how you work with information. Develop metaphors that will help you organize your workspace. You will find mapping your media space helpful here. You can build many metaphors upon the notion of media space. For example, consider it as your electronic notebook or desktop, your classroom, or your work environment. Visualize where you are getting your information from and how you are going to work with it. An information flow diagram is useful here. For example, diagram how you are going to transfer information from your data sources to the software you are working with. Also diagram how to transfer information to your product or presentation.

Visualize the realities you are working with. As noted in the last chapter, mock-ups — such as thumbnail sketches and storyboards — can help you visualize your presentations. How are you visualizing your presentation? If your model is an object, can you look at and even touch and feel a similar product? If your model involves a printed document, are there similar presentations you can use as an example of what you want to produce? How are you modeling the reality of what you are working with — the objects or processes involved? Identify the metaphors you can use to build models — an artificial reality. Are there metaphors you have no experience with? How can you gain experience with that reality? For example,

if your metaphor is a model of a landscape, can you go to that site, walk around, and develop a sense of what it is like?

This exercise will help you develop models to visualize your workspace, your information flow, your presentation, and the reality you are working with. Using metaphors will help you relate precognitive experiences to what you are doing. This can stimulate modes of thought necessary for the creative process. But it is only an introduction. The next chapter will examine the creative process further. Part II of this book comes back to these visualization techniques to help you learn to use them more effectively when working with electronic media.

page mockup

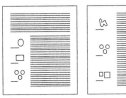

Visualize Presentations

5

The Creative Process

This chapter will discuss what researchers and writers have discovered about creative thinking. By understanding the creative process, you can nurture the ideas you generate. Knowing the process your mind goes through when developing ideas will help you learn to use new tools effectively and creatively. This will enable you to use computers to undertake complex projects. This chapter will show you ways to diagram work flow so you can clearly picture your process. There are typical syndromes you may be struggling with. Yet you can overcome them and discover how working with electronic media can make the creative process easier to carry out. The activities at the end of the chapter will help you apply the creative process to projects you can do using electronic media.

What Is Your Creative Process?

Ideation

Visualize where your ideas come from. Do you see any pattern in your own thinking when you are generating ideas? Maybe you have never thought about this before, or maybe it seems to you that creative thinking is simply chaotic. It may always seem to happen differently for you. Or you may have difficulty seeing how what you do relates to what other creative people do. There is a rich variation in how each of us approaches creative thinking. Yet there are patterns you can recognize. Understanding and building upon these patterns enables you to enhance your creative capacity. It also helps you to work creatively with other people.

Theories about the Creative Thought Process

creative process The stages your mind goes through when developing ideas. These stages include preparation (involving both first insight and saturation), incubation, illumination, and verification.

Many researchers have examined the *creative process* over the last 100 years. Creative individuals have also written about their own approaches. You can recognize similarities in how people describe this process. At the same time, examining the differences gives you divergent perspectives that may be helpful for recognizing this pattern in your own thinking. Examining some of these thinking patterns can help you develop a better understanding of the creative process. It will help you develop your own approach to creativity which you can use in your discipline and computer environment.

In the latter part of the nineteenth century, Herman Helmholtz, a physiologist and physicist, described how he arrived at his own scientific discoveries. The process he described involved *saturation*—where he became immersed in research; *incubation*—which involved thinking over what he was researching; and *illumination*—where he received that flash of insight leading to his discoveries. You may recognize this pattern as similar to the creative process you experience.

Early in this century, the mathematician Henri Poincaré took this understanding of the creative process a step further. He pointed out that the creative process involves not only *saturation*, *incubation*, and *illumination*, but also *verification*. Verification is necessary to check or test ideas to make sure they are valid or meet the criteria of what you are searching for.

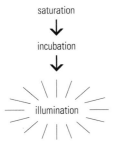

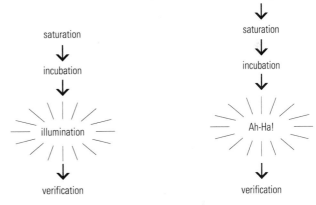

Helmholtz's Description of the Creative Process

Poincare's Description of the Creative Process

Getzel/Kneller's Description of the Creative Process

By the middle of this century, psychologists became interested in understanding creativity. Jacob Getzel recognized yet another stage in the creative process. He pointed out that creative individuals actually seek problems to solve and that this is a very necessary step for getting the creative process started. Another psychologist, George Kneller, termed Getzel's preliminary stage, involving finding or formulating problems, as the *first insight*. He observed that this applies to defining existing problems as well as to finding new ones. Getzel also described illumination as *the ah-ha*. This strange term vividly describes what we all experience when discovering a solution to a problem.

Using descriptions of the creative process that scientists, mathematicians, and psychologists experience, Betty Edwards—who is an artist, educator, and writer—integrated them in a very understandable way. In her book *Drawing on the Artist Within*, she summarized the creative process in five stages:

1. First insight
2. Saturation
3. Incubation
4. Illumination
5. Verification

Each stage can involve varying lengths of time, depending upon what you are doing.

Edward's findings correspond to what other researchers and educators have discovered. The educator Viktor Lowenfeld, for example, also believes that creativity is a common human trait for which everyone has potential. However, he acknowledges that this potential may be latent in some individuals who haven't had the opportunity to develop their talents. Lowenfeld describes the creative process as involving *preparation, incubation, illumination,* and *verification.* You can see how this corresponds to the stages that Betty Edwards described. By now, the pattern of creative thinking should be more familiar. Perhaps you are able to relate it to your own thought processes.

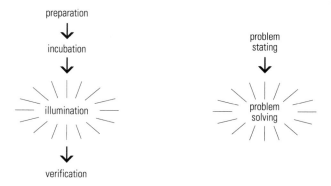

Edward's Description of the Creative Process

Lowenfeld's Description of the Creative Process

Gordon's Description of the Creative Process

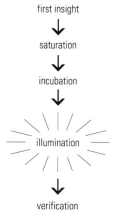

RSVP Cycles
adapted from *RSVP Cycles: Creative Process in the Human Environment* by Halprin

William J. J. Gordon pointed out in *Synectics: The Development of Creative Capacity* that the creative process can be described in even simpler terms. He said that creativity involves *problem stating* and *problem solving.* If you think about it, preparation and incubation are stages in problem stating. Illumination and verification are stages in problem solving. Yet there is more to the creative process than simply recognizing the different stages.

The creative process is cyclical rather than linear. The landscape architect Lawrence Halprin pointed this out in his book *RSVP Cycles: Creative Processes in the Human Environment.* Halprin developed his own terms for describing that cyclical process. However, the terms he uses correspond to terms that have been used by others. The *R* in *RSVP* stands for

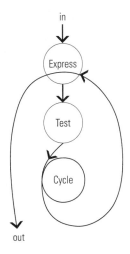

ETC Cycles
adapted from *Experiences in Visual Thinking*
by McKim

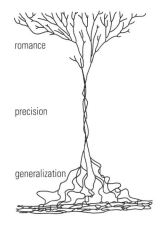

The River Metaphor
adapted from *Design for Human Ecosystems*
by Lyle

design process The stages your mind
goes through when developing design
ideas. These stages — which are
related to the stages of the creative
process — include research (involving
both problem identification and information gathering), analysis, synthesis,
and evaluation.

resources — or inventorying your information, developing your goals,
and motivating yourself — which is a form of preparation. The *S* stands
for *scoring* — which involves diagramming and symbolizing what you
are working with. This is more than just incubation. Halprin considers
scores to be "like musical scores; ways of telling others about ideas and
actions for their own performance." The *V* stands for *valuaction* — a
word Halprin coined by combining the words *value* and *action* — which
are key notions involved in illumination. Finally, the *P* stands for *performance* — involving the implementation or testing of the idea — which is
essentially verification. Some of the terms Halprin uses for describing
this process, particularly *scoring* and *performance*, relate to the performing arts. His wife is a dancer, and they have worked together developing
scores for performances. Halprin also pointed out that one cycle of this
process can lead to another — that creativity is a continuum. Consciously,
people may start at any stage in the process, drawing upon other stages
that they have internalized. For example, a dancer can perform extempo-
raneously.

People typically go through a cyclical creative process in iterations. Robert McKim, in *Experiences in Visual Thinking*, discusses the *ETC cycles*
which involve *expressing*, *testing*, and *cycling* ideas. He points out that
people typically go through a cycle, first expressing and then testing
ideas. One idea can lead to another. You can go through this cycle frequently, each time adding refinement to the ideas you are working with.

Alfred North Whitehead described the learning process as involving these
stages: *romance*, *precision*, and *generalization*. The creative process is
closely related to learning. The first insight is a *romantic stage* of the
process. Saturation and incubation involve more *precision* as you examine information that is relevant. Illumination and verification can become
a more *general stage* of the process where you make discoveries and
determine how they apply.

In his book *Design for Human Ecosystems*, John Lyle relates
Whitehead's description to the design process by using a river as a metaphor. He points out that the origin of a design flows from many sources
during the romantic stage. The flow becomes more directed during the
precision stage, which involves research and analysis. Finally, like a river
flowing into a delta, designs branch out during the generalization stage
involving synthesis of new possibilities.

The *design process* used in the design disciplines — such as architecture
and landscape architecture — usually involves:

Research (which is really problem identification
and information gathering)

Analysis

Synthesis

Evaluation

This design process is really patterned after the creative processes described by others. Each discipline typically has its own rubric for describing its design process. Your instructor or workgroup can provide you with the approach they prefer to use in your discipline. The approach may vary somewhat and the words may be different, but the basic pattern is usually very similar.

All these explanations of the creative process are summarized in the chart below. Obviously, descriptions of the creative thought processes are very abstract and not very precise. One stage flows into another; terms tend to overlap. Understanding the stages of the process is important. Being able to work with the transitions between the stages is crucial. This enables you to progress through the process. Understanding the creative process also helps you use computer applications more appropriately when doing design.

Design Process	Comparative Descriptions of the Creative Process								Learning Process
Various Disciplines	Helmholtz	Poincare	Getzel	Edwards	Lowenfeld	Gordon	Halprin	McKim	Whitehead
			first insight	first insight					romantic stage
research	saturation	saturation	saturation	saturation	preparation	problem stating	resources		
analysis	incubation	incubation	incubation	incubation	incubation		scoring		precision
synthesis	illumination	illumination	the Ah-Ha	illumination	illumination	problem solving	valuation	express	
evaluation		verification	verification	verification	verification		performance	test	generalization

Creativity in Each Phase of a Project

design phases The steps you go through when doing a design project. Each phase of design involves the design process.

Design professions such as architecture and engineering go through phases in developing design projects. For example, the American Institute of Architects identifies the phases of the basic services that architects provide as:

Pre-design

Preliminary design

Design development

Construction documents

Bidding

Construction administration

The stages of the *creative process* and the *phases of design* are intertwined. The design process relates to creativity. The phases of design services relate to the scope of work provided by design professionals. Designers go through the stages of the creative process in each phase of a design project.

For example, during the pre-design phase of a project, designers will go through research, analysis, synthesis, and evaluation. In this phase of design they can define the problems and opportunities, identify objectives, and begin to develop the program for the design.

During the preliminary or schematic design phase, designers will again go through research, analysis, synthesis, and evaluation. At this phase they can establish the design concept and basic forms.

Then, during the design development phase, designers will once again go through research, analysis, synthesis, and evaluation. Now they can refine the design and add more information — such as selecting materials.

During the construction document phase there are other iterations through the creative process. Here designers work out the precise layout and details showing how to build the project.

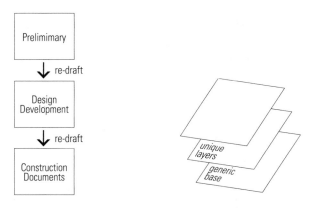

Living Documents

Layering Information

Bidding involves still other iterations of the creative process, this time finding appropriate bidders and communicating the project clearly for them to be able to research, analyze, and come up with contruction costs. These costs are carefully evaluated according to established criteria. For example, the construction contract may be awarded to the lowest bidder.

Even construction administration involves iterations of the creative process. Inevitably, problems arise in the field that need to be solved. Typically, the person doing the construction administration will have to research and analyze a problem. That person may have to synthesize alternative solutions and present them to the client's representative, the contractor, and possibly other consultants for evaluation. This might take place between job meetings. It might also take place with great urgency in an emergency meeting. For example, consider how quickly you would have to move from understanding the problem to implementing a solution

Schematic Design
research
analysis
synthesis
evaluation

Design Development
research
analysis
synthesis
evaluation

Construction Documents
research
analysis
synthesis
evaluation

Bidding
research
analysis
synthesis
evaluation

Construction Administration
research
analysis
synthesis
evaluation

Interwining Creativity and Design

if a gas line ruptured on a construction site. You need to be able to apply your creative capacity quickly in situations like these.

Many people think the creative process only involves the initial schematic design and design development phases of a project. Actually, the creative process involves every phase of a project. The focus may be different. In the initial phases of design the focus is on giving the project form. In the later phases the focus is on how to build the project. Each phase of a design project involves creative thinking, but in different ways and to different degrees.

Creativity is also involved in management. Good management involves developing insights about where the problems are in an organization or facility. People need to immerse themselves in these problems—saturation helps in understanding the problem completely. There needs to be incubation, or the chance to reflect on what is going on. There also needs to be illumination to come up with an idea to improve the management of an organization or facility. In addition, there needs to be verification to see if the management idea will work.

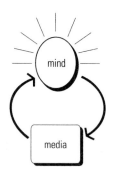

Interaction of Mind and Media

Ways to Visualize Your Creative Process

A key to working out your creative process is to visualize your approach. You can do this in several ways by listing and diagramming the procedures you are undertaking.

checklist A list of activities or items. Often called a "to do" list.

Probably the simplest way to visualize your approach is to make a *checklist* of activities. Many people call this a "to do list." You can write this list using pencil and paper. Using a word processor permits you to more easily update it, putting top priorities at the top of the list. You can also list your activities chronologically in a journal, recording the activities you have accomplished, your agenda for the day, and the activities you plan for future dates. I usually keep journals for the classes I teach and put them online using E-mail to share with colleagues and students. Doing this online makes it fairly easy to update this journal as the school

Checklist:
   top priority
   second priority
   third priority

Journal:
   record

   agenda

   plan

MONTH

M	T	W	T	F	S	S

Lists

Calendar

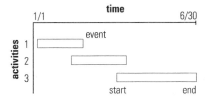

Gannt Chart

Gannt chart A bar graph that shows the duration of tasks and relates them to a time line.

work flow diagram A diagram linking activities and events and relating them to a time line. Used widely for operations research and project management.

CPM (critical path method) A procedure for determining which set of activities will take the longest to accomplish, hence constituting the critical path of activities in a project.

PERT (progress evaluation review technique) A procedure for considering what is completed on a project and relating this to a schedule.

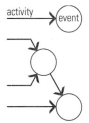

Work Flow Diagram

term progresses. Some of my colleagues make calendars for their classes, listing activities and assignments for each date the class meets.

You can also relate your checklist for a project to a time line by developing a *Gannt chart*. Simply draw a time line horizontally and identify the beginning and the end of your project. Then identify different tracks of activities you are undertaking and list them on the left side of your chart. Chart each track beginning from when you anticipate it will start to when you expect it to end. In this way you can graphically identify the duration of the tasks you are undertaking, relating them to a time line. This is useful for planning your project and managing your progress. However, a Gannt chart does not really show the interconnections of the activities.

Work flow diagrams, used widely in operations research, enable you to visualize the relationships of activities and events. You can also relate them to a time line. *CPM* (critical path method) and *PERT* (progress evaluation review techniques) use these diagrams in managing military and large manufacturing operations. Construction, and other endeavors such as launching space satellites, also uses these techniques. You can diagram activities as arrows (the length of which relates to duration). You can identify events as circles and place them at the appropriate dates on the time line. Each activity usually relates to some event or product. For example, you could diagram the activity involved in digitizing a basemap by showing an arrow on your time line which would start on the date you expect to start digitizing and end on the date you hope to finish digitizing. The product of your digitizing activity would be the map you produce. Identify that map in the circle you place on your diagram. You can describe procedures by linking activities and events. You can diagram sequential procedures, parallel procedures, and even cyclical procedures in time. This helps you determine the longest (or critical) path through a project. For example, you could link your digitizing activities to other procedures you will undertake using the base information you compile. You will see that these procedures are dependent on getting your base information digitized. So digitizing your base may be part of the critical path through your project.

Strategies for developing work flow diagrams are similar to the strategies already described for developing information flow diagrams. One strategy is to start at the beginning of a project and diagram the path by which you think you will proceed. Another strategy is to picture the end product (or final event) and then visualize what leads up to that — working backward from the final product. Yet another strategy is to list all the activities and events involved in a project. Then begin to link them, first developing subroutines and linking these modules into larger processes. As you become more familiar with various procedures, you can build these modules to shape approaches to new projects more quickly. For example, you may be able to establish some standard procedures for your discipline and computer environment and then link them creatively.

You can draw work flow diagrams on paper (by hand), or you can produce them electronically (using computer graphic software). Project management software is also available to help you manage projects. This software can even generate Gannt charts and work flow diagrams. Typically, project management software links graphic charts to databases and calendars, keeping track of your activities, events, and schedule along with the resources you have allocated. Using this software helps you design your approach to a project. It helps you evaluate your project to see what resources are necessary to carry it out. You can estimate how long it will take to do your project. In this way, you can refine your approach before you commit a real effort to it. This software can also help you manage your work as you proceed. Using project management software, you can produce a variety of reports useful for monitoring your progress.

Applying work flow diagrams to visualize creative projects becomes difficult to do with precision because there are so many unknowns. Nevertheless, having a clear picture of where you are, and where you are going, is extremely useful in any creative endeavor. Consider your work flow diagram as simply a map or a guide through your creative process. When developing a map, you can consider alternative routes and different vehicles for getting to your destination. This thinking strategy helps you decide how to proceed and you will not get lost as easily. This can give you more confidence to explore new avenues and use different vehicles. Picturing alternatives is especially important if you want to make use of new tools that are available. Often, the only way to break out of your present work pattern is to visualize alternative approaches incorporating new tools or visualizing more innovative ways to use the tools you have access to. To use computer applications effectively, you have to plan your approach. Work flow diagrams can help you do that. They help you to understand how to develop methods to mesh your mind with the media and models you are using. Work flow diagrams also help you to communicate what needs to be done so you can coordinate a team's effort. By carefully planning your approach you can save time and effort when carrying out a project — especially a team project.

Despite these obvious benefits, you may be tempted to avoid the whole procedure of visualizing your creative process. Sure, sometimes it is more fun to travel without a map, particularly if you don't mind getting lost. You probably also realize you don't follow a rigid process when thinking creatively. However, having a work flow diagram can actually give you more freedom to let your mind wander because you know where you are, and where you are going, in your approach to a project. Oftentimes you will discover some better options or new obstacles along the way. Being able to visualize your approach will enable you to reassess your goals and update how you will proceed. Now you are working more creatively. Visualizing your approach can also help you overcome some common syndromes, or behavior patterns, that can waste or block your creative energies.

Creative Process Syndromes

A number of common syndromes interfere with the creative process. I have observed these syndromes over many years of teaching design courses. I have also seen many of them in professional practice. You will probably be able to recognize them in your own work environment. Understanding these syndromes can help you identify and overcome problems you may be having in releasing your creative capacity.

The "Lack of Insight" Syndrome

To use your creative capacity you need to spark a desire to explore new possibilities. People can struggle in trying to find this spark. Some of this struggle may stem from knowing too much. Or it may result from considering only "expert opinions." This can keep you from looking at a situation freshly and synthesizing new possibilities from what you perceive. For example, it is sometimes easier to look at another person's house and visualize what might be done to improve it rather than to look at your own. Maybe you are too familiar with your own home and the constraints you are living with.

Usually, you can perceive some insight or creative direction that you feel is compelling enough to pursue. This may be more difficult to do when you stare at a blank piece of paper or empty computer screen. If this is the case—if you feel like you're drawing a blank—remember you can draw insight from what you know and can visualize. For example, think about remodeling a part of your home. You can develop a certain set of insights by sitting in the space that you want to change and looking around contemplatively. You can develop another set of insights looking at a diagram of that space and studying how it relates to other areas, how the circulation works, how the plumbing works, or how the building structure works. Architects work back and forth between these realities. They consider the actual place; then they develop diagrams, models, or plans of the place. This way they are able to develop insights and possible design directions both from reality and from representations of this reality. A good architect can quickly come up with some exciting ideas that the client may wish to pursue. Just as an architect does this, so does a writer or a painter. So do you, every day and in almost any situation. Insights constantly occur to you. Paying attention to and acting upon your insights is essential to any creative endeavor.

Let your mind go—almost in a naïve childlike fashion. Then you can discover your first insights. You have a wonderful "what if" and "why not" capability. There is a child in us all who can look at the world freshly. In addition to working with reality, using multimedia with computers enables you to draw more from your senses. Computers can augment and enhance reality. Electronic media can provide an artificial reality that can help you derive insights.

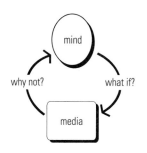

Deriving Insights

"A man should learn to detect and watch that gleam of light which flashes across his mind from within, more that the luster of the firmament of bards and sages. Yet he dismisses without notice this thought, because it is his."

—Ralph Waldo Emerson, "Self Reliance," 1844.

research

analysis

synthesis

evaluation

Analysis Paralysis

The "Analysis Paralysis" Syndrome

Usually, analysis can lead to synthesis, drawing from the information you compile. But, sometimes, key pieces of information may be missing, making it difficult to proceed. Sometimes, the more information you gather, the more difficult it becomes to synthesize. Some people find information gathering an end in itself instead of a springboard for creativity. This is typical of academic pursuits; for example, a good historian can enhance your perception and comprehension of a period of civilization, but carefully avoids inventing anything. Scientists tend to give more credence to rigorously working with the apparent facts of the matter than to take speculative intuitive leaps. It is easy to get preoccupied with finding more information rather than creatively using the information that is available. All these situations and attitudes can lead to analysis paralysis: the inability to move beyond analysis.

History considers past events, but invention can shape history. People sometimes make discoveries and inventions from previous events and findings; however, there needs to be an intuitive leap to go further. Analysis paralysis occurs when people are afraid, or somehow unwilling, to take that leap. Hypothesize! Sometimes it's necessary to make assumptions or use surrogate information to proceed.

Analysis is like breathing in, and synthesis is like breathing out. As you can relax to let your breathing flow naturally, you can also relax and let your creativity flow more naturally. Let your ideas develop with this flow. When taking in information, go ahead and make assumptions; wonder about possibilities. Be careful not to confuse facts with fabrication, but go ahead and speculate with ideas even if risks are involved.

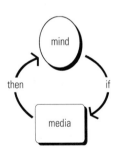

mind

then

if

media

Exploring Possibilities

You can reduce risks when working with computers. You can change assumptions and add information more easily than when working by hand. You can model possibilities using information in artificial reality before you commit the resources to act upon them. For example, suppose you are missing some numbers for a spreadsheet model, and that prevents you from getting to the bottom line. Plug in some assumptions so you can proceed. (Carefully note that these are assumptions by stating them as "if-then" strategies.) When you get better information, you can substitute it. If the new information is part of a calculation, you can automatically have it revise the bottom line.

Similarly, you can use computers for design. Electronic media can make it easier to develop designs adding new information as you proceed. You can interactively try out more possibilities, particularly if there are variations on a pattern, or procedure, that you may already be working with in the computer. Sometimes, working ahead with assumptions helps you determine what information you really need. Sometimes making mistakes or working with erroneous assumptions can even lead to fresh insights. Try out possibilities using electronic media. Don't let analysis paralysis prevent you from making discoveries.

first insight
saturation
incubation
illumination
verification

Premature Judgement

"In every work of genius we recognize our own rejected thought; they come back to us with a certain alienated majesty."

— Ralph Waldo Emerson,
"Self-Reliance," 1844.

The "Premature Judgment" Syndrome

How often do you see people kill an idea before they give it any chance of surviving? Maybe you prejudge your own ideas before you give yourself a chance to explore them. Judgment is a very important critical thinking skill. Yet you need to know when and how to use it appropriately. Premature judgment can stifle creativity.

What causes people to judge prematurely? Sometimes it is anxiety — the inability to tolerate uncertainty. Sometimes it is laziness. People prejudge so they don't have to spend time and effort exploring ideas unless they think the ideas would be immediately beneficial. There may not be a budget for exploring possibilities or for design. People often become complacent with preconceived notions. Sometimes, misguided wisdom results in premature judgments. People constantly hear pompous pronouncements of what will (or what will not) work. Final judgment is only useful in the final evaluation. Premature judgment is a curse at the inception of a creative project. However, people like to make pronouncements — maybe because they assume a certain importance — as if they were making the final decision.

Another form of premature judgment is personal preference. Obviously preferences make everyday decisions or choices easier to make. But when people develop preferences, they risk not having an open mind. People's preferences are polled both in marketing and in politics. In free markets, surveys frequently determine preferences among existing choices. Consequently, products become market-driven. These products are tailored to what people think they want, rather than taking into account new possibilities that might exist. Thus, many manufacturers mass-produce what sells rather than what adds value. Public opinion polls in democratic societies often examine positions rather than possibilities. Politicians are frequently guided by opinion polls rather than policies leading to potential solutions of difficult problems. How shortsighted are market-driven design and opinion-poll politics based on looking back on what people prefer? Imagine trying to drive forward while looking in a mirror. Mirrors provide important and useful information; however, it is dangerous to guide by them alone, particularly if you are trying to move forward. You need to develop a careful balance between making judgments based on past experiences and keeping your mind open to explore new possibilities.

Sometime people judge prematurely out of fear or inhibition. They become self-conscious. They don't look further at possibilities, but worry about what others will think. Creativity can involve a certain craziness that they fear others may misunderstand.

Computers can permit you to "get crazy" and try out possibilities. You can explore new realities, visualizing what doesn't exist. For example, sculptors can have a wonderful time building computer models of three-dimensional constructs. Scientists can visualize new molecules this way.

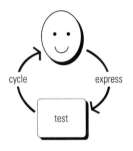

Express, Test, Cycle

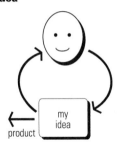

One Idea

My Idea

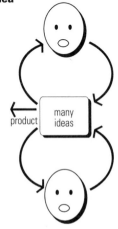

Collaboration

Engineers can build computer models of automobiles and then test them rigorously using evaluative programs that simulate aerodynamics, or crashworthiness. Designers can model new possibilities and make photo-realistic presentations. This even opens the possibilities for market surveys testing the reaction to new products before putting designs into production. Computers can enable you to try out new (even crazy) possibilities more easily, going beyond what exists.

Your personal capabilities are also enhanced when using computers. You can do more on your own without involving other people. This makes it possible to move beyond prejudgments and explore crazy ideas on your own.

The "One Idea" Syndrome

Sometimes people get one idea and are not able to move beyond it. They become very protective of "their idea." They have difficulty considering alternatives or even effectively developing their original idea. They need to be able to generate a full range of possibilities in order to determine which idea is the best option so they can develop it fully.

There are many reasons why people can become stuck on one idea. Understandably, it may have something to do with being insecure. Having an exciting idea is delightful, even relieving — especially if the people had no exciting idea before. Their idea becomes precious for them; they stick to it regardless of its merits. They worry that they may not be able to find another good idea. They may also be reluctant to change what they have done, particularly if they are using traditional media such as paper and have invested a lot of time.

Sometimes people get rather lazy. (Well, don't we all?) They quickly arrive at an idea they think is "good enough" and go with it. In some circumstances, where there are time pressures, that may be justifiable. Some people, steeped in logical thought processes like math, think there must only be one right answer. But there usually is no single answer to a good design project, or to most situations people face in life.

In some cases, people personally identify with ideas. They identify them as "my idea" or "your idea" rather than by the intrinsic merits of the ideas themselves. Egos can become a curse on collaboration. Effective collaboration requires a certain maturity or mutual respect to set egos aside. Children begin to exert their will at about the age of two when they discover the word *no* which they use to respond to almost anything a parent may suggest. Teenagers naturally search for their own identities, which may be contrary to whatever their parents identify with. This search for identity is natural, and everyone goes through it in many stages in life. Identity often becomes manifested in the ideas people generate.

Care must be taken that the "one idea" syndrome doesn't become a "my idea" syndrome. Probably the most difficult aspect of group dynamics of design teams is to get everyone to judge ideas on the basis of intrinsic merits. Teams need to do this to agree upon a direction. One has to be able to work with many ideas and transcend ego involvement. The same is true for effective teaching.

Using electronic media, you can store that one precious idea. (And you had better create a backup file.) But you can also store other ideas you or your workgroup may generate. A computer can help you compare, modify, or even combine ideas, making electronic media ideal for collaboration. Ideas developed in a computer become somewhat depersonalized because they don't have the signature of people's handwriting or drawing style. Bigger and bolder need not be a basis for being better, as can happen when considering hand-sketched ideas. Consequently, it becomes easier to evaluate ideas on the basis of their intrinsic merits.

The "Too Many Ideas" Syndrome

Some people just bubble with ideas. Everything they consider turns into another possibility. The dilemma they have is selecting the best concept and committing to develop it. Somehow, to them it can be more fun to just keep on discovering more ideas.

There is real excitement in discovering ideas. Ideas often lose their luster when the hard work of developing them begins. Because of that, you might consider the initial stage of the creative process the romantic stage. The romance is over when you work with more precision.

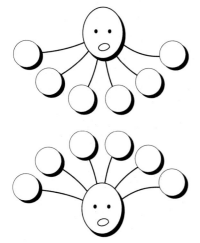

Too Many Ideas

How does one commit to ideas, and what does it take to develop them? Commitment is driven by different motives. The ideas you are working with may be compelling enough to give you the drive to proceed. This passion, or obsession, is an important part of creativity. You may also see pursuing ideas as a challenge that helps you test your potential. Abraham Maslow descibes this as self-actualization. You can even pursue an idea out of a sense of duty — part of the integrity to carry out a job, or the professionalism involved when serving a client. Of course, it always helps to visualize successfully fulfilling the ideal and realizing some reward.

Using computers may make it easier to sort out options and to commit to a concept you can work with. Once committed, you can develop concepts using electronic media. Your commitment can grow stale if it takes too long to develop a concept. You can become distracted by other problems or possibilities. Consequently, any medium that provides for quicker interaction helps focus your creative attention. Collaboration that provides positive reinforcement can also help you sustain your resolve. Electronic media can enable you to make connections with a support group which could help you sustain your commitment. Using electronic communications can help you connect with colleagues almost anywhere in the world. You can reach beyond your immediate peers who may have little interest in, or sympathy for, what you are trying to achieve.

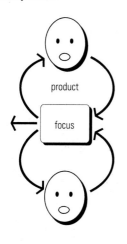

Committing

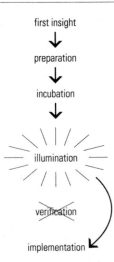

Lack of Testing

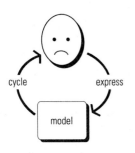

Presentation Is Irrelevant

The "Lack of Testing" Syndrome

Sometimes you may present projects where the ideas are half-baked. You may need more time and capabilities to develop and test ideas sufficiently.

An interrelationship exists between developing and testing ideas. As Robert McKim points out, a good design process involves iterative loops—expressing, testing, and cycling ideas. Engineers recognize the importance of optimizing. They learn to optimize different sets of constraints. Engineering design often involves sorting out optimal patterns of conflicting constraints. Although it takes more design effort, in the long run it is much easier to develop models to determine the optimal design. This way engineers can evaluate tradeoffs before they build.

Computers can help you work with evaluative models. Having information in a digital format enables you to test it more easily. For example, drawing files can include attributes and takeoffs. These are useful for cost estimating. Many CADD programs now link to finite element analysis (to evaluate structural integrity) and other evaluative routines. Viewing three-dimensional models is also another form of evaluation. (You can see how everything fits together three-dimensionally.) Even running text through a spell checker or grammar checker is a common form of using the evaluative tools that computers provide.

The "Presentation Is Irrelevant" Syndrome

Some people get so wrapped up in developing ideas, or models, they don't put enough thought, time, and effort into communicating them clearly. They may spend all their time visualizing their project and never bother to visualize their presentation. This can result in poor communication.

Visualizing a presentation requires understanding what your audience needs to know. On the basis of this understanding you can determine how to best package information. Often, there are different audiences you have to address. This means you may have to package information in different ways to present it effectively.

Working electronically, using computers, provides flexibility when packaging information for presentation. You can transfer information from models and mock up presentations in computers. You can develop presentations for a wide variety of output. For example, there are presentation programs that enable you to develop page layouts integrating both text and graphics. You can develop layouts for drawing sheets integrating many layers of information. You can develop slide shows, as well as animation and video presentations. You can even synchronize sound with your presentations. You can also work with multimedia presentation formats that the audience can access interactively using computers. The message needs a massage. Again, in the words of Marshall McLuhan, "The medium is the massage." Integrating both the message and massage can have far-reaching effects.

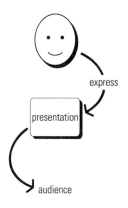

Presentation Is Everything

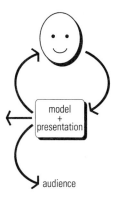

Modelling and Presenting

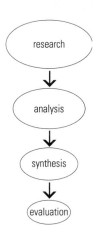

Run Out of Energy

The "Presentation Is Everything" Syndrome

Some people sense that presentation is everything. For example, in design courses some instructors tend to reinforce this when they only consider projects superficially. When working with traditional media, sometimes the design of the presentation becomes separate from the design of what is being presented. Design involves more than making something look good. A slick presentation cannot save a weak design. Design cannot be added; design should be integral to what you are doing.

In computers, design and presentation can become more integral. Model space and presentation space are intertwined. For example, it is very difficult to fudge the perspective of a three-dimensional model in a computer. You can look at it from different vantage points, or with different view angles. Some views may look better than others, but you have to work harder to distort the image. With hand-drawn perspectives, roughing out the image is usually easier but can result in distortions. Sometimes a rendering can create an image of its own. An "artist's conception" can be very misleading. Certainly, you can also create illusions with computers. However, when using modeling programs, there is a better chance of an accurate presentation of the artificial reality of what you are creating. Content is important.

There is concern that electronic media — particularly video capture and imaging — will provide instant rendering tools to use deceptively. Yet video and photo-realism — now possible with computers — can make deception more difficult because they reveal so much. Poorly conceived or deceptive designs present conflicts in content. The image may not relate to the content.

Many people think they can use presentation tools, such as desktop publishing or desktop video, without any design sense. This can result in horrible presentations that lack content. People with good design sense are often offended. They may reject the potential of these tools just because of what they see being produced. Good presentations need a design sense. Regardless of the tools, presentations are no better than their content. It may be true that "The medium is the massage"; however, the medium should contain a message.

The "Run Out of Energy" Syndrome

Commonly, people can run out of energy in the creative process. They may not be able to commit, or develop, test, or present ideas. They can run out of energy at any stage of the process.

People run out of energy for any number of reasons. Sometimes, this is due to the wasted effort dealing with the syndromes already described. Syndromes can even entirely block the flow of creative energy. More often, people run out of time or get distracted. Or they don't have the resources to act upon ideas. Pursuing ideas through the creative process involves hard work.

Plugging into electronic media literally supplements your energy. You can work through the creative process more easily. It is easier to transfer information from analytical stages to synthesis. You can, using less effort, work with large documents or massive models in artificial reality. You can test models in many different ways. Insights, derived from testing, can be quickly cycled into your model, which can continue to evolve rapidly. You can develop a wide variety of presentations using multimedia. You have a better chance of not running out of time and energy when working with electronic media — that is, unless you try to do too much.

When using electronic media, however, be careful that expectations are not too high. It is tempting to build more models, to generate more alternatives, to do more extensive evaluations, or to make more ambitious presentations because of all the tools that are available. It is tempting to use information just because you have access to it. The result is that you can still run out of energy, time, or budget — using electronic media. You should learn to work with limitations that will always be there. Learn to release your creative energy. Learn to augment it effectively with energy you can derive from electronic media.

Procedures Related to the Creative Process

The goal is to use as much of your creative capacity as possible. Now that you have gone through many principles involved in creative thinking, here are some procedures you can use to work with the creative process. These will help you develop your own approaches for using your creative capacity in your discipline and computer environment.

- Nurture your own creativity by understanding the thinking process you go through when developing ideas. This process involves problem stating and problem solving and includes five stages:

    First insight

    Saturation

    Incubation

    Illumination

    Verification

- Remember that the creative process is cyclical; you go through it in many iterations — expressing, testing, and cycling your ideas.

- Relate your creative process to the design methods you work with. Make sure you apply your creativity at each phase of a project. Pay particular attention to how you move from one phase of a project to another. Apply computer applications appropriately to your design methods.

- Develop work flow diagrams to map your approach to a project. Use these diagrams to:

  Conceive alternative strategies for carrying out a creative project.

  Evaluate how you are allocating your time and energy (resources).

  Manage your project and update the diagram when necessary.

- Overcome common syndromes, which can waste or block your creative energy.

  Use your insight.

  Move freely beyond analysis, into synthesis.

  Keep your mind open to possibilities by postponing judgment until you need to verify ideas.

  Generate more than one idea so that you will spend your creative energy developing the most promising idea.

  When you have many ideas, sort them out and commit to the best option. Focus your creative energy on developing that idea.

  Test ideas after you have developed them. From that you can derive further insights that will help you refine your design.

  Make sure the content is well presented.

  Make sure presentations have content.

  Conserve your creative energy so that you can do more with less effort.

- Work intelligently. Use your understanding of the creative process and the tools you have available to:

  Develop useful models to visualize what you are doing.

  Focus on doing what is necessary. Try not to get carried away with doing something just because you have the tools to be able to do it.

  Use information appropriately. Don't use information just because you have access to it.

- Use media effectively throughout the creative process.

  Select media that enable you to transfer information and ideas easily.

  Work interactively, following your natural creative processes as much as possible.

  Work collaboratively where you can.

Relating the Creative Process to Electronic Media

Centuries ago, civilization crossed a threshold of literacy. Many people gained access to the tools needed to work creatively on traditional media, such as paper. As a result, creativity flourished and became manifested in a period that came to be known as the Renaissance. Many different cultures have gone through Renaissances often related to people having access to new tools and media they learn to use creatively. Today, civilization is crossing yet another threshold — computer literacy. Individuals once again have access to new tools for creativity.

The media you use influence how you move through the creative process. How you can work with paper is somewhat different from how you can work with film. Different yet is how you can work with electronic media. Each has intrinsic qualities that you can use creatively. A major challenge today is to learn to use electronic media creatively.

The first part of this book focuses on the mind. It presents principles and approaches related to visualization and the creative process. This can help you understand how to link your mind with electronic media. The next part of this book deals with interactions of mind and media. It will help you develop strategies for using computers more creatively. There is a third part of the book which will help you when mastering media.

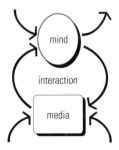

Work Interactively

Summary

This chapter helps you develop your creative capacity. There are mental processes for deriving insights and exploring possibilities. You can use these processes when working with electronic media. The creative process involves problem stating and problem solving. There are five stages: insight, saturation, incubation, illumination, and verification. These stages relate to the design process: research, analysis, synthesis, and evaluation. Creativity is a cyclical process. Express, test, and cycle ideas. Work with media interactively. The first activity at the end of this chapter will cause you to examine your present approaches to creative endeavors.

Learn to diagram your work flow. This helps you visualize your approach. Diagram your work flow to conceive alternative strategies, to involve new tools and media, to evaluate how to allocate time and resources, and to manage your project as you proceed. The second activity will have you develop a work flow diagram for a project of your own.

Overcome potential syndromes. You can do this by using your insight, moving freely from analysis to synthesis, postponing judgment, generating more than one idea but committing to the best option, testing ideas and refining them, presenting content but making sure you present it well, conserving creative energy—working smart, and working collaboratively where you can. The third activity will help you identify syndromes so you can move beyond them.

Activities

1. Describe Your Present Creative Process

Everyone has experienced the excitement involved in generating ideas — the "aha" involved in discovery. You can probably also recognize the flow experience involved as you become intrigued by the idea and work with it using whatever media you have at hand. Similarly, you can recognize the fun of sharing your idea with others, and the satisfaction of seeing your idea result in some action that makes a difference or provides an artifact that you find satisfying and can be proud of. Certainly, these qualities relate to some very satisfying experiences you have had. They may also relate to some very frustrating experiences you have had as well.

Whether you consciously consider it or not, you have creative processes you presently use to generate and develop ideas. Describe the creative processes involved in the discipline you are working with. Relate these processes to the methods you use. How do you generate your first insights? How do you saturate yourself in what you are doing? What are your approaches to incubation? How does illumination occur for you in what you are doing? How do you verify your ideas and refine them? Describe the methods you now apply in your discipline. Identify the tools and media you use. Do you see ways of developing new methods that will make use of computers and the electronic media you have available?

2. Diagram Work Flow

You can visualize how activities and events relate to the creative process by developing a work flow diagram. For example, a Gantt chart shows time lines identifying the starting date and anticipated ending of different activities. A PERT chart shows how you can link activities and events (procedures and products) over a time frame. These types of diagrams help you visualize the pattern of work involved in a project so you can plan and coordinate your efforts.

Make a work flow diagram of the procedures you will use to undertake a creative project. First identify the activities and events involved in your project. Then link them in ways that describe the paths you will follow through your project. (Ask yourself what precedes and follows each activity you have identified.) Consider how your procedure relates to each stage of the creative process. Consider the critical path and how you might compress it on the time frame. Diagram alternative approaches to your project that incorporate different strategies for using the resources you have available. Relate your alternatives to a time line. For example, how would you do this project using traditional media like paper and pencil? How would you do the project if you had access to multimedia computers? (Notice your procedures can change when using different tools and strategies.) Evaluate your alternatives by estimating the time involved and the resources required. You may find that new tools and clever strategies for using them can save you considerable time and effort. But you may also find that you need to revise your time frame (and/or budget) or your scope of work to make it work with the tools and resources you have available. You may even need to redefine your problem to get all these considerations to work together. Diagram your strategy before proceeding.

1. List activities.

_____
_____
_____

2. Link activities.

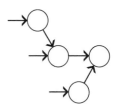

3. Refine procedures.

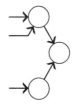

4. Develop work flow diagram.

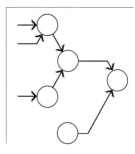

5. Revise & re-define. If necessary, change scope or change time frame.

6. Manage project. Update workflow diagram as you proceed.

Use this diagram to manage your progress. Use the diagram as a focus for group interaction, identifying the paths that each team member will pursue. Update the diagram, taking stock of where you have been and where you are going. You will continue to see new alternatives. Act upon them if you can, but try to keep your project on schedule. If you have a deadline, you may have to reaccess what it will take to complete the project. Simplify it if necessary to complete it on time. Or using your diagram, you may determine that you can justifiably extend your schedule.

Obviously, this exercise will take a long time to carry out, so come back to it again and again as you proceed with your project.

Note: You can do this exercise either by hand, with pencil and paper; with computer graphics, using a drawing program; or with project management software. Project management software can help you to schedule and track resources with more precision.

3. Identify Syndromes

The syndromes identified in this chapter provide a variety of examples that demonstrate typical problems encountered when using creative thinking skills. You can see how these syndromes will waste creative energy and sometimes block the essential processes necessary for creative thinking.

Examine what you typically do when working on a creative project. If you are having some difficulties working creatively, don't feel discouraged. Many others share these difficulties. Write down syndromes you identify with. This can help you determine what problems you may be having. Once you have identified these problems, you have a better chance to develop your own strategies for overcoming them. After you have done this exercise on your own, and have given co-workers a chance to do the same, it may be helpful to do it again together with your workgroup. The types of behavior described in the syndromes often undermine creative collaboration. Sometimes the dynamics of a workgroup can accentuate problems and cause friction among individuals. This results in the loss of productivity and, more significantly, compromises the creative potential of both the individual and collaborative effort. If a workgroup can address these problems, the group members can also help one another overcome them, thereby bringing out the best in the individuals involved in the creative collaboration. This can result in a much happier situation for everyone participating in a project.

Part II

Interacting

Part I
Thinking

provides a foundation in visual thinking and creative thought processes. This is especially helpful in **design methods courses.**

Part II
Interacting

provides approaches for involving electronic media more creatively. This is especially helpful in **case study courses.**

Part III
Mastering

provides a direction for getting the most out of your mind when using electronic media. This will help you **address change.**

6

Using Computers Creatively

This chapter helps you address the following key concerns: What media am I using? What models am I using? And, what methods am I using? It provides approaches for working with media, models, and methods that will enable you to develop your own procedures to use computers more creatively and effectively. This chapter helps you relate electronic media to your goals and develop working metaphors to define frames of reference when working with media space. It shows you how to plan transfers of information to electronic media where you can work with it interactively. It provides strategies for using computers to model ideas and mock-up your final product. In addition, it presents approaches for planning and managing your creative process which help you to clarify how to use computers effectively at different stages of your project. At first these approaches may seem a bit abstract, but once you read about them and apply them to some case study projects, you should be able to make them your own.

Integrating Your Mind and Media

There are three basic considerations when using electronic media. The first consideration centers on selecting your media for transferring information. This is especially important because you have so many choices when working with multimedia computing. You also need to set up your media space. The next consideration involves developing effective models so you can represent what you are working with electronically. The third consideration involves applying *methods* for interacting with these models using appropriate computer applications. There are basic approaches for addressing each of these considerations. Using these approaches you can develop your own procedures for doing your projects in your computer environment.

Approaches

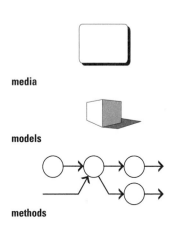

media

models

methods

Each of the three basic approaches has three steps. Combining them results in the following nine-step approach to building your own procedures:

Media — for transferring information

    1. Relate electronic media to your goals.

    2. Map your media space.

    3. Diagram information and data flow.

Models — for the realities involved

    4. Identify the realities you are working with.

    5. Develop models of reality.

    6. Mock up your presentation.

Methods — for the thought processes

    7. Define your project.

    8. Diagram your work flow.

    9. Manage your progress.

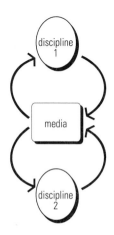

Multidirectional

You can apply these approaches to multimedia computing. They will help you engage different modes of thought. The approaches work not only with text, but also with graphics, three-dimensional modeling, animation, video imaging, and even sound.

These approaches are *multidirectional*. They address getting information into electronic media as well as getting information from it. They can help you interact with a computer as well as help your group interact in a media space work environment. They can make it easier to organize and manage the creative collaboration of a project team.

These approaches are *multidisciplinary*. They are useful for focusing the creative thinking involved in many disciplines — ranging from the arts to all the design professions, as well as the sciences. They help you use computer applications appropriately and combine expertise in effective team efforts.

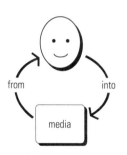

Multidisciplinary

Media
Step 1: Relate Electronic Media to Your Goals

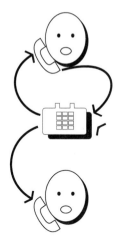

Phone

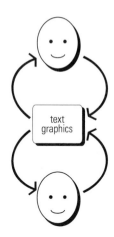

Telecommunications

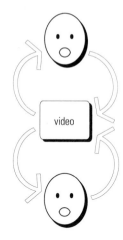

Interactive Video

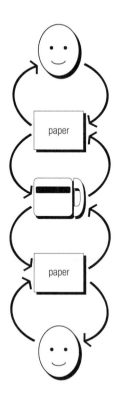

FAX

There are many opportunities to relate electronic media to your goals. Almost everyone uses the telephone. You can enhance the capabilities of the telephone with answering machines and voice mail systems. You can also use FAX machines to transfer information printed on paper. This enables you to work with handwritten documents as well as small drawings and photographs. You can also transfer digital information by using telecommunications or by handing off or mailing computer disks. Digital transfers provide files that others can work with electronically. Interactive video is emerging which will widen the range of electronic media you can transfer.

Many design professionals now use computers. This enables them to work with drawings, graphic images, and even three-dimensional models as well as text. They draw, model, and compose directly in a computer working interactively to develop their final product. Computer-aided design and other programs enable them to visualize what they are working on. Using telecommunications, they can send information directly over telephone lines.

Look for ways to use computers as a vehicle for transferring information and ideas related to your project. Learn to transfer information as directly as possible. You can do this by simply getting the information you are working with into digital formats that you can evolve into your final product. Learn to work interactively with ideas and information. Use electronic media for visualization, not just for viewing. Broaden the range of media you use to include not only text and graphics, but also modeling, imaging, video, and sound. Use computers as more than single-purpose tools; use them as workstations that integrate applications. Where possible, set up a computer work environment that you can access from many different places. For example, with a small notebook computer and modem, you can access your files and send messages from wherever you have access to a telephone line.

Look for opportunities to use electronic media collaboratively. Set up shared media space that your workgroup can access by using telecommunications or simply by sharing work disks. Try moving information instead of people where possible. Make use of the freedoms you gain over time and space, enabling people to work together without being in the same place at the same time. Use electronic media to enhance your work sessions, providing models that serve as objects your workgroup can relate to interactively.

Use computers to enhance meetings. You can do this simply by having a computer at hand which a few people can use like a piece of paper or a blackboard during a discussion. You can also enhance larger group meetings through formal setups that include a discussion leader as well as a technographer who will record the ideas generated by the group. Provided with the right facilities, a technographer can electronically project the group's ideas onto a screen for all to interact with during the meeting. The technographer can save the results of the discussion and electronically transfer or print out the files for participants to use.

Work interactively with electronic media through each stage of the creative process. Find ways to capture your first insights digitally if possible. You can always make mental notes or capture those insights with a few handwritten notes or idea sketches on paper if necessary. Transfer your ideas to electronic media as soon as possible so you can work with them interactively. Do your preparation by electronically accessing and compiling information you need. Go through the incubation stage by using computer applications that can help you analyze information. Enhance your illumination by using computers to synthesize and explore possibilities. Verify what you are doing by using computers as evaluative tools. This may be as simple as spell checking a document. Or it may be as complex as doing a cost evaluation of a design. Use electronic media for presentations. Look for opportunities to transfer your ideas and information to your audience as directly as possible. Use multimedia to help your audience experience your presentation more completely. Consider ways of interacting with your audience through electronic media.

Look for opportunities for translating your computer models into reality as directly as possible. For example, using numeric controls, engineers can link machine tools to a computer. This enables them to fabricate an object directly from a computer model. They can avoid producing the typical construction documents, a task that requires transferring the three-dimensional model to two-dimensional orthographic drawings and printing them out for a machine operator to use.

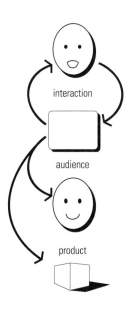

interaction

audience

product

Transfer Information Directly

Step 2: Map Your Media Space

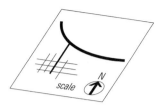

Map of Physical Space

When you are hiking in a wilderness, you need to be able to orient in a landscape in order to survive. The same is true when driving on highways, or you can get lost. Kevin Lynch observed that people develop an image of a city. They use this to navigate and find their way. As children, we can draw simple maps of what we are aware of in our neighborhood. As we grow, and learn more about our surroundings, our image of a city becomes more encompassing. We often draw a little map to show another person how to find some place. Lynch developed diagrams of what most people use to orient in cities such as Boston or Los Angeles. The implications are that we need to make cities accessible as well as provide the landmarks and other qualities that enable people to orient in urban landscapes. The same is true of media space.

We all use mental maps of our work environment. For example, you know where your classroom or office is, and where you (usually) put your tools or files. You know where libraries and other information sources are. You know how to locate advisers or consultants. This is necessary to function. As you begin to do more work electronically, you need to learn to develop a mental image of your media space work environment. This will help you learn to use tools, find files, and access information.

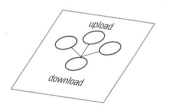

Map of Media Space

Physical location is not that important when working in media space. You may know the location of the information service you are reaching via modem, but what is really important is to know how to access the gateway to get there electronically. Where you go, through that information service, defies any relation to a physical context. It is fun to realize you can literally zoom around the world when accessing different nodes in media space. However, that realization is not particularly useful when navigating. What is significant is what you experience. The information you discover in this new media space shapes your experiences.

You need to have a clear mental image of your media space to orient and find your way. This is especially important if you want to use shared media space and let others know what you have named a file and where you have put it. You can define your media space similarly to the way

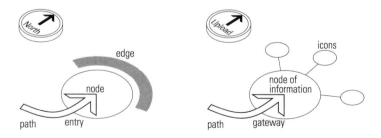

Cognitive Map of Physical Space   **Cognitive Map of Media Space**

you diagram paths, nodes, districts, and landmarks in physical space. For example, simply organizing your hard disk into subdirectories or folders helps you understand what is there and how to access it. You can also set up a file-naming system that helps you, and others, recognize programs and work files. You can also diagram the gateways you use to access information services with telecommunications. Understanding frames of reference helps you navigate within application programs as well as within your work files.

You can use computers to gain access to the information at your fingertips. A key to using computers in this way, however, is recognizing what information is there and how to access it. Without a mental map, you are likely to function with limited awareness of what is "out there." Of course, you also need computers that can provide access to media space and expand your perception. You can expand your awareness by making use of media space that telephones, computers, and other electronic devices provide. You can become the architect of your own media space, working with the information context that is available and shaping it to meet your needs. You need to develop your own mental map of media space that transcends physical reality. From this map you gain clear images that will help you orient in media space.

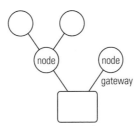

Branching Diagram of Media Space

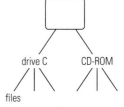

Branching Diagram of Disk Space

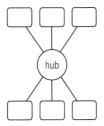

Centralized

Mainframe computers tend to centralize information. Full-time systems managers maintain these information environments. Hackers delight in finding their way around these worlds. Their approach carried over into early computer games. Originally, games like Adventure and Zork were favorites. They were interactive word games providing scenarios in which the player would go through a maze of passages, enter rooms, and find treasure and/or a variety of "life threatening" hazards. The player learned to develop mental maps to orient in this labyrinth, reaching deeper and deeper levels. Now there are also graphic versions. Games like these provide exercises for orienting in media space.

Personal computers tend to disperse information; you can maintain files at your own workstation. Graphic user interfaces are making personal computers easier to use. Personal computers become a vehicle for accessing and interacting with information in media space. As you save files to

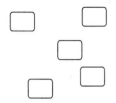

Dispersed

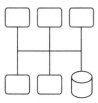

Networked

disk and tape, there is also a physical counterpart to electronic media space. You need to store these computer disks and tapes in safe and accessible ways. Both individuals and organizations need to have clear practices for doing this. People working with files stored on these media need to have access to them.

Today, information resources are becoming more dispersed as well as more interrelated. Networks and modems can link you to information stored on hard disks, tapes, and CD-ROMs in many different computers. Now, when you look at a computer monitor, you can have a window into rather extensive media space. The computer and telephone have merged. Information services such as CompuServe and Prodigy provide access to a wealth of current information. You can access library card catalogs to understand what is in these archives of printed matter. Different disciplines — such as medicine and law — have database services that professionals can subscribe to. Local area networks and modems can help you more effectively share the information that you have at your own workstation. Local hubs enable you to communicate all over the world.

Computers and television are also merging. Computer companies are buying entertainment companies to gain access to video products. Videocassette and cable television companies are already challenging broadcast radio and television networks. Communication companies are installing fiber optic systems that will provide wideband pathways for transmitting multimedia. You will no longer be limited to selecting a radio station or TV broadcast and passively listen to what they offer. Computers will enable you to interactively access video and other multimedia. In effect, you can create a new information environment.

To access information, you need to develop clear mental maps of media space. You can reach different nodes of information if you know how the nodes are organized and how to access the pathways to reach them. Understanding how to work with file directories can help you set up an organization of information you and your workgroup can relate to. In some instances, developing partitions — divisions between different types of files — makes it easier to access and explore these areas. You can also develop security for some files you wish to have in private domains. Menus — which present choices — help you select options. Icons — which graphically represent files, programs or commands — function like landmarks to help you find your way. Maps of media space relate to your understanding of your information environment. They also relate to your perception of your mindscape — the inner space of your mind. (Chapter 9, "The "Zen" of Regeneration," will help you open the doors of your inner space. It will help you develop a mindscape that links your inner space to media space.)

Multimedia do not occupy a separate nitch or application. Neither do telecommunications. Just as in reality all experience is multisensory and usually involves communication, the same is becoming true with electronic media. In the artificial reality of media space, you can derive experience from multimedia and involve communications. You can learn to navigate within this realm.

Beyond navigating around file directories, you need to learn to orient within the files. Workspace exists not only within operating systems, but within program files as well. Here you find the tools for different applications. By learning application programs you can access and use these tools. We often use metaphors — such as the *notepad*, the *desktop*, the *drawing table* or the *cockpit* — to orient in this workspace. As the workspace becomes a work environment, metaphors — such as *windows* — become more open-ended.

Notepad

Desktop

Drawing Table

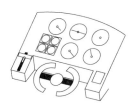

Cockpit

Window

"In another moment Alice was through the glass, and had jumped lightly down into the Looking-glass room."

Lewis Carrol, *Through the Looking Glass,* 1872.

In storybook fantasies you reach "Never-never Land" thru a window. "Wonderland" is down a rabbit's burrow. You can also enter "through the looking glass." Relating metaphors to familiar objects permits you to use your intuition by drawing upon past experiences. You can relate metaphors to all your senses.

Within your computer you can create your own artificial reality. Again, you can use metaphors such as three-dimensional spatial contexts or objects. This may be a geographic database of a region or a three-dimensional model of a product design. You can attach attributes to this context, or object, to create a very rich metaphor you and your workgroup can relate to. You can add detail that approaches virtual reality. Key maps can help you orient while you zoom in to examine detail. You can create walk-throughs and even fly-throughs of this artificial environment, enabling you to experience and explore what is there.

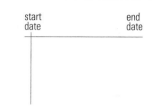

Time Line

Sequence

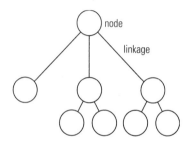

Hierarchy

macro A brief computer program that combines steps. For example, a macro can make repetitive logging-on procedures easier when using computers.

More abstract conceptual frames of reference can also help you find your way in media space. For example, you can navigate using time as a frame of reference — putting information in chronological order in a journal or on a time line. You can create linear sequences with beginnings and ends, like those in tape recordings of stories or books. You can also work with a sequence of events — such as a process or a program. More abstract frames of reference such as categories, linkages, hierarchies, or levels of abstraction also help you navigate. In databases you work with records and fields. You can set up associations or linkages for navigating in hypermedia.

You may link information to an object. For example, an interactive training program showing people how to assemble components of a computer could have an image showing the components. Clicking on components in the image could provide helpful information about those parts. Or there may be databases with categories — such as an encyclopedia on CD-ROM. When you select an item you may gain access to a picture or even a full-motion video image complete with sound showing the object you are investigating.

There are differences between navigating and authoring. When navigating, you need to orient in media space so you can find your way. When authoring, you need to shape media space so you, and others, can work with it creatively. As a navigator, you experience media space and find your way within the information context that is available. As an author, you can, in effect, become the architect of your media space. You can establish a framework and begin to organize information, adding your own insights.

Think through how you will organize your media space. Map the media space you intend to work in. How will you name your files? What directories or folders will you set up? What pathways will you use to access nodes of information you are working with? What menus or icons can you provide to help you and your workgroup navigate? How can you record where you have been? How can you let your workgroup know what is in your shared media space? How can you guide others to find information? For that matter, how can you find files yourself, once you have forgotten where you put them in media space?

Simple diagrams can show paths you can access through your network or modem. This helps you remember information you need to log on to your pathways. Using communication programs, you can develop *macros* that make repetitive logging-on procedures easier. You still need a directory of these auto-dial macros. You can also make tree diagrams of directories and subdirectories (or folders and their files) which you keep at each node.

Develop ways of naming files that permit you to sort them easily. You can manage files by using an operating system such as MS DOS, or by using file management utilities like Norton Commander or PC Tools, or a

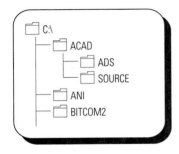

Disk Directory

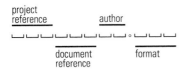

File Naming Convention

Log or Journal

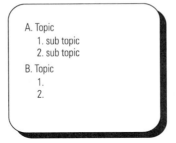

Outline

Format

user shell such as Windows. The operating system will tell you the date and time the file was last edited, as well as the file size. Programs usually automatically provide the extension that tells you the format of the document. You can also develop file-naming conventions. For example, use the first three characters in the file name to identify the project. The next three can identity the type of document. The last two characters can identify the author. Longer names may be more descriptive, but they are more difficult to sort. They also don't transfer well when you move files through different computer environments.

Keep a log of the file names you are using for a project. This log is an important way of defining your media space. You can keep it as a separate document or directory of descriptions to share with others in your workgroup. This might be part of a project journal. For example, you can keep the names of files you are accessing in your daybook just as you might keep phone numbers of those you call. Not only does this provide a guide to the media space you access, but a log or journal can also describe what you and others on your project team do, in chronological order. Using a simple word processor, you can "search" and "go to" keywords or file names you want to locate. You can do this more elaborately by setting up a database file, enabling you to search and sort it more extensively if you wish. Some software has this utility already built in. Thus, you can identify file names and other information that help you define and orient in your media space as it evolves.

In addition to knowing how to use your software, you need to establish metaphors or frames of reference for the files that you are developing. For example, a clear outline can help you relate to your word processing document. A good format can help you organize both text and graphics in a desktop publishing document. A clear two-dimensional frame of reference, or some concept of composition, enables you to do computer graphics. Paint palettes and symbols libraries provide useful metaphors for developing computer generated images. Setting up an appropriate scale, or limits, as well as a clear strategy for layering information, provide frames of reference you need when using a drafting program. A three-dimensional frame of reference, as well as a user coordinate system for viewing objects,

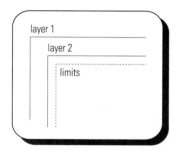

Graphic Layers & Limits

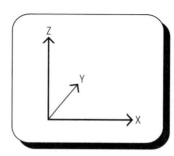

Three-dimensional Modelling

**Linking Data to Objects
or Locations**

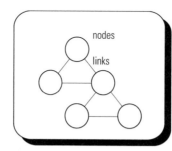

Hypermedia

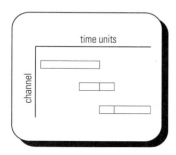

Scripting Environment

can help you do modeling using computer-aided design programs. Setting up formats for handling databases enables you to attach attributes to objects using CADD systems. Relating locational information, such as map overlays, to data bases enable you to work with geographic information systems. Linking information through key words or graphics enables you to create stacks of associated files for Hypermedia.

You can also work with a scripting environment to relate different channels of multimedia to a time frame. Time and motion are frames of reference you can use when working with animation software. Time and sequence are frames of reference you use with video. You will need to either select and capture frames to work with statically or link segments dynamically in a video production. Music and sound tracks are also composed in segments. You can mix different tracks of sound. Scripting environments enable you to create a score to integrate animation, video, and sound using a multimedia program.

You define these frames of reference; you shape the electronic environment you work in. Operating systems, communication programs, file utilities, and application programs help you manage it.

Step 3: Diagram Information and Data Flow

When working creatively with computers, you do not deal with static information. You gather information and analyze and synthesize it by adding your own insights which you can act upon. Then you evaluate the information in your synthesis and eventually package it for presentation or for implementation. You continually transform information throughout the project. Diagramming information flow can help you develop clear strategies for these transformations. Clever strategies can save time and effort. Back up data files at different stages as you use them. This provides a safety net and enables you to work more effectively with alternatives. You can also transfer information from one application program, or computer platform, to another if you understand data flow and how to translate files.

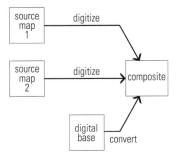

Compositing Information

Electronic media become very good integrators. You can take information from many different sources and pull it together using multimedia. For example, when working on paper, you may have difficulty with maps drawn at a variety of scales. By getting this information into a digital format (at its correct size), the question of scale no longer becomes an issue. Electronic media also enable you to use overlays on your maps or images as well as link attributes to your graphic information.

When mixing information from different sources, be careful the accuracy doesn't become corrupted. It makes little sense to mix information that is obtained with great accuracy or high resolution with information that is approximate or of low resolution. The accuracy of the result is no better than the lowest level of resolution.

Sometimes you need high levels of accuracy or high resolution, a lot of detail, or photorealism for the task at hand. But you do not always need this detail or precision. Use information appropriately. Pursuing perfection can be irrelevant and expensive. On the other hand, not having sufficient accuracy or detail can lead to expensive mistakes. When transferring information, you need to make careful judgements about the accuracy, or level of detail necessary.

Typically you change a document when you work with it. Your base information becomes combined with information you add. For example, a template is no longer a generic form document once you add new information to it. If you want to use your template again, you need to save it separately. The same is true of a basemap once you add information to it. Consequently, you have to either develop strategies for layering information or save the base information separately. A good approach is to develop stopping points for your documents at different stages of your project. Then you can save versions of your file at each stopping point. This enables you to reuse generic information more easily. It takes careful management of your file transfers not to get different versions of the same file confused, particularly if you are part of a project team working on the same set of documents.

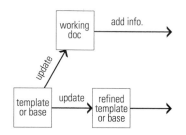

Transferring Bases

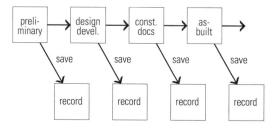

Saving at Stopping Points

Of course, you should also make sure you back up your information. Keep your backup files in different locations — such as different nodes of your network — and on separate floppy disks or tapes stored at different locations. It is easy to copy data files; it is also very easy to destroy them. The best protection of your data is to have clear backup procedures that are part of your transfer strategies.

Diagramming information flow can help you visualize your transfers. A good method is to proceed from your source information on the left side of your chart to the finished product on the right side of the chart. Grouping different types of information (related by topics or types of information) can also help provide clarity to the diagram. You may wish to use symbols to identify different types of files. Lines can provide connections showing how to transfer information through each stage of the project.

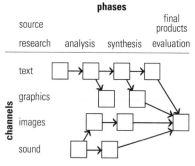

Information Flow Diagram

A typical progression for transferring information involves research (really information gathering), analysis, synthesis, evaluation, and presentation. Your information flow diagram should reflect what you are doing with your information at each stage of your project.

In the research, or data-gathering, stage, you typically begin with some source data. This may be a primary source — such as instrument readings or notes from your direct observations. Or it may be a secondary source — such as a basemap or data file from a research document. You

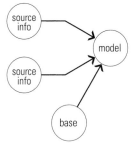

Research

should understand the accuracy of the information regardless of whether it is primary or secondary. Base information should deal with objective observations — those that can be clearly observed and measured with consistency.

The analysis stage involves interpretations. You typically take base information and interpret it. For example, you can interpret soils maps for a landscape according to fertility or permeability. Each interpretation should have clear criteria. You can bring together many interpretations to create composites of information. You can derive suitability composites (if you use positive criteria) or sensitivity composites (if you use negative criteria). Compositing interpreted data provides a way to integrate judgments of the information you are working with. This becomes the basis for synthesis.

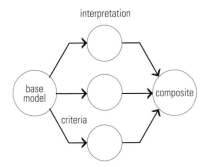

Analysis

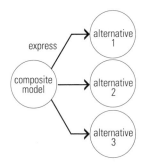

Synthesis

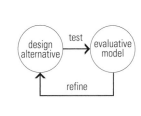

Evaluation

In the synthesis stage you need to take your composited information and, in creative projects, give expression to it. This requires drawing upon your own insights and reacting to the information you have to work with. Synthesis usually involves several iterations of expression, as discussed in Chapter 5. You typically start with a preliminary or schematic design. In design development you build upon these concepts but add more detailed information. Only then do you proceed with implementation documents.

Once you have a synthesis of your information, you can begin to evaluate it in many different ways. You can bring criteria and information you derived in the analysis stage to bear on the evaluation. For example, environmental impact evaluations of site development might have bearing on the fertility or permeability of soils interpreted in the analysis phase. You might evaluate if you are you using fertile soils appropriately. Your evaluation might evolve as you go through different phases of your project. Initially in architectural or landscape architectural projects, you may test concepts during the preliminary design phase, eventually you evaluate materials during design development, and then you focus on evaluating construction methods and costs during the construction document and bidding phases.

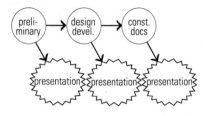

Presentation

Typically, you make presentations at each stage of the project. You have to address the question of how you are going to package information for each presentation. Information flow diagrams are particularly helpful for letting you understand what pieces to present at different stages of the project. They often help you identify the best way to package information for different audiences. Sometimes it is useful to present your information flow diagram as part of your presentation, so others you are working with can see where the information came from and how you are using it.

While this approach provides a generic method for diagramming information flow, each project is different. There are also distinct variations in how different disciplines use information. You can apply this basic approach to your discipline. It is particularly useful when working creatively with computers using multimedia.

When doing these diagrams, remember to focus on the information. Information usually manifests itself in what you produce — the documents, maps, data files, models, design drawings, mock-ups, etc. There is information content in every product of a project. Look at what you produce at each stage of a project and recognize the information it contains. Your information flow diagram should show how you transfer this information from one stage of the project to another. The object is to design your approach in a way that the appropriate information will flow easily from one stage of the project to another.

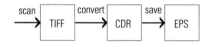

Data Flow Diagram

Although some information may already be digital, you may still need to translate these files into formats you can work with using your software. Standards are emerging that make these translations less of a problem. Conversion software also exists that provides filters between many different texts as well as different graphic formats. In some instances, the translations of files from one format to another can be frustratingly difficult or even impossible. So you need to examine the formats that you are using and make sure that you can move your data from one application program to another. Data flow diagrams can help you visualize these translations. There are often several strategies for translating files. You need to try them out to find which is most effective. For example, do you translate when you save your file, or do you translate when you open your file in a new program? Diagram different strategies and test them to determine which works the best. Do this before committing a great deal of time and effort. A data flow diagram showing key transfers can also help your workgroup communicate. Then you can work out the translations involved in using different applications and computer platforms.

Because information is continually changing, some software provides for dynamic data exchanges. These exchanges provide (more or less) seamless ways to link data from one program to another. Dynamic data exchanges will automatically change related information. For example, changing a cell in a spreadsheet will change the "bottom line." Dynamic data exchanges enable you to even link information in different spreadsheets. Some software also permits you to exchange data dynamically

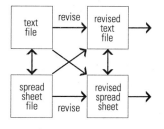

Dynamic Data Exchange

between different applications. For example, using Windows you can dynamically link a number in a spreadsheet to a word processing document. When you change the spreadsheet, the number in the word processing file will also change. Similarly, you can do this using some CADD or GIS programs. When attributes attached to objects are changed, they may change the object, or changing the object may dynamically change the attributes. It is often difficult to link information dynamically. So you need to have clear procedures that help you understand where the information you are using comes from, how you are using it, and what it will eventually be used for.

Document-oriented programs are emerging which permit you to attach data and programs to documents. This means that you need to keep track of both static information and dynamic routines for manipulating it. Some software, such as Penpoint — the Go Operating System, combines documents with pen-related applications rather automatically. For example, it attaches a drawing tool to a sketch enabling viewers to work on it. Other software, such as Hypermedia and Tool Book, permits users to build files linked to programmed routines as well as other data. Using this type of software, you may display an object and act upon it. For example, you could create a file which would enable viewers to point to an image of a bird and click upon it, setting in motion a video of the bird flying. This opens many possibilities for using multimedia to author documents which viewers can explore more interactively.

Computers can help you create objects that, in effect, begin to take on a life of their own. Programs may contain algorithms to which you can assign parameters and variables. Once you set the program in motion it can churn out number sets, color graphics, or even patterns of sound. The patterns evolve according to preprogrammed rules and the parameters and variables you use. You can set procedures in motion where the outcome is unknown. In this way you can add a lifelike element to artificial reality. This is of interest to those working with computer art, process-oriented design, and some scientific and mathematical inquires of chaos.

Models
Step 4: Identify Realities You Are Working With

When working with real life objects or situations, the reality is obvious. You derive hands-on experiences. Your tools and work environment are part of the same context. When working with representations, the question of reality becomes more complex. Many people deal with descriptions, mathematical models, drawings, or photos on paper or film. Most are also comfortable working with scale models and even mock-ups of reality. Electronic media provide new opportunities for dealing with artificial reality. To work effectively with electronic media you need to identify the realities you are involved with and think through how you

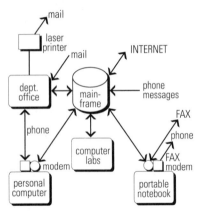

Work Environment

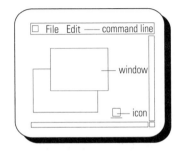

Work Space

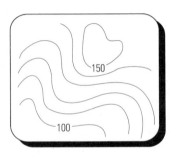

Model Space

relate to them. These realities include your work space and your model space, as well as your presentation space.

Just as you should carefully arrange furniture, tools, and files in your physical workspace, you should also carefully arrange tools and files in your media workspace. Software user interfaces present tools in media space. User shells and other utilities help you organize files electronically. Too often people neglect the organization of their physical and media workspace. Instead they focus on obtaining the fastest hardware and the latest versions of software. Yet productivity gains can be realized just by giving more attention to shaping the workspace — dealing with both the physical and the artificial realities. Not only could this help improve productivity, but also it could help overcome the anxiety sometimes produced by saving information in media space — where you don't see the information unless you access it through a computer. You feel anxious when you don't know where information is and when you are not certain it is safe. Feeling this way can undermine the confidence needed to work effectively in a media space work environment.

It is easier for me to find files in my media space work environment than in my physical work environment. I can quickly access tools and files electronically. In my physical work environment, I often find that someone has borrowed the tool I need or that the file I am looking for is at another location. For example, I can never find my stapler. And it used to be that the file I needed was usually at the university if I was working at home, or — of course — at home if I was working at the university. A media space work environment enables me to keep my tools in my computer and access information from almost any location. I can also reach my students, my colleagues, the department secretary, the library, and a variety of other information services right in my media space work environment. I can send our department secretary letters to be laser-printed and mailed without having to take them to her. (Our department office tends to be hectic.) I can also send messages directly through Internet to those who are online, or I can send them via FAX/modem to those who have FAX machines. Imagine what we could do with interactive video. Of course, I still enjoy meeting my students in class and seeing people in the hallways. Media space simply adds new dimensions to my work environment.

Another reality is your model space. This may represent the context or the object you are working with. The actual context may exist in reality — for example, a real landscape. The information context is the artificial reality you can shape in media space using a computer — the representation of this landscape using information. Typically, you would start with some concrete information which you would abstract to better comprehend what you are working with. For example, you can examine the slope and aspect of a terrain model. You can relate the objects you design to this context by creating mass models of buildings and placing them in the terrain model of the landscape.

You can develop this model or artificial reality in a computer, drawing from different sources of information. One such source is the information you can access directly through electronic media, such as an aerial survey, which exists in a digital form on disk. This may include other base information that is online. You can also transfer information to electronic media. This may include data you key in or mapped information you digitize. It can also include photographic information you scan, video images you capture, or even sound you sample. To use existing digital information, you need to know where it is and how to access and translate it. To use other information in computers, you need to know how to transfer it to digital formats.

You can also represent figments of your imagination in this model space. What you imagine can become reality if you can act upon it effectively. This is the essence of creativity and design. You can create an artificial reality using electronic media. Typically, this begins with some abstract notion. You can transform your mental images into virtual reality using many different modes of thought and expression. Multimedia computing enables you to work with quantitative models, text, graphics, three-dimensional models, imaging, animation, video, and sound, as well as music.

Presentation Space

Yet another reality is the presentation space that you access through electronic media. Although you will draw information to present from your models, it is often helpful to think of the presentation as another reality. Presentation space may involve paper space or even video space. It may also involve planning views to transfer to photographic slides or animated cells. The presentation can become a reality itself. You need to consider how to package information for presentation representing the artificial reality you are working with. This might involve a "mock-up"—perhaps a layout of a printed page, or a plotted drawing. It might involve a "storyboard" for an animation or video production. It could even become a "prototype" of a manufactured object. Presentation and production also involve many design decisions. You can work with design and production (or presentation) concurrently by addressing these different realities using electronic media as you develop your project.

Almost any project, then, involves workspace where you keep your tools and files. It can also involve model space which represents a real context as well as objects you are working with. In addition, it involves presentation space where you visualize the presentation or production of what you are working with. For example, artists' workspace may involve electronic graphics and video imaging tools, or even musical instruments. The key themes the artists work with become their models. Their product is the art they produce which may integrate many channels of expression.

People involved in publishing use a workspace that involves both text and graphic tools. Their model becomes the draft manuscript and graphics. The product is the composited document where they integrate text and graphics for publishing. Writers and graphic designers can concurrently model presentations as they develop them. In the design disciplines — such as architecture and engineering — there are computer-aided design tools.

Designers may work with three-dimensional models or drawings of the context and objects they are designing. Their presentation may be drawings they plot. Presentation also relates to the production of what they design. They can develop designs and model production concurrently — as is happening with concurrent engineering. Engineering is also integrating computer-aided design with computer-aided manufacturing.

In planning and business management the tools may involve geographic information systems with databases as well as spreadsheet programs. Planners' models may be maps, tabulations, or quantitative representations of the realities they are working with. The presentation may involve business graphics, which can take many forms, such as graphs or pie charts, depending upon the information that is presented and the audience that planners and managers are trying to reach.

Even in science, new tools are emerging related to macroscopic and microscopic discoveries. The models become the images and data that scientists acquire from reality. The presentation becomes how they package this information for others to understand.

As you can see, each discipline has realities it relates to and can model using electronic media. You need to clearly recognize each of the realities you work with so you can orient in media space. Carefully organize your workspace. Build the information context necessary to address the problem you are working with. Conceive models of your ideas so you can work with them in "model space" using a computer. Use "presentation space" to translate this artificial reality into actual reality by promoting action. In artificial reality you build with information. In reality, of course, you build with materials. Only if you have a clear understanding of each of these realities will you be able to work with them. Identifying these realities will help you visualize what you are doing.

In reality, you can work on actual objects with tools in hand. In the virtual reality that you can access using multimedia computing, workspace, model space, and presentation space are merging once again. In virtual reality the presentation can become obvious. New information environments are beginning to be created that include tools, models, and presentations together in media space. You will be able to share this media space environment with others in your workgroup as well as with your audience.

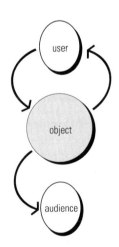

Merge Work Space, Models, and Presentations

Object-Orientation

Step 5: Develop Models of Reality

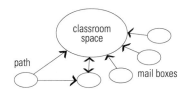

Media Space Classroom

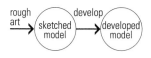

Transform Models

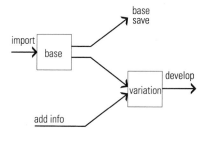

Transfer Information

Once you identify the realities you are working with, you need to develop clear metaphors and models that enable you to use electronic media.

Metaphors can help you relate to your media space work environment. For example, windows or desktop metaphors are commonly used to organize tools and files. Pen computers use a notebook metaphor. I also use mailboxes and "media space classrooms" to help my students find their way around the media space environment at our university. Simulators use the controls of an actual vehicle such as an airplane. The better you can relate these metaphors to previous experience, the more you can draw from your intuition. One difficulty is, however, that what you can do in your media space work environment often transcends your previous experience. So the metaphor must be open-ended and must make it easy to learn new activities.

Models can help you relate to the contexts and objects you are working with. When building these models, start off simply and then add complexity. For example, when writing, start with a few keywords, develop an outline, and then expand the outline into a written statement. When developing a spreadsheet model, set up your format, enter key formulas, and then add the information. When drawing, start with a few key organizing elements and then add to the composition. When working with three-dimensional modeling, build a basic wire-frame object that can serve as a frame of reference and then add to it. In this way you can develop the model you are working with more quickly and see how well it will work before you invest considerable time and effort in developing it. You can also decide how to shape your model so it is appropriate for your purposes. For example, what topics should be included in your outline? What information should be in your spreadsheet? What should be the extent of your drawing be? What are the limits of your three-dimensional model? How much detail is appropriate? Chapter 2, Exploring Media, presents many frames of reference commonly used in computer models.

Sometimes you can import or capture base information that provides a context for your model. For example, there may already be an example or draft statement you can use as a starting point. There may be a template for your spreadsheet model. There may already be a basemap or drawing in a digital format. Or there may be a three-dimensional model — such as an aerial survey that is photogrammetrically derived. Or perhaps there is an image you can use — scanned from a photo or captured from video. The challenge is to work with this information creatively. Use techniques described in Chapter 4, Visualization — A Key to Creativity. Save base information separately so you can always go back to the original. Then you can overcome inhibitions of changing it. It is also helpful if you can simplify this information. For example, with a drawing, turn off layers you don't need. Move between abstract and concrete levels of understanding. Looking at your model abstractly enables you to see overall

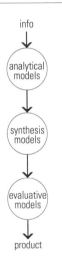

Use Models at Each Stage of
The Design Process

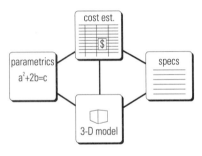

Link Models

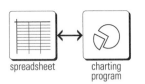

Link Quantitative and Graphical
Models

patterns. Using your model more concretely enables you to work out important details.

Keep in mind that you can use your model for each stage of the design process. Initially, your model may be useful for analysis — helping you organize and understand information. At the synthesis stage your model can help you integrate ideas and information to create new entities. As you move into the evaluative stage of the design process your model can help you test ideas. Try to transfer information from each stage of the design process to the next. Let your models evolve, but save them at different stages of the evolution. This is easy to do by creating separate files. Carefully naming the files enables you to track this evolution. It is sometimes useful to show the progression of thought. You may wish to go back to try alternatives and explore options. Develop several models and link them. Sometimes you need to show phases or movement in your model.

Three-dimensional modeling may be the most compelling, because it relates to the real world we perceive. You can also use this as a frame of reference for linking more abstract models. For example, you might attach attributes, such as specifications and cost estimates, to objects in your three-dimensional model. When working with three-dimensional models, you need to develop coordinate systems and viewing planes. CADD software enables you to do that and select vantage points and viewing angles. In this way you can model space and form, keeping track of locational information and creating objects in space. In effect you can create a virtual reality. The difficulty is that three-dimensional models take time and effort to develop; they also require more powerful computers to manipulate. Just now are people beginning to develop ways to transfer three-dimensional computer models into reality. Most designers still typically translate three-dimensional models into orthographic drawings (plans, sections, and elevations) that can be plotted or printed on paper, creating scale-accurate drawings to build from.

More abstract models sometimes have the advantage of representing phenomena you normally can't see. For example, you can model processes involving a time dimension. You can also develop quantitative models and see patterns in statistical relationships. Many people use computers for this type of modeling. The advantage of abstract models is that they are often quick and powerful. Combining them with graphic visualization can make them easier to comprehend and present. Integrated software that includes spreadsheets and charting programs enables you to do that.

Step 6: Mock up Your Presentation

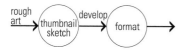

Develop Your Format

When mocking up your presentation, again start simply and then add complexity. Quick thumbnail sketches on paper are often all you need to begin your mock-ups. Once you set up a format, you can work more easily in a computer — using your format as a template to lay out your presentation. Presentation software, desktop publishing software, and desktop video or multimedia software provide ways to mockup your presentations as you develop them. They enable you to integrate different channels — text, graphics, images, animation, video, and sound — adding interest to your presentation. They guide you through many design decisions. Making these decisions requires sensitivity and training. Multimedia software programs provide the tools, but to use them effectively you need some design education. An important key to making good decisions is relating your presentation to your audience. Decide what your viewers need to know and how you can best help them understand it. You especially need to be able to visualize interesting ways of expressing what you want to relate.

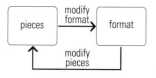

Modify Message and Format

Your mock-ups may involve page layouts integrating text and graphics on paper, or compositions of images and text for film (slides or overheads). Mock-ups can also involve three-dimensional models or even storyboards for animation or video. A typical procedure is to make a thumbnail sketch of a mock-up, quickly exploring composition. Sometimes, if you have the pieces you want to compose already in your computer model space, it is easiest to work with these pieces in the computer to see how you can compose them for presentation. Once your composition begins to work, establish parameters, making format sheets you can use to lay out the rest of your presentation consistently. (Remember, you can always break rules you establish.) Then you can integrate elements into your format to make an actual working mock-up or prototype of your presentation. This will show you how the pieces fit together. You can work with your presentation interactively by either adjusting the layout or going back and refining the pieces so they are more appropriate for the presentation.

Working with animation or video, you need to develop a script or even a storyboard that enables you to model time and sequence, combining different channels. For example, composers of music develop scores — relating different instruments to the tempo of the orchestra. Multimedia

Storyboard

Musical Score

software provides a scripting environment—relating different channels of media to time units. These channels may include text, graphic "stills" or animation, video, and audio that may involve both narration and music. You need to explore how to integrate these channels simultaneously. You can also work out transitions in the presentation. There are many types of transitions you can use. They may be abrupt or gradual. For example, metamorphoses can create fascinating effects enabling you to show in-between states of a transition.

Using computers you can integrate elements into an actual working mock-up or prototype of your presentation. Desktop publishing software helps you compose and lay out pages. Similarly, desktop video or multimedia software helps you compose and produce video presentations. You can work with your video presentation interactively by mixing tracks and sequences. Or you can go back and refine what you are incorporating into your video so the components are more appropriate for the presentation.

Prototyping or CAD/CAM software enables even you to even produce three-dimensional models. In this way you can create an actual object for presentation. There are different devices that enable you to do this, including numerically controlled lathes and stereolithography. You need to mockup your prototype by thinking through how you will fabricate and assemble it.

Begin mocking up your presentation as you start your project. My students sometimes find this strange—saying they don't yet know what they are going to present. They are used to working on paper where it is difficult to start a final presentation before they have final pieces to work with. Electronic media enable you to work on design and presentation (or production) concurrently. You can fluidly move information back and forth, trying out possibilities. This helps coordinate these phases and can reduce overall design and development time. For example, graphic designer Joe Molloy mocked up the first chapter of this book while I was still writing and developing the graphics for other parts with computer graphic artist Long Ha. This helped us work together refining the format and making sure the components we were developing would transfer between computer environments. It provided very helpful feedback that I needed to refine the manuscript and graphics. This also helped my executive editor, B. J. Clark, understand what we were working on so he could relate it to McGraw-Hill's reviewing, editing, printing, and marketing processes.

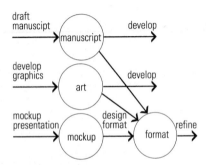

Work Flow Diagram

Now it is also possible to develop interactive presentations using hyper-media and laser disk technology. In these presentations you invite the users to explore — pursuing their own interests at their own pace. You still need to author and mock up these types of presentations, providing a framework for the user to navigate in. Again you can mock up presentations as you develop your material. In fact, these presentations can become living files that could be continuously updated. This has tremendous potential — especially for educational materials, product maintenance, or management manuals. It may even have potential for producing implementation documents.

Methods
Step 7: Define Your Project

role
goal
audience

parties
human process

site
natural process

short ⟷ long
term   term

Key Issues

Now that you have addressed your media and models, it should be easier to address your methods. If you are doing a series of projects, where you use the same type of media and models, you really only need to refine those steps and focus on the methods you use to approach a new project. In other words, the first six steps become part of your basic procedures. These last three steps become part of each proposal and your project management.

When defining your project, clearly articulate your role, the goals of the project, and your audience (users and/or client). Also identify your focus. A good way to do this is to use the models of reality that you intend to develop in your computer. For example, simply identifying a project site on a basemap is a good beginning if the project is site specific. Also, identify key processes involved in your project and think through how you can model them. These might be natural processes such as material and energy flows related to the ecosystem of a site. They may have to do with human processes such as communication, decision making, or cash flow. Describe the levels of detail as well as the scales of concern you are going to address. The life span of your design is another issue you should address. Are you seeking an immediate short-term solution? Or are you looking into the future, seeking an approach that will be more far-reaching and sustainable? You should also identify your final product. Your initial mock-ups of your presentation can be very helpful here.

Each discipline has somewhat different approaches to developing proposals. Artists and entrepreneurs will typically start their own projects. However, they should still clearly think through their approaches to get the best result. If you are writing a book, you will find publishers will want a proposal describing many of the common elements identified above. The same is true of clients seeking proposals from design professionals. In the sciences you also need to submit proposals describing these elements to obtain research grants.

Step 8: Diagram Your Work Flow

1. List activities.

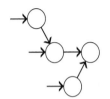

2. Link activities.

3. Refine procedures.

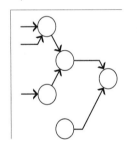

4. Put procedures on a time line and refine.

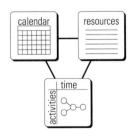

The key parts of any proposal are the scope of work and the schedule. They describe the methods you will use in your project. Chapter 5, The Creative Process, teaches you how to visualize work flow. The second exercise in Chapter 5 takes you through the steps involved in developing a work flow diagram for your project:

1. List activities.

2. Link activities.

3. Refine procedures.

4. Put procedures on a time line.

5. Revise and redefine. If necessary, change the scope or time frame.

6. Manage the project. Update the work flow diagram as you proceed.

You will find that the information flow of your project will closely relate to your work flow. Each activity results in a product. Each product has some information content. Consequently, the information flow diagram you develop for your approach to using media will help you develop your work flow diagram. It is very important to think work flow through by examining information flow. There is a tendency to go through the motions using work flow based only on your experience. (This may not make the best use of new tools and electronic media you have access to.)

You will find there are different strategies to developing work flow diagrams. For example, you can approach these diagrams as a general guide — keeping your options open. Or you can approach these diagrams with greater precision — endeavoring to pin down key events. Your own personality and the situation you are working with will dictate which approach is most appropriate. Beyond that, you can develop interactive approaches that set up more open-ended situations you can respond to. Or you can develop more integrative approaches that use established procedures as building blocks. These diagrams help you communicate your approach to colleagues and clients. Keep it simple. There are limits to how precisely you can plan a creative project. Diagramming will enable you to think through your approach more clearly, but there inevitably will be much more to discover as you proceed.

Of course, related to your work flow is your allocation of resources and an estimation of the time (and compensation) necessary to carry out the project. Project management software can help you establish your calendar, develop work flow diagrams, and track resources. Make sure that you consider not only the personnel involved, but also the computers and other devices you need to work with electronic media.

Manage Project

Step 9: Manage Your Progress

Effective management involves taking the time to review your progress. Use your work flow diagram to determine where you are and where you are going. Update your diagram as you proceed. That will help you check your progress and keep your project on track. It will help your workgroup assign responsibilities and coordinate efforts.

How you use media influences how you organize and manage your activities. It is important to be aware of different organizational structures, because they influence your mind-set which relates to using computers creatively. The major organizational approaches are presented below. Draw your own conclusions about the significance of these approaches and what they mean to you. Consider the impact of communication technology carefully, especially with regard to basic human freedoms and values. If used well, electronic media could be liberating. Used with the wrong intent, such media could become controlling and inhibiting.

Centralized approaches to organization and management typically emphasize chains of command. This style is certainly evident in military and in bureaucratic organizations. Decision makers assign tasks to members of the organization and expect them to carry out orders. Most communication is from the top down. Centralization optimizes control and can implement coordinated actions. However, centralized approaches can lead to difficulty when gathering information and addressing local concerns. Information and decisions typically pass through several levels before being acted upon. This can stifle initiative and creativity. Chains-of-command began with very limited communication systems. Originally, orders were verbal; eventually messengers carried written instructions. That simple system of written instuctions has evolved into memo-driven bureaucracies where people can spend inordinate amounts of time writing memos. Today, the sheer volume of communications can grind actions to a halt, particularly if each level of a centralized organization has to spend time documenting what it is doing. However, good communications can potentially make centralized organizations more responsive. It can enable organizations (such as military units) to act more quickly, as demonstrated in the Iraqi War. Communication can speed the distribution of orders as well as speed the acquisition of information, making centralized command more possible. However, electronic media also make it more difficult for totalitarian organizations to maintain control. For example, students in China and around the world used FAX machines and telecommunications to gain support during the Tiananmen Square uprising. Telecommunications and news services, such as CNN, now provide the public in most countries with unprecedented access to events as they occur. Totalitarian regimes have attempted to control radio and TV as well as copy machines and computers. They have endeavored to use the media for propaganda. It will be interesting to see how countries will assimilate telecommunications, particularly where the political and social order is changing.

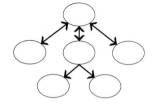

Centralized Organization

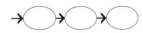

Production Line Organization

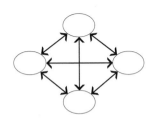

Workgroup Organization

Production line approaches to organization and management typically emphasize specialization. Each person has a position or role to carry out. Although people can make certain decisions, they are part of an organization and carry out specialized tasks (which may often be repetitive). With industrialization, this approach became manifested in the production line. Specialization can optimize efficiency. However, taken to extremes, this type of involvement may not engage the whole mind and consequently can result in personnel problems. For example, absenteeism, high turnover rates, and numbing addictions are typical syndromes found in production-lines workers. People have the potential to do much more than production-line work. Although the production line has led to a certain level of material success in the industrial age, this pattern may be changing as the information age emerges. Machines can often function better than people in production-line situations. People have the potential to carry out more creative activities which can add value.

A workgroup approach to organization and management emphasizes independent initiative. Participants relate to the whole context and the objects they are working with. This can enable people to collaborate more creatively, drawing upon more of their potential. Each person in a workgroup can assume responsibilities and contribute unique talents he or she may have. All participants can communicate directly with each other. This approach tends to optimize collaboration and creativity. It is characteristic of research groups and design teams. The key to making it work effectively is communication and the right mix of motivated people. Electronic media are making it possible to use this approach more widely. You can create networks linking people in a workgroup. For example, workgroups can use a local area network (LAN) in an office environment. A workgroup can also network using telecommunication through modems. And, of course, they can also use the telephone; however, by working with computers workgroups can relate to objects in media space. Creatively using multimedia computing could stimulate cultural changes that would de-emphasize top-down and production line mind-sets, possibly leading to more humane work habits and lifestyles. It is even possible to create effective workgroups that function independent of space and time, giving people more freedom over where and when they work.

Summary

This chapter helps you learn to develop new procedures so you can use them to manage your projects and go beyond what you have done before. You need to address the following concerns: What media, what models, and what methods are you using? Using the nine-step approach to media, models, and methods can help you develop your procedures for using electronic media more creatively and effectively. Clear procedures for using media can help you transfer information. Clear procedures for building models can help you visualize what you are working on. Clear procedures for developing your methods can help you manage projects.

The basic nine-step approach involves:

Media — for transferring information

    1. Relate electronic media to your goals.

    2. Map your media space.

    3. Diagram information and data flow.

Models— for the realities involved

    4. Identify realities you are working with.

    5. Develop models of reality.

    6. Mock up your presentation.

Methods — for thought processes

    7. Define your project.

    8. Diagram your work flow.

    9. Manage your progress.

Refining procedures enables you to adopt new tools and accept change. The following activities will help you do that. The first activity suggests you review previous projects. The second activity will help you develop your own procedures based on the nine-step approach. The third activity will help you learn to manage media, models, and methods. And the fourth activity will help you learn to refine your thinking skills for using electronic media by continuing to apply the basic nine-step approach to media, models, and methods when doing projects in your own discipline.

Activities

1. Review Previous Projects

Some people can easily demonstrate that computers are not worth the extra cost. For example, I have seen some architects mindlessly use computers to try to duplicate their hand-drafting procedures. To their disappointment they find the way they use computers inhibits their creativity and is not cost effective. Others show how multimedia computing has opened new opportunities for creativity. They find computers enable them to work with information more easily and interactively. Aside from using appropriate hardware and software for the task, another important key is how you apply your mind. This exercise will help you to develop the thinking skills for critically evaluating how to do projects when using electronic media.

Examine a case study of a creative project done in your discipline using computers. (Use your own project if you can.) Follow the approaches described in this chapter. What was the approach to handling media? What was the approach to modeling realities? What was the approach to the design methods involved in the project? What hardware and software were used? How could the project be done better?

Note: Start with an easy case study which you can examine rather quickly. The next chapter will provide more elaborate examples of case studies from different disciplines. The activities at the end of the next chapter will help you examine your discipline further and develop multidisciplinary approaches for doing collaborative projects using electronic media. Keep all of these observations in your journal.

2. Develop Procedures for Using Computers Creatively

If you can visualize how to do something, you can do it much more easily. For example, when hiking or driving, if you have a mental picture of where you are going, you can get there more easily, even if you have never been there before. The same is true in artificial reality. Your map of media space and information flow diagrams provide that mental picture of where you are going and how you are going to get there. Models help you relate to the realities you are working with. Clear methods help you manage your project.

Take a creative project you are working with and go through the following approach to develop your own procedures for handling media, models, and methods.

Media
1. Relate electronic media to your goals.
2. Map your media space.
3. Diagram information and data flow.

Models
4. Identify realities you are working with.
5. Develop models of reality.
6. Mock up your presentation.

Methods
7. Define your project.
8. Diagram your work flow.
9. Manage your progress.

This exercise will help you develop the thinking skills you need to carry out your project using electronic media.

3. Manage Your Media, Models, and Methods

There is a big difference between visualizing something and actually doing it. Consider the difference between having a mental map of where you are going and the experience of actually hiking or driving there. For example, when driving, you encounter any number of obstacles — accidents, bad road conditions, maybe your car even breaks down. You may find distractions that may get you off course. Maybe you want to change your route, or at some point you may prefer to explore. Although you can learn a great deal from visualizing your route, there is no substitute for actually experiencing it. It is especially important to compare what you visualize with what you really experience. Use this comparison to update your visualization of where you are going so you can enhance your experience.

Use these thinking skills to guide your approach to your project as you are doing it. Have project management meetings where you and your project team can regularly assess your progress using your media, models, and methods. Use this approach to guide and coordinate your procedure. Take time to update your thinking skills as you proceed.

4. Refine Your Thinking Skills

Everything continues to change —
especially the tools you have access to.
For example, computer hardware
increases in speed and capacity. Software becomes more refined, providing
new potential for using electronic
media. Your capabilities to use these
tools can change. Even your goals and
aspirations will probably change.
As this happens, you will discover new
opportunities to use electronic media.
Learning creative thinking skills will
enable you to develop strategies to
address these changes.

When you are done with your project,
go back to the first exercise in this
section and look at your project again.
Repeat the first exercise using your
own project as the case study. Evaluate
the results and refine your approach.
Where are you having problems? Can
you identify with any of the syndromes
described in this book? Can you see
changes in your media, models, or
methods, or in your software or hardware, that would be beneficial? Are
there changes in the way you organize
your workgroup that might also help
overcome problems?

Fantasize how you might do this
project if you had access to better
hardware and software and could
refine your thinking skills. Go ahead;
muster your courage and share that
fantasy with others. Try to keep your
expectations within the bounds of the
situation you are dealing with; otherwise you may breed frustration within
yourself and others.

Note: These activities can take a long
time. Schedule time for your workgroup to undertake these efforts.
Make them a part of a continuous
process for doing projects. The time
you invest in these activities can be
worthwhile, helping you reach new
levels of creativity and effectiveness.
Use the journal you started in Chapter
1 to record your thoughts. This will
enable you to see how your procedures
for using multimedia computing
evolve.

7

Case Studies—Relating to Disciplines

How do creative thinking skills for electronic media relate to different disciplines? This chapter will examine some commonalities and differences among disciplines and people. Then it will look at case studies of people in disciplines ranging from the arts to engineering and science and examine how they use computers creatively. The first case study explores how an artist does animation using computers. The second examines a collaborative project done by a team of architects, landscape architects, and civil engineers. The third case study investigates how planners and landscape architects use computers for analyzing natural resources for developing site plans. The final case study looks at how engineers and scientists use computer models to simulate designs for space platforms used for scientific investigations. These case studies demonstrate how individuals from different disciplines work with media, models, and methods. The activities at the end of the chapter let you examine your discipline, give you an appreciation of where others are coming from, and help you develop multidisciplinary approaches to team projects.

Consider Your Discipline

Consider the discipline you are pursuing. You probably recognize that there are accepted media, models, and methods for working. You also realize that certain modes of thought as well as hardware and software have become more or less accepted. Yet there is potential to do much more with electronic media.

Commonalities and Differences

Although we share many modes of thought, each discipline has its own knowledge base and emphasizes different modes. For example, the arts draw more on R-modes of thought—emphasizing inductive thinking. Design disciplines relate to both R-modes and L-modes—involving both invention and development of ideas. The sciences tend to stress L-modes of thought—emphasizing deductive thinking. People gravitate toward disciplines they are interested in learning about and in which they feel comfortable with the modes of thought that are emphasized. Excelling in any discipline typically involves a considerable knowledge base and the capacity to use different modes of thought.

art   design   science

R-modes   L-modes

Modes of Thought

ENERGIZING PREFERENCE

Extraversion
"Talk it out."
Preference for drawing energy
from the outside world of people,
activities, or things.

Introversion
"Think it over.'
Preference for drawing energy
from one's internal world of ideas,
emotions, or impressions.

ATTENDING PREFERENCE

Sensing
"Focus on specifics."
Preference for taking in information
through the five senses and
noticing what is actual.

Intuition
"Focus on the big picture."
Preference for deriving information
from a "sixth sense" and developing
insight of what might be.

DECIDING PREFERENCE

Thinking
"Make logic-based decisions."
Preference for organizing and
structuring information to decide
in a logical, objective way.

Feeling
"Make values-based decisions."
Preference for organizing and
structuring information to decide
in a personal, value-oriented way.

LIVING PREFERENCE

Judgement
"Come to closure."
Preference for living a
planned and organized life.

Perception
"Stay open for new inputs."
Preference for living a
spontaneous and flexible life.

Ranges of Characteristic Behavior
adapted from *Introduction to Type in
Organizations*, 2nd ed.
S. K. Hirsh and J. M. Kummerow
(based on Myers-Briggs Personality
Type Indicators)

mind-set Attitude; point of view.

Each discipline works with much of the same computer hardware and software. Most disciplines work with word processors, spreadsheets, and databases. More disciplines are beginning to use graphics programs, imaging, three-dimensional modeling, and even animation, video, and sound. What comes out of applications — such as CADD, GIS, and desktop publishing — is, of course, quite divergent. Disciplines use information differently while emphasizing a variety of modes of thought.

In addition to different disciplines, there is also a range of personality types. All of this makes formulating project teams and managing the group dynamic more challenging. Certainly, these are very important considerations when meshing different minds in a multidisciplinary endeavor. Katherine Briggs and Isabel Myers developed a personality-type indicator based upon the work of Jung. They found preferences in how people energize, what people pay attention to, how people make decisions, and what lifestyle they adopt. Each of these preferences has a bipolar scale shown in the chart to the left. You probably can relate this chart to the type of people you know and work with. You can also recognize how you may demonstrate different characteristics described on the chart. The characteristics may vary depending upon your mood or the situation. To some extent, these characteristics are manifestations of using different modes of thought.

How can we formulate multidisciplinary teams? Or how can we create effective workgroups even within a discipline? One strategy is to educate people to use many modes of thought and teach them skills necessary to work comfortably with a range of electronic media. Another strategy is to formulate workgroups — including people who specialize in certain modes of thought, yet who appreciate the thinking skills of others and who can communicate effectively using electronic media. Well-rounded people may be most effective on projects carried out by an individual. The multidisciplinary workgroup is necessary for large, complex projects.

The case studies presented here focus on minds. I have interviewed people from a range of disciplines to see *how* they think when using electronic media. These case studies are only a sampling. They are not entirely representative of each discipline. Nor are they fair representations of the organizations mentioned in the studies. Consider these cases only as case studies — not as models. Probably the next time these people do a project they will do it somewhat differently. Within the organizations where these people work, there are other case studies that could demonstrate many different procedures.

I found it interesting to explore different *mind-sets*. Those dealing with the arts and design obviously worked from overall perceptions. The details tended to be less interesting to them — since details were subject to constant change. There was even some impatience with articulating processes. Those dealing with engineering and science seemed to focus more on details. Credibility was a major concern. There was some reluctance to generalize or fantasize. These case studies reflect how disciplines emphasize different modes of thought.

Computer Art Case Study: Wound Healing

Image of The Synaptic Gap
adapted from animation of *The Brain*
by Jules Bister

Jules Bister, a German artist who works with computer animation, commented to me about the recognition his animation received at NCGA (the National Computer Graphics Association) and SIGGRAPH (the Special Interest Group in Graphics) where he won several awards. He said, "Credits for computer graphics always state the hardware and software used, but usually say nothing of how the artist worked." People become enamored with the tools. In fact, the impression sometimes is that the artist doesn't matter. This could not be farther from the truth.

Traditional art has transcended tools. When an art gallery displays a painting, one rarely sees a discussion of the media. There is almost no mention of what brushes were used or how pigments were mixed. Most important is what the artist expresses.

The famous photographer Ansel Adams was once asked which camera to use for capturing a particular scene. His response was simply that you should use the one you know how to use best. Photography has suffered the same technical preoccupation that is now see engulfing computer art. Presently, much computer art features technical virtuosity. This will wear off, as it has with photography, when the techniques become more commonplace. It won't be long before the artist will show through. Initially, artists explore the limits of the media. Eventually, they use the media to explore the limits of their thoughts and expressions.

Art Media

In creating the computer-animated video *The Process of Wound Healing*, Jules Bister worked with multimedia. Beiersdorf AG, the company in Hamburg, Germany, that commissioned the work, came to an animator because what it wanted to present could be neither seen nor filmed. Bister studied electron microscope images of wounds and learned about the healing process from specialists. He developed an image of the process in his mind. And because he is an animator, his mental image was a moving image. He had to work with electronic media to express this mental image.

Sketch of Blood Cells
adapted from *The Process of Wound Healing*
by Jules Bister

Previously, Jules Bister had done an animated film, *The Lymphedema*. For that project he constructed sculptural models, photographed sequences of frames for the animation, and combined that material with cell animation by double or triple exposures. Bister did not want to do what he had done before. He wished to work with computer animation; however, the experience of working with sculptured models helped him visualize what he wanted to do. In fact, for *The Process of Wound Heal-*

Animation of Blood Cells
adapted from *The Process of Wound Healing*
by Jules Bister

ing video, he ended up integrating a sculptured model. He built and filmed this sculptured model to use as a backdrop for the three-dimensional computer animation he did using a computer workstation.

As Bister learned about the healing process, he developed thumbnail sketches, or "scribbles" as he called them. These were visual notes to himself, not for presentation. "I got a friendly feeling of things in my body that I could not see." Then he thought, "What will I do when I sit at my computer? How will I do it in my computer? I had images in my head, but I had to reduce some ideas. I also found some things I could do in the computer model," things that he hadn't thought of before. In the computer, he developed a three-dimensional model with animated elements he constructed. For example, he would draw a simple form and then rotate it in the computer to construct a solid. Then he could transform it for animation. Only the background was clay, latex, and paint. He videoed the background first and then integrated the computer model into the video.

Art Models

Bister worked with several realities:

His workspace: He worked on his computer in his studio/apartment, where he did the sculpturing and had a video camera setup. There is no separation between his work and his living. His work is his life and his life is his work. Bister is so involved in what he is doing, he feels like it is not a job.

He is contemplating getting a more powerful computer system for animation. With that system he could do more in the computer and would therefore need to do less with sculpture. In effect, more of his workspace would be in the computer.

The context of the project: A medical company commissioned the animation, and a production company hired Bister's studio to do the animation. Each had its own set of requirements. More important, however, was the skin and the healing process involving erythrocytes, thrombocytes, fibroblasts, fibrin mesh, and blood vessels. Bister had to visualize this process to give expression to it.

Artificial reality: This began as an image in Bister's mind. He sketched the image on paper with quick thumbnail sketches. He sculptured some model backgrounds. He generated several three-dimensional models in the computer.

The animated video: This was the final reality. It began as a storyboard and evolved into an animated sequence to which voice and music were added. Bister's ideas went through many transformations as he created the computer-animated video. What he produced shows the transformations that skin goes through in healing a wound. Animation is an ideal medium for showing transformations.

Jules Bister and his wife, Elka, extracted portions of the animation for submission to NCGA and SIGGRAPH. These submissions were internationally recognized. The complete animated sequence was turned over to the production company, which integrated it into a longer presentation.

Art Methods

Like many artists, Jules Bister doesn't consciously think of the processes he goes through in creating his art. Nevertheless, there was a clear process. Bister's comment, when we discussed his process, was that he hadn't thought about it so clearly before. However, he recognizes that to use a computer effectively, he must plan his approach. Bister points out, "An animator must develop a feeling for time that is very different from live action shooting, or only painting one image. Everything you do in planning animations involves time. You have to have movement in mind."

The images Jules Bister developed in his mind had a mood, color, and even sound. Jules and Elka worked together to give expression to the mood. Taking care to stay in sync with the animation, Elka used a computer to write the text that was later narrated by Jay Tuck. The Bisters collaborated with composer Okko Bekker, who composed music using a computer to synthesize it. Jules used a full range of senses and gave expression to them electronically through his animation and collaboration with others. He could work with a multimedia sense of what he was creating and communicate this sense to others with whom he was collaborating. He worked from this sense of awareness, without consciously trying to measure time, light, color, or sound intensity. These variables were all manipulated intuitively.

In this project Jules Bister made a sculptured model of the background. He then made a video of the background model and integrated the computer-animated model into it. The script was written after he had the animated images, and then the music was added after that. Sometimes the Bisters follow a different procedure putting animation together. The sequence could involve composing all channels simultaneously, or it could start with other channels such as the narrative.

Jules Bister confided, "Sometimes when I start doing these things, I don't want to have too much detailed information. It stops me. I can add information later." He avoids outside influences because they may make it hard for him to come back to his first insights. "I first like to brainstorm with my wife to get an overview of what to do, then make my own ideas and work from a basic structure. And then I can incorporate some other information and build it up where appropriate. You need not have everything in the visual image; it can be in the text or music." There is a longer version of the *Wound Healing* video that uses Bister's animation. Bister strongly feels "less is more." The longer video added more information but lost the message.

Integrating Channels

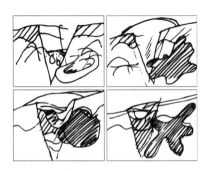

Sketch of Four Stages of Wound Healing
adapted from Jules Bister

Four Stages of Wound Healing
adapted from *The Process of Wound Healing*
by Jules Bister

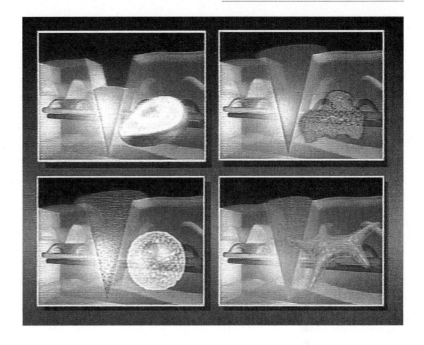

Once Jules Bister modeled the "actors" and the background, he shared representations of this artificial world with specialists and the client to get their comments. He then began to animate wire frames to test on video. In the final animation the computer models seemed to "ask" for specific movements or expressions, much like puppets do. These artificial creatures take on a character of their own. An interaction takes place between the animator and the animated object, no matter what kind of object it is.

Architecture Case Study: High School Design

Over the past several years, I collaborated on a design for a large new high school in Rancho Cucamonga, California. The architects for the project were Wolff, Lang, Christopher, Architects, Incorporated (WLC). My firm, Claremont Environmental Design Group, Inc. (CEDG), provided landscape architectural services. Derbish, Guerra and Associates did the civil engineering. The project team did most of the design work using computers.

Dale Lang, the principal architect, and Tony Palmisano, the project manager from WLC, have reflected with me upon the process we went through together. In retrospect, there is much to learn from the successes and frustrations of producing this project.

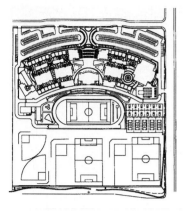

Rancho Cucamonga High School Site Plan
courtesy of WLC

Architecture Media

WLC decided to do as much of this project as possible electronically. The design media were electronic drawings, models, and video. The project itself consists of a 40-acre campus with 20 buildings totaling 230,000 square feet and an assortment of sports facilities. The documentation for this project involved 15 minutes of videotape — 100 megabytes of architectural drawings produced with AutoCAD. We produced more than 3 megabytes of landscape architectural drawings with LandCADD. The specifications took 3 megabytes of text. The final construction set was plotted on about 475 "E" sized drawings (36 x 42 inches) which used 60 pounds of paper. The specifications were printed on another 750 pages of 8.5 x 11 inch paper.

The existing site contours were scanned into a digital format to use with AutoCAD. Working with the engineers, the architects laid out the property boundaries in the computer. They also worked out the required rights-of-way and setbacks for future roads. The computer helped integrate site information that became determinants for the design.

The project group at WLC developed a three-dimensional computer model of the overall site. The group also used computers to develop plans, sections, and elevations of each building. The structural engineers used computers to add their information to the building drawing files. CEDG added the hardscape and landscape to the digital bases obtained from WLC. The civil engineers worked on plots from this site plan and developed their own drawings by hand, although they used computers for many of their calculations. The interaction between the architects, landscape architects, and engineers was therefore most effectively done in a series of meetings working with hand-drawn overlays. After these meetings, however, the civil engineers had to transfer information separately

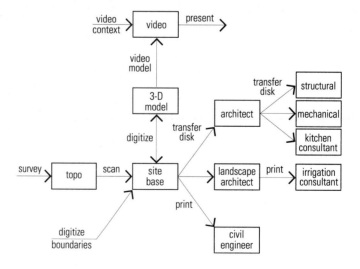

Information Flow Diagram

to their paper drawings. The architects also had to transfer this information to the electronic model for the architects and landscape architects to work with. These additional transfers slowed down some of the interaction and made coordination more difficult.

The architects developed ideas for the site plan by sketching over a plot of the base. They also tried out possibilities in the computer. The architects on the design team generated three alternative site configurations for the building masses. They selected a scheme involving concentric arcs. They could not have easily developed a scheme with concentric arcs if they had not used a computer.

Architectural Models

Rancho Cucamonga High School Shaded Model
adapted from video by Dale Lang

Having selected the form concept, the architects used computers to develop a three-dimensional model of the school. Simultaneously, they began to develop some cardboard study models of a few key buildings. At the same time the architects developed floor plan diagrams of all the buildings to review with the client. By using the computer, they could evolve the diagrams into building plans. They inserted the ground floor plans into the digital site model. Here they transposed the ground floor plan into three dimensions by simply copying the plan for each level of the building. This provided a simple three-dimensional mass model of the entire site.

Rancho Cucamonga High School Wire Frame Model
adapted from video by Dale Lang

Dale Lang spent about a week modeling the site, making simple wire-frame models of each building. By doing this he was also making many key design decisions. The 40-acre site had a consistent 3 percent slope. This resulted in about a 40-foot change in level from the north to the south of the site. Lang modeled this slope simply as an inclined plane. He set the buildings at appropriate elevations stepping up the slope. Lang also used this model to show me outdoor spaces shaped by the building masses and the different levels of the ground plane. This model became the reference we used in developing the landscape architecture.

Using a computer, Lang then developed the three-dimensional wire-frame model into a simple shaded model. The shaded model provided a clearer picture of the building masses and outdoor spaces. He used a video camera to take a sequence of views of this model directly from the computer screen. He recorded sequences by moving around in the three-dimensional model and "taking a few frames" of each view. Lang and his workgroup used this initial video simply as a visualization tool for those working on the project. It was helpful to me as the consulting landscape architect. Eventually, they showed this crude video to the superintendent of the school district, as well as to some of the school district staff.

A logical next step was to create a more refined video presentation for the school board members to view when they were to approve the design. The firm purchased a video capture system to transfer computer images directly to a video recorder. Dale Lang took the same wire-frame model he had done in the computer and refined it. By then, the architects in the workgroup had developed the building forms. Using imaging software they were able to add more detail. They also showed the soccer and base-ball fields, the basketball courts, and the swimming pool. Problems and opportunities started showing up that were not apparent in the earlier stages of design. Dale Lang took a video camera to the site and shot the context, including views of the San Gabriel Mountains to the north. He then generated similar views in the computer model and combined the video images using video editing equipment.

The presentation video started with a Gregorian chant and images of traditional schools. A sequence of views showed the existing site. This was followed by a sequence showing the computer model following the same path. The video continued back and forth between the actual site and the computer model, providing the viewer with a tour of the campus. The architects showed this video to members of the the school board, helping them understand the design.

The video also helped the design team to visualize the project. The architects developed designs for the buildings in the computer, working in a rather typical way using plans, sections, and elevations. Initially, our landscape architectural group used a plot of the digital base that WLC provided for sketching ideas for the outdoor spaces on paper. Once we had a design direction, it was easier to develop the design of the landscape in the computer. We worked with overlays on the electronic base.

In this way, we provided the architects with a development of the landscape on their digital reference drawing. They used this in refining the site plan. They also provided us with updates of this base drawing, and we could easily substitute the new version of the base for the old one in our drawing. Then we could adjust our overlays where necessary. This computer drawing was the medium for our collaboration.

We also passed a three-dimensional computer model of the entry and amphitheater back and forth. Dale Lang developed the basic form which fit into the overall site model. Working on this model of the entry and amphitheater, I developed the seating tiers, steps, and handicapped ramps. We refined this form interactively, working together in the computer. The model then became the base for our dimensioned layout plan of the walks and planters. The architects detailed the walls and related structures from this model. We added the planting and irrigation design. Working in three dimensions made it easier for us all to visualize the relationship between the ramps, the stairs, and the seating tiers. Electronic media help us develop this artificial reality.

Other types of models were also used to develop this project. A facility program was developed at the inception of the project to articulate the school district's needs as interpreted by the administration and its working committees. A financial model was developed to project anticipated costs and relate them to funding sources. The building plans were reviewed at different stages by the Office of the State Architect which addressed many code requirements for this type of public facility. The plans were also reviewed by the community of Rancho Cucamonga with regard to its planning and development requirements.

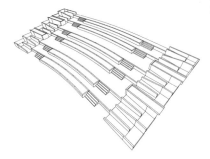

3-D Model of Entry and Amphitheater
adapted from model of Rancho Cucamonga High School by WLC and CEDG

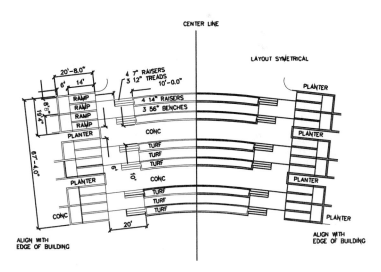

Entry and Amphitheater Dimensioned Layout
adapted from working drawings of Rancho Cucamonga High School by WLC and CEDG

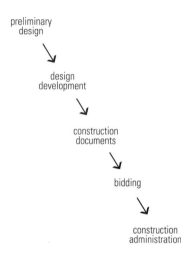

preliminary
design

design
development

construction
documents

bidding

construction
administration

**Architecture
Scope of Work**

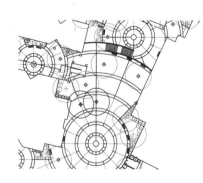

Pavement Layout
adapted from working drawings of Rancho
Cucamonga High School by WLC and CEDG

Architecture Methods

This project followed the traditional scope of work provided by architects — preliminary design, design development, preparation of construction documents, bidding, and construction administration. A design team generated the preliminary design. Then a larger team of architects went through and developed the design for each building. The same team of people worked on each building from design development through construction documents. They would focus on one or two buildings at a time. The team would use the floor plans developed in the preliminary design to generate the elevations and sections. For this project there was frequent interaction with about eight school committees — one for each department. There was a science committee, English committee, shop committee — everybody. The meeting schedule was hectic, particularly because everything had to be either plotted or laser-printed for presentation. Then the comments and sketches from the meeting had to be transferred later to the computer drawings. The digital documents evolved with minimum redrawing. Outside consultants included not only civil engineers and landscape architects, but structural engineers, mechanical engineers, electrical engineers, and food service consultants as well. There were coordination meetings involving all the consultants. The review process was lengthy. As usual, revisions were necessary to accommodate all the different (and sometimes conflicting) requirements.

At the beginning of this project WLC had computer workstations in a separate area of its office. The architects would use this work environment when working on the drawings for this project. Now, WLC has installed a local area network and is starting to integrate computers throughout its office. At CEDG, where we did the landscape architecture, we have computer workstations in one room dedicated to electronic media. We also have a drafting studio where we drew the details for this project. Our irrigation consultant, Dan Scaliter, worked on hand-drawn overlays over computer-generated bases. He did his calculations, notes, irrigation schedules, details, and specifications on a computer. He taped computer-generated transparencies on his overlays rather than hand-drafting notes, details, and schedules. A vacuum frame helped integrate computer-generated and hand-drawn materials placed on pin-registered overlays of Mylar.

A tricky element we had to deal with was laying out walkways among the curved buildings. Obviously, rectilinear walks were not going to fit well. We generated some concepts with hand-drawn sketches and came up with the idea of creating places articulated by concentric circles of pavement. I made a block of a concentric pattern in the computer. I then went through the site plan and decided where the outdoor places should be, inserting this paving pattern at each place. From there it was easy to extend and trim the pattern, adjusting it around the buildings and creating planting areas to help define the outdoor spaces. In this way we developed the layout of the walks rather quickly in the computer. Since each place had a repetitive module, dimensioning the layout plan was also easy to do. Despite this repetition, the places we created have interesting variations. Each place is different, which should help people orient in this school. If the contractor uses modular forms in the field, the design should be relatively easy to implement.

As we completed the construction documents, coordination was also complicated by the need to move the project ahead of schedule to obtain funding from a current bond issue. This necessitated submitting the drawings to the state, the local jurisdictions, and the school district and going out to bid before all the changes could be made. Although it was relatively easy to make changes, working in the computer as opposed to drawing by hand, we found it difficult to track them. It is important to adhere to a schedule for coordination and plotting, avoiding, it is hoped, the need to replot large sets of drawings.

Partial North Elevation of Multipurpose Building
adapted from working drawings for
Rancho Cucamonga High School by WLC

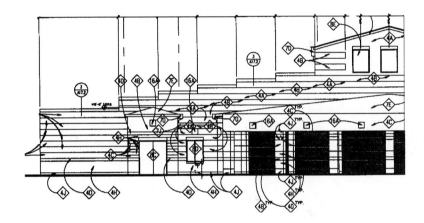

Changes in Architectural Practice

Tony Palmisano, the project manager, commented that he would like to do the next project with more extensive three-dimensional modeling of each building in the computer. He and his co-workers could use information from these models to develop the orthographic drawings needed for construction documents. A three-dimensional model can help an architect visualize the interior spaces of the building. It would also be a good tool for collaborating with clients and consultants. "We weren't to the point that we would bring something into the meeting with the computer and collaboratively change it, but next time I would like to start playing with that too," Palmisano commented.

Although at the time we started this project we simply mailed disks to each other, we are now both on the C-4 network that enables us to transfer drawings at 19,200 baud over telephone lines. Using this network, we can send drawings to each other's account at a local hub. We can also send drawing files out for high-quality and large laser plotting using this network.

Each set of construction documents weighed a great deal, making them hard to handle. The project used reams of paper for progress prints reviewed in meetings. What alternatives are there, given the bulk of paper and time consumed in printing these drawings? One alternative is to do progress reviews electronically. Client committees and consultants can collaborate using the CADD models as the media space for shared inter-action. A video projector could augment larger meetings by displaying the images from the computer monitor on a larger screen. The time may also come when review bodies, such as local planning jurisdictions or the Office of the State Architect, can review drawings electronically. Using artificial intelligence, they could check certain code requirements such as exit door spacing or the distances between fire hydrants. Programs based on specific regulations could check drawings much like spell checkers and grammar checkers evaluate written documents. For example, there are already programs that check dimensions on drawings to see if the distances and numbers match. Evaluative tools such as these could make routine evaluations easier, permitting plan checkers to focus on issues requiring human interpretation.

To make bidding more accurate, contractors could use CADD systems for construction takeoffs. Having a CADD system at the construction site would enable the contractor to query the digital documents. The contrac-tor could also make a record set, or as-builts, of a project using a com-puter right at the construction site. The owner could then use these elec-tronic documents for facilities management.

In the interim, it is more likely we could reduce the size of paper presen-tations. When working on paper, there is a limit to how small one can draw. For example, landscape architects must draw planting and irriga-tion plans at least at 1 inch = 20 feet — which is about as small as one can legibly place the information on the sheet. In a computer we work full scale in the model space and simply zoom in to work on whatever we want. We can plot most computer drawings at a half or third of the scale of hand drawings and they are still very legible. For example, a planting plan done in the computer could be legible when plotted at 1 inch = 40 feet or even 1 inch = 60 feet. Therefore, what we typically plot on a D size 24 x 36 inch sheet, we could laser-print on 8 1/2 x 11 inch paper. We can reproduce large format sheets using diazo printing. We can repro-duce small format sheets using a common copy machine. This reduces the materials and time involved. Dale Lang indicated to me that his office was doing more of its progress prints from CADD using a regular-sized laser printer. He said he would like to find an inexpensive laser printer, with a slightly larger format, for printing drawings.

My office has also been laser-printing CADD drawings at smaller scales for progress reviews. Initially, one has to get used to not having much

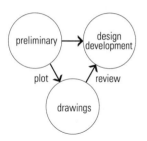

Paper Review

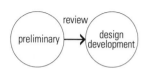

Electronic Review

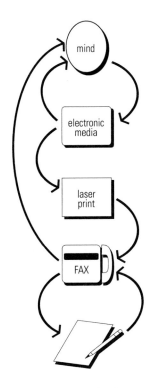

Using FAX Interactively

space to mark up the sheet, but we found we could number the corrections and relate them to comments we write on a separate piece of paper. It can actually be easier to work from a list of corrections than to chase red marks scattered all over the sheet. You can lose track of red marks unless you highlight (with a yellow marker) the ones you have resolved.

Another advantage to the smaller format is that you can easily send drawings by FAX to those who don't have a CADD system. For example, I find it helpful to FAX progress prints of drawings to clients. They can mark up these drawings and quickly return them by FAX along with their comments. Or we can have a telephone conversation using the FAXed drawings as a focus for our discussion. I have even used this approach on international projects. A simple facsimile can create a shared workspace, increasing the speed and quality of collaboration. Using computers to transmit digital models and video images could enhance this interaction.

**Planning Case Study:
Life Learning Village**

Jack Dangermond pursued the goal of developing geographic information systems. He was educated as a landscape architect at Cal Poly, Pomona, in the 1960s and then went on to the Harvard Graduate School of Design. At the time, most GIS (geographic information systems) were grid-based — the locational information was related to grid cells. Dangermond saw the advantages of developing a polygon-based GIS and formed the Environmental Systems Research Institute, Inc. (ESRI). Today ESRI is a major developer of GIS software. The institute also does many interesting projects using the tools it develops.

I went to ESRI in Redlands, California, and met with Mark Sorensen. Mark Sorensen was a student in my senior landscape architecture design class at Cal Poly, Pomona, many years ago. Since he was very interested in using computers for landscape planning, he went to work for ESRI after doing graduate work at Harvard. As we sat together in a conference room at ESRI, Sorensen related to me many of the developments he saw occurring. He talked about convergent technologies driven by multimedia. Because it is now possible to integrate both raster and vector graphics with databases, many of the barriers between GIS, CADD, computer

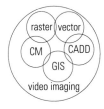

Converging Technologies

mapping (CM), and computer imaging are disappearing. New synergies are emerging for different disciplines related to common databases and tools. For example, many geographers, engineers, landscape architects, and planners and managers in city and regional governments use ARC INFO—software ESRI produces. The newest version incorporates *image integration*, enabling people to drape air photos over models of terrain, as well as overlay models with other locational information—such as soils maps, vegetation maps, and zoning maps. Users can also reference images, as well as videos and animation, to a GIS model. For example, by clicking on a spot in a GIS map, it is possible to activate a video actually taken at that location, enabling people to experience the views and the sounds one would perceive there. ESRI also now includes a grid package in the latest version of its software which enables people to do quicker manipulation of data using much smaller computers. ESRI has also developed ARC VIEW—software that permits users to view and query digital maps and models using small portable computers.

While it is interesting to sample the developments of software products that constantly evolve, the intent of this case study is not to present a company's product. The real intent is to see how people in different disciplines work with these tools.

Planning Media

One of the key goals of a geographic information system is to develop locational databases. This enables people to shift from a project orientation to a transactional orientation. With a project orientation, the *life cycle* of information relates to the life of a project. When the project is finished, so is the use of the information. A transactional orientation enables people to gather information and transfer it from one application to another. This gives the information a much longer life cycle. It is also now becoming possible to enter the information into the database as the information is generated. An example of this is the way many businesses now use cash registers to compile information on sales. They no longer just ring up single sales as if each were a separate project. Computerized cash registers now collect information on a company's inventory and revenues with each transaction. This enables a company to build very accurate models of its inventory and cash flow. The same could be done with locational models of geographic contexts. If a community could record each change as it occurred, this approach would also enable a government to model the capacity of its environment and infrastructure to do better planning and evaluate development proposals.

Sorensen told me how ESRI was working on major databases such as the Digital Chart of the World. The intent of this project is to put important environmental information on CDs for countries around the world to use to better address global environmental issues. The major cost of any project is the cost of compiling information. It is possible to distribute the cost of compiling information over many projects and also share it among

image integration The combining of visual information. For example, draping air photos over computer terrain models.

life cycle A sequence of stages that include the formation, use, and disposal of an object. Can refer to physical objects as well as to information objects developed in computers.

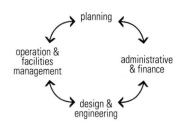

Information Life Cycle

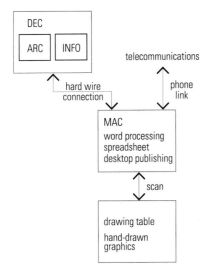

Media Space Diagram

different disciplines. Distributing costs over many applications makes good information less expensive. Sorensen sees data brokering as a growing field in information science. He sees a need for "information architects" who have an overview of many applications and know how to design and put together useful information models.

Aside from working with very sophisticated application databases, the media space that Sorensen worked in was rather simple. He did a lot of his planning and report writing using a computer with word processing, spreadsheet, and desktop publishing software. He could also access geographic information models that run mostly on minicomputers and workstations. Previously, his planning section was located in an old adobe house in Redlands, because ESRI was growing more rapidly than it could build facilities. A computer network linked the planning section to the rest of the organization. The planning section is now located in the main facility, but Sorensen has access to the outside world through telecommunications. Sorensen helped refine this case study by working with me in media space using Internet.

The case study we discussed was the Matsuda Life Learning Village for which he did an environmental assessment and conceptual master plan in collaboration with the Japan Housing Organization. On planning projects such as this, ESRI functions as the integrator of information. Although ESRI works primarily using computers, it has exchanged information with its client and planning consultants mostly through meetings and on paper. The final product is typically a report that integrates text and graphics. Some graphics are generated from GIS models. Some are scanned from other sources including pencil and pen drawings.

Sorensen also uses a video camera in the field. This enables him to take dynamic field notes, not only recording the views and sounds he perceives, but also adding verbal comments as he moves around a site. He found this particularly useful when doing projects in Japan where he often had only a very short time to visit a site and also needed to bring his impressions back to his workgroup.

On another project in Japan — this one for the Forest City of Kawauchi Kogen — ESRI used video modeling done by the Landscape Research Centre at the University of Toronto. The team took a three-dimensional digital elevation model of the site and developed a visual simulation of several lakes set into this terrain. Using this model, they were able to explore what the edge of the lake would look like and how to place development, such as a resort hotel, in this context.

One reason ESRI got involved in planning for the Life Learning Village is that it had already compiled a GIS model for Gunma Prefecture — the region where this project is to be located. Sorensen said ESRI was able to transfer information from this regional database to develop a model of the context for this project. ESRI used this to assess the environment and develop a conceptual master plan. The environmental analysis process

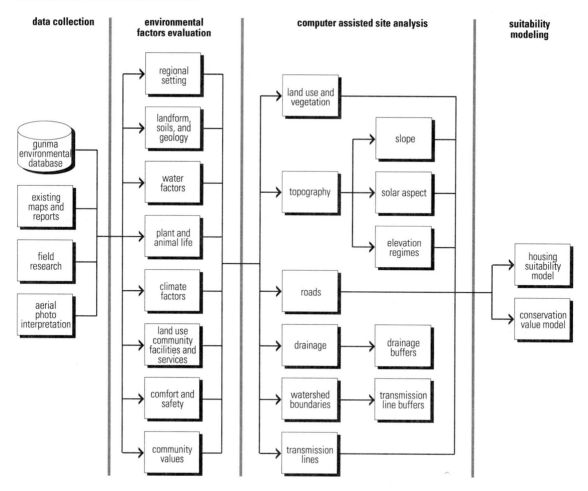

Environmental Analysis Process
adapted from ESRI

diagram shows the information flow ESRI uses for a project such as this one.

Sorensen acknowledges that while this diagram provided a frame of reference, his thought process is actually more cyclical. He finds himself often looping back to previous phases, adding and refining information as he proceeds through the project. He leaves a paper trail to document his progress.

Planning Models

This planning project addressed a number of interesting realities. First, there was the social reality that workers are living much longer than in the past — the retirement period of life can now last many years. Also, during the working period of life, employees dedicated to companies tend to be very focused — often forgoing family and personal development. The economic hope is that while workers contribute to their companies,

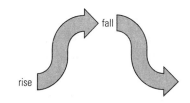

Old Model of Human Life

A Cyclical Model of Human Life
adapted from *The Global Life Learning Center*

nagaya (Japanese) Old-style Japanese "cluster housing." Places where people of all ages live in harmony with each other and the land.

ninjō (Japanese) A spirit of cooperation and neighborliness.

they can accumulate wealth to use during retirement.

The visionary Mrs. Matsuda, president of the Japan Housing Organization, founded the Global Life Learning Center. One of the purposes is the creation of a network of life learning village communities that will serve as demonstration centers for the creation of an "ageless society" which will prepare people for each stage of life. Rather then creating "leisure communities," which can become a glorified way of warehousing the elderly. Life Learning seeks ways of drawing upon people's potential at each stage of life. This can benefit both the individual and society.

The ESRI Planning Report points out: "The old model of human life has been rise and fall. In contrast, the Ageless Society operates on a cyclical model, in which each period of adult life includes not only obligations, achievements, and contributions to society as appropriate, but also includes education and preparation for the next phase of life." (See the prepare-achieve cycle on the left.) Consequently, the planning of these communities becomes very important. They need to be sustainable places of economic health, physical beauty, environmental harmony, and excellent construction.

This concept of community villages has the support of the Japanese Housing Organization because it has potential for stimulating decentralization of overcrowded urban areas. It is reminiscent of old-style Japanese *nagaya* ("cluster housing"), where people of all ages live in harmony with each other and the land. *Ninjō* (a spirit of cooperation and neighborliness) can prevail. This spirit is found in many small rural communities around the world. One can't help but wonder what new levels of humanity could be achieved if people could create a network of modern *nagaya* peacefully linked by telecommunications. The spirit of *ninjō* could flourish anew on a global scale.

Beyond these very important conceptual models, ESRI developed spreadsheet models projecting social and economic factors of the area. Workgroup members looked at demographics and did market projections and feasibility studies. They also developed a geographic information model of the physical context. Drawing from the database they had previously assembled for the region, they were able to compile overlays mapping natural features such as geology, soils, plant associations, and drainage units. They also mapped man-made features such as the utility and transportation infrastructure as well as existing land use. They used all this information to assess environmental factors on which to base the plan. In addition, they also modeled the landform in three dimensions using a computer. This helped them visualize many features of the land. For example, this helped them look at the dynamics of the drainage system.

Using this information, the project team generated a conceptual plan for Matsuda Life Learning Village. The plan addressed important land-use, access, and transportation issues. The workgroup members incorporated high nutrient compost used for soil conditioner and fertilizer for community gardens and landscaped area

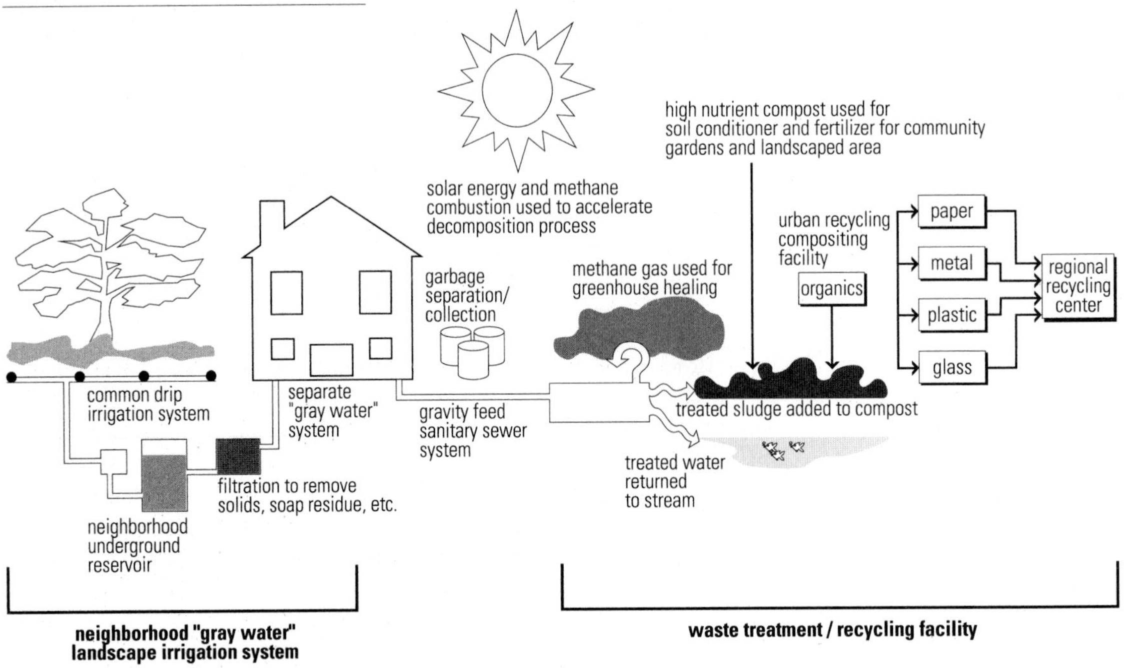

solar energy and methane combustion used to accelerate decomposition process

urban recycling compositing facility

organics

paper

metal

plastic

glass

regional recycling center

garbage separation/ collection

methane gas used for greenhouse healing

common drip irrigation system

separate "gray water" system

gravity feed sanitary sewer system

treated sludge added to compost

filtration to remove solids, soap residue, etc.

treated water returned to stream

neighborhood underground reservoir

neighborhood "gray water" landscape irrigation system

waste treatment / recycling facility

Systems Diagram of Material and Energy Flow
adapted from ESRI

environmental guidelines into the plan. They based some of these guidelines on conceptual models of material and energy flow through the community (see the systems diagram below). They derived others from checklists of environmental considerations they had generated from other projects and environmental impact assessment provisions related to CEQA (California Environmental Quality Act).

Sorensen showed me sourcebooks that ESRI uses to generate its planning documents. The sourcebooks provide models that are already in a working digital format. These sourcebooks address major categories of concerns and serve as a guideline for each project. Sorensen would use what was relevant, but also add information unique to this project. At the same time, the sourcebooks continue to evolve, and so ESRI can use them on the next project. Architects and engineers use similar approaches to developing construction specifications.

Sorensen wrote the text in a word processor, using the sourcebook files as a guide. He also gathered information from the consultants who developed economic models of the market and costs/revenue projections. Some graphics — such as illustrative drawings — were hand-drawn and then scanned into a digital format. Other graphics — such as maps showing the land resources (drainage units, vegetation coverage, etc.) — were downloaded from the ARC-INFO coverages done in a minicomputer. The workgroup used Pagemaker — desktop publishing software — to integrate the text and graphics into the final report document which was presented to the client. The key visual model was the community plan.

Planning Methods

The Japanese Ministry of Housing provided grants for this project to support decentralization. The ministry is interested in creating communities in rural areas that have urban amenities and are within three hours of Tokyo. Mrs. Matsuda provided the vision, and the Global Life Learning Center provided the organizational support. They are responding to the need to provide not only housing, but a more productive and stimulating lifestyle for those who are retiring. The center is dedicated to finding ways of creating more balanced, self-supporting, and sustainable communities — ways of overcoming the decay of family and isolation of older people that is occurring in present-day society.

The Global Life Learning Center sent ESRI a project description and basemaps with general information. Sorensen visited the site to do reconnaissance and a front-end feasibility evaluation. He used checklists to guide these efforts. He was then able to select the project team based on needs he and the client group identified together.

ESRI provided the expertise to manage the necessary information and develop site plans using the GIS tools it had developed. Working with available information, ESRI was able to do the study very quickly. Sorensen commented that this was a six-week project.

In managing this project, Sorensen used a generic work flow diagram he had developed doing previous projects. From experience he knew which activities took longer and were consequently on the critical path. For example, he knew he needed to get blockouts to the renderer early because this type of visualization took time to produce. Sorensen began the project by having a scoping session that involved his entire consultant team. They established their approach to the project and assigned areas of responsibility. In this scoping session, they would go through checklists to make sure they were covering all the key elements. They would also share insights using dry marker boards and markers on paper (which they would attach to the wall) to help focus their discussions. After the scoping session, the project team worked somewhat independently with Sorensen coordinating the team's efforts.

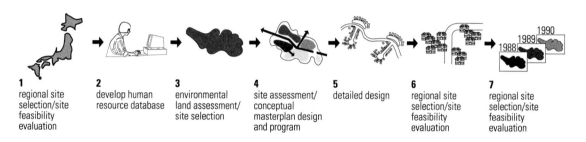

1
regional site selection/site feasibility evaluation

2
develop human resource database

3
environmental land assessment/ site selection

4
site assessment/ conceptual masterplan design and program

5
detailed design

6
regional site selection/site feasibility evaluation

7
regional site selection/site feasibility evaluation

Seven-Step Approach to Community Planning and Design
adapted from ESRI

ESRI was able to develop a model of both the existing context and the potential reality of what this community might become. Using these models, the project team worked interactively, designing from the ground up. Sorensen successfully managed a multidisciplinary, and even multinational, team.

Engineering Case Study: Space Platform Design

Space platforms house instruments for gathering information from outer space. The collectors need to be as large as 20 meters in diameter to gather light for enhancing the resolution of distant images. These structures must be lightweight to get beyond earth's gravity. This makes them prone to vibrations, caused by any type of movement. They are also subject to deflections caused by thermal expansion. Vibrations and deflections distort the platform and collector surfaces. Making these structures stable so they do not disturb instruments collecting information is a very challenging problem. There also need to be ways of maneuvering and pointing instruments. In addition, the platforms must have antennas to transmit digital information for scientists on earth. Effectively modeling these structures can help avoid costly mistakes.

I visited with Dr. Hugh Clark Briggs, who works on the Control/Structure Interaction (CSI) Program at the Jet Propulsion Laboratory (JPL) in Pasadena, California. He provided me with an overview of the work he was doing. In addition to his controlled structure design research, Dr. Briggs is developing design methodologies for the National Aeronautics and Space Administraton (NASA). We discussed the approaches he is exploring. He also gave me a glimpse of how some workgroups at JPL presently approach projects such as CRAF and Cassini. CRAF's mission is a comet rendezvous and asteroid flyby. Cassini is to go to Saturn and drop a probe onto Titan, one of Saturn's moons. Both are to use slightly modified *Mariner Mk II* spacecraft.

What I describe here is simply intended to demonstrate how researchers think and use electronic media. This case study does not represent the complex endeavors JPL undertakes, nor does it reflect JPL policy. It reports on impressions I gathered from a few interviews and some subsequent dialogue with Dr. Briggs, who generously shared with me some of the world in which he is working.

Engineering Media

Briggs is looking for ways of doing concurrent engineering to more closely integrate mechanical layout, structural design, and control system design by using computer models. As in any organization, it is difficult to find time for innovations within the framework of the funded projects. Innovation requires an investment in tools and in the training time needed to learn to use those tools effectively. It also takes an investment in effort to manage effectively. It is often difficult to factor these investments into the initial stages of project funding. These investments must also provide benefits over more traditional methods.

INTERNET links JPL to the outside world. Within the organization are many local area networks serving desktop workstations in different workgroups. These networks provide engineers and researchers with access to communications such as E-mail and information services. For example, Briggs and I correspond using E-mail. We refined this case study in shared media space. Briggs is working with others across the country sharing computer models. For example, when working with colleagues at MIT, he found that by logging onto their computer while having a phone in his ear, he could communicate, write, and transfer code, thereby helping to debug a model without having to be there physically.

The networks at JPL provide workgroups with access to shared models of what they are designing. For example, when I visited there, Mike O'Neal downloaded the CRAF/Cassini spacecraft model over the network using his workstation. (O'Neal is a member of the Mechanical Systems Development Section located in another building. However, O'Neal's physical workspace was near Briggs's office to help collaboration on CSI projects.)

**Cassini Project,
Front Trimetric View**
Courtesy of JPL

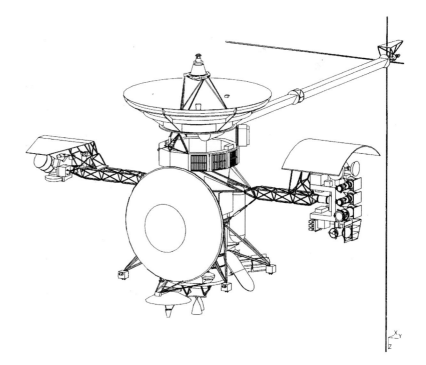

Segmented Reflector Telescope
Courtesy of Dr. H. C. Briggs at JPL

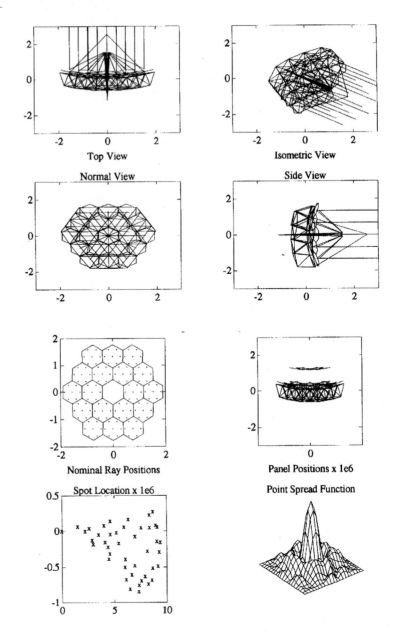

Top View

Isometric View

Normal View

Side View

Nominal Ray Positions

Panel Positions x 1e6

Spot Location x 1e6

Point Spread Function

The image of the space platform came up on the computer on O'Neal's desktop. I found it fascinating how quickly he could, using his local workstation, manipulate the wire-frame views of this 20-megabyte model, and I was also fascinated by the detail with which the computer could shade the solid model. This model mimicked the real assembly so that different teams could take the parts they were working on, refine them, and plug them back into the model again. This object, constructed in media space, provides individual team members with an overview of how what they are doing relates to the whole object. O'Neal mentioned how they used the model in group discussions to optimize the design. For example, the model made it readily apparent if an instrument would not fit into an allocated space or if the exhaust from a thruster would affect nearby parts of the spacecraft. This model can also simulate light sources to visualize shading. This is a crucial concern for both locating collectors and investigating the expansion and contraction of materials.

O'Neal mentioned they sometimes take video images of this model to share with management and NASA officials. In that way, even a standard VCR can relate to this shared media space. The model provided me — a visitor — with a very clear image of this project.

I also watched with amazement as Briggs sat at his workstation and began manipulating parameters in a computer model he had developed that described how a space platform would vibrate as a result of different disturbances. He literally could make the platform dance to different rhythms and then dampen the oscillation. Although Briggs was manipulating the model mathematically in his command window, he would look at the deformed and undeformed shapes in a graphic window that showed a wire-frame three-dimensional model of the structure he was working with. This interaction provided the response he needed to try different parameters to optimize the design of the control systems.

Briggs refers to what he calls the design food chain. Key information such as a schematic of the mechanical layout needs to be established, and then everything can feed off that. Having this information in a visual form helps people relate to the object they are creating. On the CRAF/Cassini project there were about 400 people working on 15 different teams, each responsible for a special concern. Each group used this top assembly, getting information and feeding it back so others could work with it. In this way, members of the workgroup can share ideas and information as well as transfer their components for further analysis and evaluation. The design evolves through the preliminary stages to implementation documents used for "cutting metal." For example, Briggs would work with simulations of structure (based on information he got from the shared model), run them through perturbations, find ways to solve the dynamic structural problems, and feed this information into the implementation documents.

Since most of the funds for these projects come from NASA, part of the job is to make information available to the public. Thus information must be disseminated in press releases and publications. Video is also becoming an effective mode of communication that can present the dynamics of these complex instruments in a multimedia manner. JPL is now producing videos that describe its projects and show the data acquired — such as the recent mapping of Venus. TV coverage is an important avenue for generating public support.

Engineering Models

JPL, like many organizations, is shaping new work environments. Some workgroups physically work in the same space—arranged in rooms with furniture. Other workgroups electronically access shared media space for different projects but physically may be in different places. The opportunities, constraints, and implications of doing more work in media space are just beginning to be understood.

The context of the projects the groups work on, however, is in outer space. The space platforms must perform where diminished gravity changes the behavior of structural members. There is no air—which affects light transmission and thermal dynamics. Consequently, it is difficult to test prototypes on earth. Because of the expense of making test flights in outer space, using computers to model the performance of these platforms in media space is a promising approach.

JPL uses a variety of models and simulations to visualize and test the design of space platforms. These include both computer models and physical simulations. Visual computer models include the three-dimensional solid models already described. They also include parametric models—like those Briggs works with—to explore and analyze alternatives mathematically. JPL engineers and scientists traditionally test prototypes of key components.

**Cassini Project,
Rear Trimetric View**
Courtesy of JPL

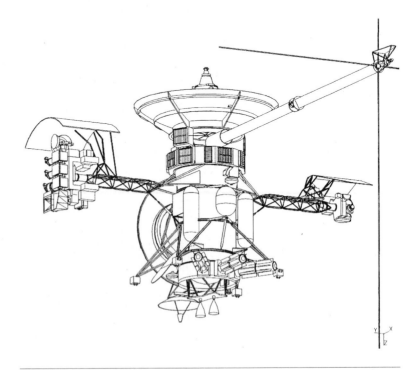

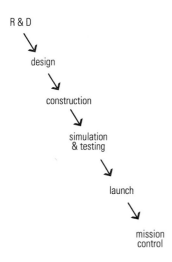

R & D

design

construction

simulation
& testing

launch

mission
control

**Space Science
Project Phases**

Engineering Methods

JPL's projects take years of lead time to plan, design, build, test, and launch. JPL begins with R&D of technology and science, looking for opportunities and gaining support to get a project moving. Only when there is strong support does a plan become a "project looking for a start." During this stage JPL will do preliminary design studies, models, and cost estimates. A start date is established when the project becomes funded. After the start date, JPL will prepare the construction documents, do simulations and testing, and start building. Eventually, many industries become involved in building the space vehicle before it is complete. Once NASA determines when a rocket or space shuttle is available, a launch date can be set. After a mission is launched, JPL is involved in guiding the space vehicle and fixing it in real time (if necessary). JPL also gets the information from outer space and makes it available to scientists. The public is probably most aware of JPL's involvement in space missions because of TV coverage of this aspect of its activities. For example, the Venus radar visualizations riveted public attention.

The life cycle of a space vehicle begins at the inception of a project, goes through the design stages, continues into production, and extends to operation and maintenance of the vehicle in outer space. Some vehicles are even modified in outer space, to correct problems or take on new missions, before their retirement into the darkness of the galaxy.

The space vehicle starts as a set of goals that a small design team transforms into candidate conceptual designs. This team works primarily with visual tools. Once the design direction is established, component teams develop more detailed models. These models most often become quantitative to provide a basis for analyzing alternatives. These detailed analytical models are linked to a three-dimensional mass model or top assembly. Engineers transform components from this model into the detailed shop drawings needed for fabricating the spacecraft.

Typically, JPL engineers do physical simulations of components on test beds, taking prototypes of components through dynamic tests such as loading vibration and radiation. These tests feed information into computers that relate the information to parametric models. The tests provide data that relate the simulations to reality. Computer models enhance these simulations by extrapolating beyond the capabilities of ground testing. They also perform functional testing. Engineers and researchers can provide artificial inputs to assembled spacecraft, or major subsystems, and run them through different mission scenarios. The intent is to achieve a virtual reality for testing the craft and its components. The results of this testing are used for further design iterations before the final craft is assembled.

JPL preserves this test bed after the launch to support flight operations and anomaly investigations during the mission. Even after the spacecraft is constructed, engineers continue to do simulations and evaluations to test all conceivable circumstances before the vehicle is launched. After launching, it becomes very difficult—if not impossible—to correct a problem because the vehicle is no longer visible to those on earth and because interaction is then by radio control over millions of miles.

Changes in Engineering Practice

How can you coordinate large complex projects and still keep the spontaneity and innovation of a "skunk works" operation? Media space can take the place of the old garage that is characteristic of a skunk works. Creating workgroups and enabling them to work in media space can provide the opportunity to explore. Relating these workgroups to one another with telecommunications can help the groups communicate more effectively.

groupware Software that enables group interaction. Helps coordinate large teams using computers to do complex projects.

Groupware that is emerging shows promise for helping coordinate large, complex projects. Briggs believes that getting engineers to think using electronic media, rather than using the back of an envelope, will make it easier to share, document, and work with more information. Computers can help engineers go from creating ideas to cutting metal.

Briggs is developing a design tool that would ultimately share data across analytical methods and integrated systems modeling. He is hoping to achieve an integrated model with a common command structure, symbol sets, and data types for conceptual design. This model would have a common presentation with the same look and feel across engineering discipline modules within the tool. For the present, he and his co-workers must use entirely different programs built by different companies with different user interfaces and different modeling paradigms. This is a common situation, but better integration of applications is beginning to occur in many engineering disciplines.

group dynamic Interaction among members of a team. Involves the members' different modes of thought.

Another challenge is the mental integration of the project team. *Group dynamics* interest Briggs. He recognizes that members of a team can display different modes of thought. He introduced me to the "personality-type indicator" discussed at the beginning of this chapter. Briggs realizes that to make the group dynamic work, the team needs members who can contribute not only specific expertise and skills, but also the capacity to think differently from other members. At the same time each member needs to understand and appreciate the value of the thinking modes of others to have effective collaboration.

Summary

This chapter has presented case studies from different disciplines. Use this approach to better understand your discipline and the media, models, and methods it currently uses. The first activity that follows causes you to examine your discipline. This can help you look for ways to use these approaches for developing your own procedures.

People have different characteristic behavior. Each discipline emphasizes a range of modes of thought. You can also use these approaches to learn where others are coming from. The approaches can help you develop effective teams that mesh different modes of thought and behavior. Doing the second activity that follows will help you appreciate where others are coming from.

You can also develop multidisciplinary approaches. Computers enable you to use media, develop models, and manage methods for multidisciplinary team efforts. Visualizing collaborative efforts can help coordination. By sharing information this information can have a life cycle that lasts longer than a single project. The final activity for this chapter will help you develop multidisciplinary approaches that include using and transferring information electronically and building models which different disciplines can share. Visualizing entire projects enables the various disciplines (and workers) to see how they fit into the entire picture.

Activities

1. Examine Your Discipline

Each discipline has its own knowledge base. Included with this knowledge base are acceptable media for handling information, familiar ways of modeling reality, and proven methods for working.

For example, artists find ways to develop their perception. For centuries they have used traditional media — such as sketching, painting, and sculpting — to represent the realities they work with. Art history continues to trace the influence of various ideas, thought processes, and techniques in different cultures. A new Renaissance may emerge as artists discover what they can do with electronic media.

Designers have divergent ways of looking at the world, depending upon whether they work with land, buildings, or manufactured articles. They use prototypes, scale models, three-dimensional images, and various types of orthographic drawings and maps as well as a wide variety of diagrams, descriptions, and databases to represent the realities they work with. Proven procedures are embodied in the standard forms for contractual agreements put out by professional organizations such as the American Institute of Architects, the American Society of Landscape Architects, and the Professional Engineering Societies. The practice of these professions is beginning to change dramatically because of electronic media.

Scientists' horizons continue to expand through electron microscopy and outer-space exploration. Scientific disciplines have many ways to model reality and rigorous thought processes related to the scientific method. Again, history provides a fascinating story of the evolution of scientific knowledge. Electronic media will have a significant impact on this evolution.

Examine a case study typical of your own discipline. Describe the media for transferring information, the models of reality, and the methods for working with the thought processes involved. Can you see opportunities that may lead to innovations? Innovations often come from finding new sources of information (or ways of acquiring it). They can also come from finding better ways to model reality so you can deal with it more effectively. In addition, innovations may come from developing new methods that enable you to work with thought processes to use tools more creatively or with greater precision.

2. Appreciate Where Others Are Coming From

In the last exercise, you examined how the knowledge base of your discipline relates to creative thinking skills. No discipline works in isolation. Most complex projects require a multidisciplinary team. For example, the construction of a building requires close collaboration between planners, architects, and engineers as well as the client, the local jurisdictions, and users of this environment, as well as — of course — the construction contractor. Even projects done individually must relate to some audience, client, constituency, or other parties to be effective. Consequently, you need to be able to recognize how to relate to the creative thinking skills others use as well. This will help you learn to use electronic media more effectively for communication and collaboration.

Examine the media, models, and methods your consultants, clients, audience, or constituencies deal with. Can you work together in shared media space? Can you set up communications electronically? Can you promote better collaboration using shared models? How do their methods relate to yours? Use this approach to determine how you might better integrate the knowledge base of several different disciplines or parties involved in a multidisciplinary project.

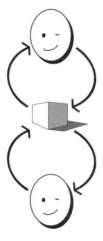

Shared Model

3. Develop Multidisciplinary Approaches

Multidisciplinary projects need careful coordination. When an orchestra warms up, there is no conductor and no score. Consequently, we hear no music (although it is important for an orchestra to warm up before it can play music). Similarly, after a team warms up there has to be coordinated efforts, or a game plan, if the team is going to be successful. We have all seen projects where chaos prevails, communication breaks down, and collaboration is impossible. Creative energy becomes dissipated, and little progress results from the effort. We need to find ways to orchestrate our efforts if we are to use the instruments we have at our disposal in harmonious ways to achieve shared objectives.

Develop a strategy for managing a multidisciplinary project using the nine-step approach presented in Chapter 6. Think through how you approach media, models, and methods. Go through the following steps as a multidisciplinary team:

Media — for transferring information
1. Relate electronic media to your goals.
2. Map your media space.
3. Diagram information and data flow.

Models — for the realities involved
4. Identify realities you are working with.
5. Develop models of reality.
6. Mock up your presentation.

Methods — for thought processes
7. Define your project.
8. Diagram your work flow.
9. Manage your progress.

Can you use electronic media to share information, to collaborate using common models of reality, and to coordinate your efforts when working toward shared objectives?

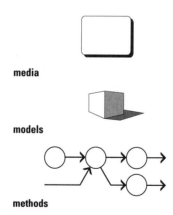

media

models

methods

8

Applications — Tools and Toys

This chapter explores the meaning of tools and toys and provides approaches for learning to use them. It explores a broad range of computer applications relating to the different channels of perception and expression. It also examines how these tools relate to each stage of the design process. To work with multimedia, using computers creatively, you need to know how to use tools for each channel. You also need to know how to relate these tools to different stages of the creative process. In addition, you will want to learn to integrate different channels as you move through the creative process in multimedia. Once you are comfortable doing this, you will find trying out new tools and toys to be a very pleasurable experience. It is like taking a new car for a spin and not getting lost. The activities at the end of the chapter will help you explore, practice, and plan how you use tools and toys.

What Are Your Favorite Tools and Toys?

You probably have a favorite computer, and on that computer you probably have some favorite software — maybe even some games. You find them to be your favorite probably because you know how to use them. Computers and software continue to evolve rapidly, and you may have the opportunity to upgrade your hardware and software. Or you may simply find you can learn to do more with what you already have. Consequently, what are presently your favorite tools may not be your favorite next year. Nevertheless you can build upon your understanding of how to work with electronic media and transfer much of this to the new workstations or applications you learn to use. This can help you learn more easily and quickly.

The Meaning of Tools and Toys

tool An object that helps the user to work. Used to optimize efficiency where cost-effective.

toy An object that enables the user to play. Used for pleasure and self development.

It is sometimes said that the only difference between adults and children is their toys. Adults' toys tend to be more expensive. But we also need to ask ourselves what is the difference between tools and toys. We use *tools* for work when they are cost-effective. Tools help us do different tasks and optimize our efficiency. We use *toys* for play when they provide pleasure and self development. Toys enable us to relate to challenges and help us perform. So the basic difference between tools and toys is the type of experience they provide.

Toys   **Tools**

A good way to learn to use tools, therefore, is to first play with them. Treat them as toys. Try out tools playfully and address challenges you find pleasurable. Then, when you apply tools to work, not only will you find using them more enjoyable, but you will also find you can be more productive. Although it may seem hard to justify playing within the context of most productive organizations, an important part of user training is giving people the opportunity to play with the tools. This helps people begin to relate to the tools in more pleasurable ways, and, as well, it helps them explore their own potential.

Most of us marvel at how quickly children learn to use computers. Probably the biggest difference between how children and adults learn is attitude. Children usually play with computers as if they were toys. They approach computers simply for the sake of having fun. Adults usually approach computers in a more pragmatic way. They frequently limit themselves to learning only applications they have to work with. Yet some older, retired people learn to use computers very quickly because they play with them.

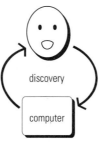 

Discovery Method   **Strategy Method**

Offices that encourage employees to play with computers set up a learning environment that actually can become very productive. Obviously, playing computer games and experimenting with a wide range of new applications during prime time can be counterproductive. But giving employees access to computers so they can play before work, during lunch, or after work can be very stimulating. Better yet, providing employees with new computer applications they can take home to play with on their own is beneficial to both the employee and the organization. I have noticed, among my own students and employees, that those who play with computers at home are remarkably more productive than those who only work with computers at school or in the office.

Many educators recognize there are different approaches to learning. One approach is the "discovery method," which encourages the student to explore. Another approach is the "strategy method," which provides guidelines or procedures.

When learning software applications, it is useful to alternate between the discovery and strategy methods. For example, while you are curious about a new application, you should explore it and see what you discover. Simply enter the program and try out menu options. Context-sensitive help commands can provide answers to some questions, but you will probably learn most by just seeing how the program works. Time can pass quickly. Before you know it, you may develop a good sense of what you can do with the program. Or you may find yourself getting bogged down with questions you can't discover the answer to. Then it is helpful to change approaches and shift to a strategy method by using a tutorial, or user guide. Typically, tutorials and user guides take you through a strategy, or pedagogical sequence. This involves a series of steps usually focused on a examples. You will find this guidance can help you avoid mistakes and keep you from getting bogged down.

Reading in the manual and working through some case studies, you can quickly find out what is difficult to discover on your own. Manuals are more meaningful after you have a chance to play and discover what the program is like. And after reading in the manual, you usually feel ready to jump into the program again and explore how you can use it for you own applications. At my office, or in my classroom, I often find that when we get stuck on some computer application problem, we will naturally try to find solutions using both modes of learning. One person will usually sit at the computer and explore options. Another person will grab the manual and search for a strategy or procedure that would be helpful. We can usually sort out a solution rather quickly that way. If that fails, however, it is nice to be able to call for technical support or get help online.

Using the discovery method, you work up from concrete experiences. Using the strategy method, you work down from abstract goals and principles. Alternate between the discovery method and strategy method when learning creative thinking skills as well as when learning to use tools and toys. You will find you can learn to use multimedia computer applications to enhance perception, visualization, and expression. The following section briefly describes what you can do using multimedia computer applications. Obviously, you will need to learn to use the appropriate hardware and software to be able to do it.

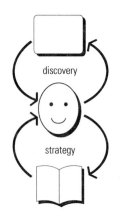

Combined Methods

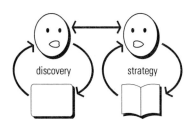

Sharing

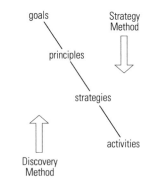

Contrasting Discovery and Strategy Methods

Multimedia Tools and Toys

Multimedia computing involves working with two or more channels of expression. Each channel has tools associated with it. For example, you use a microphone to record verbal expression, a keyboard for written expression, and a digitizer for graphic expression. You naturally gravitate to tools that deal with channels that interest you. However, you can also learn to use tools that open other channels of expression. Doing this provides more possibilities for multimedia expression. Working with a wider bandwidth of expression can involve different modes of thought. It can enable you to express richer multimedia messages regardless of your discipline.

The chart at the left shows channels of expression that are emerging with multimedia computing. Each of these channels requires different application software. Multimedia software are now beginning to emerge and integrate different channels.

To work with text, you would use a simple text editor or a word processor, entering words with a keyboard. Or perhaps you might use a pen computer that recognizes your lettering or handwriting. You can also scan written documents taken from printouts and use OCR (optical character recognition) to convert scanned letters into ASCII characters. Using online services and E-mail, you can pick up digital files directly from other sources. Using a FAX/modem, you can send text you generate in a computer directly to FAX machines anywhere in the world. You can also receive FAX transmissions and convert them to text files using OCR. Word processing software often uses its own format for saving files, fonts, and printer commands; however, most programs can now convert from one word processing format to another. You can enter numbers into a computer using a numeric key pad. You typically manipulate numbers using spreadsheets. You can also use programming languages to work with quantitative expressions. Databases enable you to manipulate both text and quantitative data. They are often integrated with spreadsheets. You can electronically transfer database files from one format to another, provided you have the appropriate program for making the transfer.

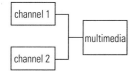

Multimedia - working with two or more channels

text
words
numbers
data

2-D graphics
drafting (vector graphics)
painting (raster graphics)

3-D modelling
wire-frame
shaded surface
solid modelling

imaging
image enhancement
rendering
holograms

animation
2-D sequences
3-D manipulation

video
still-video
full-motion

audio
voice
music
sound effects

**Electronic Multimedia
Channels of Expression**

You can digitize graphic information using a mouse, a digitizing tablet, or a pen computer. You can also scan images into digital formats. A FAX transmission is already a scanned image in a digital format which you can convert to work with using graphic programs. Scanned images usually start in raster graphic formats which may also include shades of gray or color. You can work with two-dimensional graphic images using paint programs, which are raster-based, or drafting programs, which are vector-based. Raster-based programs simply address pixels on the screen which are turned either on or off to create an image. Vector-based programs define coordinates of points on the lines which define the geometries shown on the computer screen. The advantage of raster graphics is that it can more easily handle textures and tones—like those you can generate with an "electronic spray can" you find in paint programs. The advantage of vector graphics is that you can scale images, enlarging or reducing them without losing resolution. You can also plot drawings without the "jaggies" (or *aliasing*) associated with raster graphics. Raster programs have evolved many file formats; however, filters now permit transfers between most raster graphic programs. There are also different file formats for vector graphics, although standards such as DXF and IGES permit transfers between most vector graphic programs. You can convert vector graphics into a raster image by capturing an image on a screen. A raster file can also be vectorized using auto-trace routines available in some graphic software packages. Some computer graphic programs now integrate raster and vector graphics, drawing upon the advantages of each. Formats such as EPS (encapsulated postscript) can transfer these files to laser printers and printing presses.

You can enter three-dimensional coordinates using keyboards with parametric routines to generate models. You can also build three-dimensional electronic models by entering x, y, and z coordinates using a digitizer. If you use a mouse or digitizing tablet, you need to establish different viewing planes related to our coordinate system. For example, you may draw in an x,y plane and add z coordinates. You could also draw in an x,z plane, or even an oblique plane, to define the three-dimensional surfaces you are working with. Some three-dimensional digitizers are now available. Three-dimensional surfaces can also be digitized using photogrammetry. For example, topography is commonly digitized from stereo pairs of photographs taken from an airplane. There are even some three-dimensional scanning devices that use sound or light waves to detect the form of objects and digitize them with three-dimensional coordinates. Using a CADD program, you can express three-dimensional digital information as a wire-frame model that you can view and print out with (or without) hidden lines removed. You can also create shaded models by filling in surfaces to obscure what is behind them. With shaded models you can also trace rays of light to cast shadows on surfaces from different light sources. Solid models actually define the volumes and not just the edges

aliasing Assuming the characteristics of a computer generated line. Associated with raster graphics where dots form lines by reducing "jaggies," or a steplike appearance.

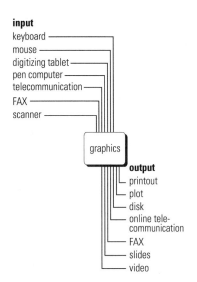

input
keyboard
pen computer
telecommunication
scanner
FAX
OCR
text

output
printout
online telecommunication
disk
FAX

Digital Text

input
keyboard
mouse
digitizing tablet
pen computer
telecommunication
FAX
scanner
graphics

output
printout
plot
disk
online telecommunication
FAX
slides
video

Digital Graphic

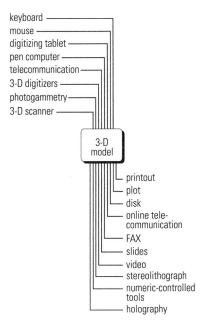

keyboard
mouse
digitizing tablet
pen computer
telecommunication
3-D digitizers
photogammetry
3-D scanner

3-D
model

└ printout
└ plot
└ disk
└ online tele-
  communication
└ FAX
└ slides
└ video
└ stereolithograph
└ numeric-controlled
  tools
└ holography

3-D Modelling

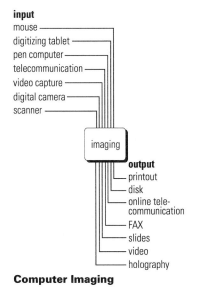

input
mouse
digitizing tablet
pen computer
telecommunication
video capture
digital camera
scanner

imaging

output
└ printout
└ disk
└ online tele-
  communication
└ FAX
└ slides
└ video
└ holography

Computer Imaging

or surfaces you are working with. This can help you understand how different volumes will connect to each other. Three-dimensional models are vector-based; however, views of a model can be captured as raster images for presentation as a two-dimensional graphic. Most CADD and GIS programs also permit you to attach attributes to the objects you are working with. In this way you can create "smart drawings" that have defined geometries integrated with databases.

You can take electronic images by using digital cameras, or by capturing them from video, or by scanning them from photographs. Once you have an image in a digital format, you can enhance it by manipulating contrast and color. This is often helpful for scientific visualization or the interpretation of aerial photography. This also provides artists a new medium for expression. You can even take a video image and render with it. You can render a view taken of a three-dimensional model and create a very realistic image, including textures and tones captured from real materials and even reflections and shadows. You can take an image of a context and place into it an image you generate using computer modeling (viewed from the same vantage point) to show what a model would look like in "reality." You can even render in three dimensions by painting on the surfaces of three-dimensional computer models.

Electronic media enable you to work with animation. You can create a series of frames or cells using two-dimensional graphics programs and then record the frames in sequence to create animation. Some computer animation programs use the traditional "onionskin" metaphor and enable you to draw over a series of images to create smooth-flowing characters. Other animation programs enable you to build three-dimensional models and manipulate them to create movement or spatial sequences. Animation software can help fill in the in-between frames (tweening) as well as create transformations of form, color, and texture. Typically, you would work first with a drawing module to outline the forms. Then you would use a painting module to fill in color. You can preview animated sequences by flipping through the images. You can also coordinate sound tracks with the animated sequences and transfer them to videotape for presentation.

The videotapes used in a VCR are in an analog format that combines a red-green-blue signal such as that received by a television. Computers are becoming sophisticated controllers for analog TV, enabling you to integrate full motion into other computer applications. But possibly more significant is what occurs when the TV image is converted to a digital format that you can manipulate using a computer. Now you have access to a vast array of tools for working with video images enabling you to do desktop video production with a computer workstation. As high-definition television (HDTV) emerges, the resolution of video images is

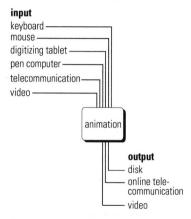

input
keyboard
mouse
digitizing tablet
pen computer
telecommunication
video

animation

output
disk
online tele-
communication
video

Computer Animation

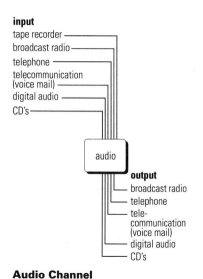

input
tape recorder
broadcast radio
telephone
telecommunication
(voice mail)
digital audio
CD's

audio

output
broadcast radio
telephone
tele-
communication
(voice mail)
digital audio
CD's

Audio Channel

improving. Although electronic images do not approach photographic quality, they are achieving resolution acceptable for publication and presentation. You can work with digital TV by capturing and manipulating single images as still video. You can also record and manipulate full motion digitally, although it is necessary to use data compression to keep these files at a workable size. Interactive video enables you to transmit video images in real time, creating the opportunity to set up telecommunication conferences that use live video.

Computers also enable you to work with sound. You can record and integrate voice messages into E-mail and other applications, making them an extension of the way you use the telephone. Voice recognition is also emerging. This enables you to use voice commands that a computer responds to. Computers can also read written text using synthesized sounds. Researchers are working on getting computers to capture verbal statements and convert them to text files. Having a computer be able to take dictation would represent a real breakthrough in working with electronic media. You can also use computers to capture and create music. MIDI (musical instrument digital interface) keyboards enable you to play music and transfer it to a computer. There you can manipulate tone and tempo and add other channels of sound to a musical composition. You can capture these additional channels by making recordings of other instruments. Using a computer, you can even generate synthesized sounds, ranging from those of traditional instruments to electronic music and sound effects. You can also integrate these effects into your musical compositions. Music programs enable you to transfer compositions you play into written music. They can also read music and play it back. Using multimedia software, you can integrate sound tracks into videos or other presentations.

Integrated Tools

Multimedia software provides tools to integrate channels of expression. For a long time (relatively speaking in the rapidly changing world of software applications) text-based programs have been available that integrate word processing, spreadsheets, and databases. There are also programs that integrate databases, spreadsheets and business graphics, combining both text and graphic channels. Many word processors now integrate graphics and may even include a simple graphics editor. Desktop publishing programs allow even more elaborate formatting, enabling you to work with both text and graphic files from many different sources. E-mail is beginning to integrate both text and graphics as well as voice messages. Graphic programs, of course, can handle text, enabling you to

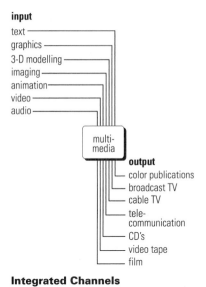

input

text
graphics
3-D modelling
imaging
animation
video
audio

multi-media

output
color publications
broadcast TV
cable TV
tele-communication
CD's
video tape
film

Integrated Channels

lay out pages or posters. CADD programs provide both two-dimensional drafting and three-dimensional modeling capabilities. Many CADD programs and GIS programs enable you to relate databases to graphic attributes for analysis and evaluation. Imaging programs accept graphics from many different sources so you can render the images. They also enable you to capture images from video. Animation programs, of course, contain graphic generators and have imaging capabilities. Desktop video enables you to take text, graphics, imaging, and animation, and combine them with live video and even sound. Music programs enable you to generate rich channels of sound that you can integrate with video. And these tools and toys continue to evolve.

Multimedia capabilities are emerging in many different manners. Computers provide the tools to work with electronic media using each channel. It is important to learn how to use these tools effectively to give expression to ideas and information by integrating different channels. To do this you need to think through how you use tools related to each channel of expression at each stage of the creative process.

Tools for Each Stage of the Design Process

You use tools differently at each stage of the creative process. No matter what computer environment you are using, or what discipline you are working with, you need to recognize how to use the tools you have appropriately. I have often seen people waste time, or even become defeated, because they were using tools inappropriately. The sometimes senseless debates over which is the better tool will frequently fail to recognize that some tools may be more appropriate for one stage of the creative process than for another. There is more to creatively using information than just accessing it and presenting it. For example, during the research and analysis stages of writing you only need a quick text editor to capture key ideas and information, generate outlines, and access many different files simultaneously. During the synthesis stage it helps to be able to move around a document quickly as you work with it, using search routines and markers. It is nice to have a thesaurus you can access instantaneously. During the evaluative stage you need to have quick access to a spell checker and possibly even a grammar checker. To put your document into a final format, you need to have the appropriate fonts and page layout capabilities so you can see "what you get" to accomplish what you are trying to do. I sometimes see people lost in formatting and layout, before they have done any real thinking or writing. Or, conversely, I will see people trying to do elaborate page layouts using primitive word processors. When doing my own writing, I find it easier to work with a small notebook computer using a quick character-based word processor when doing research, analyzing information, and drafting the first synthesis before transferring files to publishing software in the later stages to deal with fonts and formatting.

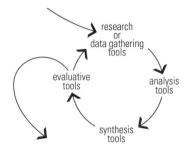

research
or
data gathering
tools

evaluative
tools

analysis
tools

synthesis
tools

**Tools for Each Stage
of the Design Process**

Of course, you need to go through many iterations of the creative process using different tools appropriately. The next section examines each stage of the creative process and shows how you would use different tools to work with each channel of expression.

Research Tools

When gathering information you need tools that help you quickly get your information into digital formats you can work with. Many research instruments now record information digitally in formats you can pick up directly with a computer. When working with text, it is helpful if you can access information online already in digital file formats you can use. Otherwise you have to enter the data by hand. Data collection may be easiest and most accurate if you can record it at the source. For example, take notes during a discussion or while you are reading. Or gather information during key transactions such as sales. Small portable computers enable you to gather information more directly. Using them effectively helps you avoid having to take field notes on paper. Although pencil and paper can be very comfortable and convenient, at some point you have to transfer your information to a digital format if you are going to work with it using a computer. The sooner you do this, the quicker and more accurate you can be. With a palm-top, pen, or lightweight notebook computer you can easily enter text during a meeting, or at a library, or even in the field.

When working with graphics, it is also helpful to use basemaps that are already in digital formats. These may be photogrammetrically derived from aerial surveys. There are also growing symbol libraries you can use that provide extensive graphic vocabularies for different disciplines. You may also scan images from existing drawings and either work with them in raster graphic formats or convert them to vector drawings. Hand digitizing from existing paper drawings can create digital files that integrate information taken from many different graphic sources. Pen computers are making it easier to work with graphics in the field. For example, using a small, but powerful, pen computer, you can take a digital basemap and field-check it. You can also do this with a notebook computer and a mouse. You can correct the digital base right on the spot and then transfer this file to more powerful workstations with full featured CADD or GIS software for analysis and synthesis. Of course, you can also mark up a printout when working in the field, but it takes time to plot and then transfer information back to the graphic file. Also, large basemaps are not always easy to work with in the field. Field notes on basemaps are not always very accurate representations. Sometimes you don't realize there are discrepancies or information is missing until you are drafting the drawing. It can be easier to work out a digital graphic representation in the field when you are relating directly to the reality you are working with.

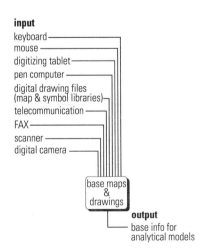

input
keyboards
numeric key pads
pen computers
research instruments
telecommunication
code scanners
cash registers

database
model

output
base info for
analytic models

Data Gathering

input
keyboard
mouse
digitizing tablet
pen computer
digital drawing files
(map & symbol libraries)
telecommunication
FAX
scanner
digital camera

base maps
&
drawings

output
base info for
analytical models

Graphic Information Gathering

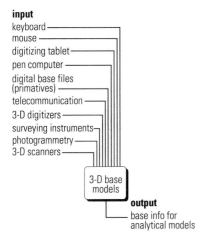

3-D Data Gathering

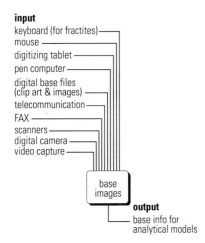

Image Gathering

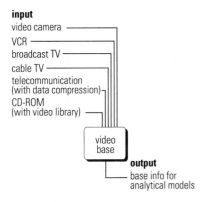

Video Gathering

Also, when working with three-dimensional models, it is nice to have the context in a digital format. For example, digital terrain models are available from aerial surveys. There are also instruments that can create digital three-dimensional models of existing objects. Symbols libraries are emerging which provide shapes and forms useful to different disciplines. Beyond that you can do field measurements. Some surveying instruments will record digital information that can be uploaded to a computer — even over phone lines. Or you can enter the data into computers by hand using a keyboard, mouse, or digitizing tablet. Notebook computers can be powerful enough to handle CADD programs, especially when you are beginning three-dimensional wire-frame models that are useful for blocking out existing spaces and forms. You can upload these models to more powerful computers once you have compiled more information, making them complex. Then you can work with shading and with solid models.

You can capture images using digital cameras and transfer the file to a computer on disk or through a port. You can also use a video camera in the field and then capture digital images you select using a computer graphics board that accepts video input and can capture frames. Taking photos in the field and then scanning them provides higher-resolution images. You can also gather a library of colors, textures, and materials in this way which you can use for rendering images. Of course, you can also sketch in the field using a pen computer or even a portable notebook computer with a mouse (although sketching with a mouse is rather clumsy).

You can use video to capture movement that becomes the base for developing animated sequences. For example, the Sports Science Division of the U.S. Olympic Committee uses video to capture performances of Olympic athletes. With computers, sports scientists can draw lines over moving video images to reveal the alignment of the body throughout movement patterns. They can closely examine the angles of the arms, legs, and torso of a figure skater during a jump. This information is helpful in teaching athletes how to match the "signatures" of winning movements. You can also record key frames using film that you can scan electronically. Animation programs can carry out the tweening or the metamorphoses (such as in *Terminator 2*). Libraries of flicks are emerging that provide segments and transitions which can become part of an animation repertoire.

Video cameras provide a relatively easy way to gather all types of information. There are almost endless possibilities for positioning cameras on different types of platforms—from outer space to deep beneath the sea. Often, video cameras can go where you cannot—thereby extending your perception. Taking good video images requires all the art and craft once associated with photography. Now that video is being integrated with computers, a tremendous range of new possibilities emerges because of the ways in which you can work with these images. Once we have analog video images on tape, we can edit the sequences using a computer as the

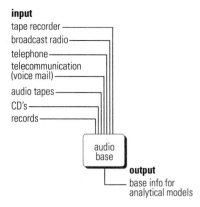

input
tape recorder
broadcast radio
telephone
telecommunication
(voice mail)
audio tapes
CD's
records

audio
base

output
base info for
analytical models

Audio Gathering

controller. To do this successfully, however, you need to start with good video images and work with tools that can maintain the quality of the images as you manipulate them. Converting the analog signal to a digital format enables you to manipulate video images more freely without the degradation that occurs when you copy analog videotapes. For example, you can capture single frames to manipulate still video digitally. With data compression, it is now becoming possible to work with full-motion digital video using computers.

Today, you can access vast libraries of recorded music and sounds. You can also make your own recordings of sounds using microphones. Fidelity is a fine art, although the tools available make high fidelity of stereophonic sound more attainable and affordable. It is relatively easy to transfer between digital and analog formats for sound recordings. In addition, you can make your own music on a keyboard and transfer it to a computer using a MIDI connection. You can even generate synthesized music and sound effects.

Analysis Tools

You can work with many different types of analytical models using multimedia computing. These representations can relate to each channel of expression. Here is an overview of how you can use these analytical tools.

When writing, it is helpful to list keywords. You can arrange lists of words according to priorities, topics, sequences, and so forth. Word processing programs not only give you a way of recording and storing lists; they enable you to search, rearrange, and add to them easily. Lists are very familiar and simple analytical models. You can expand lists into an agenda for a meeting or into a working outline for a letter or draft document. Outlines provide a topical framework to which you can add information. You can also build more dynamic frameworks using database programs. A database model contains files with information related to selected attributes. For example, card catalogs are database models of library collections you can access online using modems. They enable you to find references related to subject, author, title, etc. The French have a national catalog of art called *Mistral* (after the famous French wind). Accessing this electronic catalog by using a small computer and modem, art historians can quickly locate and analyze background information on significant paintings done in France. You can also build simple database models of your own. For example, you may keep names, mailing addresses, phone numbers, FAX numbers, and E-mail addresses as well as professions of people you wish to stay in contact with. Databases enable you to look up this information in different ways and even merge it with the correspondence you write. You can also manipulate quantitative information in databases or spreadsheet models. In fact, you can build quantitative models that help you analyze situations. For example,

keywords
lists
priority
topical
sequencial
working outline
agendas
databases
catalogs
spreadsheets
budget

Analytical Models for Text

business graphics
graphs
charts
diagrams
functional
spacial
temporal (flow)
orthographic drawings
plans
sections
elevations
locational databases
maps
layers
attributes
composites
suitability models
sensitivity models

Analytical Models for Graphics

you can use a spreadsheet model to set up a simple budget. Typically, the kind of budget most people work with is a financial budget, but you can also work with energy budgets, water budgets, or models of any other relationships you can represent quantitatively. This can help you better understand the realities you are dealing with. You can also give visual expression to quantitative information. For example, spreadsheet programs integrate business graphics, enabling you to generate line graphs, bar graphs, pie charts, and even three-dimensional charts to help you visualize quantitative information.

Working with graphics, you can quickly develop diagrams that abstractly represent relationships. This book is full of this type of graphic, which help you analyze and understand thought processes and the relationship between mind and media. To analyze existing objects or contexts, you can also work with plans, sections, and elevations. Raster graphics convey images along with the subtleties of tones and textures. You can use raster graphics to study tone, color, texture, and form. Vector graphics describe the geometries involved. Consequently, you can use vector graphic drawings to derive very accurate measurements of distances, areas, perimeters, etc., which are helpful in analysis. You can also layer graphic information to build up very complex levels of detail which you can portray in different colors. You can analyze this information by turning different layers on or off. By turning on several layers of information you can see how they relate. Turning off layers enables you to simplify the image and examine particular information. Compositing layers of information can give you new understandings of what you are working with. You can also add layers that summarize your analysis. For example, you might add an overlay that you use for calculating area takeoffs. You can do this using a computer-aided design system by drawing a polygon around areas you are calculating electronically — even listing the result — in much the same way you can do area takeoffs on tracing paper over a basemap. Using geographic information systems, you can do even more elaborate analyses of mapped information as well as link maps to databases that contain attributes you can manipulate. Geographic information systems may be grid-based — like raster graphic programs. Or they may be polygon-based — like vector graphic programs. Using either approach, you can develop map overlays of information that you can composite for analysis. Grid-based programs tend to be quick but crude. Polygon-based programs can produce more accurate representations, but they require more powerful computers to manipulate the geometries.

Three-dimensional modeling enables you to analyze space and form. You can also analyze spatial sequences and movements of objects. Designers can do very effective form studies using simple wire-frame diagrams, although to convey them clearly to others, it is helpful to render images of the model. Archaeologists and art historians can reconstruct deteriorated or lost objects by modeling them in three dimensions using a computer. They can build these models with information they have. For example, the Italians have reconstructed the Stabian Baths in Pompeii,

209

3-D based models
wireframe
shaded
solid
analytical models
finite element analysis
ray tracing
digital terrain models
slope
aspect
elevation

Analytical 3-D Models

building three-dimensional computer models even of the parts that no longer exist today. This permits the archaeologists to portray and analyze what has been lost over time.

You can also link three-dimensional computer models to other analytical tools. For example, engineers use finite element analysis taking the geometries of a structure and calculating loads to size members. Ray tracing can help you understand how light will cast shadows. Architects, landscape architects, and engineers use this to study sun and shade patterns on model surfaces. This can be very helpful when designing buildings and landscapes as well as space platforms. Graphic artists study how light and shadow will affect a computer graphic image. Solid models help you analyze how you can combine forms. You can also use solid models to analyze volumes, surface areas, and other attributes such as the center of gravity. This analysis can be useful when optimizing designs. Scientists can use solid models to visualize relationships of objects they normally cannot see because the object may be microscopic or in outer space. Surgeons can use a similar analysis to visualize delicate operations.

Imaging can also be an analytical tool. Enhancing texture, tones, and color can aid in interpreting and analyzing images. Art historians do this to reconstruct works of art without using "invasive methods" that may damage the original. For example, at the Uffizi in Florence, the Italian National Research Council is exploring "electronic restoration" to reconstruct images of the original appearance and colors of paintings and frescoes. Imaging can also be used to render studies of objects. You can paint photorealistic images on surfaces. For example, you can paint realistic textures, tones, and colors of actual building materials on images of buildings. You can even drape air photos over landforms. Scientists use electronic imaging for scientific visualization, enabling them to see what cannot normally be perceived with the naked eye. Medical doctors use electronic imaging to help interpret images taken of the human body when doing research or diagnosing diseases.

imaging base models
black & white
shades of grey
color
scientific visualization
image restoration
image enhancement
image interpretation

Analytical Imaging Models

As mentioned before, the movement of Olympic athletes can be captured using animation derived from video or film taken of their performance. Sports scientists and athletes can analyze these movements to learn optimal patterns that enhance athletic performance. Animation is also sometimes used to reconstruct events related to accidents. This is useful in courtroom testimonies to determine the cause of an accident.

scenes
positions
sequencing
tweening
transformations

Analytical Animation Models

Videotapes enable you to compile massive amounts of information. You can view and analyze analog video by accessing it interactively using CD-ROM. Using digital video, you can capture and enhance frames to examine still video more closely. Using digital video, you can analyze motion, even changing space and time. Video is becoming the medium for presenting many of the analytical models already discussed. You can present text, graphics, three-dimensional models, images, and animation all using video.

analog video tapes
digital video models
still-video
full-motion

Analytical Video Models

Similarly, using audiotapes, you can also compile massive amounts of verbal information as well as musical performances. You can now quickly access analog audio using computers to search and sort information for analysis. Using digital audio, you can analyze the quality of voices, musical instruments, and other sounds. Digital audio is useful for both artistic and scientific purposes. For example, it can help performing artists develop richer timbres, or it can even synthesize new sounds for muscial instruments. Digital audio can help engineers analyze the signatures of sounds to understand their sources, making it possible to reduce noise in motor vehicles.

analog audio tapes
digital sound
restoration
enhancement
interpretation

Analytical Audio Models

Synthesis Tools

Computers have also become marvelous tools for synthesis enabling you to work with many different channels of expression. This can help you manipulate information and reveal your insights and inspirations. The models you synthesize may represent new realities. You can develop these visions with multimedia splendor and produce books and reports, graphic designs and computer art, building and landscape plans, as well as product designs. You can also create computer generated three-dimensional models, images, animation, and video for education and entertainment. Here is an overview of how you can use computer-aided synthesis tools.

Word processing is probably the most familiar tool for synthesis using computers. You can work with deductive modes of thought by taking outlines and expanding them into draft documents. Or you can write with more inductive modes of thought by expressing ideas as they flow in a stream of consciousness and capturing them in words using a keyboard or pen. Or you may tape-record thoughts you express verbally and transcribe them to a text file. The copy, cut, and paste commands resident in word processors enable you to manipulate documents quickly as you develop them. Word processors help you revise and refine documents more easily than you could if you had to redraft a handwritten or typed document. Search routines enable you to navigate around digital documents by finding keywords. You can also select fonts and format your documents in ways that enhance the clarity of your message. You can send these digital files electronically to other computers and FAX machines. You can also transfer the working models you develop digitally, using desktop publishing software, to laser printers and even printing presses. Similarly, you can work with spreadsheets and databases to manipulate information, exploring "what-ifs" and "why-nots" to create new possibilities.

expanded outlines
draft
transcriptions
mock-ups
databases
spreadsheets

Synthesis Models for Text

In a similar way that word processing programs enable you to express yourself in writing, computer graphics programs enable you to express what you visualize graphically. You may use more deductive modes of thought working with defined geometries or graphic formats. Or you can also work more inductively by sketching or painting from your perception or insight. Computer graphic tools are becoming more portable, more refined, and easier to use, making it possible to work very interactively — even in the field. Digitizing styluses and pens are now becoming touch-sensitive, enabling the user to have more control over their graphic expression. You can also work with scanned images of sketches you may make with pencil or pen, or possibly incorporate images from other sources. Possibly the greatest advantage of working with computer graphics is being able to develop drawings by using powerful edit commands such as *copy*, *mirror*, *rotate*, *scale*, *extend*, *trim*, *erase*, *fill*, etc. You can even manipulate graphics by manipulating parameters. Once you master the tools, you can more easily develop a drawing by using computer graphics than by drafting and redrafting it by hand. You can modify drawings without a sign of erasure. You can also create many versions of the same drawing by copying or sharing the base. You can navigate around drawings using pan and zoom commands. This enables you to zoom in and work with small details or zoom out to gain an overview. You can also work with multiple views simultaneously by having several windows on your screen. You can add various fonts, line weights, textures, and tones to drawings to enhance their legibility. Binary file transfers enable you to send graphic files to other computers where you can work with these drawings using the same, or compatible, software on a computer graphic station. You can transfer raster graphic images to FAX machines. You can also transfer your digital files to color film using a slide generator, or project digital images using a video projector. Of course, you can also laser-print and plot drawings. In addition, you can even create digital files with color separations to produce color graphics with a printing press.

Using three-dimensional modeling programs, you can construct objects and define space. Again, you can work deductively by building on a framework. Or you can take pieces and inductively explore ways of assembling them. Simple wire-frame models can enhance your capabilities to visualize in three dimensions. Shaded models help you work with surfaces, and solid models help you work with volumes. You can use simple three-dimensional models to explore artificial realities that are too complex to visualize entirely in your mind. You can share some of what you experience by capturing views of the three-dimensional model, rendering and transferring the image to film or paper for presentation. It is also possible to create physical three-dimensional models or mock-ups using stereolithography and other technologies. In addition, you can also create walk-throughs or fly-throughs, transferring these sequences to videotape so they can be viewed with a VCR. It is also becoming possible to invite the viewer into a virtual reality constructed in a three-dimensional model that the viewer can enter and experience using stereo viewing goggles and navigating devices such as data gloves or bodysuits.

Imaging provides new opportunities for creative expression. You can capture images of existing contexts and work more deductively to

sketches
diagrams
functional
spacial
temporal (flow)
orthographic drawings
plans
sections
elevations
projections
locational models

Synthesis Models for Graphics

3-D based models
wire-frame
shaded
solid
representations
views
stereolithography
prototyping

Synthesis Models for 3-D

modify, enhance, or abstract them. Or you can take the vast array of color, texture, and form you can generate using imaging programs and work inductively to create new images. Computer graphic artists are now painting on three-dimensional surfaces in virtual reality. Delineators are creating images with photorealism. Using computer peripherals, they can transfer their work to paper or film. Viewers can also experience computer-generated images electronically by using video or by viewing the image directly with a computer. You can see computer-generated images every day in newspapers, in magazines, in movies, and on television, as well as on computer monitors.

Computers do not limit you to creating static images. You can create dynamic movement as well as subtle gestures through animation. Animation artists can draw two-dimensional animation in much the same way they approached animation drawing on onionskin paper or cells of film. They create a progression of computer images that, when viewed in rapid sequence, provide the experience of movement. They work both deductively — thinking through the movements from starting to ending positions — and inductively — giving subtle expressions, or "life," to the characters. Animation artists can also work with three-dimensional animation using computers. This approach is more like claymation where the animators construct models they can manipulate. After building the model, they need to develop visual sequences that involve manipulating the model or moving through it. This process can involve deductive modes of thought that are necessary to work out the progressions of movement. It can also involve inductive modes of thought when the animator explores new compositions and expressions using the computer-generated model. Computers can assist the animation artist by making it easier to copy repetitive elements and providing tweening and many types of transformation routines. They also can help the artist keep track of the massive number of frames that must stay in sequence. Animation programs help transfer computer animation to video for presentation.

Still another approach to animation is setting in motion computer algorithms that can generate computer graphic images. There is now software that enables you to manipulate the parameters and algorithms that generate fractile images. For example, "Chaos: The Software" enables the user to work with Mandelbrot sets, which are programmable representations of chaos theory. These dynamic graphic engines can present fascinating animated images. Similar engines can also generate sound. In fact it is entirely possible to create multimedia engines that can set computer animation in motion. Rudy Rucker and John Walker at AutoDesk are experimenting with *cellular automata* — generating cells that possess programmable characteristics.

Computer programs can model *anastrophic* changes, or the coming together of disparate elements to form a coherent and connected whole. In effect, computer programs are coming to life when these processes are set in motion. Scientists, such as Dr. Stuart Kauffman of the Santa Fe

---

painting
two-dimensional
three-dimensional
Imaging
abstract
photorealistic

Synthesis Models for Imaging

two-dimensional animation
three-dimensional animation
parametric models
fractiles
cellular automate
robotics

Synthesis Models for Animation

cellular automata Computer programs enabling objects to carry out functions. Empower information objects to begin to take on a life of their own.

anastrophe A change involving the coming together of disparate elements to form a coherent and connected whole. The opposite of catastrophe.

Institute, are building computer models of complex networks which, in effect, simulate life processes. Planners and landscape architects also have to deal with dynamic systems in order to understand how ecosystems function and anticipate how plants will grow so they can work successfully with natural processes and living plant and animal communities.

Life is a very pervasive archetype that people are now beginning to replicate not only through cellular automata and dynamic computer models, but also through robotics. For example, Rodney Brooks and his students at MIT are creating small robots that begin to take on lives of their own. Each robot is programmed to respond to different stimuli. At some point small robots, which you will be able to set in motion, may carry out useful functions.

Video is also an extraordinary synthesis tool. Creativity is involved in taping the images. The cameraperson needs to select the right vantage point and the right lighting and be able to pan and zoom effectively portraying the scene and activities. Computers now enable you to work with video images in ways that previously were only possible in expensive production studios. By simply working with analog video you can use computers to gain more control over selecting sequences. Working with digital video enables you to capture video images and work with still video using the approaches to imagining that I have already briefly described. You can also generate characters to superimpose text on video images as well as create transitions between segments of video. Full-motion digital video is also emerging. This enables you to work deductively, enhancing video images. You can also use inductive modes of thought to create special effects which are limited only by our imagination. You can deliver video productions using computers or video recorders or transfer them to film for viewing by large audiences.

analog video
taping
sequencing
digital video
mixing
transitioning
synthesizing
character generation

Synthesis Models for Video

Electronic sound offers still other amazing synthesis tools. Computers enable you to search and control analog sounds in ways that no tape recorder or stereo system can. Most exciting is what you can do with digital sound using computers. It is now possible to capture sounds from many different sources. These can be sounds you record; they can also be sounds of instruments with MIDI connections played by musicians. In addition, you can use computers to synthesize sounds. A computer can become a musical instrument in itself. With music programs, you can use computers to compose electronic music. You can transfer this music to written scores so musicians can play it on other instruments. You can also tape it directly from the computer so you can play it back using a tape deck or CD player. In addition you can integrate the sounds you compose into animation or video productions.

analog audio
taping
sequencing
digital audio
composing
mixing
transitioning
synthesizing

Synthesis Models for Audio

Evaluative Tools

A distinct advantage of working with electronic media is the array of evaluative tools which are emerging. These tools enable you to test and optimize what you create in virtual reality, making it less necessary to produce physical prototypes. In some situations, where it is not possible to build a prototype, evaluative tools provide ways of assessing impacts before you proceed with developmental actions. Good evaluative tools can reduce the cost of research and development by shortening the time it takes to get new ideas to an audience or to market. If used cleverly, evaluative models can more thoroughly test design ideas. You can work with many different types of evaluative models using multimedia computing. These representations enable you to test new possibilities related to each channel of expression. Here is an overview of how to use these evaluative tools.

Probably the most familiar evaluative tools are the spell checkers integrated in most word processors. They enable you to find and correct spelling errors. Grammar and style checkers can also provide helpful evaluations of your writing. For example, grammar checkers will bring grammatical and punctuation problems to your attention. They can also tell how long your document is and how frequently you are using certain words. In addition, these evaluative tools provide some measure of the reading level your audience needs in order to understand what you are writing. These evaluative tools can boost the confidence and credibility of creative spellers and writers. I refer to my grammar checker as my "heartless editor." Fortunately, I can review its comments in the privacy of my personal computer and make the corrections I find necessary, before sharing my writing with others who will, it is hoped, have a heart. There are also evaluative tools for spreadsheets which test formulas to make sure they are entered correctly. When working with written documents, a "what-you-see-is-what-you-get" environment also becomes an evaluative tool. Most word processing, spreadsheet, and database programs now enable you to preview documents before you print them out. In this way, you can evaluate the format and fonts and achieve what you want to see before you get it.

Like the programs used for working with text, good graphics programs also provide a "what-you-see-is-what-you-get" working environment. This enables you to work interactively — expressing and testing repeatedly — until you achieve the results you are looking for. Painting programs can help you evaluate colors. For example, you can electronically compare hue and density to help you precisely match color specifications. You can also layer graphic information to create composites that help us evaluate interferences. For example, in an architectural set of drawings you can check for conflicts between structural, mechanical, and plumbing systems by overlaying these drawings and evaluating them as if they were on a light table. Vector graphic programs enable you to make very accurate measurements and calculate areas of polygons using the coordi-

spelling checker
grammar checker
previews
layouts

Evaluative Models for Text

previews
layouts
composites
measurements
distances
areas
linked databases
bill of materials
budgets

Evaluative Models for Graphics

nates that are part of the drawing. You can relate this information to cost estimates, which are another evaluative tool. You can extract information from drawings and work with it in spreadsheets to create evaluative models such as cost estimates, energy budgets, and water budgets. Dynamically linking evaluative models to the drawings allows you to make changes to the drawings, and automatically update the evaluation.

Three-dimensional models help you to visualize forms and spaces. A three-dimensional model, in itself, can be a wonderful evaluative tool, enabling you to work interactively to refine the forms and spaces you are viewing in a computer until you achieve the results you are looking for. Surface models help you evaluate how surfaces interrelate and examine considerations like shading. Solid models help you evaluate how objects interrelate and examine attributes like center of gravity. There are also dynamic evaluative models you can use with three-dimensional models. For example, engineers can move a part through a full range of movement. They can also simulate crashes. Many other evaluative models can help optimize the performance of designs. For example, racing teams are using evaluative models to test the aerodynamics of cars for the Indianapolis 500 to quickly refine and optimize their designs. Sailboat racing teams are using similar programs to evaluate the efficiency of sailboat hull designs for the America's Cup race. You can use these types of evaluative tools to create simulations. Some simulations are passive, which enable you to only watch the effects. Of course, you can use what you learn to change the design later. Some simulations are becoming interactive, enabling you to modify and optimize the model of the design during the simulation.

Imaging enables you to express design ideas with photorealism. Most people relate more readily to realistic images than to abstract ones. A realistic image enables them to see objects that don't yet exist. For example, photorealistic images showing proposed buildings in context can be very useful evaluative tools for reviews by local jurisdictions. It is also a good way of getting market reaction to a product before building it. These crucial evaluations can provide critical feedback which helps determine the success of plans and designs.

You can use animation to provide an even more realistic experience by adding movement to your evaluative models. In this way you can examine all sides of an object — as if you were rotating it in your hands. You can check moving parts going through a range of movement. You can also move through spaces and experience what it would be like to be there and look in different directions. You can produce this animation by creating a series of views and saving them in a computer or transferring them to videotape. You can also experience movement by entering a three-dimensional model and moving around it. You can do this with stereo viewing devices and controls, such as a data glove, which enables you to navigate in this three-dimensional space. In effect, you can create a virtual reality that gives you the sensation of being there.

form visualization
forms
space
wireframe models
edges
surfaces models
planes
shades
solid models
shapes
volumes
massing
dynamic models
growth simulators
aerodynamics
fluid dynamics
thermo dynamics

Evaluative 3-D Models

photorealism
abstraction
interpretation

Evaluative Imaging Models

movements
deflections
viewing
walk-through
fly-through
virtual reality
experiences
mandellas

Evaluative Animation Models

You can use video to present almost any of the evaluative models already described. Transferring these models to videotape enables your audience to view them using simple VCRs. Consequently, you can reach a wide audience. You can even transmit analog video to television sets using air waves or cables. With data compression and fiber optics you will be able to transmit digital video via telephone lines. This has many potential applications. For example, installation details might be clearer in a video form. Consumers or workers could watch videos to learn how to assemble a product. This could make the transfer of information clearer and more certain. Customers could actually see how to assemble products they purchase in components. Construction workers would not have to know how to read abstract working drawings. In addition, architects and engineers can also use video as a medium for construction administration. Capturing video images during inspections provides a convenient medium for storing a visual as well as a narrative description of a project. This is a very useful tool for evaluating progress. It provides a rather inexpensive record. Architects and engineers can extract images from these videos and, using a computer, integrate them in construction reports. Construction reports evaluate progress and provide information to both the contractor and client to keep a project on track. Using digital video, you can capture frames to examine the still-video image more closely. Or you can change the speed of full-motion video to examine movements. We can even work with time-lapse images to evaluate change.

instruction
inspection
video models
still-video
full-motion
time lapse

Evaluative Video Models

Audio is not often thought of as an evaluative tool; however, we all make judgments about what we hear. Think of all you determine just from the tone of voice in a telephone conversation. Certainly a music connoisseur critically evaluates the quality of the performance and fidelity of a recording. With digital audio, you can examine the quality of sounds. For example, you can provide speakers, musicians, and other performers with graphic feedback showing the richness of the sounds they produce. This feedback can help musicians create more overtones to produce richer sounds.

audio recordings
sound sampling

Evaluative Audio Models

Using a Progression of Tools

To avoid wasting time and effort, you need to apply tools effectively and also work with them in appropriate progressions. People don't always do this. For example, when using a word processor, there is the tendency to format documents before spell-checking or editing them. Obviously, edits will throw off a format that you may labor over. (Although, it can be useful to mock up a document or final draft to get a sense of how it lays out.)

You need to develop clear progressions for using tools so your effort and information will flow in a effective sequence. You can do this by carefully selecting your medium, developing useful models, and clarifying

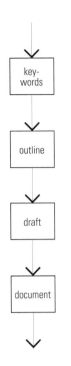

Producing Written Documents

your methods for working on your project. Two progressions are described below — one for producing written documents, which is probably already familiar to you, and then one for producing video, which is more complex.

When working with text in a computer you can find quick ways to gather information as well as capture keywords to express your insights. While this may involve simply taking mental notes, you can also take written notes in a small computer, or tape record keywords and statements. Once you have some information and insights to work with, you can find ways to organize your thoughts. Here, using a word processor to arrange lists, outline, and expand outlines is helpful. Then you need fluid ways of expressing your thoughts. One way is to dictate into a tape recorder and transcribe what you have recorded. Using a word processor you can edit while you transcribe — in effect making the transcription a second draft. Another way is to write with a word processor, getting your thoughts down and sorting them out as you work. Try to express ideas quickly with minimal distraction. Postpone serious testing of your ideas until you have given yourself a chance to express them. Then you can use evaluative tools, such as spell checkers or grammar checkers, productively. There is a tendency to use evaluative tools as a diversion, which can unfortunately distract you from your train of thought. Once you have the substance in order, then you can refine the format before you print out or transfer your document. You may want to transfer your file to desktop publishing software to produce your final document.

When working with video to make a multimedia production, you also need to find effective ways of gathering information, capturing images and sound as well as recording your insights. You can do this by taking mental notes, but also by working with a small portable computer, a tape recorder, video camera, or even film or digital cameras. Stephen Eiffert, who teaches a Padgett-Thompson workshop on video script writing, suggests you begin writing video with a mission statement — identifying your objectives, your audience, and the results you expect. You should then write a treatment which is a verbal and visual outline of what you have in mind. You can draft the mission statement and the treatment using a word processor. Once you have information, images, and insights to work with, you will need to develop a script. This may begin as a presentation script, describing each scene — video-audio, video-audio. You will need to develop your presentation script into a production script to provide the necessary direction. A storyboard can also help you visualize your production and coordinate how you will combine different channels of media. There is software for writing scripts. You can also develop your own template for script writing using a word processor. You can use graphic programs to develop storyboards, working with simple images you draw, photographic images you scan, or even video images you capture to describe each scene. You then need to work with different synthesis tools to develop your ideas in the various media you are working with. (This may be a team effort involving people with expertise in different

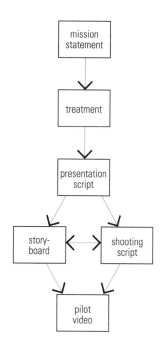

Producing Videos

media—graphics, animation, video, music, voice, acting, etc.) Once you have the components of your presentation developed, you will then want to integrate them. You can use your storyboards and production script to direct the effort on a set or in a well-equipped production studio if you are interested in a broadcast quality production. Multimedia software is emerging which has tools for doing storyboards and enables you to link your storyboards to files which contain the segments of your production. Using this software you can put your video production together right in a computer. You will want to evaluate how well the presentation plays to your audience. A good multimedia presentation will require considerable refinement.

As you can see, there are almost endless possibilities for applying electronic tools to the creative process. The key to doing this successfully, however, is to not only recognize how to use these tools appropriately as you progress through a creative process but also to work with them appropriately at each stage of a project. For example, you can use a computer-aided design program as a research tool to compile information, as an analytical tool to explore relationships graphically, as a synthesis tool to come up with new designs, and as an evaluative tool to do take-offs and present your work. You can also use the computer-aided design program at each phase of a design project—for preliminary design, for design development, for preparing construction documents, evaluating bids, as well as for construction administration. You can even use the computer-aided design program for facility management once the project is completed. Select your media and set up models you can transfer from one stage of the creative process to another, as well as through each phase of the project. Develop clear methods which use your media and models to advantage.

Setting up Tools

There are different approaches to setting up tools which significantly influence the way you use them.

Tool-based approaches which most people are accustomed to working with involve working directly with tools in a physical context such as a desk or drawing table. It is here that you use writing and drawing instruments, or file cabinets. Perhaps, you have cut and pasted text produced by typewriters, Linotype machines, and other single-purpose tools, integrating images to produce "camera-ready" composites for photo-offset printing. Perhaps you have created multimedia presentations photographically using tools like slide and film projectors synchronized with sound.

Or perhaps you have put together a video production using video editor. Many people may use a computer as a single-purpose tool—usually for word processing—or as a personal assistant to keep a daybook.

Tool-based Work Environment

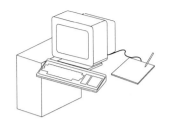

Workstation-Based Environment

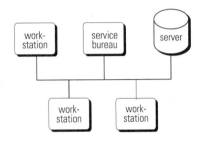

**Media Space-Based
Work Environment**

Computer-based approaches integrate tools in application software. Computers can integrate many tools enabling you to work with multimedia. For example, computer-aided design, desktop publishing, hypermedia, and desktop video are multimedia applications which provide the tools needed to integrate media electronically — all within a computer. Many people may do much of their work with integrated applications, but may not transfer files beyond their workstation.

Media space–based approaches include computers with integrated software connected to servers, providing access to services and information in many different locations. You can access this media space using local area networks or from wherever you have a computer with a modem. The tools you use may not even be located in your personal computer or workstation, but may reside in servers or service bureaus that you access electronically. With a media space work environment, you can work electronically on shared media and models. This can dramatically redefine your approach to using tools, and can give you new freedom over where and when you work.

Although this chapter has focused on tools to show you the range of possibilities, you will need to carefully select which tools you use to deal with your case study projects. You will need to set them up appropriately. Your choice will probably be limited to tools you have access to. Keep in mind, however, that the tools you have access to and your approaches to using them will continue to evolve. Consequently, you need to explore new tools and toys, and set them up in productive and pleasurable ways.

In the beginning you may wish to just consider new computer applications as toys and play. That is a wonderful way to explore their potential. Once you have a feeling for that potential, and for your own, then you will be able to figure out how to apply them appropriately.

Work Habits

The first part of the book presents creative thinking skills. This second part of the book provides approaches for applying these thinking skills to use computers creatively. The next step is to develop appropriate work habits.

The last part of this book helps you develop those habits through mastering media. Chapter 9, The "Zen" of Regeneration, teaches you how to relax when using electronic media and draw from deeper levels of your mind. Chapter 10, The User Interface, helps you to master interfacing with computers so you can work more creatively using electronic media. Chapter 11, Mixing Media, provides approaches for effectively integrating different channels of expression. The final chapter, Change, discusses how you can use some of these emerging tools to change your educational and work environments.

Summary

Explore new computer applications. There are approaches to learning how to use them which draw upon different modes of thought. The discovery mode is more experiential. The strategy mode is more logical. The discovery mode proceeds from concrete experience to an abstract understanding. The strategy mode starts with abstract goals and principles which can lead to successful experience. The first activity at the end of this chapter encourages you to explore computer applications, which you may find both interesting and fun.

Practice using computer applications to learn to use them better. You may have a preferred mode of learning, but you can also adopt other modes. Often you learn most from combining or sharing modes to learn new computer applications. Have workgroups share methods. Integrate practice into games or case studies. Practice can make using computer applications more pleasurable. The second activity at the end of this chapter provides some guidance for achieving flow, which can lead to more pleasurable experiences when using computer applications.

You need to relate capabilities to tasks. One way to do this is to chart applications related to channels of perception and expression at each stage of the design process. This will help you use a range of electronic media and work with computer applications at each stage of the design process. You can emphasize learning by using different channels at each stage of the design process. Or you can optimize a workgroup's production by having team members specialize in different capabilities. The last activity in this chapter will help you use these approaches to plan ways to work appropriately with computer applications at each stage of the creative process.

As you can see, there are more electronic multimedia tools than you can easily master. Select those that are most useful to you in your creative endeavors. Remember that learning to use new tools can be fun.

Activities

1. Explore

You can discover how to use electronic media in different ways. Artists typically immerse themselves in media to experience what the possibilities are. For example, painters will explore different brushes, pens, pigments, and surfaces to find which they like the best for different applications. You too can explore electronic media in this way. On the other hand, scientists typically develop procedures for experiments which enable them to focus their attention. They use heuristics that are well thought out. In the same way, computer manuals offer carefully thought out procedures and strategies for learning applications.

Play with multimedia computers that enable you to explore electronic media. Consciously select programs that involve different channels of perception and will cause you to use modes of thought you may not commonly use. Try out different approaches to learning. One approach is to explore the program and see what you can discover. Another approach is to follow a strategy or example outlined in a manual or user guide. You may find it most productive to learn by using both approaches alternatively. You might first play with the program until you gain familiarity. Next use the manual to work through some examples. Then develop a goal of your own and explore again.

Or you might work together with another person. One of you can play with commands to discover what they can do. The other person should read the manual to learn strategies or approaches for using the commands. After a short time, discuss what you each have learned. Then switch learning methods. The person who was playing should read, and the person who was reading the procedures should have a chance to explore them on the computer. This "buddy method" can be a very effective way of quickly sorting out how to use new commands in application software.

2. Practice

You have had the experience of mastering some tool or toy. It may be a simple pencil, a musical instrument, skis, a bicycle, or an automobile. You have played with it or worked with it until it feels like a part of you. You probably no longer consciously think about how you use it. Your actions flow through this instrument as if it were part of you. You find the experience of using this tool intrinsically rewarding.

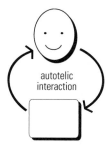

autotelic interaction

Take a familiar computer program or select a new application you find potentially useful and enjoyable. Practice with it until you achieve flow experiences. You will experience flow when you find engaging challenges that require skills you can master. Your actions and awareness will merge. You can develop clear goals and obtain feedback in reaching these goals. You can concentrate on the task at hand. You will experience a relaxed control and overcome self-consciousness. You will lose the sense of time. Out of this can come the rewarding *autotelic* experience that Mihaly Csikszentmihalyi describes in his book *Flow: The Psychology of Optimal Experience*. People pursue autotelic experiences because they enjoy them as opposed to *exotelic* experiences which they do only for external reason (such as their employer requires it). Typically, people do things for a combination of reasons. Working with computer applications may begin as a purely exotelic experience, but you can find this experience becoming more autotelic — particularly if it engages your whole mind.

3. Plan

Each tool has certain capabilities. You need to understand these capabilities to use tools effectively. For example, you cannot use a screwdriver effectively when you really need a wrench. Similarly, you can't use a spell checker when you really need a word processor. A spell checker is an evaluative tool. Writing requires synthesis which a word processor enables you to do. An application program often integrates many tools, but you need to know how to use them effectively. You use different tools for each stage of the creative process.

Take the computer applications you are presently using. List them on a chart according to different channels of perception. For example, list the application programs you use for working with text or with numbers. List programs you use for working with graphics, or images, or three-dimensional models. Can you also list programs you use for animation and video? Can you list programs you use for working with sound or for composing or playing music? Determine which channels strongly interest you.

Now take your chart and list the tools you use for each stage of the design process. For example, identify your analytical tools. Identify your synthesis tools, as well as your evaluative tools. Again determine where your strengths are. Determine how new tools would fit into your repertoire. Next, develop strategies for rounding out your own capabilities or putting together a team that can cover other important aspects if you prefer to specialize. Make sure you take into consideration your typical approach to projects. You can also develop a more detailed chart for a specific project. It can help you clarify your approach to a project by taking into account the composition and dynamics of the workgroup and the tools you are going to use.

stages of design process

channels		research	analysis	synthesis	evaluation
	text				
	graphics				
	3-D modelling				
	imaging				
	animation				
	video				
	audio				

Chart Applications

Visualizing a Mental Image
Star Trek
Courtesy of Richard Helmick in memory of his son Steve

Visualizing the Natural Environment
Parametric Trees Inserted into the Image of a Park
Courtesy of Onyx Computing, Inc.

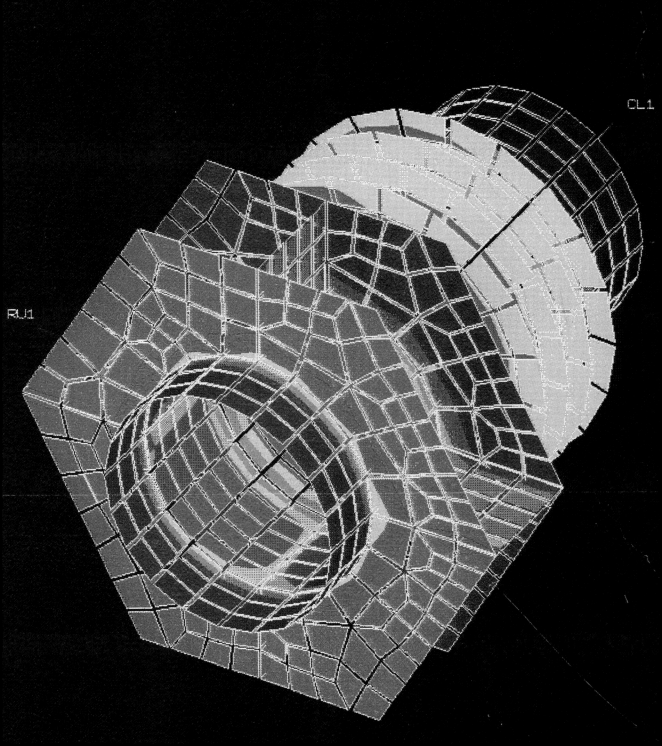

RU1

CL1

Visualizing Our Changing Planet
San Francisco Bay Area
Courtesy of Silicon Graphics
Satellite image processing by Environmental Research Institute of Michigan

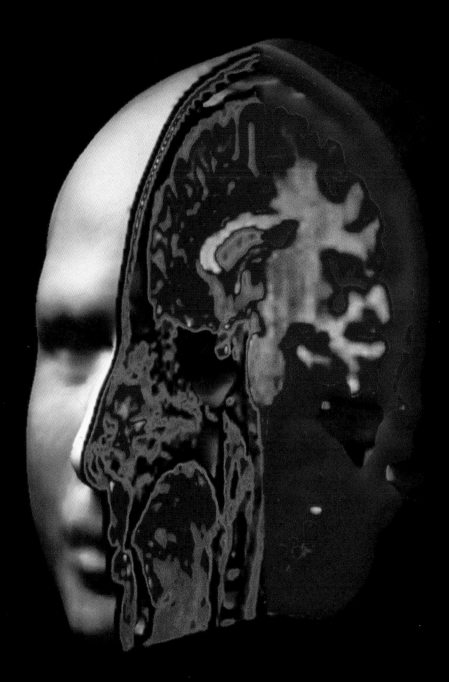

Visualizing the Anatomy of the Brain
Enhanced MRI Image
Courtesy of PV-WAVE

Part III

Mastering

Part I
Thinking

provides a foundation in visual thinking and creative thought processes. This is especially helpful in **design methods courses**.

Part II
Interacting

provides approaches for involving electronic media more creatively. This is especially helpful in **case study courses**.

Part III
Mastering

provides a direction for getting the most out of your mind when using electronic media. This will help you **address change**.

9

The "Zen" of Regeneration

This chapter will take you beyond the cognitive methods and strategies already presented in this book. It will show you how to relax when using computers and how to release your mind to think creatively. It will help you discover your unconscious creative drive. You can discover your own inner space by focusing deeply within yourself, working actively with your imagination and dreams. Then you can transfer insights and visions from your inner space to the electronic media space you have available. The activities at the end of the chapter will help you learn to do this.

Consider How You Use Computers

You may have noticed that when you use computers you may sometimes find it difficult to relax, to release your mind, and to draw upon the creativity within you. Other times you may find that you become immersed in what you are doing and lose track of time as you interact with your ideas on the computer monitor. What is happening? How can your mind work creatively sometimes and not others?

Exploring Your Inner Realm

Mastering: combine media space & innerspace

You may already be going beyond the strategies described in this book, and developing your own approaches for using computers creatively. However, you will soon realize that thinking skills involve more than just working with conscious modes of thought such as the R-mode and L-mode — more than techniques for visualizing what you perceive. They involve drawing upon your inner vision.

Your inner spirit is a highly personal realm. You can explore it on your own. I will simply open the door and help you peer into that realm. Just as you can develop a mental map to navigate in media space, you can also develop an inner sense to navigate in your own inner space. We may be fellow travelers in media space; however, you become your own way-

R   L   conscious

         unconscious

The Inner Realm

inner space The mental realm that relates to human memory and spirit. Just as people can develop a mental map to navigate in media space, people can also develop an inner sense to navigate in their own inner space.

farer in your *inner space*. It is there that you will discover the spirit you need to work creatively. You will also find others with kindred spirits with whom you can relate personally.

Regeneration

Computers need time to regenerate images. People also need time to recenter and refocus. How impatient we become with computers as they churn away, generating fonts, digital patterns, or vectors. We want everything to happen instantaneously, or at least in rhythm with our conscious thought processes. However, if you look at the rhythm of your own thought processes, you realize there is also a need for human *regeneration*. Physically, mentally, and even spiritually you cannot be constantly on "go." You need time to contemplate — time for "so." Ideally, you can relate your own rhythms to the rhythms of the computer.

regenerate To form again or renew. To be spiritually reborn. For example, while computers regenerate images on a screen, human minds recenter and refocus — regenerating mental images in rhythm with conscious thought processes.

One strategy for relating rhythms, of course, is to have faster and faster machines — so the computer will be waiting for you. In this way the user dictates the rhythm. This is fine in theory. However, faster hardware spurs the development of more extravagant software and more ambitious applications. So, again, you will find yourselves waiting. This will continue to be true as you move into virtual reality and work with video despite great gains in the speed of computers. Some applications, however (such as word processing), now have almost instantaneous response times, if you are willing to pay for the faster computers.

human regeneration

rhythm

computer image regeneration

Interactive Rhythm

Another strategy is to learn to pace yourself with the computer. You can relate your regeneration time to the computer's regeneration time. You can regenerate while your computer is accessing or saving files, receiving or sending information, scanning, printing, or plotting. You also have time available when the computer is just working through some very large routines.

Probably the best approach is to combine both strategies. Use the fastest computers you have available for the task. And also learn how to pace yourself relating your regeneration time to the computer's regeneration time. In other words while the computer is regenerating, use the time to regenerate your own body, mind, and spirit. How you can do this is the subject of the rest of this chapter.

Relaxing Your Body

You become physically tired using a computer, though there is very little physical activity involved. As tiredness sets in, you make mistakes more easily, which compounds your physical stress. This also affects your

Out 5

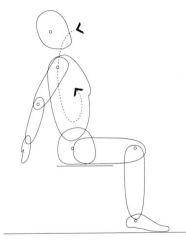

In 5

mind and spirit. Obviously, you should limit your work sessions on a computer to what you can do comfortably. However, there are ways of relaxing your body that enable you to maintain peak performance for a longer time. Deep breathing is a good way to begin.

Breathing Deeply

People usually breathe very shallowly when working on a computer. You may compound this by slouching in a poorly designed chair, or possibly hunching over to look at a monitor positioned too low. Poor posture collapses the chest cavity, reducing the volume of the lungs. Breathing provides oxygen to burn the energy you consume. Therefore, if you breathe shallowly for a long time, you begin to feel sluggish. Your mind becomes dim, and your spirits may be low. You will probably find yourself involuntarily stretching and yawning when your body senses oxygen depletion. You can consciously learn breathing exercises that will help keep you alert. You can do these exercises during your regeneration time.

A simple breathing exercise begins with exhaling to a count of 5 until you can press your navel toward your spine while rolling your shoulders forward to collapse your chest. Inhale to another count of 5, filling your whole abdominal and chest cavity with air by stretching your arms back to expand your chest. Even yawn if you need to. Pause briefly, and then repeat — slowly exhaling and inhaling — until you feel you are completely alert.

You will notice as you do this breathing exercise that your posture will naturally improve. Maintain good posture to sustain good breathing.

Rolling the Spine and Balancing the Body

Good posture is a key to staying alert. You can improve your posture by rolling your spine into straighter alignment starting at the base of your

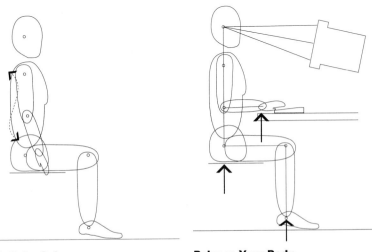

Roll the Spine   **Balance Your Body**

back, then slowly working up to the area between your shoulders and finally stretching your neck by gently pointing your chin to the ceiling. Think how gracefully a cat stretches its body. Enjoy the sensation of your muscles relaxing, causing your blood to circulate freely and energize your body. Remember the feeling of having your body balancing easily on the base of your spine and retain this posture. Properly position your chair, keyboard, and monitor so you can easily maintain this feeling. Also make sure your hands have a place to rest so your neck and shoulders can remain relaxed. It is especially important that your wrists are straight when using a keyboard. Repetitive finger strokes through bent wrists may damage the carpel tunnels through which your tendons move.

Looking Beyond the Monitor

You use your eyes intensely when working with computers. Poor contrast, poor resolution, flicker, and glare from a computer monitor compound eye strain. Therefore, it is not surprising after working with a computer for awhile that your eyes can become tired. We may begin to lose focus or feel spasms.

You can resolve some of this by carefully adjusting the monitor. And some of it must be taken care of by controlling external light sources to reduce glare. Appropriate eyeglasses can correct focusing problems. Beyond that, you should limit your work sessions to what you can do without straining your eyes. Some simple eye relaxation exercises can help you rest your eyes as you work. Again, you can do these exercises during regeneration time.

Each time your computer is scrolling or regenerating, get into the habit of fixing your eyes on something in the distance, causing them to refocus. When working with a very fast computer that takes little time to regenerate, look away from the monitor periodically. This is easiest to do if you are in a room that is spacious, offering longer views. You can also do this by looking out a window. However, make sure the light level of your monitor and that of the outside view are similar, so you don't suffer glare when changing your view. Even without a long view available, you can change your focus by imagining that you are looking at something far

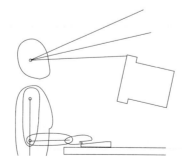

Look Beyond the Monitor While it Regenerates

beyond the monitor. You will notice the monitor go out of focus when you do this. Using your peripheral vision, you can perceive when the scrolling or regeneration has stopped. Then, if your eyes feel ready, you can refocus on the monitor and proceed with your work.

Relaxing Eyes and Ears by Palming

Palming is another excellent way to relax your eyes. Bring your head to your knees and cover your eyes with the palms of your hands. Keep your eyes open so you are sure not to press your eyeballs. Peering into darkness, move your eyes slowly and rhythmically from side to side and then in circles. Doing this, you will notice that the afterglow of light and color disappears. Without the external stimulus, your eyes soon relax. (Eventually, light and even colors may re-appear once you are able to focus deeply within yourself, drawing upon your inner energy.) The warmth of your hands and the movement of your eyes stimulate blood circulation in this crucial area. Make sure you have a proper diet, since eyes are high consumers of vitamins. Because palming takes a little longer than refocusing, you can get in the habit of doing this while you are saving large documents or sending or printing files.

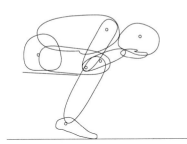

Palm Eyes

To protect your ears when working with sound and music programs, you should have a good sound system that can accurately reproduce subtle acoustical qualities. Also you should adjust the volume appropriately. High volume can cause hearing loss, temporarily and even permanently, depending on the intensity and duration of the exposure.

Computer-related noise such as fans, hard disks, and printers can also be hard on your ears. Some of these sounds can be shielded at their sources. You can also mask some sounds with music. Earplugs are a last resort. The persistent hum of a roomful of electronic equipment can become quite irritating. Here are some exercises that can help deal with noise.

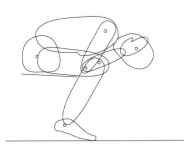

Palm Ears

Try palming or cupping your ears. Cover your ears with the palms of your hands. Do it firmly, but be careful not to cause pressure or suction on your eardrums. You will find that external sounds subside. Suddenly, you notice the sounds inside your head. Lower your head to your knees and close your eyes. Rest there, listening to the sounds in your head. This silence gives your ears a chance to rest. Also the warmth of your hands and the lowering of your head cause blood to flow to your ears, bringing renewed energy. This can also relax your neck and back. Do this while the computer is printing. It is a good way to avoid the noise of a printer. You will notice you can focus on your breathing when palming your ears.

If anybody asks you what you are doing, tell them simply that you are doing the "zen of regen." — seeking to refresh your mind, like your computer refreshes the image on the monitor. (If you are in California or Japan, don't move under your desk while lowering your head to your knees. People will think there is an earthquake.) By now you realize these exercises may be most suited for personal computing, done in the privacy

of your study. Some of the exercises such as breathing and changing the focus of your eyes are subtle enough to do among strangers. On the other hand, some of the exercises, if done among strangers, can make you the center of unwanted attention. If possible create your own support group where everybody accepts these exercises. Workgroups and classes can get in tune with these simple means of regenerating your body and mind. People can learn to understand and accept them. Most important, others can provide positive reinforcement by also doing these exercises to stay relaxed. It is easier to do these things if you see others do them as well. I once had outsiders, looking at my class through a glass enclosure, believing we were holding some kind of seance having to do with worshiping computers. With that said, let's move on to exercises that appear really weird. Once you do them, however, you will find they can be beneficial.

Certain muscle groups can become tense because of the repetitive actions typical of using computers. These usually are in the areas of the neck, back, shoulders, arms, hands, and fingers. Relax and stretch these areas at frequent intervals while seated at your computer. Here are some exercises you can do to regenerate while waiting for the computer to regen and carry out its tasks.

Rolling Your Neck and Twisting Your Torso

Neck

Relaxing
Rub your neck. Make it warm.

Stretching
Roll your head slowly from side to side. (You may notice a crunching sound. This is normal.)

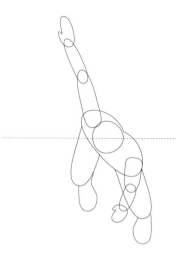

Torso

Relaxing
Rub your sides and back with your hands. Even gently pound your torso. Make it warm.

Stretching
Twist your torso by gently exerting leverage against your knee. First stretch your lower back; then slowly continue to your upper back. Then twist your neck by turning your head. Finish by moving your eyes to look as far behind you as you can. Repeat. Slowly twist in each direction.

Rolling Your Shoulders

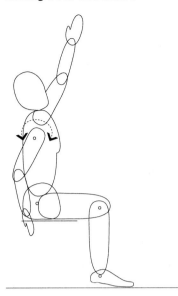

Relaxing
Rub your shoulders down to your elbows. Make your shoulders and upper arms warm.

Stretching
Slowly roll your shoulders forward and back. Push your chest out as you roll your shoulders back. Then reach your arms toward the ceiling and alternately stretch each side of your torso by extending your hands as if you were picking fruit from a high branch.

Rotating Your Arms, and Shaking Your Wrists

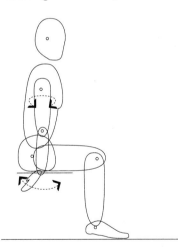

Arms and Wrists

Relaxing
Rub your forearms. Massage your wrists by gently twisting and kneading them with your hands.

Stretching
Move your hands in a circular motion, gently stretching your wrists. Then hang your arms limply at your sides and shake out your wrists by rotating your arms.

Opening Your Hands, Stretching Your Fingers

Hands

Relaxing
Rub and knead each hand with your opposite thumb, fingers, and palm. Work your thumb around

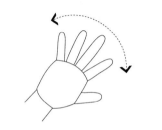

Open Hand

your palm. Then run your thumb up the valleys on the back of your hand between the bones connected to your fingers. Rub in the direction of your heart.

Stretching
Open your hands, spreading your fingers as wide as you can. Repeat this slowly several times.

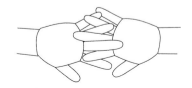

Stretch Fingers

Fingers

Relaxing
Use the thumb from your opposite hand to gently rub your fingers toward your heart. Make sure you rub each finger and thumb.

Stretching
Clasp your fingers together and stretch by gently turning your hands inside out as you sometimes see a pianist do before a concert.

Breathe normally as you do these exercises. Do not hold your breath or force any of the stretches. Stop if you feel any pain. The stretching sensation is actually quite pleasant. Take time to enjoy it. Think of yourself as a concert pianist warming up at the keyboard as you gracefully move from one exercise to another.

In addition, get up and take breaks. Consider fitness part of your daily routine. Relaxation and fitness are like sleep and good nutrition. You don't function very well without them.

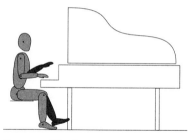

Concert Pianist

Releasing Your Mind

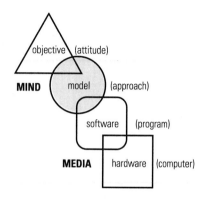

Mind / Media System

Your mind may tense when you start to use computers. This can have both internal and external causes. Internally, you may not be comfortable with the hardware, the software, or even your thinking skills. You may be uncertain about what the computer will do — "Will it malfunction?" You may not know how to work with the software — "Now, what was the command for . . . ?" You may not know the approach you need to proceed — "Where do I begin, and where am I going?" You may not be at ease with all these components of the computer system. In addition, the setting may not be right. There may be discomforts or distractions that bother you.

Overcoming the internal causes takes confidence. You gain confidence with experience. You need to know the computer will perform if you use it properly. Software commands need to become second nature. You need

approaches that enable you to visualize how to proceed. After you have experienced success, or at least understand where you have failed, you can build up your confidence. This begins to put your mind at ease when using computers. You also need to make sure the setting works for you.

Avoid building up anxieties about everything that could go wrong. Some people, with considerable successful experience, can conjure up imagined problems leaving them almost paralyzed. You almost need to develop the "invincible" frame of mind so typical of teenagers. There is something to be said for the peace of mind exemplified by the statement "Hey, no problem!"—though this is often said with great naïveté. Sometimes, however, your mind is more at rest if you can anticipate problems or are at least confident you can deal with them when they inevitably occur.

Overcoming external distractions takes sensitivity. First, you have to be aware of what might be distracting you. Then you have a better chance of controlling distractions or interruptions. Music may help you relax if you are doing routine tasks. And there are ways of using the imagery from music to stimulate your thoughts. However, music can become a distraction if you are trying to listen to your inner self. I know from experience that this is very difficult to explain to my students and children in a way that they will truly believe. Typically, they will only believe it once they experience it. Ask yourself, do you really hear your stereo when you are deep in thought? Then maybe it isn't adding anything to your thinking. And maybe you will find it detracting from your thinking when you recognize a tune you like. However, some computer work environments are full of noise. Stereo earphones may provide a means for masking sounds that you cannot control in other ways.

Masking Sounds

There are many techniques for relaxing and releasing your mind. Some traditional relaxation techniques are found in the practice of yoga and similar exercises where you learn to respond to your body. Some techniques involve biofeedback where you can use electronic devices to monitor key indicators of your mind and body stress levels. Learning to respond to this feedback can help you relax.

Letting Go of Your Body

A traditional mental relaxation exercise involves focusing on breathing and letting go of your body. Begin by taking two or three deep breaths, exhaling to the bottom of your lungs each time. While sitting, you can cultivate controlled relaxation by sequentially letting go of each part of your body to the forces of gravity, as opposed to letting your whole body go limp like a rag. For example, start by releasing your legs, allowing them to rest motionlessly on the floor. Next release your lower back, putting all the muscles in that area of your body at ease. After that, release your torso by carefully balancing on your spine. Release your neck by carefully balancing your head on your body. Release your arms, allowing them to hang at your sides. Then relax your jaw — even letting your mouth hang slightly open. Next turn your attention to your eyes — which

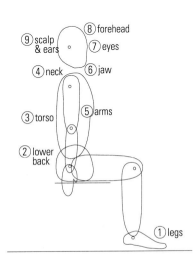

Release Progressively

you can close gently. Then focus on your forehead, which you should put at ease without furrows. Similarly releasing your scalp and ears may cause them to tingle because of the added blood flow. Your body will provide clues to indicate you are relaxing. Your limbs will feel heavy, and you will experience a sinking sensation as your body responds to gravity. You will naturally begin to balance yourself with good posture if you are sitting or standing. You will feel a warm sensation as your blood circulation improves. Your breathing will become deeper and more rhythmic — as it does when you are beginning to fall asleep.

Working with Biofeedback

biofeedback Technique for responding to indicators of mental and body stress. For example, therapists use biofeedback to help patients learn how to relax and overcome physical and mental problems.

electroencephalograph (EEG) A device that measures brain waves. Can help people learn how to produce alpha waves, which indicate the brain is in a relaxed state.

EEG

Electronic Encephalographs

electromyograph (EMG) An instrument that measures muscle tension. Can help pinpoint areas of tension and help people learn how to release that tension.

EMG

Electronic Myographs

galvanic skin response (GSR) A physiochemical change in the skin that can be used to assess arousal. Can help people learn to control arousal related to anxiety or agitation.

GSR

Galvanic Skin Response

Biofeedback devices can measure key indicators of mind and body stress. Therapists use biofeedback to help patients learn how to relax and overcome physical and mental problems. For example, *EEG* (electronic encephalographs) measure brain waves. Using these devices, people can learn how to produce alpha waves, which indicate the brain is in a relaxed state. *EMG* (electronic myographs) measure muscle tension. They can help pinpoint areas of tension and help people learn how to release that tension. *GSR* (galvanic skin response) assesses arousal. It helps people learn to control arousal related to anxiety or agitation. For example, you commonly experience this when you blush due to embarrassment. Hand-temperature feedback systems can teach you to control circulation. This is especially helpful to people who suffer from cold extremities or headaches resulting from poor circulation due to stress. We have all experienced cold hands when we become nervous.

There is already computer software that can help people learn to relax by providing feedback that users can respond to. Other software applications may emerge that will incorporate biofeedback into user

interfaces. In effect, the software could become user friendly to the extent that it actually responds to your physical and mental state. This might help enhance the user's performance.

Releasing your mind is important for relaxing and being able to work at peak performance for longer periods. This can also help you explore your inner space so you can learn to relate it to media space.

Reviving Your Spirit

Sharon Stine, a colleague — who formerly was my student — conceded she felt rather "mindworn" after learning many mental approaches to computers in a graduate design course I taught. Her reaction was understandable considering the rigors students are subject to in the name of education. Computers can compound these rigors. First, they present a new array of tools to learn how to use. Then, they trick the user into increasing expectations to match (and usually exceed) exciting new capabilities. Then, computers can fail miserably, for any number of reasons, causing severe depression just when you are beginning to depend upon them. No wonder your spirit can suffer when you deal with these devils.

Aside from having difficulties dealing with computers, you may lack motivation. You may not be comfortable with the task at hand. This sets up internal struggles you need to learn to resolve. You use computers most effectively if you can work with them using your body, mind, and spirit. Creativity and curiosity are some of the motivating drives that cause people to become interactive computer users, authors, and tool makers (such as programmers) as opposed to being just passive viewers and casual tool users. Here are some other approaches to reviving your spirit.

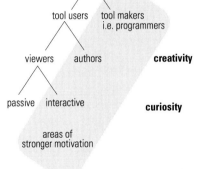

Motivation Factors

Most cultures have traditions related to meditation. Certainly major religions — Buddhism, Christianity, Hinduism, Islam, Judaism, and Taoism — involve this type of experience. Religions have developed rituals for meditation — be they simple prayers or mystical experiences. Aside from the religious implications (which vary), the common theme is learning to access deeper levels of consciousness and becoming a wayfarer in your inner space.

witness To experience personally. Can involve centering on where you are, to become fully aware of your senses.

Witnessing

You can also do this through witnessing, contemplation, and transcendental meditation. *Witnessing* involves centering on where you are, to become fully aware of your senses. For example, you can sit in a beautiful landscape and absorb all of what you perceive — the play of sunlight, the sound of birds, the fragrance of the air. Witnessing

contemplate To access different modes of thought through meditation. To reflect upon what you experience and understand.

Contemplating

can also be useful when interacting with multimedia computers. *Contemplation* enables you to access different modes of thought through meditation. In this way you can reflect upon what you experience and understand. For example, you might contemplate an event in your life by replaying it in your mind's eye and relating what you understand and how you feel about the experience.

transcendental meditation A way of thinking that enables people to access altered states of consciousness. To project into unconscious modes of thought.

Transcendental Meditation

Transcendental meditation enables you to access altered states of consciousness. You can do this through active imagination and dream work. For example, you can take fantasy flights into your imagination and discover things you were not even conscious of. In this way you can project into unconscious modes of thought.

There is an important body of literature behind these beliefs and approaches to meditation which you may want to explore further. The following is only one approach to getting in touch with your inner self.

Inner Space: The Source of Your Creative Drive

Your unconscious levels are an important part of your being. They are the seat of your values and the source of your motivation. Energy derived from these levels is what fuels your creative drive. You can explore your unconscious; there are many ways of doing this. You can also transfer insights derived from your unconscious inner space to conscious levels of awareness. This enables you to express your insights in media space where you can work with them interactively.

Part III: Mastering

The psychologist Carl Jung provided a model for understanding the unconscious in his works *Archetypes of the Collective Unconscious* and *Man and His Symbols.* Jung identified *archetypes* that are symbols of the inner being. He derived them from observations of people's dreams and imagination. He also noted how these symbols have recurred in many different cultures over time. He developed approaches for relating to this inner world. For example, therapists use these approaches to help people understand dreams and to resolve conflicts between their conscious and unconscious levels of being.

archetype In psychology, according to Jung — a symbol of the inner being that manifests ideas inherited from human experience. These symbols recur in many different cultures over time.

In his book *Inner Work: Using Dreams and Active Imagination for Personal Growth*, Robert A. Johnson, who is a Jungian analyst, provides

approaches for integrating the conscious and unconscious selves. He does this by using dreams and active imagination. Some people do inner work under the guidance of a counselor as therapy for resolving internal conflicts they may have. Other people do inner work as a means for understanding themselves better to stimulate personal growth. Here we will approach inner work only as a means for drawing upon creative energy.

Creative thinking skills relate to conscious as well as unconscious mental forces. You can learn approaches to exploring your own inner space so you can transfer energy from your unconscious to images you can work with consciously in media space when using computers. Examine your basic motives and spiritual values on your own, or with the help of philosophers, ministers, shamans, and sages.

Imagination

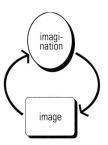

Active Imagination

Imagination is probably the most useful way of reaching your unconscious to stimulate creativity. Robert Johnson, in *Inner Work,* provides a four-step procedure for what he calls "active imagination." Active imagination involves an interaction or dialogue with your unconscious levels that results in some action. This is different from a passive fantasy.

As Johnson puts it, "The essence of Active Imagination is your *conscious participation* in the imaginative experience." Passive fantasy is simply daydreaming — watching a stream of fantasy going by as if you were watching TV. You don't act on passive fantasies. They may repeat without being resolved because you don't interact with them. As Johnson points out, "The whole function of the imagination is to draw up the material from the unconscious, clothe it in images, and transmit it to the conscious mind. Whatever comes up in the imagination must have been living somewhere in the fabric of the unconscious before it was given an image-form by the imagination."

You can do inner work using a variety of computer programs such as word processing, color graphics, or music programs. Actively record your mental images or even your dreams. Computers are not just a TV set for passive viewing; they are a multimedia vehicle enabling you to participate consciously in imaginative experiences. You can use computers to participate actively in the artificial reality of your imagination with all of your feelings and emotions. You can also translate interactions with the artificial reality of media space to actions in the real world. Computers can provide a vehicle for getting back and forth between the inner world of imagination, or dreaming, and the external world of human life in this universe.

How can you apply this procedure to thinking skills for using computers creatively? Here is Johnson's four-step procedure for active imagination:

1. Invite the unconscious.
2. Dialogue and experience.
3. Add the ethical element of values.
4. Make it concrete with physical ritual.

Step 1: Invite the Unconscious

Establish where you are going to work — you need privacy. Learn to relax your body, release your mind, and reflect on your inner spirit. Use the techniques already described for human regeneration.

Decide how you are going to record your active imagination. Try to transfer your mental images into electronic media as directly as possible. Remember you can do your recordings electronically or by using any media you may be comfortable with. You can invite your unconscious verbally using a tape recorder, or with text using a word processor. You can also record your images graphically using a painting, drawing, or drafting program. You can also work with three-dimensional models using a CADD program. You can even record your mental images musically using a music program. Work on paper with traditional tools (like a pencil or a pen) if you find that more comfortable to start with. However, transfer to electronic media as soon as you can. By recording your inner work electronically, you will have these images in a form that you can work with interactively, consciously using computers. You can also transfer them to formats that you can share. You can work collaboratively if you are ready to invite others to share your unconscious images.

Remember, however, that the images that you initially generate are for your eyes only. They may be very personal. Use symbols and shorthand notations, perhaps ones that only you understand. Don't worry if your images seem incomplete. Be careful not to judge them in any way. Avoid superfluous concerns such as presentation formats, fonts, and spelling. You can deal with these concerns more consciously later. They are significant only for presentation. Again, this first step of the procedure is for your eyes only.

Johnson offers some suggestions for getting started; however, he cautions, "Once you have found the image and started the inner dialogue, you must relinquish control. Once the invitation is made and the image appears, you can't dictate the focus of your imagination and you can't push it in any particular direction." Here are some techniques he suggests for getting started:

Use your fantasies.
Visit symbolic places.
Use personifications.
Dialogue with dream figures.

Johnson's frame of reference is understandably more psychological and interpersonal than the approaches mentioned previously. Yet his techniques relate to visualization skills already discussed in Chapter 4. For example, you can find in them the fantasy, symbolic, and personal analogies that William J. J. Gordon writes about. You can also use direct analogies for getting started. These may be based on the intrinsic order of space and time you see in nature. The models you can develop in a computer can become a focus for both your conscious and unconscious mind. These archetypes, based on intrinsic order, can be particularly useful to artists, designers, engineers, and scientists, who often relate to objects as well as people.

Step 2: Dialogue and Experience

Having invited your unconscious, you should now be open to having a dialogue with it. Experience what it reveals. Make sure you listen and observe. Record what you are experiencing. This will capture these insights so you can work with them later. It will make these images more vivid in your mind. Participate fully using all your senses. You should get the feeling that what you are experiencing is actually happening.

Johnson points out that active imagination involves complete experiences. Each has a beginning, a middle, and an end—similar to dreams. There is usually a problem statement, interaction with the problem, and finally a resolution of the conflict or issue. Johnson says, "This may take place in one session, or it may require a series of sessions that continue for days or even years." This relates to my experience working with design. You probably can relate it to experiences you have had with your own imagination and dreams.

As with any dialogue you must learn to reply. Learn to interact with what you experience. As Jung points out, there should be an interaction between your ego, or consciousness, and your unconsciousness. Neither should dominate. You should not let your ego manipulate your subconscious. Similarly, don't let what you experience in your unconscious overwhelm your ego. Strive to achieve a unified balance. This balance is dynamic, however, alternating between conscious and unconscious levels of thought throughout the dialogue. This experience should be interactive. As the unconscious provides images, the conscious can clarify these images and add more information. This in turn can provide new stimulus for the unconscious.

Active imagination is open-ended. It enables you to discover what is in your unconsciousness. You should not confuse it with guided imagery, which is scripted. Guided imagery is useful for getting your reaction to different situations. You should also not confuse active imagination with the guided creativity of the design process. Active imagination happens without "a priori." The design process usually has a set of goals, and sometimes even schedule and/or budget constraints. Use active imagination as a technique for working with different stages of the design process.

Step 3: Add the Ethical Element of Values

After you have entered into a dialogue and derived experiences from your unconscious level, then you can judge them. This enables you to decide how you value these experiences. This is an important step to considering how you will act upon them. Make sure the dialogue is complete before you start judging. Otherwise you are likely to disrupt the dynamic balance and stop the flow of images prematurely.

Your judgments can flow from either conscious or unconscious levels of your mind. You may consciously judge something to be possible or practical; you may unconsciously judge something to be desirable or ethical. Possibility and practicality are cognitive considerations you can calculate according to criteria. On your unconscious level, desirability relates to basic drives that are archetypical to most human beings. The word *ethics* is derived from the Greek word *ethos*, meaning the "essential character or spirit" of a person or people. It is on this basis you make unconscious judgements.

You need rigor to do good cognitive evaluations. You should also strive to nurture and preserve human values. Be careful to proceed only with actions you find are physically sound and morally correct.

ethic (From the Greek word ethos) The essential character or spirit of a person or people. The basis upon which people make unconscious judgments.

Step 4: Make It Concrete with Physical Ritual

Having made judgments, you are now ready to act on this experience. There are many ways of doing this. You can do it symbolically through rituals. You can do it physically with concrete actions. You can even act experientially in artificial reality using media space accessed by computers. However you do it, there must be a vivid enough connection to your life's experience to make it seem real.

Johnson offers this guidance:

> To incarnate your imagination, during this fourth step, does not mean to act out your fantasies in a literal way. It means, rather, to take the essence that you have distilled from it — the meaning, insight, or basic principle that you have derived from the experience — and incarnate it by doing physical ritual or by integrating it into your practical life. You can get into trouble and cause harm if you fail to make this distinction. You must not take this fourth step of Active Imagination as license to act out your fantasies in their raw, literal form.

Dreams

You can access your unconscious through dreams. This is something that we all experience regularly. Working with your dreams can be very helpful to your mental health and personal growth. Since dreaming is an aspect of creativity, it can also be useful for developing your creative capacity.

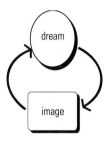

Dream Work

Johnson outlines the following four-step procedure for what he calls "Dream Work":

1. Make associations.

2. Connect dream images to inner dynamics.

3. Interpret.

4. Do rituals to make the dream concrete.

Briefly, the procedure involves recording the images in your dreams and making associations. The first step is to make these associations directly with the images in your dream. Do not make associations with associations. Then select those associations that seem to "click." You have a sense of what fits, or what satisfies your intuitive forces. You will find that all the energy of your mental impulses seems to resonate in harmony when you find this fit. This can help you release the creative energy you can derive from your unconscious level.

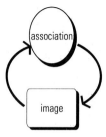

Make Associations with Images

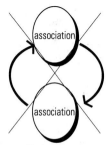

Avoid Associations with Associations

The second step involves connecting each dream image to what is going on inside you. In this way you can begin to derive some meaning from the dream that you can work with at more conscious levels.

The third step involves interpreting the dream. This interpretation should tie the meanings you have derived from your dream into a unified picture. In *Inner Work*, Johnson provides principles for validating interpretations of dreams:

Choose an interpretation that shows you something you didn't know.

Avoid the interpretation that inflates your ego or is self-congratulatory.

Avoid interpretations that shift responsibility away from yourself.

Learn to live with dreams over time — fit them into the long-term flow of your life.

The fourth and final step of dream work involves rituals to make the dream concrete. These rituals are very similar in nature to the rituals discussed before for active imagination. Make the experience you derive from your dream real.

The Art Spirit

Your creative spirit — or the art spirit — like many inner drives, can be very pervasive. Yet it is very difficult to describe. A creative spirit, like love, is a deep-seated feeling you experience in many different ways. Just as you can find and experience love, you can also discover and experience your own creative spirit. You can even recognize it in others. Permit me to share a very personal experience.

My daughter, Kirsten, wrote me a cheerful letter from the south of France where she was studying art in the LaCoste Program. She was ecstatic by what she was creating in stone working in the hot and dusty limestone quarry each day. She described herself as tanned, but skinned. While carving the limestone, she had skinned her knuckles and knees. The medium of stone enthralled her, despite the physical demands.

The Art Spirit
sculpture by Kirsten von Wodtke

Kirsten's letter caused me to reflect on our artistic spirits. Each medium presents challenges that require some creative drive to overcome. Electronic media, although not physically demanding, are full of traps that breed frustration. As you probably know by now, nothing described in this book is particularly easy. No doubt you also have experiences using computer hardware and software that you would prefer to forget. But, overcoming these frustrations lets you enjoy the fruits of your creativity. With an artistic spirit, you can learn to use almost any medium creatively. Success breeds a bonding to the medium. If one can find form within stone and give expression to a vision, certainly one can organize information electronically and synthesize a new creation. This may be text, a tune, a graphic, or any object you can visualize.

In her letter, Kirsten described how she labored on a piece of limestone. The sculpture broke as she was completing it. Fortunately, with help, she pinned it back together in a way one hardly could notice the fracture. This reminded me of the electronic files my students have lost and how we were sometimes able to recover them.

I received Kirsten's letter when I was having the configuration blues. Nothing was going right as I was upgrading software and installing new drivers for an old laser printer. My patience was worn raw — much like my daughter's hands. At the time, I was not ecstatic, but her letter made me realize we can endure hardships and frustration. We need an artistic spirit to give expression to our creative drives. Kirsten was working in stone and loving it. I was working electronically, and — at the time — was rather frustrated. Soon my frustration faded. I realized how the artistic spirit can prevail. This art spirit can help you meet both physical and mental challenges to work creatively.

Summary

This chapter provides approaches for relaxing your body. Relaxation invigorates your body and helps you develop interactive rhythms when working with computers. You can relax your body by:

· Breathing deeply — in 5, out 5
· Rolling your spine, balancing your body
· Looking beyond the monitor
· Relaxing your eyes and ears by palming
· Rolling your neck and twisting your torso
· Rolling your shoulders
· Rotating your arms, shaking your wrists
· Opening your hands, stretching your fingers

The first activity at the end of this chapter guides you through these exercises for relaxing your body.

The chapter also provides approaches for releasing your mind. Releasing revitalizes your mind. Merging mind and media can link your inner space and media space. You can release your mind by letting go of your legs, lower back, torso, neck, arms, jaw, eyes, forehead, scalp, and ears. The second activity at the end of this chapter helps you to release your mind.

In addition this chapter presents approaches to reviving your spirit. Reviving regenerates your spirit so you can draw upon your mental energy and enhance it using electronic media. Look inward through witnessing, contemplating, and practicing transcendental meditation. You can revive your spirit by:

· Inviting the unconscious
· Dialoguing and experiencing
· Adding ethical elements of values
· Making it concrete through rituals

The final activity in this chapter will help you revive your spirit by working with your active imagination and dreams. You will find that curiosity and creativity provide strong motivating factors.

Activities

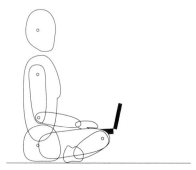

1. Relax Your Body

Sometimes when you work at a computer, everything goes really well. However, you probably also have had work sessions that were disasters. The difference often relates to your mental and physical state. When you are relaxed, your mind and body can respond to the tasks at hand. Relaxed attention helps you work at peak performance.

You can develop a rhythm when working with computers that enables you to relax and regenerate. You can set the pace if you work with fast machines. The computer will wait for you. You can also learn exercises that will help you regenerate while the image on the computer screen is regenerating or while the machine is carrying out tasks.

Before you begin, check out your workstation to make sure it is ergonomically correct for you. Is your body position comfortable? Are your hands supported? Is your monitor in the right position, enabling you to see it while you are in a relaxed posture? Are the contrast and color adjusted correctly? Have you eliminated glare? Are you avoiding disturbing noise? Is your sound system adjusted correctly? If you work at a stationary workstation, you can set up these conditions — although you still may have to do some minor adjustments if you share this workstation with others. If you work with a portable computer, you will need to make sure you optimize these conditions wherever you are working. In the right setting, you will find using a small notebook computer can be very relaxing.

Develop a rhythm for working with computers that incorporates the exercises described in this chapter to help you relax your body. Breathe deeply; practice breathing exercises such as "out 5 — in 5," described in this chapter. Maintain good posture to help sustain your deep breathing. Get in the habit of looking away from the monitor when the screen is scrolling or regenerating. Practice palming to rest your eyes and ears. Do the exercises described in this chapter to relax your neck, back, shoulders, arms, hands, and fingers. As you wait for the computer to respond, exercise the parts of

your body that feel tense. Make sure you do both the relaxing and stretching part of each exercise. Develop a support group in which everyone does the exercises. Assimilate regeneration exercises until they feel natural and you do them almost automatically. Make sure you take breaks and combine fitness into your daily routine.

When you do these exercises, you will feel vitality flow into your body and mind. Because electronic media can become so absorbing, make sure you occasionally turn attention to yourself and determine how you are doing. If you can't regenerate a feeling of vitality using these exercises, it is time to take a break.

2. Release Your Mind

Keeping a journal, sketchbook, collection of images, or even compositions of sounds can be a wonderful way of releasing your mind. Make it a habit to look into your mind and reflect upon what you are thinking. It can help you sort out your goals. By doing this using computers, you can also develop more confidence in electronic media. Practice can help you master applications for creative expression such as word processing, graphics, modeling, or music programs. You will become more comfortable using these tools to express yourself.

Of course, you don't need a computer to release your mind. You can do it by simply meditating, talking to others, or using other media such as paper. Look at published examples of journals such as those done by John Muir when he was in Yosemite Valley. Or find published sketchbooks and journals done by famous designers such as LeCorbusier and Halprin. Remember, the journals you see in bookstores are refined for publication. Your journal will be in a much more original form — as the published ones were at their beginning. The advantage of

working with electronic media is that you can record your insights in very flexible formats. You can refine ideas and transfer them to your work more easily. You can also use different channels — recording not only words, but drawings, paintings, models, images, and sounds — all of which you can work with interactively.

One of the activities at the end of the first chapter of this book suggested you write your goals in a journal. Go back to that journal and see how your goals are evolving. Also use your journal to sort out your approaches to electronic media as you did in the case study activities at the end of Chapters 6 and 7. View your journal as an integral part of whatever you are doing.

Develop your personal journal. You may do this with electronic media using a personal computer. This enables you to work with different channels of expression, exploring tools you wish to work with. For example, you can do it in a written format using a word processor or in a graphic format using a drawing or painting program. You can also do it in spatial models using a CADD program or in movement using an animation program. You can collect and play with images using a video imaging program. You can also collect and compose sounds using a music program. Your journal could contain any mode of expression. Find ways to release what is on your mind.

This journal is for your eyes only. You can decide if you want to share parts of it with others. Begin by cultivating the controlled relaxation described in this chapter. Put yourself into a mental state that enables you to reflect. Then record your understandings and insights. Date your entries so you will see how your understandings and insights evolve. Practice witnessing where you are—physically, mentally, and even spiritually. Contemplate your observations. Center on key ideas or themes that fascinate you. Broaden the bandwidth of your expression by using different channels as much as possible. Work with both representational and abstract statements. Reflect on your feelings and insights in a descriptive way. Release your mind — let it wander.

Your journal can help you clarify the problems you are contemplating. Use your journal as a place to record your insights and ideas as they occur. Don't worry if your representations are crude, messy or not refined. Let your journal reflect how your ideas develop, identifying what is influencing you and helping you shape your thoughts.

Learn to share your better insights and observations. Put them into letters you write to others. Transfer selected ideas to media space you share with your workgroup so they can become part of a team project. Incorporate your insights into your own works of art or solutions to problems you are dealing with. This approach to expressing your thoughts can serve you well throughout a professional career.

You might also develop a group journal for transactional writing and modeling in shared media space. For example, a workgroup or project team can keep a project journal. This journal should be on a computer that each team member has access to. Your team may wish to have a project manager who is responsible for keeping the project journal, gathering input from the group. Or your team may wish to work collaboratively in your shared media space. Try out different modes. Sometimes you may interact individually in media space for communication—getting messages from or writing messages to your team members. Sometimes you can work collectively as a group, using the computer and media space like chalk and a blackboard for collaboration. Try to get everyone's ideas down when you do this together. Brainstorm in a relaxed environment; then work together to organize the ideas. Sometimes it is important to evaluate ideas and generate an outline or summary that reflects your group decisions. In this way you can provide a record of your collaboration. Keep your collaborative journals on separate files from your personal journals. If you are working electronically, it can be relatively easy to transfer files from your personal media space to your shared media space. You will probably want to refine your ideas somewhat before you present them to others.

Electronic media provide a place to develop ideas—both individually and collaboratively. Use representations (or models in artificial reality) as a vehicle for focusing both your individual attention and your group's collaborative efforts. Journal writing provides a way to release your mind. Getting into this habit offers an approach you can use to free your thoughts. This can be stimulating, yet very relaxing. You will find satisfaction in discovering what you are all about and realizing how you can contribute to group efforts. Your personal journal provides a means to draw upon your individual creativity. Group journals provide the means to work with your group's shared creativity. Your journal can help you find the inner strength or resolve your need to carry on. This vision can help carry you through difficult phases of a project. A shared vision, which all members of your workgroup relate to, is often a key to successful group dynamics.

3. Revive Your Spirit

Probably you experience imagining things that can become very real to you. This may occur through your active imagination. It may also occur as a result of dreams that have aspects that come true. These forms of transcendental meditation are energizing. You can use this energy to nurture and revive your creative spirit.

Focus on a project you are comfortable daydreaming or even dreaming about. Try to start off with no expectations at all — just open yourself up to see what you might discover. Allow yourself to enter different states of mind through transcendental meditation so that you can explore your inner space. Transfer ideas from your inner space to media space using the following approaches:

a. Active Imagination

Have you ever had your imagination "run away" with you? Of course you have. You might reflect upon when this happens. You probably recognize that it helps to relax (although sometimes being scared will cause your imagination to run wild). A familiar activity — such as walking or driving a car — can stimulate your imagination. So can good music, an interesting painting, a beautiful landscape, a wonderful person, or an absorbing film. Conversations or group discussions — brainstorming sessions — (when people are comfortable with each other) also will stimulate your imagination. Consider how you could run away with your imagination.

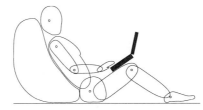

Try focusing your active imagination on a creative project you are working on. As a starting point, jot down some keywords or make concept diagrams. You can do this either on paper or with electronic media. Then let your mind wander. Follow it, taking notes. These may be mental notes you take while walking or driving, but be careful not to become too distracted. It is safer to follow your imagination when sitting with a sketchpad or at a computer. You might invite others to collaborate, either by having them sketch with you or by using computers together to access shared media space. The important thing is to have some comfortable way of recording where your imagination is taking you.

Use Johnson's four-step approach for active imagination:

1. Invite the unconscious. You can do this by contemplating or reflecting upon some stimulating feelings, ideas, or concepts.

2. Dialogue and experience. Here electronic media can be particularly effective because you can work with information so interactively using computers. For example, you can write, draw, or build electronic models representing what you are imagining. This becomes a representation of a new reality that you can experience, further stimulating your unconscious mind. Can you become conscious of your unconscious by recording your insights? Can you record your thoughts in ways you, and others, can interact with?

3. Add the ethical element of values. What insights have value relative to the problems at hand? Are they practical? Are they feasible? And, ultimately, are they ethical?

4. Make it concrete with physical ritual. Can you create an image that will help you visualize your insight more clearly? For example, incorporate it into what you are writing, drawing, or modeling. Use your insights in the image you are rendering or even music you are composing using computers. Can you incorporate this image into some artificial form of reality you are creating to experience it more thoroughly? This way you could also invite others to experience what you are imagining.

You can use your imagination very simply and quickly, or much more elaborately over a longer period of time. It is not always easy, however, to use a computer to develop quick and simple representations of what you experience drawing from your unconscious thinking. Sometimes it is easier to start with simple mental notes, verbal statements, or hand-drawn sketches. (You can also do this electronically, once you are comfortable using computers.) The advantage of using computers is that you can work more interactively with increasingly elaborate models of what you imagine. Evaluate how you are recording your insights. Make sure you find approaches that are both comfortable and interactive. Develop strategies for communicating your insights and transferring ideas to the objects you are creating.

b. Dreams

Leonardo da Vinci experimented with sleeping for short periods so he had more time to pursue his creative endeavors. By sleeping and waking more frequently, his mind went between dream and conscious states more often. It seems that machines he dreamed about were hundreds of years ahead of their time.

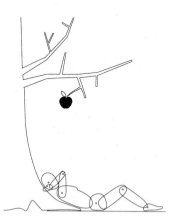

Try your own experiments with sleeping. You might find special places where you can do this, such as a couch in your study, a secluded cabin, or even a comfortable place outside — perhaps under the proverbial apple tree. Immerse yourself in a project before you go to sleep. Contemplate it as you are dozing off. You might keep a sketchpad or notebook computer nearby so you can take notes that will help you remember insights you derive from your contemplation. (You can use a notebook computer very well when you are lying down, although sometimes it is better to get up and use a desk or computer some place else, particularly if you are sleeping with another person and your insights become very compelling.) After you have slept, take the time to reflect on what you were dreaming about. Again use a sketchpad or computer to take notes that will help you remember your dreams. Do this even if the dream doesn't seem related to the project you were contemplating when you went to sleep.

Use Johnson's four-step approach for interpreting your dreams:

1. Make associations. How might the dream relate to what you are contemplating (or to anything else in your life that matters)?

2. Connect dream images to inner dynamics. Does the dream reflect insights that concern you?

3. Interpret. What conscious feelings or ideas can you derive from the dream?

4. Do rituals to make the dream concrete. Can you create an image of your dream that will help you visualize it more clearly? Again, can you incorporate it into what you are writing, drawing, or modeling? Can you use it in images you are rendering or even music you are composing using computers? How else can you act upon your dream to experience it through some form of reality?

You may find that you already do some of this naturally. Probably the most difficult thing is taking the time, finding the right place and relaxing — getting in the right mood. Notice the times, places, and thought patterns that help you do dream work. Also notice that stimulants like coffee, alcohol, or drugs are counterproductive. They may overstimulate your mind or thrust you into a stupor, making it much more difficult to derive insights from your dreams.

The focus of this effort is to explore your inner space and to transfer some of what you discover to media space. It is an exercise in making you conscious of your unconscious. You never know what you will discover in unconscious levels, which makes this effort very intriguing. Once you connect with your imagination, or a dream, you can begin to work with insights more consciously. You can do this by interpreting them, modeling them, and making them real using a variety of computer applications. The virtual reality of electronic media can provide a wonderful vehicle for doing this. Draw upon the creative energy in the unconscious levels of your mind by learning to use symbolic imagery. Nurture a creative or "art" spirit. Recognize this energy in yourself and in others.

For further guidance on relating to your inner space you may wish to refer to *Inner Work: Using Dreams and Active Imagination for Personal Growth* by Robert A. Johnson. If you encounter problems when exploring your inner realm, seek the guidance of a qualified clinician.

10

User Interfaces

How can you master the user interfaces emerging for computers? Most people master simple tools like pencils and pens. Let yourself become absorbed using electronic media. You can master computer interfaces once you become comfortable with the devices you use. Interfacing involves your body, mind, and spirit. Multimedia workstations can interact with many of your senses. The personal computer can now be a multimedia workstation connected to large work environments. When working with computer applications, you will find there are different levels of involvement. To work with computers creatively, you need to find ways to bond with them. This chapter will help you visualize your dream machine and open your mind to new realities. Computers can provide access to media for constructive collaboration, enabling you and your workgroup to become more productive and creative. The activities at the end of this chapter can help you explore how to interface with computers and access media space..

Interfacing

physical interface In computer applications, that which relates to the way people work with the hardware devices.

human factor A characteristic related to people. Especially concerning how people interface with tools such as computers.

ergonomics The study of how energy is spent. Pertains particularly to human energy expended for doing work.

mental interface In computer applications, that which relates to software procedures and thinking skills.

spiritual interface In computer applications, that which has to do with a sense of attachment, empowerment, and meaning.

The previous chapter put you more in touch with your body, mind, and spirit. This chapter will help you put your whole being in touch with computers, giving you better access to electronic media. There are different ways to relate to computers and electronic media. At one level there is the *physical interface* — which relates to the way you work with the hardware devices. Physical *human factors* and *ergonomics* are very important here. At another level there is the *mental interface*, which has more to do with software procedures and thinking skills. At still another level is the *spiritual interface*, having to do with a sense of attachment, empowerment, and meaning. This level is harder to articulate, although you can relate to this awareness. Each level influences how you interface with computers and electronic media.

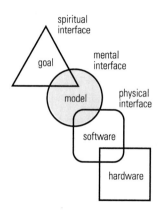

Interfaces

CRT Monitor

LCD

Projector

Just as you can learn to nurture your body, mind, and spirit, you can also learn to work with interfaces physically, mentally, and even spiritually. This chapter, and the activities which follow, will help you do that. Let us begin by exploring how you use computers and some of the interfaces which are emerging. Each of us has considerable capacity to master user interfaces if they are well designed. Build upon what you already know and are comfortable with. Learn to apply familiar user interfaces in new ways. Also, be open to learning new user interfaces that will allow you to work with different media. This will open new channels for thinking and expression.

The Look: Relating to What You See

A rapid evolution is occurring in computer monitors. CRTs (cathode ray tubes) now provide higher resolution and the capability to display more colors. By working with colored light, instead of reflected color, it is possible to display hues that are even more vivid than one can find in paintings on canvas. Computer monitors with progressive scanning reduce flicker. The result is that regular computer displays are almost as easy to read as images on paper. Enhancements of images using computers can even help the visually impaired. Flat panel technologies, made possible through LCDs (liquid crystal displays) now also offer color as well as shades of gray, making small notebook and pen computers increasingly appealing and useful to many people.

Computer images can also be projected onto screens for workgroup interaction or presentation to larger audiences. Small projection systems let individual workers, such as machinists, work with see-through displays, which enable them to align images of templates with parts they are working on.

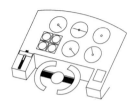

Stereo Goggles **Simulator**

real-time Movement which occurs at the speed it would in reality.

Computers also provide three-dimensional viewing capabilities. Devices such as three-dimensional glasses, or headsets with stereo goggles enable you to use your binocular vision. Booms with binoculars let you peer into three-dimensional space without being encumbered by a headset. By using fast computers, you are able to experience *real-time* movement. Virtual reality lets you become immersed in information environments, navigate in them, and even manipulate them using computer interfaces. Some virtual reality devices are integrated into simulators that provide realistic experiences useful for training. For example, they may be part of flight simulators for training jet pilots.

We are all familiar with remote control devices for TVs and VCRs. The possibilities for interacting with video can go way beyond that. Myron Krueger an artificial reality pioneer has conceived what he calls *videoplaces*. His goal is to permit people to interact with these places using their natural senses and body movements. He is exploring ways of doing this with sensory floors, and data tablets — basically surfaces that you can work on — when in a video environment.

videoplace An artificial reality that you can enter and experience using video.

HDTV (high-definition television) is establishing new standards that are going to affect both commercial television and computing. These standards include not only spatial resolution, with a high density of square pixels, but also temporal resolution, with a high frame rate to capture movement. In addition, these standards address aspect ratios — the width of the image divided by the height. Wider-screen images, like those you see in wide-screen cinemas, fill your field of vision to heighten your experience. Place your hands at the extremities of your cone of vision and you will define a space that roughly has a 16-to-9 aspect ratio. HDTV is

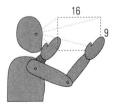

Cone of Vision

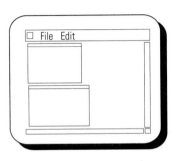

Multiple Windows **Video**

adopting a wider aspect ratio as part of the new standard. Using digital technology, you will be able to move higher-quality images, not only via air waves, but also via cable, videotape, and CD-ROM. Data compression using CODAC (coders and decoders) is making this possible.

Software now enables you to view multiple windows so you can work with multiple documents and even do *multitasking*. Modeling programs simultaneously provide multiple views of an object. You can couple multidisplays with multimedia. "Multi-multi" makes it easier to work in media space. It can help you relate to what you see on a monitor.

It is now even possible to view video on a computer monitor. You can integrate live video into documents. You can enhance and transform digital video images when making multimedia presentations. It is likely that interactive video — which enables you to both hear and see (like using a telephone with a TV camera and monitor) — will also become more widely available.

There are even performance animation systems that link your gestures to computer animation. Recently, I was sitting in the front row of a computer show. At the beginning of this demonstration, the announcer asked me my name and where I was from. Then the demonstration began, and an animated cartoon character appeared — projected on a large video screen. This character knew my name. Throughout the demonstration he would add comments about Professor von Wodtke from Cal Poly, Pomona. Needless to say, I had to find out how this was done. It turned out there was an actor behind the screen who could see me and my reactions. The actor was wearing a special face mask that recorded his eyebrow, cheek, head, chin, and lip movements. These gestures were linked to the face of the cartoon character on the screen. When the actor spoke, the cartoon character spoke — with all the appropriate gestures. And I thought I was seeing the Wizard of Oz.

Other visual media are also becoming interfaces for working with computers. For example, the Xerox company has developed software that enables you to control a computer by writing on forms you can FAX to the computer from remote locations. You can transfer images from paper to a computer using a scanner or a FAX machine. Character recognition software can read typed fonts and convert them to digital formats with fairly good accuracy. As noted before, software is emerging which enables you to train a computer to even recognize your handwritten characters. This requires training the machine and, of course, forming characters in a consistent way. You can also scan photographic images so you can work with them using digital drawing and painting programs. In addition, you can capture video. And, of course, you can transfer digital information to paper using printers, plotters, FAX machines, and even color printing presses. You can use film recorders, as well as video recorders, to convert digital information into images you can see. These devices for working with paper, film, and video become extensions of your computer user interface.

multitasking Using more than one software application at the same time. For example, some computer user interfaces permit people to work with different applications using different windows.

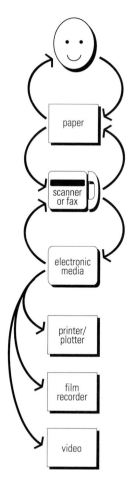

Extended Interface

The Sound: Relating to What You Hear

The sound systems of computers are rapidly improving. Coupled with good speakers, or ear phones, computers can play high-quality stereo sound. They can control analog tape recorders and play digital sound from CD-ROM disks. Many stage productions now use computer-controlled sound systems. Computers are too expensive to use solely as individual tape or CD players. There are many consumer electric devices that do a fine job of playing recorded music. The real advantage of computers is that they can also convert sounds to digital formats. This enables you to work with sound in ways that were never possible before. It provides tremendous potential for composing music. You can record sounds of vocalists and traditional acoustical instruments and work them into musical compositions. Using a MIDI keyboard enables you to synthesize electrical sounds and compose with them mixing many channels of sound.

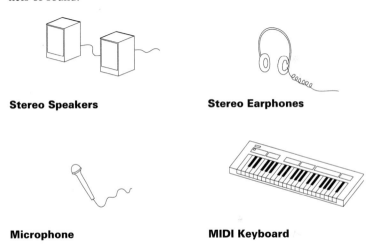

Stereo Speakers   **Stereo Earphones**

Microphone   **MIDI Keyboard**

Computer programs, games, and simulators have auditory feedback that provides users with important cues. Initially, these sounds were electronic beeps and buzzes. Now the sounds can become more pleasant or even more realistic.

Telephones are now an interface for computers, providing voice mail capabilities. Also, by using a microphone attached to a computer, you can record and embed verbal messages in computer files. You can play these messages back interactively. Voice synthesizers can convert digital information into verbal messages. In the 1970s Texas Instruments began using voice synthesis in children's educational games such as Speak and Spell. Now, telephone information services routinely use voice synthesis. "The number is. . . . "

Telephone

Voice Mail

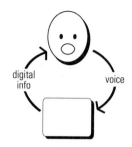

Voice Recognition

Earphone/Mike

Voice recognition is probably the most promising development for using sound as a computer user interface. Programs are available that will recognize voice commands. These have particular potential for applications like CADD, where you fully occupy your hands. With voice recognition you can speak a command without having to point and click with the pointing device you are drawing with. To use this interface, you have to train the computer to recognize your voice. Sometimes this also requires training yourself to speak clearly and consistently. It may become entirely practical to work with a computer verbally, not only by using verbal commands, but also by having computers take dictation and provide verbal responses. Often, in science fiction, interaction with computers is not bound by the keyboard, pointing devices, and computer monitor. Effective voice recognition could make these fantasies real. It could open new possibilities for personal computing providing yet other ways of interfacing with computers.

The Feel: Relating to What You Touch

Keyboards have become the standard computer user interface. The difficulty is that keyboards require typing skills. Now pointing devices are available which provide a user interface that responds to more natural gestures.

Many different types of pointing devices have emerged. There is the simple mouse popularized by the Macintosh System. Computer games have popularized joysticks. There are now also roller balls, which use less desk space. Digitizing tablets with styluses or multikeyed pucks are especially useful for drafting. Some of these devices are pressure-sensitive—for example you can make denser lines when you press harder on these pen-like styluses—making them more suitable for painting. Some pointing devices can also respond to rotation and tilt, providing some of the subtle controls of traditional drawing instruments. Pen computers are

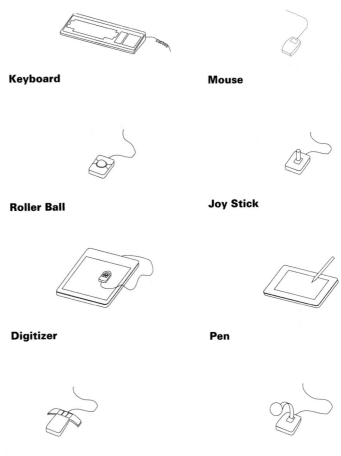

Keyboard **Mouse**

Roller Ball **Joy Stick**

Digitizer **Pen**

Flying Mouse **Control Ball**

now emerging, permitting you to gesture directly on the computer display in a more comfortable position than with the original touch-screen monitors. This provides more direct interaction with your work.

Pointing devices now even work in three dimensions, enabling users to build digital spatial models more easily. For example, flying mice and control ball devices can detect positions in three dimensions. It is no longer necessary to use two-dimensional digitizers and type in the third dimension (usually with a keyboard) or change coordinate systems to digitize in three dimensions. There are also sonic digitizers that can scan existing three-dimensional forms.

Beyond that, data gloves and even body suits can detect your movements in ways that you can, in effect, create the experience of being in virtual reality. Some researchers use treadmills and stationary bicycles in this way. You can link elaborate simulators to computers to provide very realistic experiences for visualization and training. Some simulators even provide tactile feedback.

Data Glove

The Setting

Computer Lab

Comtemplative Environment

People often ignore the setting in which they use computers. But the setting is actually an important part of the user interface. For example, the computer labs at the university where I teach are crowded and noisy, resulting in frequent interruptions. There is glare due to poor lighting. The heating and ventilation systems work poorly. These conditions compromise human performance regardless of the computer interface. You wouldn't expect people to read a book or write with pencil on paper in these conditions. It is not surprising to me that my students have an aversion to our computer labs. I, too, can barely read E-mail and have difficulty writing thoughtful responses when working there. I find it remarkably more productive accessing the same programs in the privacy of my study using a modem at home in Claremont. For me, it is even easier to write when reclining in the loft of my cabin at Big Bear Lake, in the San Bernardino Mountains of California, with a notebook computer on my lap. In this quiet environment, I can occasionally gaze into the woods by Metcalf Creek and watch wildlife while I reflect upon what I am writing. Parts of this book have emerged on my small notebook computer while I write here at my cabin. I also wrote for almost a month using my notebook computer while in Lerici, Italy, by the Mediterranean Sea.

Evolution of Work Environments

Everyone is familiar with a tool-based work environment. Setting up tools in a space where you can physically work with them is as old as recorded history. Primitive societies still do this, even around camp fires. Monks in monasteries, as well as craftsmen in guilds, perfected tool-based work environments long ago. Tool-based workshops, factories, and offices became the mainstay of the industrial revolution. A tool-based work environment may be a desk with file drawers where you can use common office tools. It may be a drafting station where you use drawing

The Desk

The Drafting Station

instruments. In many offices people have added computers to a tool-based work environment, using them only for data processing, or as a word processor or a drafting machine. These tools have a real-world focus and can enhance human capabilities. Yet their potential is limited if they are used only as single-purpose tools. With a change in mind-set you can draw upon more of your mental capacity when using computers.

The Computer

A computer workstation represents the next stage of evolution of a work environment. Computers can integrate the tools used and provide access to them. Computer interfaces have emerged in the last part of this century. At first there were mainframe computers, with punch cards and keyboards. Now, there are powerful desktop workstations with graphic user interfaces. For example, X windows works with the Unix operating system. Next uses a windowing environment called Nextstep. The Macintosh System provides access to tools using a desktop metaphor. Windows also provides access to different applications in an MS DOS computer environment. In addition there is OS/2—the operating system IBM has developed. Using graphic user interfaces, you can access a growing array of writing, drawing, drafting, modeling, imaging, animation, audio, and video tools. Even basic workstations can integrate a word processor with a dictionary and thesaurus. They also can integrate spreadsheet and database programs for quantitative modeling. In addition, they can integrate simple drawing, painting, and presentation programs for graphics. Advanced workstations integrate many more powerful tools, enabling you to do desktop publishing, create computer-aided design, do video imaging, and even compose music. You can work with geographic information systems, as well as animation, hypermedia, and multimedia applications, which can produce desktop video. The arts, design, engineering, and the sciences often require specialized workstations.

Although it takes a somewhat different mind-set to use a computer workstation, there are distinct advantages to being able to work with information digitally. You can develop this mind-set in any discipline using the approaches to media, models, and methods described previously in this book. You need to learn how to relate electronic media to your goals and how to navigate using different applications. You need to develop models you can use in your computer workstation which are meaningful to the realities you work with. You also need to develop methods for using computer applications so you can readily visualize your work flow.

The World

As the twenty-first century approaches, an information revolution is occurring. A media space work environment is emerging where computers become a vehicle for moving information. You can access information online. Tools like the telephone and FAX machine are now becoming integrated with computers. The worlds of computers and video are also merging. Consumer electronics will provide players that enable people to view multimedia information interactively. A new array of authoring tools is emerging for electronic media. This is making it possible for yet another mind-set to emerge—one in which space and time

can be treated differently. No longer do you have to work in the same space at the same time. You can hand off information electronically. You can link your operations to service bureaus that provide enhanced capabilities you could not afford to maintain on your own. It is now becoming possible for creative individuals to work independently of large organizations by drawing upon the support they can find in a media space work environment. This provides a whole new range of possibilities for when and where you work. Media space work environments that are emerging can provide new freedoms and flexibility.

Each of these work environments will continue to exist. There will always be a need for tool-based work environments where people can meet and work with tools in a physical context. Fabrication, construction, and nurturing of organizations require this. And people also need the stimulation of real-life interaction with other people. At the same time, computer workstations will become even more useful. You can reach your computer by using a phone or FAX machine. It also is now possible to package a tremendous number of tools into a small box (such as a powerful notebook computer) and take this workstation with you no matter where you go. This enables you to use a wonderful array of media including not only text, but also graphics, three-dimensional models, animation, images, and even video and sound. Beyond that are growing opportunities to create a media space work environment. Computers can be linked using networks as well as telecommunications.

Technologies are merging. The voice capabilities of the telephone are becoming integrated into computers that can also control digital sound systems. Video is merging with computers. All of this is being enhanced by improved communication systems which include fiber optics and data compression. Increased transmission speeds are making it possible to transfer a wide bandwidth of media almost instantaneously. Consumer electronics can provide the masses with multimedia devices enabling them to look in on this media space and view multimedia interactively. Computers can empower creative people to express themselves in multimedia and work collaboratively through telecommunications.

In effect, your ideas can travel almost at the speed of light. It is interesting to see what you can do with these new freedoms. Obviously, your choices are tempered by what you can afford. Although this technology is becoming less expensive, computer work environments are feasible only if you can develop the mind-set to use them effectively.

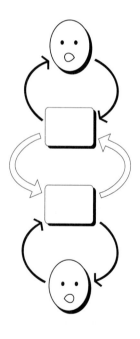

Multimedia Communication

Hierarchy of Tools

Connectivity is the key to a media space work environment. The physical connection requires a network or modem, but there is also a mental connection requiring the realization of what you can do with these tools. You may need to change your mind-set to be able to relate your goals to a

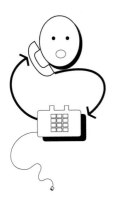

Stand-Alone Phone

media space work environment. Using your computer as a stand-alone tool is much like using your telephone attached only to an answering machine. You could record and play back information, but you could not send it. Obviously, you want to attach your telephone to an outside line. Similarly, you should recognize the potential of hooking up your computer so you can work online in media space.

A dizzying array of multimedia tools is emerging. The challenge is to find the simple tools for tasks you wish to do and yet make sure they relate to the larger picture. Just as integrated transportation systems are important, it is important to look for ways to create integrated communication systems. Automobiles have not made shoes, bicycles, or public transit obsolete. There is a hierarchy of vehicles in a good multi-modal transportation system. Each serves certain purposes best. Each can become part of a larger system helping you physically move through space. Similarly, computers have not made other modes of communication obsolete. Instead they are becoming integrated with devices such as the telephone and television to provide vehicles for moving information through media space. Both verbal communications picked up by microphones and simple gestures of pointing devices or pens are becoming inegrated into this communication system as well.

Transportation System

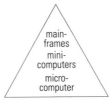

Computer System

Communication System

Merging of Personal Computer and Workstations

The many levels of computing are also becoming more integrated. There are terminals for mainframe computers and minicomputers. There are workstations and personal computers that are broadly considered microcomputers. The distinction between personal computers and workstations blurs as workstations become more affordable and personal computers become more powerful. Workstations and personal computers can also function as "smart terminals," enabling you to work using mainframe computers.

Personal computing is becoming more accessible. At first personal computers were desktop devices. Then portables emerged. Now there is a proliferation of lap-top, notebook, subnotebook, pen, and even palm-top computers. A new genre of consumer electronic devices is growing out of portable radios, TVs, tape recorders, and CD players, enabling users to listen and view electronic media more interactively. Cellular phones are beginning to take on new dimensions of wireless connectivity as they

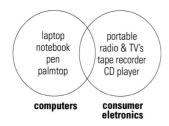

Merging of Computers and Consumer Electronics

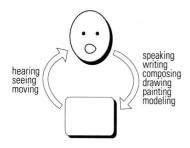

Wideband Interaction

become able to transmit not only voice, but also FAX and telecommunications as well. There is also a proliferation of new peripherals including scanners, digital cameras, and video recorders for getting information into digital formats. In addition, there is an amazing array of peripherals for transferring digital information to paper, film, videotape, and disks. Small FAX-modems included with personal computers enable users to transfer information digitally using existing telephone systems. Developments in data compression and fiber optics promise to make these conduits for communication even faster and capable of carrying a broader bandwidth of media—such as interactive video.

These tools bring amazing power to your fingertips. Many of these devices can "dock" with larger devices that add to their capabilities. Telecommunications enables you to tie them together electronically. In this way your physical work environment can become completely integrated with your media space work environment. You can be on another continent and still access a document you have filed at your home office. You no longer have to be where a document is to use it. And you no longer have to be at the same place at the same time to interact with other people. You are gaining greater freedom over mobility and the use of time. The emerging user interface enables you to work locally and communicate globally in ways that were never possible before.

Levels of Involvement

You will find different levels of involvement in anything you do. For example, actors will at first just read the lines and become acquainted with a character. Then they learn the lines. Good actors can master lines and become the character. Or take a sport like skiing for example. When you begin, your skis are clumsy attachments to your feet. Soon you learn basic turns to maneuver. Eventually, good skiers feel a harmony with the terrain, the snow conditions, and the gravitational forces acting upon them.

It is fascinating to watch children learn to play computer games. You can also reflect on how you learn computer programs. Drawing from those observations and experiences you can realize there are also different levels of involvement when using computers. When you begin, your persona and the computer are separate—there is a distinct boundary. As you become more familiar with the program, you begin to relate to the computer through the user interface. Eventually, you feel that the program is part of you. Ultimately, you can even feel that you become part of the world you experience though the computer.

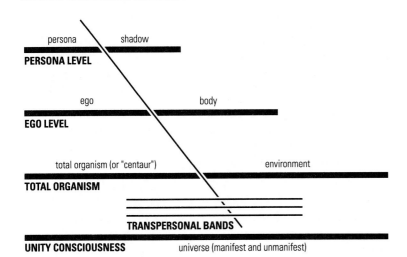

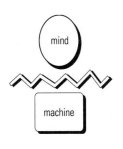

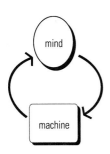

In his book, *No Boundary: Eastern and Western Approaches to Personal Growth*, Ken Wilber provides a map of the spectrum of consciousness. He points out the different levels of consciousness as you move deeper into your subconscious:

Persona level

Ego level

Total organism

Unity consciousness

The Spectrum of Consciousness
adapted from *No Boundary* by Wilber

Persona Involvement

Ego Involvement

Persona Level

At the persona level, humans and machines are separate. Each has boundaries. There is little or no interaction. The relationship between humans and computers seems unnatural, even impossible.

Books on hardware, of course, focus on the machine. They are typically written at a persona level of involvement. "This is the hardware. . . . These are its parts. . . . Its specifications are. . . . When this happens, try. . . . " Not surprisingly most people have difficulty relating to hardware manuals. They present an entity separate from your persona. You need to have a certain fascination with machines to relate to them as an entity in themselves.

Ego Level

At the ego involvement level, humans and machines begin to interrelate through user interfaces. The interface relates to your organs of perception and to your organs of expression. At this level, however, a person's ego may not be comfortable relating to the person's own perceptions and expressions, let alone to using a machine like a computer.

Books on software applications are usually written for the ego level of involvement. They focus on the user interface. "Here is how you work with this application. . . . Use this command to. . . . The routine or procedure is. . . ." People interested in computer applications relate to these books. However, there is usually little in these books to help the users go to deeper levels of involvement and draw upon their creative capacity. Chapters on advanced applications usually discuss more complex routines along with more "tips and tricks."

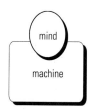

Total Organism Involvement

Unity Conscious Involvement

Total Organism Level

At the total organism level there is a union of humans and machines. Familiar repetitive tasks, like data entry, seem almost automatic. The users begins to feel that the computer is part of their being. The boundaries, however, are the standard applications that the users have mastered.

This book on creative thinking skills can help you achieve deeper levels of involvement. It provides the principles and cognitive techniques to coordinate your capabilities with a computer. Visualization enables you to learn to function as a total organism using a computer.

Unity Consciousness Level

At the unity consciousness level the computer user's inner space and the electronic media space can merge. The machine is transparent. The user begins to feel a part of the artificial reality he or she is accessing through the computer. The only boundaries are the limits of awareness and imagination.

Creative thinking skills also can help you reach levels of unity consciousness when working with computers. They provide metaphors and ways of mapping media space to guide you through cognitive domains. You also need to learn to find your way in your own inner space. For this you can refer to many different sources, such as Abraham Maslow's classic book, *Toward a Psychology of Being*. Or you can refer to the other books on personal development already mentioned by Johnson or Wilber. You may find some religious and mystical works helpful as well.

I have even observed children approaching a unity consciousness level of involvement when relating to computers. For example, children using computer games playfully experience the merger of their inner space and the media space. They can move into a transcendental state, unaware of time and their physical environment. Only certain games provide the richness for children to achieve that level of involvement. Those are the games that children often naturally select. This level of involvement can become almost addictive.

Children may move to deeper levels of consciousness more easily than adults because they haven't yet developed a strong persona. They are still learning and exploring their relationship to their organs of perception and their organs of expression. They can easily learn new patterns because they are not locked into habits. They are comfortable with bonding whether it is to a person—like their mother or a friend—or to a machine. Their awareness and imagination are unencumbered by experience. Consequently, they can focus on the "now." They are open to any new experience. The notion of entering artificial reality is not strange to them.

Thinking about your own experiences with computer programs (maybe even computer games). You will realize that you too experience different levels of involvement. The levels you work at may be different depending

upon the computer or the programs you are using. They may also change during a work session as you become more or less involved in what you are doing.

Not all computer programs (or games) enable you to achieve unity consciousness. Some are not sufficiently interactive, or the user interface may be too difficult (maybe even impossible) to master. Not all environments are conducive to this level of concentration. (As I have mentioned, some computer labs are uncomfortable and filled with distractions.) You will find favorite programs that you can master, using a preferred workstation in a comfortable place. These can include word processing, graphics, CADD, animation, music, and other programs. Some programs take a long time to master. It may take months, even years, of practice to achieve deeper levels of involvement. Yet that experience can be very satisfying. Virtual reality hardware and software may make this easier to achieve.

Here are some indications of achieving unity consciousness as you master a computer program:

- You realize that you are able to move beyond standard routines.

- You develop a sense of becoming engrossed in the program.

- You lose a sense of time during at least some of the session.

- You become oblivious to your physical surroundings during the session.

Unity Consciousness

- You relate to and remember what you experience in artificial reality as if it had the richness of real-life experience.

These encounters can become addictive — you may feel a craving to express your creative urges in this way. Make sure you relate to computing at the unity conscious level as you would relate to normal urges for hunger or sex. Enjoy the exercise of adventures in media space as you enjoy the exercise of adventures in reality.

Bonding: Mind, Machine, and Media

bonding Connecting or holding together. The formation of close interpersonal relationships involving the whole being. People can also bond with objects related to computers, and with places in reality or virtual reality.

You usually develop relationships with people — your parents, your spouse, your children, your friends. You can also relate to places — such as your home, or the place where you grew up, or the school you attended. You develop relationships with other beings — such as pets. You relate to your apparel — like your favorite shoes. You may even relate to the tools you use — your favorite pen — your favorite toys — maybe a tennis racket, a golf club, or a pair of skis. Close interpersonal attachments are sometimes referred to as *bonding*. That notion can extend to include places and objects as well. You bond with what attracts you and what you become familiar with. Common experiences give you some comprehension of how someone, or something, behaves. Bonding involves your whole being. You feel like someone or something becomes part of you. It

can add a fullness to your life. Bonding has physical, mental, and even spiritual dimensions.

You can also bond with computers. You need to do this to use electronic media creatively. There are fundamentally different approaches to relating to a computer.

One approach is to try to anthropomorphize the computer — to give it human traits. In that way you can begin to relate to a computer somewhat like you would relate to another person or to a pet. Using this approach, researchers strive to give the computer artificial intelligence and set up another being (a robot or droid). In some situations robots and droids may be useful. "Let the computer do it" (as if it could do it all alone). People begin to talk about computer designs, rather than computer-aided design.

Another approach is to use computers as an extension of yourself to enhance your being. You can learn to relate to computers in the way you relate to clothes. For example, a shoe is not a replacement for your foot. You wear different shoes for different functions. You also select certain shoes because you like them. You might even use attachments like skis or roller blades to enhance your capabilities. Your interface with the earth is most often literally through your shoes, but you can go barefoot. It is always possible, and even pleasurable, to feel the comforts and discomforts of the earth directly beneath your feet. How delightful it is to walk in surf feeling wet sand beneath your feet. Similarly, although you may use computers to work with models that are an artificial reality, you should always tune your senses to the realities these models represent. You may seek to create a unity between you and this machine. This means you use the computer to expand your perception, augment your intelligence, and enhance your actions — rather than create another entity. The idea is to let the computer become integral with, and an extension of your being. To do this, you must learn to integrate it with your body, mind, and spirit. And realize that computers do not have a will of their own. They have certain operating characteristics that you should not confuse with a spirit or will. With this approach, the human mind is the key component of computer applications. Computers aid your design capabilities; they don't replace them.

How should you relate to personal computers then? Are computers like pets, or apparel? Are they an entity that can function on their own, or are they an extension of their user? Should you use computers instead of design, or should you use computer-aided design?

Today's computers are very limited when functioning on their own. Typically, computers can only learn what you teach them and can carry out only programmable procedures. This can be useful in some situations. These situations might involve procedures that are repetitive — too boring or menial for humans to do. Some procedures have to be done with speed or accuracy that humans are not capable of. Other situations might involve hostile environments — perhaps far out in space or deep under

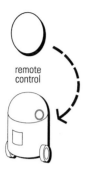

remote
control

Separate Being

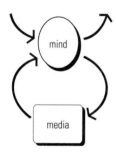

mind

media

Integral to Our Being

Move beyond
standard routines.

Become engrossed.

Loose sense
of time.

Become oblivious
to physical surroundings.

Create rich experiences
in virtual reality.

Unity Consciousness

the sea. In these situations it might be justifiable to create another entity that can be controlled remotely. Not surprisingly, though, many people perceive other entities as a threat. They may fear competition, or, even worse, replacement. They may fear that computers will take over the world. Essentially, they may fear losing control (as if anyone really has control). Subconsciously, people struggle with conflicts between their being and the artificial being they are creating. They worry that the computer might generate a spirit or a will of its own. Classic mythical themes of "dealing with the devil" emerge from their deeper levels of consciousness. Science fiction feeds on this fear. There are many scenarios about computers becoming entities out of control.

Creative activities, such as designing and planning, involve using computers as an extension of your mind. Computers can become tools for enhancing perception, tools for stimulating thought, and tools for amplifying actions. Of course, here you confront classical themes related to gaining mystical powers. You also have to be careful that when you step into the realms of artificial reality, you don't lose touch with actual reality. You have to be careful that you don't become so dependent on the enhanced capabilities computers provide that you can't function without them. For example, have you tried to add long columns of numbers without a calculator lately?

Although this book discusses the emerging computer technology, you may not have access to all these tools. Futhermore, you may not be particularly interested in learning to use all these tools even if you had access to them. So your options are limited by access and interest. Having an awareness of the possibilities is good because limitations are constantly changing. You may find ways of gaining access to tools you didn't have access to before. You may also find yourself becoming interested in media and applications you didn't consider seriously until you could relate them to your goals. That should be an outcome of using this book.

Although the best tool for a job is often the one you can use the best — the one you feel most comfortable with — this is not the ideal strategy for developing new capabilities. You need to try new tools to develop your capabilities. Initially, most people are not comfortable using computers — that is, not until they have the chance to work and play with them. Your projects can provide opportunities to explore new tools. The learning curve for some computer applications can be quite steep. However, when the learning curve is steep, you can be gaining the most capabilities in the shortest time. I tell my students that learning computer applications is like climbing mountains. Although it may start easy, it can become strenuous during steep ascents. Then your learning efforts will level off as you reach new heights of accomplishment. Just as you can derive satisfaction from climbing a mountain, you can also gain satisfaction from learning new computer applications. Classroom situations can provide the positive reinforcement needed to climb this learning curve.

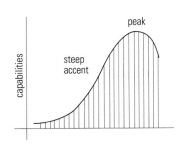

Limiting Factors

The Learning Curve

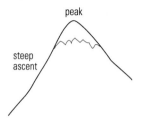

peak

steep
ascent

Mountain Climbing

They can help you reach your goals. You can also find positive reinforcement from colleagues or from computer user groups in your work environment. As with climbing a mountain, it is sometimes easier to hike with others who can spur you on; similarly, it can be easier to learn to use new computer applications with others. I know people are sometimes tempted to revert to using old tools and techniques they feel more comfortable with to finish their projects. I try to encourage my students to continue their ascent despite difficulties they may encounter. In school they have a chance to become familiar with new approaches. In practice the product will become more important. Emphasizing the product often makes people take fewer risks and not try new procedures. Yet personal development and progress can come from taking risks and learning better approaches. There is a delicate balance between bonding with tools in order to perfect approaches and developing new approaches to expand your capabilities. With an appropriate attitude, you have the potential for developing new relationships throughout your life with tools such as computers.

Summary

This chapter helps you use computers to interface with electronic media. You can set up work environments to do this. You can regard computer applications as integral to your being. You can use media space to work in collaboration with colleagues. The first activity at the end of the chapter will cause you to examine how you are using computers to access electronic media.

Use multimedia. Multimedia engages a range of modes of thought. Work toward wideband interaction involving multimedia. The second activity that follows will help you open new channels of media by using a variety of computer interfaces.

Get involved more deeply. Your tools become part of you. There is a spectrum of consciousness that enables involvement at different levels. These include:

- Persona involvement

- Ego involvement

- Total organism involvement

- Unity consciousness involvement

Become aware of different levels of involvement by relating to experiences you already have. Transfer this awareness to new computer interfaces and applications. The third activity that follows will help you seek deeper involvement.

Unity consciousness is the deepest level of involvement. Work toward unity consciousness. Computer interfaces include not only a physical interface, but also a mental interface and a spiritual interface as well. Work with all aspects of the interface. Bond with computers. Yet stay open to new possibilities. Interest and access are limiting factors when using electronic media. Stimulate your interest in computers and gain access to electronic media. The last activity in the chapter will help you bond with your computer. This will stimulate your interest in accessing electronic media.

Activities

Tool

Workstation

Media Space Environment

1. How Are You Using Computers?

Some people use computers only as a specialized tool — for example, only for word processing. Other people use computers as a workstation that gives them access to a variety of tools they find in a stand-alone computer. Still others are learning to use computers as a media space work environment through which they can gain access to information and work collaboratively. You will find your work environment can evolve. You may be drawn to computers because of a particular application and then discover other applications you can also use and enjoy. Ultimately, you can use computers to access media space and journey in a virtual reality you can help shape. Some people are hands-on computer users who like to take hold of the controls. Others work through computer operators. They prefer to be chauffeured when they journey into media space.

Consider how you use computers. What type of work environments are you involved with? Are you using computers only as a specialized tool or are you using them as a workstation? Are you using computers to access a media space work environment? Can you enhance the work environment you access with your computer? Are you presently chauffeured — working mostly through computer operators? Can you take hold of the controls so you can become more self-sufficient when you interface with media space?

2. Open New Channels of Media

Some people work primarily with a single channel of expression. They may do only word processing or computer-aided drafting. There are long traditions of people who have mastered a variety of media, drawing upon a range of expression. For example, Renaissance men — such as Leonardo da Vinci — wrote, sketched, painted, sculpted, and developed models and even prototypes of machines. Today, computers are making it easier for you to be a new type of Renaissance person, enabling us to work with different channels of expression — and use more of your mental capacity.

How can you use different channels for work and play? Can you give expression to ideas and information using multimedia? Can you transfer primary — or more intuitive — gestures directly to electronic media? Can you develop ideas, working interactively with electronic media, to refine more conscious actions? Can you integrate the media you are working with into a coherent presentation? Examine the look, feel, and sound of the workstations you have access to. Think about how you could use these computers to integrate the media you are using. Are there changes you could make in your thinking skills, software, and hardware that would enable you to integrate more channels of electronic media to effectively use more of your mental capacity?

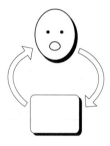

Wideband Interaction

3. Seek Deeper Involvement

When you read or listen to the radio, you experience different levels of involvement. If you don't recognize the language, you get no message — you just see the letters of the words or hear sounds. At some level you begin to comprehend patterns and learn to connect literal meaning with the message. At another level you easily comprehend the message and can relate to the nuances of what you read or hear. At still another level you lose the sense we are reading or listening. You actually visualize you are there.

You can relate these levels of consciousness to your level of involvement with computers. In his book *No Boundary*, Ken Wilber describes different levels of consiousness. He identifies these as the persona level, ego level, total organism level, and unity consciousness level. You can relate these levels to the different levels of consciousness you experience when working with computers. At the persona level, there is a distinct separation between humans and machines. Each has boundaries. No doubt you experienced this separation when you first tried to use a computer. At the ego involvement level, you begin to interrelate with machines through a user interface. Although initially you may find yourself not completely comfortable functioning at this level, you can at least interact with the computer. At the total organism level, a union occurs between you and the machine. Familiar repetitive tasks, like data entry, become almost automatic. And, finally, at the unity consciousness level, the machine becomes transparent. You feel as if you have entered the artificial reality of media space. The boundaries become only the limits of your awareness and imagination.

Persona Involvement

Ego Involvement

Total Organism Involvement

Unity Conscious Involvement

You can involve different levels of consciousness when using multimedia computing. Try to move beyond your persona and make the computer an extension of your being. Beyond that, try to achieve unity consciousness by actually visualizing that you are in media space. For example, when working with a spatial model, visualize actually entering the model and moving around it. By doing this you will draw upon more of your senses and use more of your mental capacity. Working toward unity consciousness will help you to derive more from experiences in artificial reality and remember them more vividly. What is exciting about achieving unity consciousness using a computer is that you are not just a passive observer as you would be when reading a book or listening to the radio. You can become an active participant in a virtual reality you are experiencing.

Work with tools in ways which induce different levels of involvement. First use a familiar tool or program. Then transfer this awareness to computer programs you wish to master.

For example, take a familiar tool such as a pencil and use it in a different way. For example, change hands — use the pencil with your left hand if you are right-handed. Note how your persona relates differently to the pencil in your "wrong" hand — how there seems to be a boundary between you and this object. Now take the pencil in your "normal" hand. Feel the qualities of the pencil — its length, its balance, the quality of the point, the softness of the lead — notice how your ego becomes involved. Use that pencil for a familiar task — write your name, for example. Notice how the pencil becomes part of your total organism as you become involved in the task at hand. Now, with that favorite pencil in hand, relax and reflect. Let the ideas you are generat-

ing in your head flow from the pencil. Let this flow be doodles or words— whatever comes naturally from your unconscious. Let there be a unity between your inner space and the media space you are working with on paper.

Now use the same procedure with different computer programs (even a computer game if you wish). Work toward deeper levels of involvement with each program. Work past your persona to achieve ego involvement with the program. Do familiar tasks, until they become routine and you and the program begin to function as a total organism. Finally, let your inner space merge with the electronic media space to achieve a unity consciousness level of involvement. (Be patient; it may take you months—even years—of practice to achieve this with more complex programs.)

4. Bond With Your Computer

Bonding occurs among people—the devotion and intimacy of a happily married couple, the attachment of a young child to his or her parents, or even firm friendships. People have a natural tendency to develop strong emotional ties. Similarly, people can become attached to some objects. For example, you may have a favorite pencil or pen, or even a fantastic car. You may also have a preferred computer. Bonding with computers can be both positive and negative. It can be positive because it is this type of relationship that enables you to build up the familiarity and confidence you need to work effectively with computers. But it can be negative, because hardware and software are evolving so rapidly that you need to keep yourself open to accept better computers you can bond with.

Consider how you relate to your computer(s). What does it mean to you? Have you found a computer you feel you can bond with? Are they becoming an extension of your being? Fantasy is also important in any emotional relationship. Poets are sometimes more enamored by their fantasy than by their real love. Yet fantasy helps you envision an ideal. It can be healthy to imagine your "dream machine." What would it be like? How could you use it to open your mind? Can you imagine artificial realities through which you could explore unity consciousness? Can you develop a vision of the potential you have to use computers creatively? Obviously, you need to balance your ideal with reality. You need to keep your attachment to computers in balance with the rest of your life and not lose touch with reality. You may also find other people regarding your computer jealously because of the attention you devote to it.

Bonding

11

Mixing Media

This chapter will discuss strategies for integrating media. The channels through which people move information are changing. Old transfers are becoming obsolete. The work environment is also changing as a result of electronic media. Clarifying and refining ways to delegate tasks can help people work with new media. There are opportunities to work concurrently, reducing the time it takes to get new ideas to market. Expectations are rising in response to the new opportunities that are emerging. People want quicker results (even more color and sound). You can learn strategies to mix media in effective ways. If you don't learn to master the media, the media may master you. The activities at the end of the chapter provide you with opportunities to engage in strategies for mixing media and apply them to projects you are working with.

Choices of Media

We all share ideas and information verbally — conversation is a basic medium we sometimes take for granted. When recording ideas and information, we usually choose paper, film, or electronic media. There are other media, of course. Sculptors and building craftsmen have long traditions of using materials such as marble.

Paper

People have used paper for centuries. Traditional media — such as paper — works better with linear processes. We need to draft and re-draft documents when we work on paper. It has the advantage of being inexpensive and available. You can carry it with you and write on it simply with pencil or pen. However, it is opaque so you can only work with a few layers at a time. You can send it through the mail. Paper is flammable, absorbs moisture, and changes size slightly with humidity. Some paper deteriorates in time. You can use printing presses and copy machines to reproduce information on paper. Most paper is made from the pulp of trees and is recyclable.

Film

During the last century and a half, people have learned to use film. You can take photographs or moving pictures with a camera using film coated with light-sensitive emulsions. You can also draw on films such as Mylar — working on more layers than you could if you were using paper. Drawing on overlays allows you to re-use base layers of generic information and then add overlays with unique information. Architects and engi-

neers use pin-registered overlays. Artists even integrate photographic images with hand-drawn images done on film. Animators draw on film to create moving images overlaid on stationary backgrounds. Film is dimensionally stable and does not deteriorate (although some inks and photo emulsions do). Like paper, you can send film through the mail. Working on film is more expensive than working on paper. Most films are made of oil. People could recycle this plastic, but usually they don't.

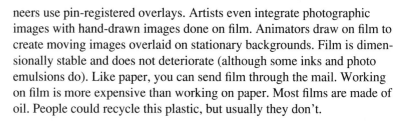

Electronic Media

Now, new electronic media which is emerging enable you to work more interactively and with unlimited layers of information. With electronic media you can produce a wide range of vivid colors. You can work with alphanumeric data, as well as graphics and images. You can create three-dimensional spatial models. You can also work with animation, video, and sound. Of course, to do this you need an appropriate computer workstation. You can also send digital information electronically using networks, telephone lines, or even air waves. Digital information, such as drawings, can be extremely accurate. You can store large amounts of information on small magnetic disks and tapes. Magnetism, dirt, and heat can destroy the information stored on disks, but you can copy digital files easily and store backups in different locations. Most electromagnetic tapes and disks are reusable. Optical discs are more permanent. They can also store even more information than electromagnetic tapes and disks. For example, one compact laser disc can store an entire set of encyclopedias (about 600 megabytes of digital information).

Transforming Media

transform To change the form or condition of something. For example, computers can transform information from paper to electronic media, or from one file format to another.

input-output matrix A chart relating "what comes in" to "what goes out." Can help people consider all possible connections.

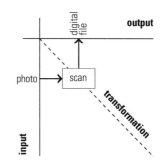

Input-Output Matrix

Because there are so many different formats and devices for working with electronic media, you often need to develop clear strategies for *transforming* it onto something you can use in your work environment. A simple *input-output matrix* can help you understand how you transform information. You can do this by identifying the format for receiving information, identifying how you transform it, and identifying your output. A matrix, like the one shown to the left, can help you to examine each channel of information you are using. For example, you may have a photograph you want to work with. With a scanner you can transform it into a digital format. You will also need to work

out the details of which digital format to use. This may depend upon the graphic software you want to work with in the next step. You can examine key transformations in this way. An input-output matrix also provides you with ways to examine how to integrate media. For example, you may take video clips and sound segments and, using a video editor, transform them into a video production.

input-output diagram A diagram showing the paths through which material and energy (such as information) moves. Can help people visualize how computers, with the appropriate hardware and software, can transfer and transform information electronically.

A simple *input-output diagram* can also help you visualize how computers, with the appropriate hardware and software, enable you to transfer and transform information electronically. For example, you can pick up telephone messages through voice mail, and you can pick up digital information through a modem. Of course, you can digitize information yourself using a keyboard or digitizing tablet. With a MIDI keyboard you can even digitize musical compositions. You can also receive information from paper through a FAX machine or a scanner. In addition, you can scan photographs or capture video images. You can also work with video and sound segments.

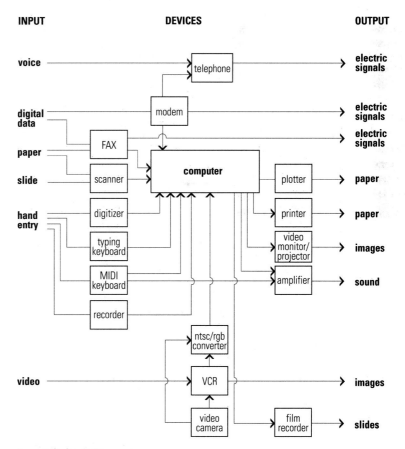

Input-Output Diagram

Using computers and related peripherals you can transform information to produce a variety of output. You can print and plot documents on paper. You can even link computers with photo-offset printing processes for publishing. And it is possible to transform files into different digital formats, as well as into FAX. You can transfer images to film using film recorders. Slides or transparencies enable you to project images for large-group presentations. You can also use video projectors to show groups what is on the monitor. With sound systems you can produce music. And desktop video now enables you to produce video you can transfer to videotape or compact disc. Computers can also drive numerically controlled tools to produce prototypes of physical objects.

Electronic media presents you with both *analog* and *digital* information. Analog is a format for replicating sound or images using electrical impulses which modulate current. Digital is a format for replicating information using primarily on-off signals, transmitted electronically or through fiber optics. Audio and video tapes have electrical analogs of sounds and images. Television also currently transmits analog images. CD players and computers use digital information. Today the technological trend is toward digital information because of the potential for higher quality and possibilities for working with it more interactively.

Digital graphic images can be either *raster* or *vector*. Raster images are bit maps indicating which pixels to activate on a computer screen. Vector images are developed using algorithms which generate the geometries you see on the computer screen. You can work with *raster* or *bit map images* and interactively manipulate contrast, color, and texture. Using *vector images* you can manipulate geometries—rotating, mirroring, and changing their scale. You can also convert vector graphics to raster images or even raster to vector using the appropriate computer software. With *digital video* you can speed up or slow down movement and create transformations. This metamorphosis can result in the seemingly magical special effects you see in movies and on television. You can also interactively manipulate *digital sound*—changing pitch and rhythm—masking noise and mixing sound tracks. While much of this has been done in specialized studios, computer hardware and software are emerging which can empower you to work with your perception interactively at a desktop. You can put information into formats that you can store, manipulate, and transfer more easily.

analog That which corresponds to something else. For example, in electronic media, a format for replicating sound or images using electrical impulses that modulate current.

digital Relating to that which uses a binary system to replicate information using primarily on-off signals, transmitted electronically or through fiber optics. Can represent numbers, text, graphics, images, video, and sound.

raster image Computer graphic composed of a bit map indicating which pixels to activate on a computer screen. Sometimes called a *bit map image*. Enables people to manipulate contrast, color, and texture.

vector image Computer graphic developed using algorithms that generate the geometries you see on the computer screen. Enables people to manipulate geometries—rotating, mirroring, and changing their scale.

digital video Still or full motion images composed of binary information processed by computers. Enables people to speed up or slow down movement and create transformations.

digital sound Sound composed of binary information played by special consumer devices and computers. Enables people to change pitch and rhythm, mask noise, and mix sound tracks.

When working with computers, you usually need to have information in digital formats, although we sometimes access and control analog sound and video using computers. More and more information is becoming digitized. Presently, this includes the following:

Computer databases (such as mailing lists,catalogues, and files)

Hypertext and hypermedia (encyclopedias,expert systems)

Electronic mail

Electronic bulletin boards

News services (including sports and weather)

Stock market information

Reservation services

Product support and purchasing services

Computer programs

Video and computer games

Digital drawings

Digital maps and geographic information

Digital models

Digital sound

Digital video

By the end of the century, much of the information used in offices in the United States will likely be in a digital format.

If your source information is not in a digital format, how do you transform it to electronic media? This may involve simply typing text files or hand-digitizing graphics files. You can also scan documents. Using OCR (optical character recognition) software, you can translate text into ASCII files. You can scan graphic or photographic images in either black and white or color. You can also make use of digital cameras. Scanned images create raster graphics files; however, software is available that enables you to transfer scanned images to vector graphic files. You can even photogrammetrically derive information for three-dimensional modeling in computers. Aerial surveys are done in this way. Photogrammetry is now also being used for archaeological sites and historic buildings. Sonic digitizers enable you to gather three-dimensional information for modeling existing objects. In addition, you can capture video images and work with them as still frames. Or you can work with video sequences. You can also record sounds, voice, or music tracks. You can use these in either an analog or a digital form. All sorts of scientific and medical monitoring and imaging devices provide information directly in digital formats. These include everything from electron microscopes to remote sensing devices in space satellites.

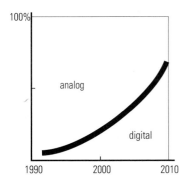

Information Format

Strategies for Media Integration

As shown previously, when using multimedia you go beyond gathering information in written notes. You can also gather information graphically, or in three-dimensional models, or in realistic images. Using electronic media, you can now gather moving images using animation or video. You can also capture sound. You can gather information electronically using most of your channels of perception.

cut & paste
multimedia slides
analog video

desktop publishing
computer-aided design
animation

hypermedia
desktop video
music programs

Approaches to Media Integration

Once you have multimedia information, you can follow many approaches to analyzing that information using different modes of thought. There are techniques for outlining written information as well as for sifting databases or navigating through topics of interest. Synthesis is also a multimedia endeavor. Ideas often come in the form of images. You can express ideas and emotions using words, graphics, forms, sequences, or even sounds.

Electronic media also enables you to test ideas — to create virtual realities that you can try out in different ways. Some evaluations are quantitative models such as cost estimates, energy budgets, or water budgets. Some of the evaluations involve experiencing what a design would be like. You can create models that people can look at from different vantage points. You can even create models which people can walk through. You can also integrate views of objects into a context you can show in video. Using multimedia, you can set up experiences. People can interact with what they experience through electronic media. They can become engaged in what they see and hear.

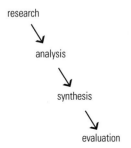

research

analysis

synthesis

evaluation

The Design Process

Some people think of multimedia as only a presentation tool; yet its real benefits involve integrating the whole design process — transferring information from one stage to another. You can draw upon multimedia from each stage of the process. It is often too costly to use multimedia only for final presentations unless you have information in electronic media you can draw upon. The use of multimedia becomes more feasible when you can relate costs to benefits derived from the entire design process — enhancing research (or information gathering) as well as analysis, synthesis, and evaluation. Multimedia presentations can happen more easily if you can develop the project using multimedia computing. Then presentations become a matter of integrating the media you are working with in ways your audience can relate to.

Tool-Based Strategies

Many disciplines have developed very clever strategies for compiling information using what is now considered traditional media. The media involved are mostly paper and film. You can work with paper by writing or drawing on it, pasting up text and graphics, and copying the composition. You can work with film by drawing on overlays and by compositing photographic images. There are many ways to make prints on paper from

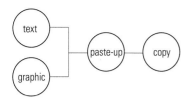

Paper Procedures

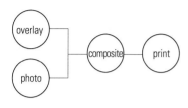

Film Procedures

film. You can also make transparencies or slides to project for your presentations. You may make paper models or even prototypes of designs using other materials such as wood. You can edit video offline using analog videotape recorders. Multimedia thinking has been around for a long time. Working with more traditional tools and media can help develop creative thinking skills for using electronic multimedia. In many teaching situations where multimedia computer workstations are not readily available, students can still learn multimedia thinking skills by developing clear approaches to the media they have access to. For example, I have taught students layering techniques using Mylar. Students can also learn to manipulate symbols libraries, using common copy machines and pasting paper presentations on poster board. They can also use small computers to produce text as well as some graphics. They can laser-print this computer output and integrate it into their poster composition. No doubt people will continue to use traditional media in some tool-based environments especially in business offices, drafting studios, and in printing, film, graphic reproduction, and prototyping shops.

As people assimilate computers into their tool-based work environments, they typically use computers as specialized tools. Following this strategy, people commonly use computers to produce text or graphics. Or they may use computers to search databases, or they may use them as electronic spreadsheets. People usually print the information out and integrate it with traditional media. They store paper documents in file cabinets or flat file drawers. The information they access is primarily what they store physically in their study or work environments. They organize papers in notebooks, project files, or office archives. For example, architectural offices may do drawings by hand. They may produce certain elements — such as notes — in a computer but then attach this information to their drawings. They will have a drafting studio set up with the tools they need to do integrated hand drawing production. They will also have flat files for storing the media they work with. There are reprographic procedures and ways of distributing paper documents by courier or through the mail.

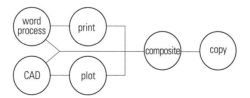

Electronic Tool Procedures

The models used in a tool-based work environment provide a variety of representations. They can range from mock-ups on paper, to mathematical models compiled in reports, to even physical scale models and prototypes. These artifacts are very tangible products of people's efforts. For example, architects love to produce scale models and architectural renderings. The profession has refined these representation techniques for

centuries. Some tool-based techniques are especially effective for taking field notes where you can only jot down keywords or make quick sketches. Using sketching techniques, you can capture initial impressions and ideas. You can also create thumbnail sketches and storyboards of how you are going to lay out a page that combines text and graphics. Or you can create storyboards for hand-drawn animation productions.

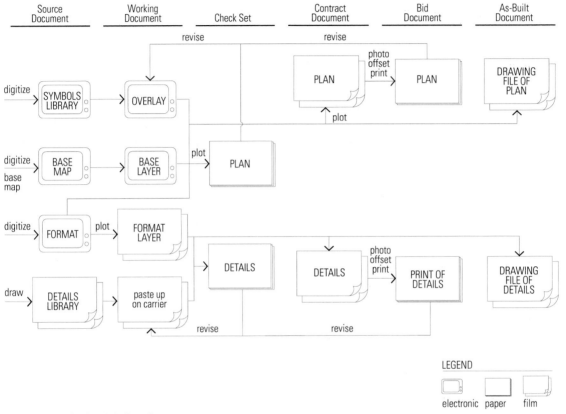

Combining CAD with Overlays

To work effectively with tool-based strategies, of course, you need to have the tools and the space to work with them. Traditional tools are typically less expensive than electronic tools, which can make them more feasible for simple endeavors. Yet simple traditional tools, such as drafting instruments, may not have the potential of more powerful tools such as computers. Most present-day office practices revolve around established methods. For example, most offices have set up procedures for producing and reproducing multimedia documents using traditional tools. Computers are now augmenting many of these procedures. Strategies that use the computer in this way will undoubtedly continue for some applications where traditional methods continue to be cost-effective. Simple tool-based techniques may require less training, although it does take a long time to master traditional skills such as drafting. Let it suffice to

acknowledge these time-tested methods and recognize that you can enhance them using computers as specialized tools. The real potential for multimedia computing, however, lies in strategies that use computers as workstations and access a media space work environment.

Workstation-Based Strategies

Using computer workstations, you can run applications that effectively integrate electronic media. For example, word processors now enable you to work with both text and graphics in a what-you-see-is-what-you-get environment. Spreadsheet programs link quantitative information to business graphics. There are programs that enable you to produce slide presentations. There are also many drawing and painting programs that enable you to work with color graphics and photorealistic digital images, as well as text. Desktop publishing software enables you to produce more refined page layouts for large documents such as books. Computer-aided drafting programs also enable you to produce documents that integrate both text and graphics — although the emphasis is on drafting. In addition, by using computer-aided design, you can construct three-dimensional models and even attach attributes to objects in your drawings and models. Geographic information systems enable you to go even further, linking attributes to spatial models. All these applications enable you to integrate media in a computer workstation. Yet there are even more possibilities.

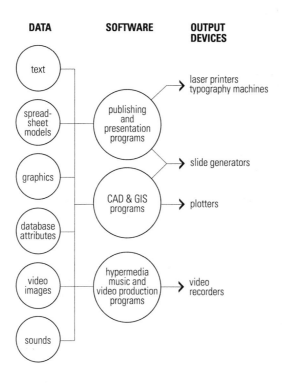

Workstation Procedures

The multimedia workstations that are now emerging enable you to work with video images and sound as well as text and graphics. Hypermedia such as Hypercard or Tool/Book enable you to explore topics using associative frames of reference. Using this software, you can navigate through linkages accessing text, graphics, audio, and video stored on CD-ROM. You can access collections such as Bookshelf and MediaSource. You can

Media
1. relate electronic media to your goals.
2. map your media space.
3. diagram information and data flow.

Models
4. identify realities you are working with.
5. develop models of reality.
6. mock up your presentation.

Methods
7. define your project.
8. diagram your work flow.
9. manage your progress.

Nine-Step Aproach to Multimedia

text

graphics

animation

music

video

Dominant Media

also use these tools to author your own multimedia presentations. You can also use animation programs to produce movement, and music programs to create compositions. In addition, desktop video programs are emerging which enable you to capture and manipulate video images. You can make presentations by doing online editing to integrate what you produce electronically. Full-motion digital video is also becoming available. You can save video on disk and view it interactively using a computer. You can also store video on tape and view it using a VCR. Some purists consider only applications that integrate text, graphics, animation, video, and sound to be true multimedia computing. These applications certainly reveal the real potential of multimedia computing. You can see there are many different ways of mixing media using a computer workstation environment. To use a workstation strategy effectively, you need to develop clear approaches to the media, models, and methods you use.

Select the media you wish to use and relate them to your goals. Make sure your computer workstation can handle them effectively. Sometimes it is helpful to use a dominant medium to which you can relate others. For example, your project may be predominantly a written document in which you incorporate graphics. Or it may be predominantly a drawing in which you incorporate some text. Or you may be working primarily with animation or music. Video is becoming a dominant medium you can use to integrate many others.

The media space of a computer workstation is usually memory and disk space. Make sure you have enough space to work, because multimedia applications are very memory-intensive. Name your files so you can easily refer to them. Make sure you can keep track of different types of files as well as different versions of the same file. You may be working with many types and versions of files in a multimedia production.

Consider the models you are going to use. These models should relate to the reality you are working with. For example, architects designing an object—such as a building—should use models that represent that building. They may start with some images of the site as well as a listing of the project goals and building program. Diagrams of key spatial relationships as well as three-dimensional models are useful for picturing the design. Plans, sections, and elevations help them develop the design and

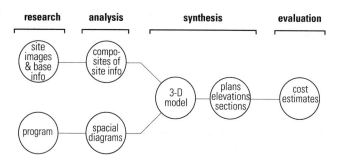

Architectural Workstation Procedures

prepare construction documents. A cost estimate provides a useful evaluative model for budgeting purposes. These models are useful for research analysis, synthesis, and evaluation.

You also need a model of your multimedia presentations. For example, say the architects (using workstations for the models already mentioned) wished to make a multimedia presentation to a corporate client. Preproduction involves charting the flow of information, storyboarding, and script writing for this presentation. It identifies the key notions to communicate and relates them to the time frame of the presentation. The architects can draw from the working models they are using and figure out how to include them in the presentation. They might begin their storyboard with some images of the site to show how they view the context. They might have some frames that quickly summarize the goals and program for the building project. Then they might walk the client through a three-dimensional model of the building using the design model that they have already produced. This can enable their client to experience the spaces. The architects could then show plans and sections so the client could see how the functions fit into the spaces provided. The architects could end their short video presentation with a brief look at the budget recommendations, graphically showing a chart for allocating the construction funds. At that point the presentation probably needs to include some soothing music.

Postproduction involves all the final elements of a multimedia presentation. Computers can become a vehicle for creating these productions using a workstation-based strategy. Presentations can draw upon digital information you are working with. You can hand off these presentations in the form of videos which can quickly convey key ideas by using multimedia. You can also create other documents such as drawings and reports to provide the background material necessary to move a project forward.

Each discipline can use multimedia in different ways. For example, artists may use a workstation environment to create graphics for pages or paintings on a digital canvas. They may construct sculpture in virtual reality of media space or create animated objects. They may even compose music. Artists can transfer their work to many different media or present it in a digital form on disk or videotape. Architects and engineers can use computer workstations to do preliminary designs, design development, construction documents, bidding, and construction administration using some of the mock-up procedures already described. Planners may use workstations to map important information as well as to develop and manage plans. Scientists may use computer workstations to research the phenomena they are working with. They may develop computer models of what they are working with using quantitative analysis. They may also use scientific visualization for image enhancement and spatial modeling. They can use these models to generate multimedia presentations. Health care professionals can use workstations for medical imaging. Business people can use multimedia to market products and to present their

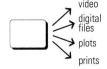

video
digital files
plots
prints

Output Options

financial picture. Educators can use multimedia workstations to create books as well as interactive presentations that can engage students in learning. Educational material is becoming available on video and CD-ROM.

Media Space – Based Strategies

You can also use computers as a vehicle for working in media space. As you learn to integrate voice mail and FAX with computer telecommunications, as well as with video and HDTV, you can work in a multimedia information environment. This provides access to information sources and service bureaus you may not be able to maintain on your own.

To work in a multimedia information environment effectively, you need to map your media space to develop a mental picture of that environment. You need to know how to navigate around it and access the information there. You also need to know how to transfer information from one computer environment to another — working with documents in different formats. Data flow diagrams provide a tool for visualizing these transfers. Transfers may involve simply accessing voice mail with a telephone or sending a FAX to your computer to store or access information. Local area networks enable you to share data files, as well as software, making the transfer of information more seamless — without having to translate files. It is possible for several people to be working together on the same documents. You can transfer digital files of written documents, drawings, images, animation, or music so you can share them with others you may be working with. Wide bandwidth transfers will even include video transmissions.

The transfers may also involve accessing information services all over the world. These service bureaus may provide up-to-the-moment information — such as news, stock quotations, weather, airline schedules. They may also provide services — such as online banking, translations of file formats or even translations of written languages, editing, and generation of color slides. In addition, online services can provide goods — the way mail order does. (Except the entire transaction can take place electronically, reducing overhead and giving customers access to a larger selection of merchandise.) You can also use a portable modem with a notebook computer to access information services or to send and receive FAX, E-mail, or other files. In this way you can stay in touch and work with your media space environment while you are traveling. A small computer you carry with you can provide all the tools you need to work in this information environment. By simply using a phone, you can stay in touch. By using a portable computer you can stay in action — gaining new freedom over where and when you work.

You can develop models to work on collaboratively in shared media space. A model might be a document, a graphic diagram, or an image. It might also be a three-dimensional model of an object or site that a team

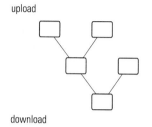

upload

download

Map Media Space

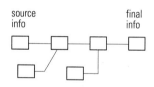

source info

final info

Diagram Information Flow

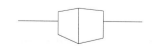

Model Objects

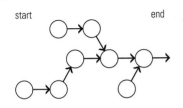

start   end

Diagram Work Flow

of professionals work on together—each responsible for certain considerations or parts. It might also be a video production that people work on together. This production might evolve—in much the same way messages on a bulletin board evolve as participates interact. Or the production might be a composition artists or professionals create for a particular audience. Once the work is complete, the audience can access the information in media space and explore this creative work.

Whole new methods for working collaboratively and communicating are emerging. People no longer have to be in the same place at the same time to collaborate effectively. You can engage in these new opportunities by clearly picturing how you are going to proceed. Diagramming work flow can help you do this. It can also help communicate how to delegate responsibilities among your workgroup.

Representing Final Presentation

mock-up A representation. Enables people to visualize a final product before producing it.

Page Mockup

storyboard Graphics and text that portray scenes. For example, when used for a multimedia presentation, a storyboard helps people portray the content, composition, and sequence of a presentation.

Storyboard

Useful models for developing multimedia presentations are *mock-ups* and *storyboards*. They can help you examine the content, composition, sequence, and timing of your presentation. If your presentation involves page layout, a mock-up can help you decide how to integrate text and graphics on the page. You can look at the format of your whole document in this way. If your presentation involves live action with a narrative, you may need to write a *script*. The storyboard can help you integrate different channels of media and sequence images and sounds in your presentation (as when you produce a video). You need to be able to preview and access collections of video clips and sound segments. Video images and keywords can help you search collections of media quickly in nonlinear ways. You can store segments either on tape or on computer disk. If you are working with analog information, you have to concern yourself with frame rates and resolution. If you are working with digital information, you have to deal with file formats and data compression. Most of the desktop video software that is emerging is starting to make the handling of different media more seamless. This software also provides tools for editing images while you work with them. For example, most video editors enable you to copy, cut, and paste as well as crop images. Working with your storyboard, you can plan the sequence and timing of your presentation. You can create transitions such as wipes and dissolves. You can switch from one track to another, even combining tracks if you wish. You can create special effects such as generating characters superimposed on full-motion video. You can even create animated overlays. Multiple-track support enables you to synchronize sound and video. Some video editing programs automate different types of sequences to make them easier to use. Other programs, however, offer more control through time-line editors. Your audience can view video sequences you produce either on videotape or on computer disk. Disk storage space is still a problem because of the massive amounts of data involved in full-motion video. Data compression schemes and new data storage devices

script A written document describing a performance. For example, when developed for a multimedia presentation a script can help people integrate different channels of media such as video and audio.

Script

are emerging to address this problem. Desktop video technology is beginning to offer some of the production capabilities of professional production studios. While some video production work is beginning to take place on computer workstations, many animation professionals are still using more tool-based approaches with specialized production tools. Computers are more often used as tools to build segments and plan productions in broadcast-quality studios. As professional-quality video editing becomes more available on affordable computer workstations, there will be a shift toward workstation-based strategies.

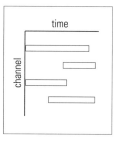

Production Score

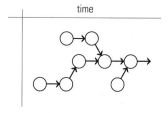

Workflow Diagram

You also need clear methods to work effectively with multimedia. Work flow diagrams can help you picture procedures and develop your methods. They can help you discover clever ways of using media for your presentations. Work flow diagrams help you move through the process so you can manage what you do more efficiently. In addition, they make it easier to delegate tasks and coordinate effective team efforts. You need clear strategies for developing these methods.

Handoffs—Transferring Information

transfer To convey or send. For example, using electronic media you can transfer text, graphics, images, video, or sound.

The strategy for *transferring* information is crucial. It determines how much time and effort you invest in communication. It also determines how timely you send and receive information. The pace and volume of correspondence are increasing in most industrialized countries. Communicating more effectively can help you compete. It is also becoming more cost-effective to transfer information electronically using media space than to transfer it physically by truck, train, boat, or airplane. Savings are a result of how you produce correspondence as well as how you deliver it. There are other impacts as well.

Data flow diagrams help you picture how to link what you get from one transformation to what you put into another. Picturing connections is especially important when you are trying to work through file transfers involving different software formats or computer environments. It also can help arrange transfers of information among a project team. For example, in producing this book I developed the data flow diagram

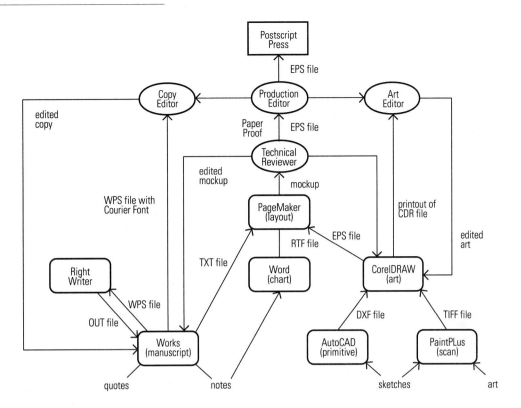

Data Flow for Concurrent Publishing

shown above. This helped me visualize how we were going to move digital information through the project team to produce the book. Since we worked with different computer environments and a range of software, it was important to make sure the files would transfer without a problem. I did most of the writing using a simple character-based word processor. I also found feedback from a spell checker and grammar checker to be helpful. I worked with an assistant, Mary Reeves, to refine the manuscript before submitting it as an ASCII file to Joe Molloy, my graphic designer. He layed out the mock-up of the book. At the same time, I worked on the graphics with Long Ha, who did most of the computer graphics. Some of the time I would start the diagrams by doing primitives in the computer and then hand them off to Long Ha, who would develop them electronically. Once we had developed a graphic vocabulary together, I could simply make quick hand-drawn sketches of the diagrams, which he would then develop electronically. We scanned in some graphics, used a bit of clip art, and worked with drawing files from other sources. We would transfer the graphic files in an EPS format that the graphic designer integrated into the layout of the book. We used the mock-up of the book to involve the technical review team and refine the design and content. The document was also edited by Judy Duguid, the copy editor, and proofread by production editors.

Concurrency

Learning to transfer information more fluidly using electronic media opens new opportunities. It allows you to move beyond some of the linear procedures related to traditional media. It allows you to work concurrently on several stages at the same time. For example, with traditional media there is usually a distinct division between design and production. It is typical to work on production only after completing design. Being able to transfer information more easily using electronic media is beginning to change that. *Concurrency* makes it possible for more people to work together with the same information. It is also easier to transform documents as you add more precision. You can create and work with very realistic models. This helps design and production people collaborate more effectively. The benefit can be a reduction in the amount of time it takes to get ideas and information to market. You can also improve the quality of collaboration, prevent mistakes, and avoid costly changes at later stages of the design and production processes.

concurrence Happening together. Agreement; accord. Concurrence makes it possible for more people to work together with the same information.

Engineers have discovered that by working with computer models they can concurrently develop the design and the production processes. This can reduce the time it takes to go from research and development to production. It also can result in better design. Usually engineers will use quantitative models for the initial research and design development. Once they have generated a form, they can model it three-dimensionally using a computer. This provides an object that the design team as well as the production and even the marketing team can relate to and work with. This object continues to evolve until it becomes a reality. Using computer models, engineers can make "soft prototypes"—electronic models they can easily change. Using numeric controls, they can make "hard prototypes"—physical mock-ups of objects to see how they fit together. Then they can set up manufacturing processes with greater confidence.

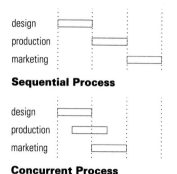

Sequential Process

Concurrent Process

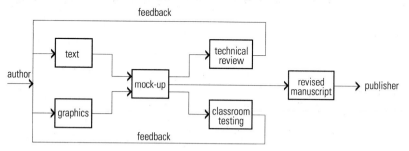

Data Flow Diagram

Concurrency also works for producing publications. For example, my graphic designer, computer graphic artist, and I mocked up the layout of the text and graphics for the first chapter of this book, long before I completed the entire manuscript. We sent this mock-up to New York so the publisher's production people could review it and provide feedback for

developing the document. While we completed the manuscript and art, the graphic designer integrated them—mocking up each part of the book. I distributed these mock-ups to the technical review team. I also used portions of the mock-up in courses I taught. This enabled me to test material in a classroom situation. Working with this feedback, I made some revisions to the text and graphics before submitting it to the publisher for copy editing. Mocking up the document enabled the entire workgroup involved in producing this book to develop a clear picture of what it would be like. It also provided a prototype for testing. Computers made it fairly easy to change. Consequently, I was able to incorporate comments from the workgroup and my students at almost every stage of the process. Electronic media will also make it easier to update this book as multimedia computing evolves.

Concurrency also has potential for construction. Design/build and fast-track construction are nothing new. But computers can improve the quality of what is produced using these techniques. You can work interactively with virtual reality to make it a reality. Virtual reality enables you to picture alternatives. You can see what the outcome would be before committing resources to build it.

Concurrency means agreement—getting a group to work together using common media, models, and methods to achieve common goals. Electronic media are opening new opportunities to do this. Consequently, work patterns are changing.

Delegation—Transferring Tasks

delegate To entrust another person with a task.

stop point The point at which one task ends and another begins. Identifying stop points can make it easier to delegate tasks.

Because computers enable you to do more, there is a tendency to do just that. But doing more doesn't always lead to happiness or increased productivity. You can become bogged down trying to do it all: draft the document, edit the document, produce the document, and distribute the document. You may enjoy doing all of this, and if you don't have organizational support, it may make sense to do it that way. If you have an organization behind you, however, using electronic media may actually cause your productivity to decline if you do not effectively *delegate* tasks. You can quickly find yourself consumed by tasks you might have delegated if you were working by hand. You need to determine *stop points* in documents. For example, you can draft a document and then turn it over to someone who can spell-check, grammar-check, and proofread it for you. Then you can review the document (without printing it out) and refine it before you turn it over to someone who can format and print it. Of course, you may want to check the final format of the document before you release it. Someone else can produce and distribute it electronically or on paper.

You can find similar stop points in all types of electronic documents. Because the media transfers are often seamless, you may need to establish these stop points artificially by clearly identifying the tasks you are

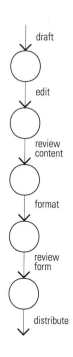

draft

edit

review
content

format

review
form

distribute

Stop Point

transferring. Sometimes, this can be difficult to do. You may want to be too helpful and spend time looking up details that someone else could look up. You may want to check your spelling or grammar before you share a document with anyone. You may be worried that you will lose control of your document if others edit it. Or you may have some very definite ideas on how you want it formatted and wish to work that out yourself. You also may be anxious to get the document out without delay and personally want to make sure everyone gets it. If you have organizational support, though, it can be more efficient to delegate these tasks to others who have talents you can trust. Think how much easier it now is for support staff than it used to be when you handed off illegible pencil drafts to be typed and retyped and retyped.

Why Mix Media?

Expectations rise as better tools become available. You often find yourself having to meet other's expectations as well as your own. Immediately isn't soon enough. Letter quality is passé. Text and graphics beg for integration. Composition cries for interesting formats. Videos want sound tracks. Networks and telecommunications are like open doors. By mixing media you can create three-dimensional models or even whole environments. More realism is within reach. You can work in virtual reality . . . and so it goes. There are exciting ways to mix electronic media. There are also new opportunities to engage other people by delegating through electronic media. You can even reach service bureaus electronically and engage them as if they were part of your organization.

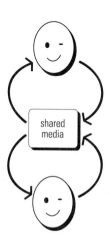

shared
media

Workgroups

Electronic media also provide new opportunities for collaboration. You can create object-oriented workgroups using computers to provide each person with an overview of the whole project. This helps people identify with the final product. That way the workgroup can draw upon everyone's perception, ideas, and expertise. Each person should find fulfilling roles and contribute to the best of his or her abilities. This can be different from a production line where people work like robots turning a bolt. Or from the stenopool where typists type endlessly. Or from the drafting room where people turn rough drafts into final drafts. Not only can electronic media change how you use space and time — where you work and

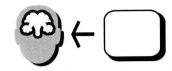

Passive Viewing

Interactive Exploration

when you work—they can change how you organize. You can build new realities, each person in a workgroup can relate to those realities. You can expand your capabilities by visualizing what we can do in the time you have.

Electronic media are making it possible for people to work with information more interactively. We are all familiar with passive presentations—the audience sits and listens. However, electronic media can be participatory—engaging the audience in truly interactive ways. There are interesting differences between passive viewing and active exploration. For example, television tends to provide passive viewing, whereas video games can involve active exploration. Considering this dichotomy at more sophisticated levels, differences exist between a presenter/audience relationship and collegial collaboration or a workgroup relationship. This has tremendous implications for communication, education, and workgroup productivity. In general, the more people are involved, the better they communicate, the more they learn, and the more productive they are.

Legal Rights

quotes
documents
data
graphics
images
sound tracks
animation
video

Copyrights

The issue of copyrights is an old one. You need to get permission to use material others have created. You should also credit the source properly. Copyrights can pertain to quotes and written documents, as well as to data, graphics, images, sound tracks, animation and video. While the material is easy to copy, sometimes it can be more difficult to obtain permission to use existing material than to create original work. There are clearinghouses that make materials available for multimedia productions. For example, you can get images, video clips, even sound segments or musical themes. Some of the material is public domain, which means you don't have to get permission to use it. Some of it provides compensation for the author or creator. McGraw-Hill is making published material available in a digital format through its Primis program. Segments of books (such as this one) are available through this publishing program. This way people can adopt material and repackage it for their own audience.

There is also the ethical matter of crediting those who collaborated on a project. This becomes more complicated as you create shared media space work environments. For example, the workgroup that helped me put this book together extends across North America with some contributions from Europe and Japan. I have done my best to acknowledge these people throughout the text and graphics.

Some fear electronic media may degrade creativity with rampant copying. Others fear that workgroups may make the individual anonymous. While these are significant concerns, abiding by established laws as well as moral and ethical mores can extend human values into the use of electronic multimedia.

Artistic Quality

As electronic multimedia tools become easier to work with, they empower amateurs to produce more. This has the potential for compromising artistic qualities. This has happened with desktop publishing. Suddenly, there are newsletters of every description — some with very little sensitivity to the subtleties of fonts and layout. This is also occurring with computer graphics, electronic music, and desktop video. Creative thinking and sensitivity can result in truly artistic expressions. People learning to use multimedia can move beyond simply learning technique. As with any art form, it can take a while to discover the true qualities of electronic media.

Summary

This chapter helps you transform media efficiently by clarifying your procedures. Input-output diagrams help sort out key transformations of media. Efficiency can improve by transforming media into digital formats and working as directly as possible. The first activity at the end of the chapter will help you to transform media more cleverly.

You can also learn to integrate media effectively. Media integration can involve paper, film, or electronic media. Mock-ups of presentations identify the dominant media and help integrate other channels. Integrate media using paper (cut and paste), film or analog video (linear editing), electronic tool procedures (composite printouts), or electronic media procedures (in workstations). Clarify procedures by diagramming information flow, modeling objects, and diagramming work flow. Picture presentations by using scores, storyboards, and scripts. Visualize transformations by using input-output matrices and diagrams. Work digitally using desktop publishing, CADD, or video programs. The second activity that follows helps you integrate media using the tools you have access to.

You also need to learn to delegate tasks appropriately to improve productivity and job satisfaction in workgroups. Media space can help develop object-oriented workgroups. Electronic media can help you work concurrently and hand off tasks. Evolve concurrent processes where possible and delegate effectively. The last activity in this chapter will help you and your workgroup delegate tasks more effectively.

Activities

1. Transform Media

Mindlessly transforming media can result in substantial losses of productivity. For example, some people may take handwritten notes, then draft a letter by hand, and finally have it word-processed in a computer. Then, they may edit a printout with a pencil and hand it back for revisions. After their document is revised in a computer, they will have it printed out again. Finally, they may FAX it to different people — running it through a FAX machine again and again, waiting to enter the phone number by hand each time. In effect, they are going from paper, to electronic media, back to paper, then back to electronic media, then back to paper which they transfer to FAX repeatedly. An alternative strategy is to take the handwritten notes and draft the letter in a computer. Next either edit or have support staff spell-check, grammar-check, edit, and format the text file right in the computer for your review. Then automatically convert this file to FAX and distribute it electronically to all the numbers you wish to send it to. Another strategy is to transmit the file directly using telecommunications, assuming the people you want to reach are online. Of course, you may receive a handwritten response by slow boat. Or you may receive a phone call that may cause an interruption or not find you there. It might be nice to have a reply on electronic mail waiting for you when you want to receive it. You could even include it electronically in a document you are working on.

Consider how you transform media. Diagram your transformations using input-output diagrams. Attach costs to each step. Compare alternative strategies. Which are quickest? Which are most cost-effective? Could you relate what you do in your media space work environment more directly to others you are collaborating or communicating with? Given the tools your workgroup has access to, what is the best way to transmit the messages you are sending? Could you use telecommunications to enable your audience to access your message directly through electronic media? Can your workgroup access shared media space? Could you use computer-aided design and computer-aided manufacturing to link your design information more directly to production? Would your presentations be more effective if you used video? What could you do with interactive video or TV?

2. Integrate Media

To integrate media effectively you need to visualize transformations of your media and models. Clear strategies can help you transform source information into your presentation, or final product, more easily. One strategy is to use computers as production tools but still integrate your output on paper or on film. You can do this by pasting up your printout, even integrating photos or hand-drawn graphics. Another strategy is to integrate information using a computer workstation. You can do this using desktop publishing or the desktop video programs that are emerging. You can also use hypermedia, computer-aided design, and geographic information systems to integrate visual digital information and related attributes. Still another strategy is to integrate information and deliver it electronically. Using a media space work environment enables others to pick up information online, or through local area networks, or simply by getting your file on a disk. Programs are emerging that even enable you to create virtual reality your audience can experience.

source   product

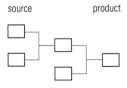

Develop a data flow diagram to picture a clear strategy of media integration for a multimedia project you are doing. Consider different strategies. Once your diagram describes a clear strategy, do a pilot study. Make sure you can make all the transfers involved using the software and hardware you have access to before you commit a major effort to your project. Some digital formats are not compatible. You may need to modify your strategy to make it work. The universal thinking skills behind different strategies for media integration will enable you to evolve new approaches. Ask yourself what strategy is most effective given the tools you are working with.

3. Delegate Tasks

Computers can make you more self-sufficient. It is tempting to try to do many things because you have access to the programs that enable you to do them. Yet electronic media also set up new opportunities for collaboration and delegation. For example, you can develop workgroups without the limitation of finding a common place and time to meet. In fact, your workgroup may be all over the globe. In addition, you can access bureaus that can provide information, services, and products you may not have readily available in the organizations where you work.

The members of a workgroup need to develop clear approaches to the media, models, and methods they are using. Choose the smallest functional workgroup in your organization; for example, this may be a project team. Sit down with the other members of the workgroup and discuss how your minds can interact on a project you are doing together using computers. One way to focus this group discussion is to have a chalkboard or a large pad of paper where the group can record ideas for everyone to consider. A larger group could benefit from a "taking part workshop" format developed by Lawrence Halprin and Jim Burns. (See Halprin and Burns, *Taking Part: A Workshop Approach to Collective Creativity,* MIT Press, Cambridge 1974.) Another way to focus group discussion it to use a shared computer setup to augment your meeting. For a small group you could simply pass a light, portable notebook computer around a coffee or conference table—take turns being the recorder. Or you could use a computer conferencing setup which includes a video projector, so everyone can see what the technographer enters into the computer reflecting the group discussion. (See Bernard DeKoven's publication on *Connected Executives*, available from the Institute for Better Meetings, Palo Alto, California.) Have your workgroup discuss the following.

upload

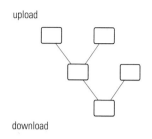

download

Media

How does multimedia computing relate to your workgroup's and organization's goals? Who has access to computers? Where are they located? How is the media space organized? Make a map of your shared work environment. Consider both the layout of your physical workspace and the organization of your media space information environment. How does information (data) flow through your organization? Can you develop typical information or data flow diagrams that describes what you are doing? Can you visualize who your audience is?

Models

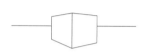

Identify the realities your group is working with. How do you model this reality? Can you each access these models and interact with them? Can all the members of your workgroup relate to the artificial reality you are using to model the reality of your real world situation? Do you all have a clear picture of how to transfer information from the models you are working with to your reports or presentations?

Methods

start   end

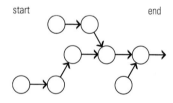

Can you identify areas of responsibility? Can your workgroup diagram the work flow typically involved in your projects, showing the progression of activities and events and areas of responsibility for different members of the group? Use this work flow diagram to help clarify how to delegate tasks among the group.

Once you have developed a general overview of your typical approach, take a case study that you are all familiar with and evaluate it carefully. Consider how you might transfer information more effectively. Consider different models you could use to represent what you are working with. Diagram better strategies for information flow and work flow. Notice how information and work flow affects your entire organization. How could you use multimedia computing to change the way you organize your workgroup and to delegate tasks more effectively?

Go beyond recording your meetings with "minutes" of who said what. Instead, strive to create objects or models that you can all relate to and act upon. For example, formulate a set of common goals and responses that you agree upon; make a map of your shared media space; develop information or data flow diagrams for key transfers and transformations. Also depict the models of the reality you are working with that you all accept. Define areas of responsibility as well as diagram work flow in ways that will help you manage your collaborative activities.

Note: These activities have the potential for enhancing both productivity and job satisfaction of white-collar workgroups. Although this activity may involve a significant investment of time, engage all the members of the workgroup in this activity collaboratively so they can delegate tasks and establish the training necessary to carry out changes. Students can learn to relate to workgroups by using this approach when doing collaborative case studies in their academic environment.

12

Change

New tools for using electronic multimedia are rapidly evolving. Your mind can help shape these tools. At the same time, these tools change the way you think. As with making any change, there are both risks and rewards. This chapter addresses issues which are compelling change. It examines how change can benefit you and what you can do to guide change. A new Renaissance is emerging that is, once again, relating the arts and the sciences and influencing design. You can become a part of this Renaissance. There are exciting possibilities for using computers to learn the knowledge base of a discipline more easily, as well as to enhance your creative capacity. This chapter will help you visualize some of the implications of the changes that are occurring. The activities at the end of the chapter challenge you to manage these changes in humane and environmentally sound ways.

Consider How Your Information Environment Is Changing

You probably realize that the way in which you are gathering and working with information is changing dramatically. Think of what you were doing just a few years ago — before you knew anything about computers. Think of what you are doing now. Better yet, think of what you might be doing if you had access to all the hardware and software you would like to use. One factor, which is common to us all, is change. We are each working through some rather far-reaching changes.

The Evolution of Media

Cave Drawings
found in Lascaux, France

You are involved in an astounding evolution! Tools and media for human expression have evolved for centuries, beginning with the first gestures and utterances of your ancestors. Prehistoric people left evidence of primitive visual expression on cave walls. They scratched images using blunt objects, smeared pigments from clays and berries, or scribed with charcoal from burning sticks. Since that time, visual and verbal languages developed. Eventually, written languages emerged — probably first etched on tablets and then later scribed with pigments on skins. Papyrus evolved into paper. With paper came the use of pen and pencil as well as the printing press. Today you use pens, pencils, and markers on paper as

Printing Press

Typewriter

Copy Machine

FAX machine

Portable Computer

well as on plastic film. You also use film treated with light-sensitive chemicals to capture photographic images. There are many ways to make copies of what you produce. Colorful media have evolved enabling you to show realistic pictures. For centuries, artists have worked on canvas and fresco with brush and blade. There has been a continuous evolution of pigments and paints. Color photography and movies emerged this century and, more recently, color TV. Now you have access to electronic media with color video capabilities.

Ancient cultures created artifacts. Some painted on canvas; some sketched on paper. Some carved in wood or stone; some formed clay or metals. Many of the objects that were created are treasured today for their artistic expression. Since the industrial revolution, mass-produced objects have been replacing hand-made objects. Many of these objects, like endangered species in nature, are also valuable because of the information they contain. Today, objects can be modeled electronically before they are produced. They can be manufactured directly from electronic models.

The printing press was probably the most significant tool in the development of written language. Printing enabled people to record knowledge in writing, spurring the development of today's cultures. Now, you can record and transmit information electronically; you can also publish it from a desktop.

Long ago, musical keyboard instruments—such as cathedral pipe organs—evolved in extremely sophisticated ways. Classical musicians mastered many complex musical interfaces—keyboards, stops, foot pedals—without much comment on user friendliness.

Keyboards became accepted, not only for musical instruments, but also for writing instruments. The typewriter became a tool for quickly putting words on paper. With the typewriter and the printing press came a proliferation of books, newspapers, and magazines. Now, the typewriter has evolved into the word processor. You can work with verbal expression in a digital form. You can check, format, and distribute documents electronically. You can store digital information electronically on disk or on tape. You can store even more multimedia information on laser disks. TV, video, and computers are becoming integrated into multimedia machines combining text, graphics, visual images, and sound.

Copy machines have evolved in this century. This development has been a boon to both written and graphic expression. Images are easy to manipulate—enlarge, reduce, rotate, mirror—providing new possibilities for quick graphic reproduction. With the right hardware and software, it is even easier to copy and manipulate images electronically than it is to use a copier.

Computers first did calculations—processing numbers and data in a digital format. Now computers digitize words and sounds as well as visual images. You can build models to simulate objects and explore space and time electronically. You can create interactive multimedia

programs integrating text, graphics, three-dimensional modeling, animation, imaging, video, and audio. Electronic media provide new opportunities for exploring images of the mind. These new media for creative expression herald the beginning of a new information age.

Changing Tools

Development Cycle

Changes in computer hardware are occurring at an increasingly rapid pace. The development cycle for some hardware is now under two years. This evolution seems continuous. Driven by a very competitive market, breakthroughs sometimes occur that offer leaps in performance. Increasingly powerful chips provide new levels of speed. Peripherals become more sophisticated; interfaces become more refined and easier to use. With each new development come new capabilities. While these changes are welcome, they pose challenges to those acquiring and learning to use computers. Equipment becomes obsolete. User interfaces change. Because of this rapid change, one needs to look beyond a particular computer or hardware configuration.

Software, too, changes at a rapid pace — although not quite at the pace of hardware. The computer industry must first introduce the hardware before it can fully develop the software. Hence, there is a lag in the development of software for each new type of workstation. New software and revisions provide added capabilities and refinements to the user interface. Often there are fixes for previous problems. Software is now beginning to settle into some standard user interfaces, making it easier to learn. As hardware evolves, new software applications become possible. Those applications, once only possible on mainframe computers or minicomputers, become popular on more powerful personal computers. Applications only dreamed of are now becoming commonplace. Each new realm of possibility stimulates new dreams.

Word processing became popular because of the personal computer. As personal computers became more powerful, the spreadsheet craze took off. Spreadsheets became integrated with databases, and business graphics became more widely used. Laser printers opened the doors for desktop publishing. More speed and higher-resolution color monitors brought computer-aided design capabilities to personal computers. Now more powerful personal computers compete with workstations as platforms for three-dimensional modeling. It is now possible to make multimedia productions using desktop video capabilities that are emerging.

Operating systems are also evolving to provide better performance. MS-DOS continues — extended to provide access to more memory. Graphic user interfaces have become the norm. The Macintosh System and Windows offer more consistent user interfaces, making applications easier to learn. Multitasking capabilities enable the user to command the computer to perform more than one task at a time. OS/2 and personal computer user shells provide multitasking. Unix and other minicomputer

operating systems have migrated to more robust desktop workstations, offering multitasking as well as better networking capabilities. Mainframe computer operating systems also now offer point and click user interfaces with window environments. Other interfaces using your voice or a pen are emerging. And so change continues; there seems to be no end in sight.

Changing Thinking Skills

Learning Curve

Changes in thinking skills are slower than technological changes. It takes years for some people and societies to accept new tools. In addition, people may need several more years to master complex applications. Those who are excited about the possibilities will start to change their approaches. Change begins with an awareness of new tools, but it takes a desire, or commitment, to learn to use them. This requires time and patience.

Presently a shift from verbal to more visual modes of thinking and expression is occurring. Traditionally, western cultures have had a verbal dominance. The written languages of these cultures use phonetics. One learns to read by using syllables to sound out words. Eastern cultures, on the other hand, have had more of a visual base to their written languages. One learns to read by recognizing graphic characters. (Recognizing graphic characters draws on different parts of the brain than does employing phonetics.) Researchers have done interesting studies to see how learning languages with a visual base influences thinking. For example, John O. Regan, a linguist at the Claremont Colleges, has determined that Chinese children can recognize abstract visual characters with greater fluency than can American children. Presumably, this is a result of their language training. Children around the world today are being exposed more and more to visual images. Perception of real-life experience is highly visual. This is now augmented by passively viewing TV. Through computers, however, both the audio and visual tracks are becoming interactive, tapping into a whole range of visual capabilities. Parents and educators note that Johnny doesn't read much any more. He is watching TV or may be playing video games. The readership of newspapers is also declining, but viewing TV news is on the rise. Although verbal capabilities seem to be declining, visual capabilities seem to be increasing. Educators with a verbal bias are lamenting this shift. As an educator who teaches visual thinking and design communication, I find it quite interesting. How will education respond to the shift that is occurring? The challenge might be to teach both verbal and visual literacy. This would provide children with a better base for effectively using the tools that are emerging.

I am hoping to see more computer literacy courses emerge in primary and secondary schools — courses which don't just teach computer programming languages such as Basic, or application skills such as word

The Core of Computer Literacy

processing, spreadsheets, databases, or even computer-aided drafting. Teaching computer literacy must go beyond teaching skills — which buttons to push. Computer literacy also involves learning how to use new tools effectively. What is needed is a "mind primer" for computer literacy courses in primary and secondary schools. This could help young people learn creative and critical thinking skills that they can draw upon when they use electronic media.

Consider the evolution of visual expression. The primitive images found on cave walls provide insight into the thinking skills of the cave dwellers. The images they expressed were simple and symbolic. An understanding of scale is demonstrated much later in the history of art. People have refined this understanding of scale today and use it extensively in architectural and engineering drawings. Computer-aided drafting makes precision even more possible. An understanding of detail has also grown continuously over the centuries. This understanding extends into microscopic and macroscopic realms. Perspective was not completely understood until the Renaissance. Today, with the use of video and three-dimensional modeling, perspective is becoming almost automatic. Light was not fully comprehended until the Dutch masters portrayed more subtle effects of candle- and daylight. Today, computers can be used to simulate light with ray tracing and even calculate energy transfers. The notion of animation was not widely worked with until early in this century. Then, animated drawings and film launched a whole new art form and industry. Today, television and video are commonly found in homes. Passive viewing is evolving into interactive involvement with video games and hypermedia.

Consummate realism came with photography and video. Ironically, by dealing with realism people also became more aware of the powers of abstraction—working with simpler images. The mind will continue to evolve to make use of new technology. As tools and toys change, they reshape the way people work and play. This in turn changes the tools and toys people create.

Risks and Rewards

There are both risks and rewards when embracing new technologies. You only need to consider the impact of the automobile or television to realize this. Automobiles provide welcome mobility. Yet indiscriminate use of automobiles in urbanized areas results in gridlock and environmental pollution. Television provides access to information in a compelling multimedia format. Yet indiscriminate programming of TV results in appalling drivel that can pollute the minds of children and adults.

Interactive multimedia provide new freedom over space and time. You can experience and even work with artificial reality. Yet there are also risks in this new world if you don't learn to use electronic media discriminately. George Felton's perceptive essay "Time-Shifting Is a Mortgage on My Future" (published in the *Los Angeles Times*) discusses

dilemmas of using VCRs. Some of the "top 10" ways Felton finds VCRs are hazardous to his health include:

> 10) They create the illusion of consequence-free living, then make me pay for it. "Time-shifting" just mortgages my own future to pay for double dipping today. But at a restaurant, almost hearing my VCR whir "Twin Peaks" into readiness, I continue to believe I'm living two lives and getting away with it.

> 9) VCRs let me tape while I sleep, so I can keep in touch with David Letterman, yet still be nodding into dreamland by 11 (pm). Ah, what a wonderful world! Until I realize that not only has my waking self been taping future obligations, but my unconscious mind has, too. The more I sleep, the behinder I get.

> . . .

> 4) "Live" no longer has any meaning whatsoever. Somebody's "live" is somebody else's "taped." Such disbelief adds to my sense of unreality and paranoia. Diane Sawyer and Sam Donaldson on "Prime Time Live" don't have their intended effect because I don't believe they're live.

> 3) Zipping and zapping with the remote control switch takes my already short attention span and teaches me to make it even shorter. I want to zip slow moments in life and aim my pointer at talkative friends, hurrying them to their point. Having become God in a very small space, I am petulant about my lack of control elsewhere.

These dilemmas are not new. Similar dilemmas have arisen with printed material. Many of us have stacks of "must-read" material stashed on reading stands or in our studies. In the future these dilemmas will be compounded as TV and computers become more integrated.

In the book *The Age of Missing Information*, Bill McKibben compares what you experience on television with what you experience in nature. McKibben asserts:

> Our society is moving steadily from natural sources of information toward electronic ones, from the mountain and the field toward the television; this great transition is very nearly complete. And so we need to understand the two extremes. One is the target of our drift. The other is that anchor that might tug us gently back, a source of information that once spoke clearly to us and now hardly even whispers.

It is important to realize that although you may gather information from artificial reality, it is essential to stay in touch with reality. Actually, as a landscape architect, I find exploring electronic sources of information can enhance exploration of the real world, particularly when I can get involved interactively. You don't need to choose between electronic media and nature. You can explore both the artificial reality of media and the reality of nature.

William Gibson's science fiction novels *Neuromancer* and *Mona Lisa Overdrive* describe traveling into the computer-generated universe known as cyberspace. These adventures are not all that appealing. Many of the horrors of present-day reality are emerging in cyberspace — and then writers invent others almost beyond comprehension. *Lawnmower Man*, a film that is introducing the masses to virtual reality, unfortunately also portrays experiments gone awry. It serves as a reminder that the sinister side of human nature can also enter virtual reality. But virtual reality can also be used to create a world that might, in some ways, be better than the real world. And virtual reality can be used to visualize ways of overcoming real-world problems.

Why Change?

A number of issues compel change—issues we must address as individuals and as societies. These key issues involve economic survival, fulfillment of human potential, and sustaining a healthy environment.

Economic Survival

To address changes in the workplace, U.S. Labor Secretary Lynn Martin established a Commission on Achieving Necessary Skills. The commission's report described five learning areas of increasing importance in the workplace. Development of these learning areas depends on more basic abilities. One of the foundations discussed in the report includes thinking skills: "Creativity, making decisions, solving problems, seeing things in the mind's eye, knowing how to learn, reasoning." A basic job skill identified in this report involves information: "Acquiring and evaluating data, organizing and maintaining files, interpreting and communicating and using computers to process information."

Economic survival in an information society requires being able to work with media, by using computers to navigate and move information effectively. It requires being able to relate to and build computer models that address the realities you are working with. It means being able to work with methods that involve computers and a wide range of electronic devices that enable you to communicate and collaborate effectively using electronic media. These thinking skills coupled with hardware and software application skills are becoming the computer literacy essential for survival on many levels — essential for individuals to survive in an information society, for individuals to compete in the job market, for the enterprises of workgroups to be competitive in the marketplace, and for countries to compete in the global community.

Another key to future economic survival is finding efficient ways to use limited physical resources. Applying information can help determine how to use materials and energy more cleverly. The countries that are thriving are no longer just those fortunate enough to have an ample natural

resource base and a limited population. They are the countries that develop innovative ways of applying information to add value to resources. For example, Japan is producing more with less energy. Germany is using information to simulate new materials. In the United States, inventors such as Paul MacCready have shown it is possible to design solar cars and airplanes. For example, MacCready's *Gossamer Albatross* demonstrated the potential of human power by flying across the English Channel. Creative minds can find innovative ways to address physical constraints. Coupling these minds with electronic media can help them do that.

Michael Schrage points out in his essay "The Capital in Capitalism Is Intellectual" (published in the *Los Angeles Times*) that improving an economy involves more than capital spending. It involves getting a good return on that capital. Schrage says, "Increasingly, it takes intellectual capital to animate financial capital; it takes ingenuity and innovation to get financial capital to yield up its returns." Thus, it makes sense to invest capital in education that enables people to use tools — like computers — creatively. Supporting the arts and design professions can help provide new visions. In addition, investing in research can provide the base information for further advancements in science and technology.

Fulfillment of Human Potential

There is more to life than survival. Creative individuals are constantly searching for ways to fulfill their human potential — what Maslow calls *self-actualization*. Electronic media provide many avenues for exploration and expression. Electronic media set up opportunities for people to interact with each other and with the world around them. They enable people to perceive, think, and act in ways that are considerably enhanced. This can help us and our societies reach new levels of accomplishment.

self-actualize To release your inner needs and potential. Psychologist Abraham Maslow places self-actualization at the top of a hierarchy of human needs.

It takes a while for people to discover the qualities of a new medium. It takes some confidence and conviction to work with these qualities. It can take longer for the public to accept these qualities and embrace them aesthetically. People are just going through that process with electronic media. Many artists are discovering these qualities; initially, they find it less risky to work with computers in more or less conventional ways. But, eventually, new images emerge. These emerging images can take many forms. For example, writers can produce hypertext accessed with computers instead of producing books. Graphic artists can produce hypermedia accessed through computers instead of producing prints. Composers and musicians can synthesize sounds that no longer emulate traditional instruments. Sculptors, or environmental artists, can produce artificial realities experienced through computers instead of creating real objects. Artists can experiment with computer art to create new realities. As in the past when civilization assimilated other media (such as canvas, paper, or film), art can influence other fields. Artists working electronically can open new opportunities for expression in planning and design,

as well as science and medicine. As with the Renaissance 500 years ago, today many new forms of art are emerging.

New media provide new ways to share ideas and information. Hypermedia distributed on laser disks could become a standard form—as common as books. (They are less expensive to reproduce, distribute, and store.) Audiences can view computer-generated images and animation in large auditoriums and theaters. Galleries can set up three-dimensional viewing of artificial realities using holography and other three-dimensional viewing devices. Telecommunications, video or TV over air waves, and cable can all deliver ideas and information to homes and schools. Computers integrated with HDTVs can enhance the image and sound quality and permit people to view more interactively.

Sustaining a Healthy Environment

Our civilization must also sustain the environment upon which we depend for survival. We need to recognize our environment as part of us—a source of sustenance and inspiration. Electronic media enable people to gather information on which to base better decisions. These media enable us to model the effects of developmental actions, evaluating potential outcomes before committing resources to them. They enable us to manage complex operations with more precision and less waste. We need to be able to do this in order to help sustain the ecosystems upon which we depend for life—and enjoy a life worth living.

The world is at a crucial point in evolution. Bill McKibben eloquently points out in his book *The End of Nature* that the consequences of human activity touch all parts of this planet. The changes people have wrought on the composition of the atmosphere, and the likely effects on global climate, are impacting all ecosystems on earth. Humans have, in effect, ended nature, or viewed another way have become intertwined with it. Given this realization, society must accept the awesome responsibility of sustaining the world. To meet this responsibility it is vital to be able to model plans and designs and evaluate their effects before committing materials and energy to carry them out. It is imperative to consider the consequences of local actions while developing a global awareness to guide this planet safely into the future. Artificial reality provides a means to plan for and design a better future. In that regard, thinking skills and especially values are of utmost importance.

Planners and landscape architects can develop databases of environments using geographic information systems that provide an accumulation of information. As demonstrated in John Lyle's book *Design for Human Ecosystems*, they can draw upon this information to create better plans for our built environment. They can carefully access natural and cultural resource bases. Planners and designers can model changes to natural processes, and to community infrastructures, and evaluate impacts. They can monitor and manage the effects of human actions.

Architects can use artificial reality to model buildings and environments. They can build with information before materials and energy are spent. In this way architects can simulate, test, and optimize plans and designs without suffering the consequences of building mistakes. They can provide clients with a better sense of what they are investing in. They can provide local jurisdictions with a better understanding of a project during the review process. They can provide those responsible for building with a clearer vision of what should be done.

Engineers can develop simulations that will enable them to test and optimize designs of manufactured articles more quickly. In this way they commit less time and resources than it would take to develop prototypes or a series of production models. They can link computer-aided design with computer-aided manufacturing.

By working in electronic media space, planners, architects, engineers, and designers can work in collaboration with one another. Each can more easily draw upon the information provided by scientists and incorporate expression provided by artists. Multidisciplinary workgroups can work in media space. These workgroups can focus on objects, collaboratively designing them in artificial reality before implementing them in the real world. By working with shared media, each discipline can more easily contribute its expertise, and help to sustain a healthy and stimulating environment.

What's in It for You?

You can enhance your own economic potential by learning to use electronic media cleverly. Being able to work with information effectively enables you to compete in the job market. Setting up your own media space work environment can give you access to an amazing array of electronic tools that are emerging, as well as access to information online. You can learn to build models of the realities you are working with, giving you ways to work with information more effectively, explore ideas, and test alternatives. You can develop methods that make use of new avenues for communication which can save you time. New opportunities for collaboration can provide access to other's expertise as well as more opportunities to share your own. By learning to work in media space, you will gain more freedom over time and space, permitting you to access information when you need it, from wherever you want to be. Imagine having a small portable computer that has in it the basic tools you need as well as files related to your current projects. Imagine being able to use a modem to access your media space from wherever you are. Imagine being able to access information services and service bureaus, transfer files, and send FAXs. You can do this by employing your mind to gain control over the media you have access to.

You can explore your creative potential. Curiosity and creativity are strong motivating forces enabling you to find out more about the world as well as more about yourself. Electronic media provide you access to entertainment and to an emerging information environment which you can explore. Multimedia computing opens channels for working with almost all of your senses, involving many modes of thought and enabling you to mix many channels of expression. Imagine being able to easily integrate text and graphics; three-dimensional modeling, imaging, and animation; as well as video and sound. By learning to work the new media that are emerging, you can become part of a new Renaissance in computer art and music, architecture and engineering, scientific visualization, medical imaging, or whatever discipline you pursue.

You can also do your part to help sustain the environment. Working in media space enables you to save resources. You can set up in smaller and more comfortable, and even portable, work environments. You no longer need a writing desk, a typewriter stand, a drafting table, and large file cabinets for papers. A computer workstation can give you access to all this and more. A small but powerful notebook computer enables you to take what you need with you and use it wherever you want to work — in a classroom, in an office, at home, or even in an "electronic cottage" in a place you care for. Using telecommunications you can save trips, moving information and ideas instead of materials and people. It takes fewer resources to arrange electrons on disk than to arrange carbon on paper. It takes fewer resources to transmit electronic messages than to send mail by truck, train, boat, or plane.

You can gather information to make better consumer decisions — considering the efficiencies and environmental impacts of what you purchase. For example, you can avoid using chlorine bleached paper. As documented by Ed Ayres in an article published in *World-Watch* ("Whitewash: Pursuing the Truth About Paper," September–October 1992) chlorine bleaching produces dioxin and other chemicals which "pose serious threats to both human health and the environment." You can work with electronic media using information and building models to make better decisions regarding your environment. You can work with financial budgets, energy budgets, water budgets, etc., using electronic spreadsheets. You can work with locational models of environments viewing maps or using geographic information systems that can reveal a great deal about the natural resources and infrastructure of an area. You can build models of developments and products using computer-aided design, and test these models before committing the resources to building them. Collaborative teams can combine the expertise needed to address serious environmental problems. Electronic media can help people think globally and act locally — as individuals and as teams.

Shaping the Information Society

Viewed abstractly, the world consists of materials, such as water, oxygen, and carbon, and energy, usually derived from sunlight or fossil fuels. The movements of material and energy contain information about the environment. When scientists use computers for scientific visualizations, they are using the information about an environment without investing what it would take to physically reconstruct it. This enables scientists and medical researchers to model and simulate many situations to understand them more clearly. Gene pools provide another important source of information, which is one more good reason to preserve species.

Until recently, and particularly during the industrial age, there has been a tendency to use materials and energy more readily than information. For example, it has always seemed easier just to get more fuel rather than use information to develop more efficient ways to use fuel. Historically, people have typically used empirical procedures — trying things out and testing them in reality — rather than optimizing designs with models before choosing which to implement. While empirical testing is useful, it can result in excessive expenditures of limited resources. A related issue is the accepted practice of sacrificing living things. For example, it has been common practice to dissect a live frog for teaching anatomy rather than to model and simulate the information that entity contains.

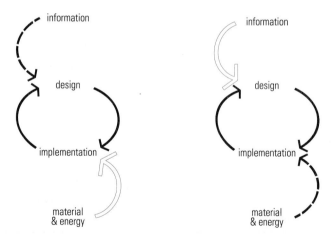

Industrial Society   **Information Society**

Computers provide tools for dealing with the information needed to optimize designs. It takes information to create designs that will reduce the long-term consumption of material and energy. It takes information to understand the result of extracting resources and releasing emissions. It takes information to understand how to integrate human life support systems into the natural process of the planet in a sustainable way. People can apply this information through computer models that enable them to

visualize alternatives. This can be a catalyst for constructive change. In this way people can nurture the will needed to develop ways for securing and sustaining a more certain future.

Civilization needs to shift away from paying for, and trying to protect, high-material and energy-consumption patterns. The massive amounts of resources used by past industrial societies have resulted in environmental pollution and the degradation of nature. This period of history is also characterized by global conflicts over resources. We need to be willing to invest in more sustainable and appropriate technologies that can reduce material and energy consumption. In the long term this would be better for both the environment and the economy. It could reduce international conflicts. We have had a tendency to want to pay very little for information, planning, and design. Countries, when developing, have wanted to reduce installation or construction costs; and, as a result, they are unwittingly paying high operation and maintenance costs they can no longer sustain. Our governments have spent absurd amounts for the so-called defense of national interests to secure extended resource bases. Nations can no longer afford to do that. We need to develop a more sustainable civilization.

Future information societies should be characterized by planning and design to reduce the consumption of material and energy. They must be ready to shift to more available resources that are sustainable. For example, Christopher Flavin and Nicholas Lenssen point out in "Beyond the Petroleum Age: Designing a Solar Economy" (Worldwatch Paper #100) that we could shift to a more sustainable and cleaner solar-based-energy economy using hydrogen as fuel. Economic evaluations must take into account life-cycle costs, such as the costs of finding and processing fuel, building and decommissioning ways of using the fuel, as well as disposing of wastes. Evaluations also must factor in externalities, such as water and air pollution — costs that are frequently excluded from economic models.

An information society could lead to international cooperation where countries could share information to reduce demands on the planet's resources. It could communicate ways to protect and enhance the environment, improving the quality of life. An information society could also lead to a more sustainable agriculture that could better support the world's population. An information society will need to disseminate birth control information to help stabilize population growth. It could use information to improve public health through prevention. Freedom to access information is the basis for democratic forms of government.

As present-day society evolves into an information society, there can be a new integration of art and science. Art uses information in expressive or evocative ways. Science uses information in rational or logical ways. Each draws upon different facets of the mind. Multimedia methods and approaches for using computers creatively enable you to use all these facets. There is sense in an animated art sequence. There is beauty in

scientific visualization. You can learn to combine both art and science using more of your mental capacity.

In the 1950s the architect Richard Neutra wrote a book called *Survival through Design*. Neutra's book describes approaches to shaping the built environment to meet human needs.

In the 1980s John Lyle, my colleague in the Department of Landscape Architecture at Cal Poly, Pomona, wrote the book *Design for Human Ecosystems*. Lyle's book describes approaches to shaping our built environment to sustain the ecosystems upon which we depend for life. His more recent book, *Regenerative Design for Sustainable Development*, tells how we can shift from the present paleotechnic era that uses degenerative technology, drawing upon fossil fuels and one-way flows that result in resource exploitation and pollution. Lyle, and others going back to Patrick Geddes, envision a neotechnic era that uses regenerative technology to draw upon solar energy and sustain more cyclical material flows.

Now in the 1990s we have a chance to develop the thinking skills to shape media space to meet our communication needs. Our information environment mirrors our society. This new reality will be as good, or as bad, as humanity makes it. It is hoped that we will use electronic media in wise and ethical ways. Careful design of our information environment can help sustain a healthy economy. It can give us new avenues for creative expression involving verbal, visual, and even musical modes of thought. Especially important, it could also help us manage the world's resources in more regenerative ways so we can sustain our physical environment for future generations.

You can become an architect for shaping the information society in a neotechnic era. You can begin by changing your work environment. Relate electronic media to your goals and learn computer applications that will help you meet those goals. Set up a media space work environment that you can access using your own computer. Change your work patterns so you can use these new tools and your media space work environment more effectively. You can also find constructive ways to change the organizational structures you relate to. Changing the way you transfer and transform information by using new media can change organizations. Productivity can improve by focusing on objects (or models of objects) and information transfers — not on an organizational structure based on a hierarchy of positions. When the focus is on objects, workgroups provide the most efficient organizational structure. An organization based on a flexible workgroup, rather than a rigid hierarchy, lends itself to finding the most effective ways to organize and move information. Workers no longer have to settle for "the way it is done" but rather can choose "the way that makes sense."

"International Expositions are independent kingdoms in their corporate relation with other countries of the world. They are phantom kingdoms wherein the people do everything but sleep. They germinate and grow with phenomenal energy. Their existence is established without conquest and their magic growth is similar to the mushroom and the moonflower; they vanish like setting suns in their own radiance. Thousand of neophytes of every race, creed and color come with willing hearts and hands to do homage and bear manna to nourish the sinews of a phantom kingdom. . . .

If building Phantom Kingdoms symbolizes man's highest aims on earth, than the same is true when building Real Kingdoms. Architecture and the sister arts are the most reliable barometers in recording human thought. They are direct exponents of a universal language wherein national progress is most clearly read.

People who build Phantom Kingdoms look hopefully for universal approval by all mankind."

Quote by Louis Christian Mullgardt FAIA from *The Architecture and Landscape Gardening of the Exposition*, published by Paul Elder and Company, San Francisco, 1915.

Mullgardt wrote these comments reflecting upon the Panama-Pacific International Exposition which grew out of the ruins of the San Francisco earthquake and fire at the beginning of the twentieth century. The same could be said of computer expositions, today, which raise from the present paleotechnic era. Will we be able to say the same of virtual reality — the "Phantom Kingdom" emerging in a neotechnic era of tomorrow?

Education and Evolution of the Mind

Change requires additional effort to overcome inertia, be it physical or mental. Physical change involves the creation of new technology. With regard to electronic media, both the inventiveness of the hardware and software makers and the market of the computer industry drive this change. Research also helps the computer industry better understand the human thought processes behind using new applications for computers. Presently Xerox, Apple, Autodesk, and others are doing this type of research. Consumers also need to become more sophisticated to stimulate the development of better tools. Users can learn approaches for visualizing how to apply new tools creatively. A good vehicle for changing mind-set is education. This may occur within the context of colleges and universities. It may also occur through corporate training and continuing education programs. It can even occur through the self-development of dedicated individuals.

Education's most important mission is to help people develop their mental capacity. To this end there should be more focus on creative thinking skills. User training for specific hardware and software often becomes dated within a few years. You will find it more important to develop thinking skills that will enable you to continue to learn to use computers to reach your full creative potential.

develop
mental capacity

develop
technical skills

Education's Mission

Schools find it difficult to keep abreast of the latest developments in hardware and software. It is not easy to write off the expense of computer workstations against productivity gains in education, although corporations and professional organizations can combine practice and production. Integrating computer applications can actually complicate classroom teaching. On the other hand, computer-aided instruction can help transfer some knowledge more efficiently by drilling and testing basic skills. It can also provide a medium for enhanced learning by enabling students to explore and gain knowledge. We can all experience new information using multimedia in ways that make learning easier and more interesting.

However, the real benefits of having computers in a classroom environment go far beyond computer-aided instruction. Computers give you access to media space and the tools for creative activity. Although difficult to measure, this can provide substantial benefits to an educational environment. It may be easier to justify the expense of computers in education by considering what it would cost to provide physical workspace, tools, and experiences comparable to those simulated in media space. For example, consider a simple game like Microsoft's Flight Simulator. As a game this program is worth what you pay for it — about $50. But it is worth considerably more if you consider it as computer-aided instruction for aviation. You can learn about navigation without getting lost. In fact, because you can even crash and survive, this program may be priceless. Obviously, though, it can only supplement real flight training.

It takes funding to acquire and update hardware and software. But more than just funding is needed. In addition, you need to be able to make full use of the hardware and software. To do this you need to be able to think creatively and develop a clear picture of how to mesh your mental capabilities with the tools that are emerging. Creative thinking skills can help you go beyond being a passive viewer and teach you to become more actively involved. Families, schools, workgroups, corporations, communities, and even countries can nurture this creative capacity, and each in its own way imparts the values necessary to use creativity constructively.

Learning

You may have heard stories about prisoners kept in solitary confinement. There, they had little opportunity to perceive anything and almost no opportunity for action. Some could retreat to inner images and draw upon experiences, visualizing new opportunities for action. A concert pianist, for example, practiced demanding pieces of music in his head. Upon his release he could perform them. A golfer, confined in prison, imagined playing the holes of his favorite course. Upon his release, he found that his golf scores were much the same as if he had been playing regularly on his favorite course.

Visualization is an important aspect of learning. Anybody learning to master a sport realizes this. Diving, for example, requires rather precise body movements. One has to learn by visualizing these movements. It is painful to learn to do a somersault off a diving board without having a mental picture of the complete movement.

Timothy Gallwey has written a widely read book called *The Inner Game of Tennis*. The book presents approaches to visualize winning tennis. It helps the player see both strokes and strategies for this game.

The inner game approach can also apply to learning to ski. One needs to visualize how to turn and use the terrain. Visualization can even help people overcome fear when skiing by helping them see how to get down a steep mountain. People may become afraid when they can't visualize how to do something. However, sometimes they may become scared afterward when they visualize what might have happened in a dangerous situation.

I remember a ski coach who showed me the line to take through a treacherous series of gates on a giant slalom course. Ice in a gate and a tree nearby concerned me. This coach told me to focus on the line I should take through the gate. He pointed out that if I thought about the ice and the tree, that is where I would end up. I saw the line and made it through. Since then, I have come to realize we can apply visualization to learning many things — even learning to using computers creatively.

There are three general approaches to teaching people to work with computers. One approach is to do it. Another approach is to learn about it.

And yet another approach is to visualize it. You can see some aspect of these approaches used in almost any school or office training program.

Doing It

You have probably seen a computer training course with many students — each sitting at a computer. The instructor begins: "Using the keyboard, type *cd\acad*." Or "Using the mouse, click on *file, open*." This course requires enough computers for all the students to get their hands on. It also requires a text that reads like a software manual. The instructor needs enough patience to teach every move. The students need to be willing to be told what to do — down to the keystroke. They must be willing to work through a series of exercises that are usually boring and may be unrelated to anything they want to do.

Doing It

Knowing about It

You are probably also familiar with a computer survey course. In this course, students read a textbook which may begin, "The first computer was invented in. . . ." The instructor lectures on the differences between mainframe computers, minicomputers, and microcomputers — maybe even getting into interesting topics starting with *aliasing* and continuing to Z. This course requires a lecture facility that has, it is hoped, some audiovisual capabilities. The instructor must keep current to lecture on a rapidly evolving topic. Students must be willing to listen and take notes so they can play them back on the exam.

Knowing About It

Visualizing It

Maybe you know of a course in some professional or academic discipline that integrates computer applications into the coursework. Students use computer applications when they work on projects for this type of course. The instructor might begin, "Here is a procedure, or an example of the kind of approach, you use applying a computer. You may want to familiarize yourself with the application using a tutorial. Then develop an approach for how you can apply this tool to your project. Once you visualize your procedure, we can sit down together and work on it using the computer." This course requires providing students access to appropriate hardware and software as well as tutorials and technical support in small-group settings. It requires a text that teaches thinking skills for using computers in addition to the regular text or reference material covering the knowledge base of the course. The instructor needs to encourage students to picture new approaches although students may encounter difficulties in executing them. The students must be willing to take the initiative and visualize how to proceed. They must also accept the challenge of trying to make what they visualize work. They should realize they can also learn from what doesn't work. They should not be afraid to try innovative approaches.

Visualizing It

Contrasting Approaches

No doubt, you recognize which approach I prefer. It is interesting to contrast these approaches for teaching computers. Each approach has certain strengths and weaknesses. Students can benefit from knowing how to use computers. They can benefit from knowing about hardware, software, and the history of computers. And they can also benefit from visualizing methods and approaches. Ideally, education involving computers should integrate user training for hardware and software, the teaching of appropriate knowledge bases, and the development of creative thinking skills.

Training courses are best for learning techniques. Often that is what is necessary to get started or to learn to use hardware and software. However, there is a danger of losing sight of what you can really do with these tools. Some students feel that what they are doing is gaining marketable skills; however, there is more to life than getting an entry-level position as a computer operator. Training can quickly grow stale. It may also become obsolete when the software or hardware is updated or superseded. Many educational institutions have difficulty maintaining up-to-date training facilities. The better training facilities are often in training centers and vocational schools.

Survey courses can provide background knowledge about computers and related topics. Traditional learning focuses on terminology and techniques before expecting someone to use tools creatively. This broader understanding, for example, gives you an appreciation of what has gone into the development of these amazing tools. It can provide a sense of where the computer industry is moving. The problem is, students may know about everything, but they may be unable to do anything. Even worse, they may not even visualize their potential or imagine what they might be able to do with these tools. They haven't learned that answer because they haven't developed their capacity to think creatively.

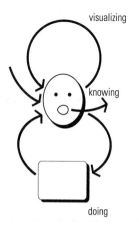

visualizing

knowing

doing

Combined Learning

Courses teaching thinking skills can help you learn to use computers creatively. These courses help you visualize how to use electronic multimedia in your discipline or area of interest. They enable you to play and picture possibilities as well as learn terminology and techniques related to your computer environment. You can also use visualization techniques for self study. You can develop your own inner game — even on paper — without having access to computer hardware and software. We are all prisoners of different sets of circumstances, but that should not limit the possibilities we can envision. Try to transcend limitations in facilities. Develop thinking skills that will transfer as hardware and software evolve. Then your capabilities will flourish. Develop a real feeling for media by working with media intimately. Acquire the basic techniques you need to function effectively. User training can be helpful. You may become frustrated with your own technical inabilities or the limitations of the tools you have access to. However, you can grow beyond that.

Media Space Classrooms

In her book *Transformations: Process and Theory*, Doreen Nelson has developed an object-oriented approach to education. She uses a model of a city as the focus for teaching students to develop their creativity. The model is also a vehicle for interconnecting subjects and teaching students a great deal about the environment. She reverses traditional learning by first immersing students in the design of an object and then drawing them into historic research that they then find relevant. The philosophy behind this approach relates to educational theories put forth by John Dewey, Hilda Taba, Benjamin Bloom, John Guilford, and Jerome Bruner. The typical framework of education tends to lose many of these ideas. Curriculum is more influenced by scheduling—organizing time and space.

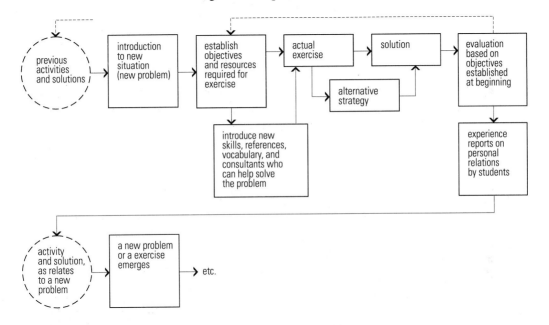

Project Development Feedback Loop
adapted from *Transformation: Process and Theory* by Doreen Nelson

As we move into electronic media space, we can transcend certain physical limitations like time and space. There are new opportunities to implement some of these educational theories. For example, one limitation of using objects—such as a model of a city or a project like those done in a design studio—is that they take up classroom space. Another is that they may be messy. And there is no place for storage. (If you can save models, you can share them with others or use them as a starting point or example for the next year's class.) The typical classroom environment does not work well for object-oriented teaching. Most classrooms must be sched-

uled for different groups, or used to teach different subjects, satisfying "classroom utilization formulas." There is also usually no real time to get different groups to work together on these objects when collaboration could be desirable.

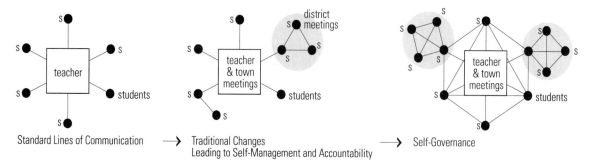

The Process of Decentralization in City Building Education
adapted from *Transformation: Process and Theory* by Doreen Nelson

What if students and teachers create objects, like a city model, in electronic media space? The cost of purchasing computers for accessing and maintaining media space is probably less than building, maintaining, and accessing the physical classroom and studio space (which usually isn't available). You can schedule media space with much greater flexibility than you can schedule physical classroom space. You could create virtual realities for project- or object-oriented education. Computer simulations, such as Sim City, are even commercially available. Maxis has sold over a million copies of this educational game invented by Will Wright.

Researchers and educators are bringing the computer into the classroom at all levels of education. Apple Computer, Inc., has funded research for what it calls the Vivarium Program, based at the Los Angeles Open Magnet School. As part of the program, Alan Kay — an Apple fellow, Doreen Nelson — a professor from Cal Poly, Pomona, and other researchers have been exploring how elementary school children learn to use electronic media as part of their classroom environment. Enrique Godreau, a researcher from Xerox PARC, has been working with junior high school children in the San Francisco Bay Area. He has developed a program that enables children to use multimedia for gathering and assimilating information as well as for authoring their own presentations. In higher education, Rensselaer Polytechnic Institute (RPI) is fostering interactive multimedia courseware across the curriculum. Dr. Jack Wilson, director of the Anderson Center for Innovation in Undergraduate Education, is guiding this effort. The students are using multimedia particularly for simulations and projects related to science, engineering, and architecture. (When I graduated from RPI, we did experiments in laboratories and projects in studios.)

**Object / Project-
Oriented Teaching**

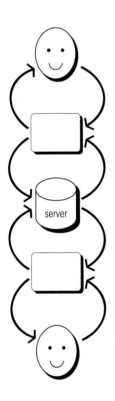

**Media Space
Teaching Environment**

Unfortunately, an object- or project-oriented pedagogical approach can be more difficult to carry out in a structured academic curriculum where survival depends upon acquiring measurable knowledge. However, design education has long traditions of project-oriented learning. Studio courses like the ones I teach are project-oriented. They involve guided creativity. This type of course provides the foundation for design education in many disciplines such as studio arts, graphic design, architecture, landscape architecture, planning, product design, and, in some places, engineering. These courses encourage students to focus on projects and explore media creatively. Projects are the vehicle for teaching creative thinking skills and design communication. Students taking these courses can experiment with multimedia and work on their projects in electronic media space. Students should be able to access this media space from their classroom or a computer lab. If students have a personal computer, they can also work on their projects where they live. If their computer is small and portable — like a notebook computer — they can work electronically wherever it is convenient for them. They can even access shared media space via modem wherever they connect to telephone lines. With the right equipment, they can also view video presentations on cable TV. The design studio no longer needs to have walls.

The availability of computers, as well as audio-video and TV equipment, is growing. There is potential for using media space as an extension of the teaching environment in primary and secondary schools, as well as in colleges and universities. Right now, the tendency is to use video just for presentations of information, which, for the audience, is like passively watching TV. There is also a tendency to use computers for repetitive drills and testing of basic knowledge and skills. While these applications of electronic media can be useful, people can use these tools much more interactively, given the nature of computers. Many levels of education and many disciplines can use these tools for creative explorations in media space, enabling students to visualize objects or projects and work on them interactively. From this, people can learn to use productive tools, while learning creative thinking skills and gaining a knowledge base related to the subjects they are studying.

An experimental project-oriented approach is also difficult to begin under the pressures of a typical office environment where survival depends on productivity. However, workstations in offices are often idle during lunch hours, evenings, and other off-times. Play and experimental projects are beneficial. Better yet, employers could encourage employees (and even financially assist them) to get their own personal computers. Employees could play to their hearts' content on their own time. They could also access shared media space from their homes. In this way they could work on projects, and even interact with workgroups, while at home. This could reduce the need to commute during peak hours. Employees could gain additional freedom to work when and where they wish. Employers could benefit from increased productivity and additional computer capacity.

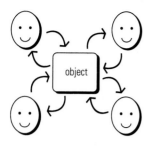

Object-Oriented Workgroup

The whole notion of using media space for organizing object-oriented workgroups has great potential. Sometimes the most interesting approaches for using computer applications come from those who have not learned so-called standard procedures. New approaches can come especially from those who don't know what supposedly can't be done. For example, children have a naïveté that opens their minds to new discoveries. Those who focus on user training may perfect certain procedures. The challenge is to go beyond these procedures and grow with the new tools that are emerging. You can develop the thinking skills that will enable you to visualize how to grow. You can become the architect of your own media space, shaping it to meet your needs.

"So far as a man thinks, he is free."

—Ralph Waldo Emerson
The Conduct of Life: Fate (1860)

Summary

The goals of this chapter are to help you evolve more humane work environments, evolve better work patterns, and evolve more responsive organizations. These goals are really intertwined — changing one aspect will cause changes to the others. We are caught in a wave of change that is both challenging and exciting. Products go through cycles. Learning evolves. Organizations adapt. Change is continuous and pervasive. The question remains: Can we constructively guide change in ways that will be beneficial?

There are issues that compel change. These issues include achieving economic survival, fulfilling human potential, and sustaining the environment. There are opportunities to change in ways that will help you become more productive and help you be able to draw upon more of your creative capacity. There are also opportunities to change in ways that can reduce the impact you have on your environment. Industrial societies use more resources but less information. Information societies can use fewer resources but more information. Education's mission is to develop mental capacity and technical skills to work creatively with information. There are different approaches to learning: doing it, knowing about it, visualizing it, or combining approaches. Individuals using new tools and media can stimulate change. These changes, if guided by good values, can improve both human conditions and the environment. You can guide change constructively.

You can help implement key strategies for change within the context of educational institutions and organizational training programs. Shift from traditional learning, which emphasizes understanding terminology and techniques, to more natural learning, which also involves playing and picturing possibilities. Case study or studio courses enable students to play and picture possibilities through object- or project-oriented teaching. Media space classroom environments can make this more possible to do in colleges and universities as well as in corporations and professional organizations. You can become the architect of your own media space. You can become an agent for positive change.

These final activities at the end of this chapter are really more challenges than exercises. They challenge you to use creative thinking skills to change your work environment, work patterns, and even organizational structures. The hope is that these changes could reverse some of the trends related to demoralization of humanity and degradation of the environment. The changes you make might help you lead a more satisfying, creative, and environmentally conscious life. Although changes are challenging, they could contribute to your happiness and productivity.

Activities

1. Change Your Work Environment

You can change your work or class-room environment. For example, I have set up virtual classrooms in media space on one of the central computers at the university where I teach. Each of my students has a personal account through which he or she can receive and send electronic mail. These accounts are private — only the students have the password. It is much like having their own mail-box or locker in our classroom. My students can access this account through terminals in computer labs all over the campus. They can also gain access using telecommunications from personal computers. Some students have computers and modems. The equipment may be in their dorm room, in their apartment, at their parent's home, or even at the office where they may work part-time. Small portable notebook computers with modems permit students to access our virtual classroom from wherever they can connect to a telephone. They can also access library card catalogs and out-side information services using a computer. They can download infor-mation and work with it in their per-sonal computer using their own software.

In addition, each class has a shared account on this university computer which all students in that class can access. Each student in the class knows the account name and password. Here we keep material we share as a class. This may be course materials, base information, even some three-dimen-sional computer models that students may work with. Students can access this virtual classroom any time of the day. They can access it from wherever they can use a computer with telecom-munications. Presently, the pathways we use limit us to text and smaller binary files. But this enables us to transfer formatted documents, public domain programs, drawings, and small three-dimensional models. Eventually, as communication speeds increase, this may enable us to transmit video and other multimedia images. Then we will be able to create a more realistic virtual classroom we can work in together.

One reason I have set up media space classrooms is because we lack physical classroom space in our College of Environmental Design. Most of my design students do not have worksta-tions (of any kind) at school. We meet in shared labs, which makes it difficult to keep course materials such as mod-els or maps for the class. Most of my students can use the lab only for the three-hour period on the assigned days they have their design class. Yet my students can access our virtual class-room whenever they want (twenty-four hours a day), and they can get there without having to commute to campus. Although we are working to get more studio and classroom space for our college, the progress is frustratingly slow. It takes a long time to get approval and funding for physical facilities. It is much quicker and less expensive to add the communication infrastructure needed to teach in virtual classrooms. We can do a great deal in media space; however, it is still impor-tant to have good physical space where students and faculty can interact directly.

Consider your work environment. The challenge is for you to shape your media space, developing a sense of place that would be appropriate and helpful to you. You can become the architect of your own media space. You can organize how you arrange files in the computers you have access to and select the pathways you use to link them. In your files you can fashion models to address the realities you deal with. Your media space may contain places where you can put programs and information. You can also create objects or models you can use to explore possibilities. It is even becom-ing possible to experience these mod-els as if they were virtual reality. For example, if you are an artist, your

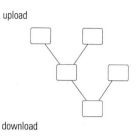

upload

download

Map Media Space

media space may contain your studio and your tools as well as what you are creating. If you are a designer, archi-tect, or engineer, your media space may contain the objects you design. Your media space may even be an entire landscape if you are a landscape architect. And if you are a scientist, your media space may contain models of the reality you are working with. Eventually these models may enable you to enter molecules, walk through environments, or even take journeys into outer space.

Working in collaboration with others, you can also set up shared media space for your classroom or work environ-ment. Identify the pathways individu-als can use to access it, and share information from their private domains. Organize your shared media space in ways that enable you to navi-gate around it. Make sure the members of your workgroup can access it and can orient themselves as well. Your workgroup may include project teams and even consultants who could access this shared media space. Build frames of reference and use metaphors that will help you navigate. Begin with simple transfers of text. As you gain access to multimedia workstations and faster channels for communication, explore how you can transmit multi-media. Use creative thinking skills to work with multimedia, drawing upon all your mental capacity. This will empower you to use computers more creatively. It will help you shape your work environment and your destiny.

2. Change Your Work Patterns

The media space we have set up in our classroom environment is changing our work patterns. For example, students can send messages to classmates, and members of their workgroup involved in team projects, and can receive messages from them as well. I send students course materials and updates for the schedule of class meetings or field trips. (This way we can more easily arrange a meeting anywhere.) Students send me messages regarding the schedule, their progress, and questions they may have. I have even sent students exercises to think about and respond to using E-mail. However, we usually meet in our design studio for real discussions and reviews. I also communicate this way with the faculty with whom I team-teach. Since we are not scheduled in class at the same time, we can contact each other via E-mail without having to find meeting times in our busy schedules. We can also prepare course materials by working together in media space and can distribute these materials directly to our students.

People can work together in media space. Although students may work independently on their own files, they can link their activity in shared files. Sometimes I have encouraged my students to write a personal journal (for their eyes only) which they can keep in their personal media space. I also have them write a journal summarizing the activities of their workgroup which they can keep in shared media space. If they wish, they can share ideas they generate in their personal journal with their workgroups. They can do this by simply extracting and distributing segments from their journal or by adding their thoughts to what the workgroup is doing. I also have students submit work electronically which I can review and hand back the same way. This may be a draft of a report or a small drawing. I can review their submission, leaving my initials with each comment so they can easily search for it, using their word processing program. I can also mark up drawings by adding a

new layer. The students can turn that layer off after they have responded to my comments. Once you are set up for telecommunications, it is actually easier and quicker to send files than to print them out and hand papers in. Electronic files also take up much less space in my faculty office. I can get these files from many locations. Small notebook computers make access more convenient. We are gaining new freedoms for using space and time.

Another circumstance is that our department has a limited support staff and budget to produce course materials. (This is typical of many organizations.) Because we have access to a networked information environment, it is often easier and less expensive to distribute information electronically. A media space work environment involves fewer transfers, saving time and effort. Education and research networks help me stay in touch with colleagues around the world — a definite advantage since we have very little travel budget. More frequently, we can save local trips by using telecommunications. This has distinct advantages in an often gridlocked, smog-bound, urbanized area such as the Los Angeles Basin. We can also reduce our use of paper. Some of my students and I also like to think of all the trees we are saving. We are beginning to realize (as noted before) it takes less energy to arrange electrons on disk than to distribute carbon on paper. We can even erase disks and reuse them more easily than paper.

The challenge is to set up new work patterns — to find more freedom over how you use space and time. Look especially for ways of doing more with fewer resources. Consider how your individual and group work patterns could change once you establish your media space. Try out these changes using the computer work environment you have access to. Begin with changing your personal work patterns. Then find others who are also making these changes so you can work together.

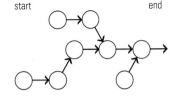

start   end

Diagram Work Flow

3. Change Organizational Structures

Changes in the work environment and in work patterns are also changing organizational structures. For example, it is no longer necessary to get my class together to make announcements. I can distribute messages via E-mail. If I forget to announce something (and I often do), I can easily add it later. Students can ask questions without finding me, and I can provide answers without finding them. I know I can reach them in media space. I can schedule meetings with individual students and workgroups and let the others know when I can meet with them. That way we can all organize our time more effectively. We can now schedule our meetings more flexibly — making them more meaningful and taking less time when students have to wait around to see what is happening. They can be where they are most productive. These are some of the new freedoms we have over space and time.

Faculty members can prepare courses by working on shared materials in media space. This provides the potential for new levels of collaboration. It can be easier for each member of the faculty team to contribute, review, and distribute information. There is also potential to do committee work using telecommunications, reducing the number of seemingly endless meetings that fit into nobody's schedule and often have no tangible result. Working electronically can avoid trips that add to meeting time. It can save production time involved in delivering the results of collaborative efforts.

A new sense of community can evolve related to media space. One only needs to look into electronic bulletin boards to see how they link special-interest groups consisting of people from all over the world. I have found, within my own classes, that media space provides another avenue through which students can communicate and build a sense of community. This is particularly helpful on a commuter-oriented campus where many of the students live over a wide area. It amazes me what I find out from students via E-mail. They will share

jokes and problems, congratulations and gripes. Students know they can reach me and that I will respond. They have control over what they tell me (they can always erase the message before they send it). There are some students who have good typing skills but who may be quiet in class. I sometimes hear more from them in our media space classroom. Other students who are more vocal in class may feel hampered if they lack good typing skills, but a student's typing improves when he or she uses telecommunications regularly. Using this medium also causes everyone to write, which has considerable benefit in an educational environment.

Some schools and offices may have better computing environments than what I am describing here. Others may have computing environments that are not as good. The key question is how you use what you have. You also need to make sure your organizational structures relate to what you are doing. Multimedia computing will continue to evolve rapidly, making better computer environments more available. You will be able to work with more channels of perception and expression, drawing upon more of your mental capacity. The new boundaries become the limits of your imagination.

The challenge here is to consider your own organizational structure. Examine how it might evolve to respond to new work patterns that could result from the media space you are shaping. Begin with pilot projects where you consciously try new approaches. Evaluate the results; improve your approaches; then implement changes within your organization.

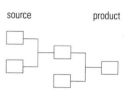

Diagram Information Flow

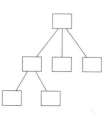

Diagram Organizational Structure

Appendix A:
Overview

Mind over Media: Creative Thinking Skills for Electronic Media

Goals:
What you might be able to do as a result of reading each chapter, i.e., the purpose.

This appendix contains an overview of goals, principles, strategies, and activities—in summary, the approaches presented in this book. Use this overview to help understand the focus of each chapter. This appendix also reveals the pedagogical sequence— that is, how the approaches build from one chapter to the next. By doing the progression of activities at the end of each chapter, you will translate the approaches you are reading about into experiences you can relate to. Each activity builds upon previous ones. Going through this sequence helps you develop creative thinking skills for electronic media.

Let's start by clearly defining what we mean by goals, principles, strategies, and activities. Then, the following pages will lay out the chapters in each part of the book.

Principles:
Natural tendencies.
Fundamental truths, laws, doctrines, or motivating forces upon which others are based.
The essential elements, or qualities, especially ones which produce specific effects.
A beginning. A mind-set.

Strategies:
Plans and directions for operations prior to action.
Methods involving thinking skills.
Ways you can use thinking skills.

Activities:
Actions you can do to pursue goals, try out principles, and experience different strategies.

Part I: Thinking

Chapter 1: Exploring The Images in Your Mind	Chapter 2: Exploring Electronic Media	Chapter 3: Perceiving, Thinking, and Acting
Goals: Become more aware of mental energy. Realize you can look and interact. Decide to use media more interactively.	**Goals:** Picture media space. Learn to navigate in it. Learn to transfer information there.	**Goals:** Employ a range of electronic media. Use different modes of thought. Develop models to represent objects.
Principles: You can simply watch electronic media without responding. Or, you can interact, alternately viewing and doing what you visualize. There are techniques, methods, and goals related to using any tool. When using computers, you must learn to work with software, and information models, as well as clearly identify your objectives. This involves both media — which you access using your computer — and mind — your thinking skills and attitude. Ideas come from your mind. Conventional computing emphasizes logical modes of thought. Multimedia computing draws upon the whole brain. Couple your whole mind with media.	**Principles:** You can establish both personal and shared media space. Maps of media space can help you navigate through workspace you access in computer applications. Understanding syndromes can help you overcome problems related to transferring information and working with electronic media. Information flow diagrams help you visualize transfers of information. Data flow diagrams show transfers of files from one format to another. Phone/FAX, computer, video are all vehicles for accessing media space. You can use shared media space for creative collaboration.	**Principles:** Multimedia stimulate channels of perception and expression which relate to each of your senses. You can use both understanding and your feelings to work creatively. Multimedia draw upon both deductive and inductive modes of thought. Your mind enables you to absorb, contemplate, and express ideas. Media enable you to work with ideas and refine them interactively. Models can represent objects you are working with. Use models of objects as a focus for collaboration. Reality can relate to virtual reality. Physical space can relate to media space. Real objects are multisensory. Computer models can be multimedia.
Strategies: Become more aware of electronic media. Experience multimedia wherever you can — on TV, in movies, with video games, with computers, and through telecommunications. Relate electronic media to your creative endeavors. Work interactively, linking your mind to electronic media. Develop goals which will enable you to enhance your creativity. Improve productivity by adopting new approaches and attitudes when working with electronic media.	**Strategies:** Map media space to develop a mental picture so you can navigate. Use shared media space to receive and present information. Look for direct ways to transfer information into electronic media. Identify transfer syndromes so you can overcome common problems. Use information flow diagrams to visualize alternative methods. Use a matrix as a frame of reference. Diagram forward from sources or backward from your final product. Use data flow diagrams to figure out transfers between formats. Access media space using a phone or FAX, computer with modem, or video. Use shared media space for creative collaboration.	**Strategies:** Use multimedia to draw upon a wider range of perception and expression. Use multimedia to stimulate different modes of thought. Develop models of objects to represent the realities you are working with. Mock up multimedia to visualize how you can integrate your presentation. Use models as a focus for collaboration.

Activities:
1. Get the Picture
2. Play Games
3. Identify Creative Endeavors
4. Develop Goals
	Activities:
	1. Map Media Space
	2. Diagram Information Flow
	  a. Impressions
	  b. Expressions
	3. Diagram Data Flow
		Activities:
		1. Explore Different Media
		2. Use Different Modes of Thought
		3. Develop Models to Represent Reality
		3. Mock up Multimedia Presentations

Chapter 4: Visualization—A Key to Creativity	Chapter 5: The Creative Process	Chapter 6: Using Computers Creatively
Goals: Learn to work with patterns. Visualize abstractly and concretely. Coordinate actions by visualizing.	**Goals:** Develop your creative capacity. Learn to diagram your work flow. Overcome potential syndromes.	**Goals:** Learn to develop new procedures. Use procedures to manage projects. Go beyond what you have done before.
Principles: You can recognize patterns. The perception of patterns relates to all your senses. Patterns reflect the intrinsic order of what you are working with. Picturing patterns helps you to comprehend what you perceive. Modeling patterns helps you to visualize and develop concepts you conceive. You can visualize abstractly and concretely using cognitive models. Initial cognitive models are fast, crude, and holistic. Later cognitive models become more deliberate, attentive, detailed. You can transform models to create new entities.	**Principles:** There are mental processes for deriving insights and exploring possibilities. You can use these processes when working with electronic media. The creative process involves problem stating and problem solving. There are five stages: insight, saturation, incubation, illumination, and verification. These stages relate to the design process: research, analysis, synthesis, and evaluation. Creativity is a cyclical process. Relate creativity to each stage of a project. You can diagram your approach. You can overcome common syndromes.	**Principles:** Basic approaches can help you address the following concerns: What media, what models, and what methods are you using? Using the nine-step approach to media, models, and methods can help you develop your procedures for using electronic media more creatively and effectively. Clear procedures for using media can help you transfer information. Clear procedures for building models can help you visualize what you are working on. Clear procedures developing your methods can help you manage projects. Refining procedures enables you to adopt new tools and accept change.
Strategies: Develop models which relate to the intrinsic orders you need to work with. Use computers to build the models you are working with. Alternate between abstract and concrete models. Use computers to transform models. Save different versions of models as you proceed. Use models to focus your perception, to compile information and ideas, and to coordinate your actions. Use your models as a focus for collaboration. Involve your audience in experiencing your model. Transfer the model to reality as directly as possible.	**Strategies:** Express, test, and cycle ideas. Work with media interactively. Diagram work flow to visualize your approach for conceiving alternative strategies, to involve new tools and media, to evaluate how to allocate time and resources, and to manage your project as you proceed. Overcome common syndromes by using your insight, moving freely from analysis to synthesis, postponing judgment, generating more than one idea but committing to the best option, testing ideas and refining them, presenting content but making sure you present it well, conserving creative energy—working smart, and working collaboratively where you can.	**Strategies:** The basic nine-step approach involves: *Media—for transferring information* 1. Relate electronic media to your goals. 2. Map your media space. 3. Diagram information and data flow. *Models—for the realities involved* 4. Identify realities you are working with. 5. Develop models of reality. 6. Mock up your presentation. *Methods—for thought processes* 7. Define your project. 8. Diagram your work flow. 9. Manage your progress.

Activities:
1. Develop Visual Comprehension
   a. Abstract Images
   b. Develop Images
2. Clarify Thinking through Visualization
3. Coordinate Actions Using Visualization Techniques
	Activities:
	1. Describe Your Present Creative Process
	2. Diagram Work Flow
	3. Identify Syndromes
		Activities:
		1. Review Previous Projects
		2. Develop Procedures
		3. Manage Media, Models, and Methods
		4. Refine Your Thinking Skills

Chapter 7: Case Studies—Relating to Disciplines	Chapter 8: Applications—Tools and Toys	Chapter 9: The "Zen" of Regeneration
Goals: Understand your discipline. Learn where others are coming from. Develop multidisciplinary approaches.	**Goals:** Explore new computer applications. Practice to use them better. Relate capabilities to tasks.	**Goals:** Relax your body. Release your mind. Revive your spirit.
Principles: Each discipline emphasizes a range of modes of thought. People have different characteristic behavior. You can develop effective teams which mesh different modes of thought and behavior. Computers enable you to use media, develop models, and manage methods for multidisciplinary team efforts. Information can have a life cycle which lasts longer than a single project. Visualizing collaborative efforts can help coordination.	**Principles:** Approaches to learning draw upon different modes of thought. The discovery mode is more experiential. The strategy mode is more logical. The discovery mode proceeds from concrete experience to an abstract understanding. The strategy mode starts with abstract goals and principles which can lead to successful experience. You may have a preferred mode. You can also learn other modes. You can combine modes of learning. You can also share modes of learning. Practice can make using computer applications more pleasurable.	**Principles:** Merge mind and media by linking your inner space and media space. Draw upon your mental energy and enhance it using electronic media. Relaxation invigorates your body. Releasing revitalizes your mind. Reviving regenerates your spirit. Look inward through witnessing, contemplating, and transcendental meditation. Curiosity and creativity provide strong motivating factors.
Strategies: Develop an understanding of the media, models, and methods your discipline currently uses. Use these approaches to develop your own procedures. Appreciate approaches other disciplines are using. Develop multidisciplinary strategies for using media, models, and methods collaboratively. Use and transfer information electronically when possible, avoiding the time and expense of printing or plotting on paper. Build models which different disciplines can share. Visualize entire projects so each discipline (and worker) sees how they fit into the entire picture.	**Strategies:** Try out different methods for learning applications. Combine methods when learning. Have workgroups share methods. Integrate practice into games or case studies. Chart applications related to channels of perception/expression and stages of the design process. Use a range of electronic media. Work with computer applications at each stage of the design process. Emphasize learning by using different channels at each stage of the design process. Optimize a workgroup's production by having team members specialize in different capabilities.	**Strategies:** Develop interactive rhythms. *Relax your body by:* Breathing deeply—in 5, out 5 Rolling the spine, balancing body Looking beyond the monitor Relaxing eyes and ears by palming Rolling neck and twisting torso Rolling shoulders Rotating arms, shaking wrists. Opening hands, stretching fingers *Release your mind by* letting go of your legs, lower back, torso, neck, arms, jaw, eyes, forehead, scalp and ears. *Revive your spirit by:* Inviting the unconscious Dialoguing and experiencing Adding ethical elements of values Making it concrete through rituals
Activities: 1. Examine Your Discipline 2. Appreciate Where Others Are Coming From 3. Develop Multidisciplinary Approaches	**Activities:** 1. Explore 2. Practice 3. Plan	**Activities:** 1. Relax Your Body 2. Release Your Mind 3. Revive Your Spirit a. Active Imagination b. Dreams

Chapter 10: User Interfaces	Chapter 11: Mixing Media	Chapter 12: Change
Goals: Interface with electronic media. Use multimedia. Get involved more deeply.	**Goals:** Transform media efficiently. Integrate media effectively. Delegate tasks appropriately.	**Goals:** Evolve more humane work environments. Evolve better work patterns. Evolve more responsive organizations.
Principles: Your tools become part of you. Set up work environments—both in physical space and in media space. Multimedia engages a range of modes of thought. A spectrum of consciousness enables involvement at different levels. These include: Persona involvement Ego involvement Total organism involvement Unity consciousness involvement Unity consciousness is the deepest. Interest and access are limiting factors when using electronic media. Computer interfaces include not only a physical interface, but also a mental interface and a spiritual interface as well.	**Principles:** Media integration can involve paper, film, or electronic media. Efficiency can improve by transforming media into digital formats and working as directly as possible. Diagram media, models, and methods to clarify procedures. Mock-ups of presentations identify the dominant media and help integrate other channels. Input-output diagrams help clarify transformations of media. Electronic media can help you work concurrently and hand off tasks. Media space can help develop object-oriented workgroups.	**Principles:** Products go through cycles. Learning evolves. Organizations adapt. Change is continuous and pervasive. Industrial societies use more resources but less information. Information societies can use fewer resources but more information. Education's mission is to develop mental capacity and technical skills to work creatively with information. There are different approaches to learning: doing it, visualizing it, knowing it, or combining approaches. Individuals using new tools and media can stimulate change. These changes, if guided by good values, can improve both human conditions and the environment. You can guide change constructively.
Strategies: Regard computer applications as integral to your being. Set up a media space work environment you can use in collaboration with colleagues. Work toward wideband interaction involving multimedia. Become aware of different levels of involvement by relating to experiences you already have. Transfer this awareness to new computer interfaces and applications. Work toward unity consciousness. Stimulate interest in and gain access to electronic media. Bond with computers. Work with all aspects of the interface. Stay open to new possibilities.	**Strategies:** Integrate media using paper (cut and paste), film or analog video (linear editing), electronic tool procedures (composite printouts), electronic media procedures (in workstations). Work digitally using desktop publishing, CADD, or video programs. Clarify procedures by diagramming information flow, modeling objects, and diagramming work flow. Picture presentations by using scores, storyboards, and scripts. Visualize transformations by using input-output matrices and diagrams. Evolve concurrent processes where possible and delegate effectively. Develop object-oriented workgroups.	**Strategies:** Shift from traditional learning, which emphasizes understanding terminology and techniques, to more natural learning, which also involves playing and picturing possibilities. Develop more case study or studio courses which enable students to play and picture possibilities. Use more object- or project-oriented teaching. Set up media space teaching environments which make this more possible to do both in our colleges and universities and in our corporations and professional organizations. Become the architect of your own media space. Become an agent for positive change.
Activities: 1. How Are You Using Computers? 2. Open New Channels of Media 3. Seek Deeper Involvement 4. Bond with Your Computer	**Activities:** 1. Transform Media 2. Integrate Media 3. Delegate Tasks	**Activities:** 1. Change Your Work Environment 2. Change Your Work Patterns 3. Change Organizational Structures

Appendix B:
Glossary of Terms

abstraction An operation of the mind involving the act of separating parts or properties of complex objects. Enables you to simplify information and clarify relationships you perceive.

actual prototypes Three-dimensional physical models.

aikido (Japanese) A martial art that focuses on three elements: **Ai** refers to harmony or coordination; **ki**, spirit or inner energy; and **do**, the method or the way.

aliasing Assuming the characteristics of a computer generated line. Associated with raster graphics where dots form lines by reducing "jaggies," or a steplike appearance.

analog That which corresponds to something else. For example, in electronic media, a format for replicating sound or images using electrical impulses that modulate current.

anastrophe A change involving the coming together of disparate elements to form a coherent and connected whole. The opposite of catastrophe.

animation program A computer application that enables users to portray movement.

anthropomorphic Related to human-like forms or attributes.

archetype In psychology, according to Jung — a symbol of the inner being that manifests ideas inherited from human experience. These symbols recur in many different cultures over time.

artificial intelligence The ability to carry out programmed responses. Computers can carry out programmed responses.

artificial reality Models or graphic representations people can access from different places to interact with objects and with each other. People can develop these representations using information in media space.

attribute A property, quality, or characteristic that describes an object.

bandwidth A range. Typically refers to the transmission of a signal, but may also refer to the richness of a message. Multimedia encompass a wide bandwidth.

biofeedback Technique for responding to indicators of mental and body stress. For example, therapists use biofeedback to help patients learn how to relax and overcome physical and mental problems.

bonding Connecting or holding together. The formation of close interpersonal relationships involving the whole being. People can also bond with objects related to computers, and with places in reality or virtual reality.

bubble diagram A graphic representation that shows the relationships between functional areas. Can describe patterns evident in a map or a plan.

cellular automata Computer programs enabling objects to carry out functions. Empower information objects to begin to take on a life of their own.

checklist A list of activities or items. Often called a "to do" list.

cognitive Knowing; recognizing what you perceive. Cognitive computer applications use primarily deductive modes of thought.

cognitive map A visual representation of your perception. A cognitive map can show spatial or conceptual relationships.

collaboration The act of working together. Electronic media offer new opportunities for workgroup collaboration.

computer-aided design and drafting program (CADD) A computer application that enables users to model and develop drawings of designs.

concurrence Happening together. Agreement; accord. Concurrence makes it possible for more people to work together with the same information.

contemplate To access different modes of thought through meditation. To reflect upon what you experience and understand.

CPM (critical path method) A procedure for determining which set of activities will take the longest to accomplish, hence constituting the critical path of activities in a project.

creative process The stages your mind goes through when developing ideas. These stages include preparation (involving both first insight and saturation), incubation, illumination, and verification.

cyberspace Media space connected to the human brain, enabling people to experience this information environment interactively.

data flow diagram A graphic representation to visualize how to transfer digital files. Especially helpful when working with different file formats where it is necessary to figure out the best way to move files from one program or computer platform to another.

database program A computer application that enables users to sift information by selecting attributes.

delegate To entrust another person with a task.

design phases The steps you go through when doing a design project. Each phase of design involves the design process.

design process The stages your mind goes through when developing design ideas. These stages — which are related to the stages of the creative process — include research (involving both problem identification and information gathering), analysis, synthesis, and evaluation.

desktop publishing program A computer application that enables users to lay out and integrate text with graphics.

desktop video program A computer application that enables users to create multimedia productions involving text, graphics, images, video, and sound.

dichotomy A division into two parts. A set of two (usually opposites).

digital Relating to that which uses a binary system to replicate information using primarily on-off signals, transmitted electronically or through fiber optics. Can represent numbers, text, graphics, images, video, and sound.

digital sound Sound composed of binary information played by special consumer devices and computers. Enables people to change pitch and rhythm, mask noise, and mix sound tracks.

digital video Still or full motion images composed of binary information processed by computers. Enables people to speed up or slow down movement and create transformations.

direct analogy A similarity or likeness that involves similar physical characteristics or processes that relate to different contexts.

directory A guide. The directory of a computer disk will provide a guide to its contents.

document-oriented interface The DOI focuses on documents rather than on applications. Object-oriented applications, as well as attributes, are imbedded in documents which users can work on using a variety of computers.

download To transfer digital information from a server (or mainframe computer) to a local computer.

drawing and painting programs Computer applications that enable users to draw and paint digitally.

dynamic data exchange The automatic transfer of information from one application to another as you work in any of the applications linked by the exchange.

electroencephalograph (EEG) A device that measures brain waves. Can help people learn how to produce alpha waves, which indicate the brain is in a relaxed state.

electromyograph (EMG) An instrument that measures muscle tension. Can help pinpoint areas of tension and help people learn how to release that tension.

E-mail (Electronic mail) Messages transmitted to an account, usually from a computer that is online. These messages can be picked up anytime, from anywhere, using a computer that can access the account.

encapsulation Combining both data and procedures in an object-oriented program.

ergonomics The study of how energy is spent. Pertains particularly to human energy expended for doing work.

ethic (From the Greek word *ethos*) The essential character or spirit of a person or people. The basis upon which people make unconscious judgments.

fantasy analogy A similarity or likeness that relates to an ideal.

file management utilities Computer programs that help users navigate around their information environment. Permit pruning of the branching structure of file directories and easily move branches and files.

flow diagram A graphic representation that shows the sequence of a process. Can describe movement of material or energy in natural processes.

galvanic skin response (GSR) A physiochemical change in the skin that can be used to assess arousal. Can help people learn to control arousal related to anxiety or agitation.

Gannt chart A bar graph that shows the duration of tasks and relates them to a time line.

geographic information system (GIS) A computer application that enables users to develop spatial models with layers of information linked to databases of attributes.

gestalt, pl **gestalten** (German) The recognition of integrated patterns that make up an experience. The overall style or personality that one senses. This whole is more than a sum of the parts.

group dynamic Interaction among members of a team. Involves the members' different modes of thought.

groupware Software that enables group interaction. Helps coordinate large teams using computers to do complex projects.

hara (Japanese) A reference to a person's center. Your center of gravity, as well as your focus of concentration, and even your spiritual center.

hardware The computer and its peripherals such as the central processing unit and monitor; includes input devices such as the keyboard and mouse and output devices such as a printer.

hierarchy The governing or intrinsic order. Can be categorical as well as spatial and temporal.

human factor A characteristic related to people. Especially concerning how people interface with tools such as computers.

hypermedia A collection of keywords, graphics, images, video, and sound linked by associations. Used to present digital information in ways a user can explore interactively.

hypertext A collection of keywords linked to information. Used to present associated information so a user can quickly access what he or she is interested in, using a computer.

icon A graphic representation. Used in graphic-user-interfaces to represent files, disks, or objects which the computer user can pick.

image integration The combining of visual information. For example, draping air photos over computer terrain models.

imaging program A computer application that enables users to work with and enhance digital images.

information flow diagram A graphic representation to visualize how to transfer information from one object to another. Especially helpful when integrating information from many different sources and using computer document-oriented interfaces to transform it into a range of products.

inheritance Enabling objects to have the characteristics of a class of objects.

inner space The mental realm that relates to human memory and spirit. Just as people can develop a mental map to navigate in media space, people can also develop an inner sense to navigate in their own inner space.

input-output diagram A diagram showing the paths through which material and energy (such as information) moves. Can help people visualize how computers, with the appropriate hardware and software, can transfer and transform information electronically.

input-output matrix A chart relating "what comes in" to "what goes out." Can help people consider all possible connections.

interact To view and do what you visualize.

interactive video Video that is both sent and received. Enables users to interact in real time involving both audio and video transmitted electronically.

intrinsic order The natural or inherent order. Recognizing the intrinsic order of what you are working with enables you to model or represent it using a computer.

lateral thinking An approach to creative thinking typically involving consideration of alternatives.

life cycle A sequence of stages that includes the formation, use, and disposal of an object. Can refer to physical objects as well as to information objects developed in computers.

macro A brief computer program that combines steps. For example, a macro can make repetitive logging-on procedures easier when using computers.

mandala A video setting you walk into and interact with.

map To represent spatial order.

map of media space A visual representation of your information environment. Shows how to connect with and navigate in media space. Can include what is accessible on disk, as well as what is accessible through networks and via telecommunications.

media space The information environment connecting real and imaginary places, objects, and the people within them. The context in which people can use representations to work with artificial reality.

medium, pl **media** The intermediate material for expression. Using computers people work with ideas and information expressed in electronic media.

mental interface In computer applications, that which relates to software procedures and thinking skills.

menu A list of choices. Provides pathways and commands to help computer users find their way and function in their information environment.

metaphor Transferring to one situation, the sense of another. For example, transferring to a computer application, the organization of a desktop. Helps you relate to previous experience upon which you can build familiarity.

mind That which thinks, perceives, feels, or wills; combining both the conscious and unconscious together as the psyche. The source of thought processes that facilitate the use of computers for artistic expression, design, planning, management, or other problem-solving and issue-resolving applications.

mindscape The inner world of your own mind, involving both conscious and subconscious levels.

mind-set Attitude; point of view.

mock-up A representation. People use mock-ups to show how the pieces of an object or the parts of a presentation come together. Enables people to visualize a final product before producing it.

model To represent functional order.

model space The information environment where you work on your models.

mosaic A series of images. Used to preview a collection of digital graphic files so a user can select an image to call up on a computer.

multidirectional Involving more than one direction. Enabling computer users to both receive and send digital information.

multidisciplinary Involving more than one discipline. Enabling disciplines to work together.

multimedia Integrating more than one medium. Computer systems can enable the integration of electronic media combining text, graphics, animation, spatial modeling, imaging, video, and sound.

multitasking Using more than one software application at the same time. For example, some computer user interfaces permit people to work with different applications using different windows.

music program A computer application that enables users to compose and mix sounds digitally.

nagaya (Japanese) Old-style Japanese "villages." Places where people of all ages live in harmony with each other and the land.

n ī n j o (Japanese) A spirit of cooperation and neighborliness.

object-orientation A focus on products, documents, or data to be processed. People can work with representations of objects in media space using computers.

object-oriented programming An approach to computer programming that enables people to build from modules that have attributes that transfer from one program to another.

operating system The programmed interface between computer hardware and application software. It permits the software to function on the computer and enables the user to perform simple functions such as searching for, copying, or deleting files.

paper space A representation showing what you will see when you print a document on paper.

parameter A key variable that governs the shape or performance of a model.

personal analogy A similarity or likeness that involves your identification with elements of a problem.

PERT (progress evaluation review technique) A procedure for considering what is completed on a project and relating this to a schedule.

physical interface In computer applications, that which relates to the way people work with the hardware devices.

po A positive maybe.

polymorphic tweening A change in morphology (or form) of an object, showing all the different shapes in between.

polymorphism Having objects represent different things.

presentation reality The information environment others will perceive. This may involve the layout of pages or drawings you produce on paper, or it might be the sequence of a video production.

principle A fundamental truth upon which others are based.

process-orientation A focus more on procedures or actions to be performed. People can program procedures using computers.

project management program
A computer application that enables users to keep track of resources, activities, and time for doing projects.

raster image Computer graphic composed of a bit map indicating which pixels to activate on a computer screen. Sometimes called a *bit map image*. Enables people to manipulate contrast, color, and texture.

regenerate To form again or renew. To be spiritually reborn. For example, while computers regenerate images on a screen, human minds recenter and refocus — regenerating mental images in rhythm with conscious thought processes.

renaissance Rebirth; revival. The revival of art, literature, and learning in Europe during the fourteenth, fifteenth, and sixteenth centuries, marking the transition from the medieval to the modern world. The term can also refer to a revival of creativity and understanding stimulated by multimedia computing, empowering individuals to make a transition into a new information age.

rendering program A computer application that enables users to add colors and textures to graphic images.

script A written document describing a performance. For example, when developed for a multimedia presentation a script can help people integrate different channels of media such as video and audio.

self-actualize To release your inner needs and potential. Psychologist Abraham Maslow places self-actualization at the top of a hierarchy of human needs.

simulation A computer hardware and software setup that represents real environments. Enables users to work with computers to rehearse what it would be like to do something, like fly an airplane, in reality.

soft prototypes Three-dimensional models built in media space using computer software.

software Computer code that transfers instructions. The program that enables the computer to carry out commands.

spiritual interface In computer applications, that which has to do with a sense of attachment, empowerment, and meaning.

spreadsheet program A computer application that enables users to organize information in rows and columns and do calculations.

stop point The point at which one task ends and another begins. Identifying stop points can make it easier to delegate tasks.

storyboard Graphics and text that portray scenes. For example, when used for a multimedia presentation, a storyboard helps people portray the content, composition, and sequence of a presentation.

subdirectory A folder contained within a directory. A computer disk can be divided into many subdirectories.

symbolic analogy A similarity or likeness that involves abstract qualities that you can relate from one situation to another.

syndrome (From Greek, *syn*, together, and *dromos*, running) Conditions running together. A number of symptoms which together characterize a problem.

technographer A technical recorder for computer conferencing. This person uses electronic media to record a group's thinking, so the group can work interactively to collaboratively develop a document.

telecommunications Electronic transfers of information. Can take the form of FAX, E-mail, or especially binary transfers of digital files such as programs, formatted documents, or drawings.

template A standardized format that presents generic information. For example, this could be as simple as a form or clip art that computer users can add information to and modify for their own purposes.

tool An object that helps the user to work. This may be a traditional tool — such as a pencil — or a computer tool — such as hardware and software for word processing, computer-aided design, animation, and many other applications. Used to optimize efficiency where cost-effective.

toy An object that enables the user to play. Used for pleasure and self-development.

transcendental meditation A way of thinking that enables people to access altered states of consciousness. To project into unconscious modes of thought.

transfer To convey or send. For example, using electronic media you can transfer text, graphics, images, video, or sound.

transform To change the form or condition of something. For example, computers can transform information from paper to electronic media, or from one file format to another.

transformation A change, or visualization of change.

trilogy A discourse consisting of three parts. A set of three.

upload To transfer digital information from a local computer to a remote server (often a mainframe computer).

user shell A computer program that provides a user interface making an operating system easier to use. Most user shells incorporate metaphors such as a desktop or windows to help users relate to the interface more intuitively.

vector image Computer graphic developed using algorithms that generate the geometries you see on the computer screen. Enables people to manipulate geometries — rotating, mirroring, and changing their scale.

vertical thinking An approach to creative thinking typically involving a linear, logical progression of steps.

video space A representation showing what you will see when you integrate media to produce a video.

videoplace An artificial reality that you can enter and experience using video.

virtual reality Simulations using information to provide multisensory experiences. People can create these simulations by using computer-generated images in media space.

visual thinking skills Approaches that help you comprehend what you perceive, and help you give expression to patterns. Visual thinking skills enable people to work with representations — drawings, diagrams, models, animation, video, and sound — so they can use multimedia.

visualization The formation of a mental image that can help you coordinate your mental and physical activities.

visualization technique Ways to perceive and comprehend based largely on pattern seeking and pattern recognition.

voice mail Verbal messages transmitted to a computer account, usually from a telephone. These messages can be picked up anytime, from anywhere, using a telephone.

witness To experience personally. Can involve centering on where you are, to become fully aware of your senses.

work flow diagram A diagram linking activities and events and relating them to a time line. Used widely for operations research and project management.

word processing A computer application that enables users to compose statements by writing and editing digital files.

Appendix C:
Bibliography

Adams, James L.: *The Care & Feeding of Ideas: A Guide to Encouraging Creativity*, Addison-Wesley, Reading, Mass., 1986.

Adams, James L.: *Conceptual Blockbusting: A Guide to Better Ideas*, 2nd Ed., W. W. Norton, New York, 1979.

Alexander, Christopher et al.: *Pattern Language*, Oxford University Press, New York, 1977.

Arnheim, Rudolph: *Entropy and Art*, University of California Press, Berkeley, 1971.

Arnheim, Rudolph: "A Plea for Visual Thinking," in *The Language of Images*, W. J. T. Mitchell (ed.), University of Chicago Press, Chicago, 1980.

Arnheim, Rudolph: *Visual Thinking*, University of California Press, Berkeley, 1969.

Ayres, Ed: "Whitewash: Pursuing the Truth about Paper," *World Watch*, vol. 5, no. 5, September–October 1992.

Myers, Isabel Briggs, and Peter B. Myers: *Gifts Differing*, Consulting Psychologists Press, Palo Alto, Calif., 1980.

Brooks, Rodney A.: *Model-Based Computer Vision*, UMI Research Press, Ann Arbor, Mich., 1984.

Bruner, Jerome: "The Conditions of Creativity," in *Consciousness: Brain, States of Awareness and Mysticism*, Scientific American, Harper & Row, New York, 1979.

Bylinsky, Gene: "Saving Time with New Technology," *Fortune*, Dec. 30, 1991, pp. 96–104.

Carroll, Lewis: *Alice's Adventures in Wonderland & Through the Looking-Glass* (originally published in 1872), republished by Macmillan, New York, 1966.

Cianchi, Marco: *Leonardo's Machines*, Becocci Editore, Florence, 1988.

Corsi, Pietro (ed.): *The Enchanted Loom: Chapters in the History of Neuroscience*, Oxford University Press, Oxford, 1991.

Csikszentmihalyi, Mihaly: *Flow: The Psychology of Optimal Experience*, HarperCollins, New York, 1990.

de Bono, Edward: *Lateral Thinking: Creativity Step by Step*, Harper & Row, New York, 1970.

DeKoven, Bernard: *Connected Executives*, Institute for Better Meetings, Palo Alto, Calif., 1988.

Dewey, John: *Art as Experience*, G. P. Putnam's Sons, New York, 1934.

Doblin, Jay (ed.): *Design in the Information Environment*, Knopf, New York, 1985.

Doebler, Paul D.: "The Living File," *Computer Publishing Magazine*, vol. 5, no. 8, November 1990, pp 42–51.

Drucker, Peter F.: *The New Realities*, Harper & Row, New York, 1989.

Edwards, Betty: *Drawing on the Artist Within*, Simon and Schuster, New York, 1986.

Edwards, Betty: *Drawing on the Right Side of the Brain*, J. P. Tarcher, Los Angeles, 1979.

Emerson, Ralph Waldo: *The Conduct of Life: Fate*, Houghton, Mifflin, New York, 1904.

Emerson, Ralph Waldo: *Journals of Ralph Waldo Emerson*, Houghton Mifflin, New York, 1909–1914.

Felton, George: "Time-Shifting Is a Mortgage on My Future," *Los Angeles Times*, Oct. 20, 1990, p. B7.

Fezler, William: *Creative Imagery: How to Visualize in All Five Senses*, Simon and Schuster, New York, 1989.

Flavin, Christopher, and Nicholas Lenssen: "Beyond the Petroleum Age: Designing a Solar Economy," *World Watch* Paper Series, paper no. 100.

Franck, Frederick: *The Zen of Seeing*, Random House, New York, 1973.

Galluzzi, Paolo (ed.): *Leonardo da Vinci: Engineer and Architect*, Montreal Museum of Fine Arts, Montreal, 1987.

Gallwey, Timothy: *The Inner Game of Tennis*, Random House, New York, 1974.

Getzel, Jacob W.: "The Psychology of Creativity," Carnegie Symposium on Creativity, Library of Congress Council of Scholars, Pittsburg, 1980.

Gibson, William: *Mona Lisa Overdrive*, Bantam Books, New York, 1988.

Gibson, William: *Neuromancer*, Berkley Publishing Group, New York, 1984.

Gleick, James: *Chaos: Making a New Science*, Penguin Books, New York, 1987.

Goldman, Glenn, and Michael S. Zdepski (ed.): *Reality and Virtual Reality*, proceedings from ACADIA '91 held at UCLA, Los Angeles, 1991.

Gordon, William J. J.: *Synectics: The Development of Creative Capacity*, Harper, New York, 1961.

Halprin, Lawrence: *RSVP Cycles: Creative Processes in the Human Environment*, Braziller, New York, 1969.

Halprin, Lawrence, and Jim Burns: *Taking Part: A Workshop Approach to Collective Creativity*, MIT Press, Cambridge. Mass., 1974.

Hanks, Kurt, and Larry Belliston: *Draw! A Visual Approach to Thinking, Learning and Communicating*, William Kaufmann, Los Altos, Calif., 1977.

Hanks, Kurt, and Larry Belliston: *Rapid Viz: A New Method for the Rapid Visualization of Ideas*, William Kaufmann, Inc., Los Altos, 1980.

Hayakawa, S. I.: *Language in Thought and Action*, Harcourt Brace Jovanovich, New York, 1978.

Helsel, Sandra: "Virtual Reality and Education," *Educational Technology*, May 1992, pp. 38–42.

Henri, Robert: *The Art Spirit*, J. B. Lippincott, Philadelphia, 1923.

Hirsh, Sandra K. and Jean M. Kummerow, *Introduction to Type in Organizations*, 2nd ed. Consulting Psychologist Press, Palo Alto, California, 1990.

Hofstadter, Douglas R.: *Gödel, Escher, and Bach: An Eternal Golden Braid*, Random House, New York, 1980.

Huxley, Aldous: *The Doors of Perception*, Harper & Row, New York, 1954.

Jaynes, Julian: *The Origin of Consciousness in the Breakdown of the Bicameral Mind*, Houghton Mifflin, Boston, 1976.

Johnson, Robert A.: *Inner Work: Using Dreams and Active Imagination for Personal Growth*, Harper & Row, New York, 1986.

Jung, C. G.: *Man and His Symbols*, Doubleday, Garden City, N.Y., 1964.

Kahl, Russell (ed.): *Selected Writings of Hermann von Helmholtz*, Wesleyan University Press, Middletown, Conn., 1971.

Kepes, Gyorgy (ed.): *Vision + Value Series: Education of Vision*, Braziller, New York, 1965.

Kepes, Gyorgy (ed.): *Vision + Value Series: The Nature of Art of Motion*, Braziller, New York, 1965.

Kneller, George: *The Art and Science of Creativity*, Holt, Rinehart and Winston, New York, 1965.

Koberg, Don, and Jim Bagnall: *The Universal Traveler*, William Kaufmann, Los Altos, Calif., 1976.

Krueger, Myron W.: *Artificial Reality*, Addison-Wesley, Reading, Mass., 1983.

Laseau, Paul: *Graphic Thinking for Architects and Designers*, Van Nostrand Reinhold, New York, 1980.

Lowenfeld, Viktor: "Basic Aspects of Creative Thinking." in *Creativity and Psychological Health*, M. F. Andrews (ed.), Syracuse University Press, Syracuse, N. Y., 1961.

Lu Cary: "Objects for End Users" *BYTE*, Dec 1992, Vol. 17, No. 14, pp. 142–152.

Luther, Arch C.: *Digital Video in the PC Environment*, 2nd ed., Edition, Intertext Publications/McGraw-Hill, New York, 1991.

Lyle, John: *Design for Human Ecosystems*, Van Nostrand-Reinhold, New York, 1985.

Lyle, John: *Regenerative Design for Sustainable Development*, John Wiley & Sons, New York, 1993.

Lynch, Kevin: *Image of the City*, M.I.T. Press, Cambridge, Mass., 1960.

Martin, Lynn, et al.: "On Achieving Necessary Skills," U.S. Labor Secretary's Commission Report, Washington, 1991.

Maslow, Abraham: *The Farther Reaches of Human Nature*, Penguin, New York, 1976.

Maslow, Abraham H.: *Motivation and Personality*, Harper & Row, New York, 1970.

Maslow, Abraham H.: *Toward a Psychology of Being*, Van Nostrand, Princeton, N.J., 1968.

McKibben, Bill: *The Age of Missing Information*, Random House, New York, 1992.

McKibben, Bill: *The End of Nature*, Random House, New York, 1989.

McKim, Robert: *Experiences in Visual Thinking*, Brooks/Cole, Monterey, Calif., 1972.

McLuhan, Marshall, and Quentin Fiore: *The Medium Is the Massage*, Bantam Books, New York, l967.

Michell, William J., and Malcolm McCullough: *Digital Design Media*, Van Nostrand-Reinhold, New York, 1991.

Minsky, Marvin: *The Society of Mind*, Simon and Schuster, New York, 1988.

Montgomery, Geoffrey: "The Mind in Motion," *Discover: The World of Science*, vol. 10, no. 3, March 1989, pp. 58–68.

Moravec, Hans: *Mind Children: The Future of Robot and Human Intelligence*, Harvard University Press, Cambridge, Mass., 1988.

Mullgardt, Louis Christian: *The Architecture and Landscape Gardening of the Exposition*, Paul Elder, San Francisco, 1915.

Naisbitt, John: *Megatrends: Ten New Directions Transforming Our Lives*, Warner Books, New York, 1982.

Naisbitt, John, and Patricia Aburdene: *Megatrends 2000: Ten New Directions for the 1990's*, William Morrow, New York, 1990.

Neisser, Ulric: *Cognitive Psychology*, Prentice-Hall, New York, 1967.

Nelson, Doreen G.: *Transformations: Process and Theory: A Curriculum Guide to Creative Development*, Center for City Building Educational Programs, Santa Monica, Calif., 1984.

Neutra, Richard: *Survival through Design*, Oxford University Press, New York, 1954.

Nielsen, Jakob: *Hypertext and Hypermedia*, Academic Press, San Diego, 1990.

Odum, Howard T.: *Environment, Power, and Society*, John Wiley & Sons, New York, 1970.

Odum, Howard T., and Elisabeth C. Odum: *Energy Basis for Man and Nature*, McGraw-Hill, New York, 1976.

von Oech, Roger: *A Whack on the Side of the Head*, William Kaufmann, Los Altos, Calif., 1983.

Ornstein, Robert, and Paul Ehrlich: *New World New Mind, Moving toward Conscious Evolution*, Doubleday, New York, 1989.

Papert, Seymour: *Mindstorms: Children, Computers, and Powerful Ideas*, Basic Books, New York, 1980.

Patterson, David A., Denise S. Kiser, and D. Neel Smith: *Computing Unbound: Using Computers in the Arts and Sciences*, W. W. Norton, New York, 1989.

Penrose, Roger: *The Emperor's New Mind: Concerning Computers, Minds, and the Laws of Physics*, Oxford University Press, Oxford, l989.

Poincaré, Henri: *The Foundations of Science; Science and Hypothesis, the Value of Science, Science and Method*, George Bruce Halsted (trans.), Science Press, New York, 1921.

Prueitt, Melvin L.: *Art and the Computer*, McGraw-Hill, New York, 1984.

Rasmus, Daniel W.: "Relating to Objects," *BYTE*, Dec 1992, Vol. 17, No. 14, pp. 161–165.

Rico, Gabriele L.: *Writing the Natural Way: Using Right-Brain Techniques to Release Your Expressive Powers*, J. P. Tarcher, Los Angeles, 1983.

Rodriguez, Walter: *The Modeling of Design Ideas: Graphics and Visualization Techniques for Engineers*, McGraw-Hill, New York, 1992.

Rucker, Rudy von Bitter: *The Fourth Dimension; A Guided Tour of the Higher Universes*, Houghton Mifflin, Boston, 1984.

Sagan, Carl: *The Dragons of Eden: Speculations on the Evolution of Human Intelligence*, Random House, New York, 1977.

Schmitt, Gerhard: *Microcomputer Aided Design: For Architects and Designers*, John Wiley & Sons, New York, 1988.

Schon, Donald A.: *Educating the Reflective Practitioner: Toward a New Design for Teaching and Learning in the Professions*, Jossey-Bass, San Francisco, 1987.

Schon, Donald A.: *The Reflective Practitioner: How Professionals Think in Action*, Basic Books, New York, 1983.

Schrage, Michael: "The Capital in Capitalism Is Intellectual," *Los Angeles Times*, Business Section, 1991.

Schrage, Michael: *Shared Minds: The New Technologies of Collaboration*, Random House, New York, 1990.

Sorkin, Michael: "The Electronic City," *I.D. Magazine*, June 1992, pp. 71–77.

Spring, Michael: "Informating with Virtual Reality," in *Virtual Reality: Theory, Practice, and Promise,* by S. K. Helsel, and J.P. Ruth, Meckler, Westport, Ct., 1991.

Springer, Sally P., and Georg Deutsch: *Left Brain, Right Brain*, W. H. Freeman, New York, 1981.

Stalley, Marshall (ed.): *Patrick Geddes: Spokesman for Man and the Environment; A Selection*, Rutgers University Press, New Brunswick, N.J., 1972.

Starfield, Anthony, Karl Smith, and Andrew Bleloch: *How to Model It: Problem Solving for the Computer Age*, McGraw-Hill, New York, 1990.

Stauffer, Russell G.: *Teaching Reading as a Thinking Process*, Harper & Row, New York, 1968.

Stults, Bob: *Media Space*, Xerox Corp., Systems Concepts Laboratory Technical Report, Palo Alto Research Center, Palo Alto, Calif., 1986.

Taylor, Gordon Rattray: *The Natural History of the Mind*, Dutton, New York, 1979.

Tufte, Edward: *Envisioning Information*, Graphics Press, Cheshire, Conn., 1990.

Tufte, Edward: *The Visual Display of Quantitative Information*, Graphics Press, Cheshire, Conn., 1983.

Unterseher, Fred, Jeannene Hansen, and Bob Schlesinger: *Holography Handbook: Making Holograms the Easy Way*, Ross Books, Berkeley, Calif., 1987.

Wayner, Peter: "Brave New Desktop" *BYTE*, Dec 1992, Vol. 17, No. 14, pp. 153–160.

Westbrook Adele, and Oscar Ratti: *Aikido and the Dynamic Sphere*, Charles E. Tuttle, Tokyo, 1970.

Whitehead, Alfred North: *Modes of Thought*, Macmillan, New York, 1938.

Whitney, Patrick (ed.): *Design in the Information Environment: How Computing is Changing the Problems, Processes and Theories of Design*, Knopf, New York, 1985.

Wilber, Ken: *No Boundary: Eastern and Western Approaches to Personal Growth*, Shambhala Publications, Boston, 1979.

Wilson, Jack, and Edward F. Redish: "The Comprehensive Unified Physics Learning Environment: Part I. Background and System Operation," *Computers in Physics*, vol. 6, no. 2, March/April 1992, pp. 202–209.

Wilson, Jack, and Edward F. Redish: "The Comprehensive Unified Physics Learning Environment: Part II. The Basis for Integrating Studies," *Computers in Physics*, vol. 6, no. 3, May/June 1992, pp. 282–286.

Wurman, Richard Saul: *Information Anxiety*, Doubleday, New York, 1990.

Yager, Tom: "Information's Human Dimension," *BYTE Magazine*, vol. 16, no. 13, December 1991, pp. 153–160.

Acknowledgments

The following acknowledgments credit the work of others. Reference to their work may also appear in chapters other than the one where the credit is acknowledged here.

Chapter 1

References to "Saving Time with New Technology," by Gene Bylinsky printed in *Fortune*, Dec. 30, 1991, pp. 96–104 are reprinted with permission from FORTUNE Magazine. References to *The Medium is the Massage*, by Marshall McLuhan and Quentin Fiore, first published by Bantam Books in l967, are reprinted with permission from Jerome Agel. Excerpts and diagram from *FLOW, The Psychology of Optimal Experience* by Mihaly Csikszentmihalyi, copyright 1990 by Mihaly Csikszentmihalyi, are reprinted by under license from HarperCollins Publishers.

Chapter 2

References to "media space" relate to the work of Steve Harrison et al., Xerox Corporation, Palo Alto Research Center. Reference to "Cyberspace" is used with permission from William Gibson, author of *Neuromancer,* which was first published by Ace Books in 1984. References to "Virtual Reality" are used with permission from Jaron Lanier. Reference to comments by Peter Drucker are used with permission from Peter Drucker. Material adapted from *The Image of the City,* by Kevin Lynch, first published by The MIT Press in 1960, are reprinted under license from MIT Press. References to *Shared Minds, The New Technologies of Collaboration,* published by Random House Inc., in 1990, are used with permission from the author, Michael Schrage. References to *Power Meetings, an Introduction to the Computer-Enhanced Meeting,* are made with permission from the author, Bernard DeKoven.

Chapter 3

References to *Drawing on the Artist Within*, published by Simon and Schuster in 1986, are made with permission from the author, Betty Edwards. References to *Drawing on*

the *Right Side of the Brain*, published by J. P. Tarcher in 1979, are made with permission from the author, Betty Edwards. Material from pp 63, 82–83, 91–93, and 119 in *Experiences in Visual Thinking*, by Robert H. McKim, are reprinted under license from PWS-KENT Publishing Company. References to *Design for Human Ecosystems*, published by Van Nostrand-Reinhold in 1985, are made with permission from the author, John T. Lyle. References to *Information Anxiety*, published by Doubleday, New York, are made with permission from the author, Richard Saul Wurman. Reference to *Envisioning Information*, by Edward Tufte, published by Graphics Press in 1990, is made with permission from Edward Tufte. Reference to *Hypertext and Hypermedia*, by Jakob Nielsen, published by Academic Press in 1990, is made with permission from Academic Press. Reference to a student project done at Cal Poly, Pomona, is made with permission from former students David Briley, Tony Diaz, and Gary Tom. The quote from "Information's Human Dimension" by Tom Yager, printed in *BYTE Magazine* December 1991, volume 16, number 13, is reprinted with permission from BYTE Magazine.

Chapter 4

References to the work of Russell G. Stauffer, copyright 1969 by the author, reprinted by permission of HarperCollins Publishers. Excerpts from *Lateral Thinking: Creativity Step by Step*, by Edward de Bono, copyright 1970 by Edward de Bono, are reprinted by permission of HarperCollins Publishers. References to *Synectics: The Development of Creative Capacity*, published by Harper in 1961 are made with permission from the author William J. J. Gordon at SYNECTICS: SES Assoc. 121 Brattle St. Cambridge, MA. References to *Cognitive Psychology*, by Ulric Neisser, published by Prentice Hall Press in 1967, are made with permission from Prentice-Hall. References to *A Pattern Language: Towns, Buildings, Construction*, by Christopher Alexander et al., published by Oxford University Press in 1977,

are made with permission. Material from *Energy Basis for Man and Nature*, by Howard T., and Elisabeth C. Odum, published by McGraw-Hill in 1976, are used with permission from McGraw-Hill. Calligraphy for the Japanese characters was done by Takeo Uesugi.

Chapter 5

Materials from *RSVP Cycles: Creative Processes in the Human Environment*, by Lawrence Halprin, published by Braziller in 1969, are used with permission of Lawrence Halprin.

Chapter 7

The chart adapted from S. K. Hirsh and J. M. Kammerow was used with permission of Sandra Hirsh and Consulting Psychologist Press. References to the work of Jules Bister, are made with permission of Jules Bister. References and illustrations of the work of Wolff, Lange, Christopher, Architects Incorporated are used with permission of Dale Lang. Comments by Tony Palmisano are used with permission of Tony Palmisano. References to the work of Scaliter Irrigation Engineering are made with permission of Dan Scaliter. References to the work of ESRI are made with permission of Jack Dangermond. Comments by Mark Sorenson are used with permission of Mark Sorenson. References to the work of Dr. Hugh Clark Briggs at JPL are made with the permission of Dr. H. C. Briggs.

Chapter 8

Reference to the work of Rudy Rucker and John Walker are made with their permission. Reference to the work of Rodney Brooks and his students at MIT are made with permission of Rodney Brooks. Material from a workshop on "Video Scriptwriting" by Stephen Eiffert, put on through Padgett-Thompson, is used with permission of Stephen Eiffert.

Chapter 9

Comments by Sharon Stine are used with her permission. Material from *Inner Work: Using Dreams and Active Imagination for Personal Growth*, by Robert A. Johnson, published by Harper & Row in 1986, is used with permission of both the author and HarperCollins Publishers.

Chapter 10

Reference to the work of Myron Krueger is made with his permission. Material from *No Boundary: Eastern and Western Approaches to Personal Growth*, by Ken Wilber, published by Shambhala Publications 1979, is used with permission from Ken Wilber.

Chapter 11

Reference to *Taking Part: A Workshop Approach to Collective Creativity*, by Lawrence Halprin and Jim Burns, published by MIT Press in 1974, is made with permission from MIT Press.

Chapter 12

Reference to the work of John O. Regen is made with his permission. The quote from "Time-Shifting Is a Mortgage on My Future," by George Felton, published in the Oct. 20, 1990 edition of The *Los Angeles Times*, is used with permission of George Felton. Material from *The End of Nature* and *The Age of Missing Information*, by Bill McKibben is reprinted under license from Random House, Inc. Reference to "Whitewash: Pursuing the Truth about Paper," by Ed Ayres, published in *World Watch*, vol. 5, no. 5, September–October 1992, is used with permission of Ed Ayres. Reference to "Beyond the Petroleum Age: Designing a Solar Economy," by Christopher Flavin and Nicholas Lenssen, paper no. 100, published in the *World Watch* Paper Series, is made with permission from Christopher Flavin. Reference to *Survival through Design,* by Richard Neutra, first published by Oxford University Press in 1954, is made with permission from Dion Neutra. Quote from *The Architecture and Landscape Gardening of the Exposition*, by Louis C. Mullgardt FAIA, published by Paul Elder and

Company in 1915, was provided through the courtesy of Dr. William R. Larson, Professor Emeritus of Behavior Sciences, Cal Poly, Pomona. Reference to *The Inner Game of Tennis*, by Timothy Gallwey, published by Random House in 1974 is made with permission from Timothy Gallwey. Material from *Transformations: Process and Theory: A Curriculum Guide to Creative Development*, by, Doreen G. Nelson, published by the Center for City Building Educational Programs in 1984, is used with permission from Doreen Nelson. Reference to the work of Alan Kay, Apple Research Fellow, is made with permission from Apple Computer. Reference to the work of Enrique Godreau, Xerox Research Fellow, is made with permission of Enrique Godreau. Reference to the work of Dr. Jack Wilson, Director of the Anderson Center for Innovation in Undergraduate Eduction, is made with permission from Dr. Jack Wilson.

Index